"In this era of multiple and overlapping crises – social, health, ecological, military, economic, political and others – a new edition of Marchand and Runyan's classic collection could not be more timely. Completely revised, this new edition provides critical and cutting-edge analysis of the gendered nature of the global economy and the ways in which it is being restructured. Contributors to the volume do not leave us in despair, but also provide insights into specific examples of women's and feminist resistances to neoliberal and neoauthoritarian policies and practices. As these authors show, these creative and inclusive forms of resistance have the potential to dislodge and subvert dominant actors and provide hope for more egalitarian and sustainable futures."

Laura Macdonald, *Professor, Department of Political Science and Institute of Political Economy, Carleton University, Canada*

"*Gender and Global Restructurings*, in its third edition is a timely, robust and nuanced feminist response to capitalism's various crises and how we can understand and resist these. In its reach, analyses and hopes it underlines the importance of feminist work on global capitalism and its pitfalls in its intersectional manifestations as well as how these pitfalls can be addressed through activism and solidarity. A book that clearly responds to the biggest challenges of our times and will therefore be of interest to students and all those who wish to understand our current dilemmas."

Shirin Rai, *Distinguished Research Professor, Department of Politics and International Relations, SOAS University of London, UK*

"This third edition of *Gender and Global Restructurings*, which includes several new chapters, powerfully reminds us of the many ways global capitalism intertwines with so many other processes of our time: From racial, homo-, and disaster capitalism to philanthro-, surveillance, and gore capitalisms, the feminist scholars in this volume continue to call out the most problematic capitalist logics and seek ways to imagine more just socioeconomic, political, and ecological futures for us all."

Amy Lind, *Mary Ellen Heintz Professor, Department of Women's, Gender, and Sexuality Studies and former Director of the Taft Research Center, University of Cincinnati, USA; one of the Editors-in-Chief of the* International Feminist Journal of Politics

Gender and Global Restructurings

In the new edition of this bestselling text and scholarly reference, new and revised chapters reflect shifts in the gendered, classed, racialized and sexualized nature of ongoing global restructurings.

Through fresh intersectional feminist analyses of widening health, climate, care, inequality, democracy and knowledge crises since the Great Financial Crisis and the deepening of many forms of capitalism, this volume stresses the complexities of multiple restructurings which demand new ways to think across sightings, sites and resistances. Some of each of these elements are in every chapter, which take the reader to different sightings, such as of neoliberalizations, neoauthoritarianizations, multipolarizations, financializations and migrations. They also bring into view different geographic sites, such as Hong Kong, sub-Saharan and North Africa, Canada, Mexico, Bangladesh and the trade blocs of the European Union and the BRICs, and different nongeographic sites such as productive and reproductive economies and the virtual economy of finance and digitalization. They further highlight different forms of women's and feminist resistance, such as local and national labor organizing, regional and multipolar organizing, reimagining infrastructure design and broadening noncapitalist community and solidarity economies. Many chapters critique problematic constructions of women's empowerment, and all challenge the machinations of neoliberal capital that undermine most women, marginalized peoples and the planet.

Providing a coherent and challenging approach to contemporary gendered globalization, better understood as global restructurings, since the last edition over a decade ago, *Gender and Global Restructurings* will be of interest to students and scholars of international political economy, international relations, economics, development and gender studies.

Marianne H. Marchand recently retired from the Universidad de las Américas Puebla, Mexico, where she held a chair in international relations and directed the Canadian Studies Program. She is currently an adjunct research professor at the Institute of Political Economy at Carleton University, Canada, after having held a visiting professorship there. In addition, she is widely recognized in the Americas for her scholarship on feminist international relations and is a member of the UNU-CRIS Hub México–CIDE, as well as academic editor of *Third World Quarterly*, one of the most important academic journals on issues related to the Global South.

Anne Sisson Runyan is Professor Emerita in the School of Public and International Affairs at the University of Cincinnati, USA. A recognized eminent scholar in the field of feminist international relations, she has published widely in the areas of feminist international political economy and peace and security studies, held multiple fellowships and a Fulbright Research Chair position, headed women's studies and politics departments, and served in leadership roles for the International Studies Association, the *International Feminist Journal of Politics* and the American Association of University Professors.

RIPE Series in Global Political Economy

Series Editors: Susanne Soederberg *(Queen's University, Canada)*, Adrienne Roberts *(The University of Manchester, UK)*, Samuel Knafo *(University of Sussex, UK)* and Naná de Graaff *(Vrije Universiteit Amsterdam, the Netherlands)*.

For almost two decades now, the *RIPE Series in Global Political Economy* published by Routledge has been an essential forum for cutting-edge scholarship in International Political Economy, which we understand to be a broadly defined area of research that may cut across other disciplines. The series brings together new and established scholars working in critical, cultural and constructivist political economy. Books in the *RIPE Series* typically combine an innovative contribution to theoretical debates with rigorous empirical analysis.

The RIPE Series seeks to cultivate:

- Field-defining theoretical advances in International Political Economy.
- Novel treatments of key issue areas, such as global finance, trade, and production, both historical and contemporary.
- Analyses that explore the political economic dimensions of relatively neglected topics, such as the environment, gender, race, and colonialism from both Western and non-Western perspectives.
- Accessible work that will inspire advanced undergraduates and graduate students in International Political Economy.

Political Economy as Theodicy
Progress, Suffering and Denial
David L. Blaney

Residential Capitalism
Rent Extraction and Capitalist Production in Modern Spain (1833–2023)
Javier Moreno Zacarés

Gender and Global Restructurings, Third Edition
Sightings, Sites and Resistances
Edited by Marianne H. Marchand and Anne Sisson Runyan

For more information about this series, please visit: www.routledge.com/RIPE-Series-in-Global-Political-Economy/book-series/RIPE

Gender and Global Restructurings

Sightings, Sites and Resistances

Third Edition

Edited by
Marianne H. Marchand and Anne Sisson Runyan

Routledge
Taylor & Francis Group
LONDON AND NEW YORK

Designed cover image: © Marianne H. Marchand

Third edition published 2025
by Routledge
4 Park Square, Milton Park, Abingdon, Oxon OX14 4RN

and by Routledge
605 Third Avenue, New York, NY 10158

Routledge is an imprint of the Taylor & Francis Group, an informa business

First edition published by Routledge 2000

Second edition published by Routledge 2011

British Library Cataloguing-in-Publication Data
A catalogue record for this book is available from the British Library

ISBN: 978-0-367-47759-2 (hbk)
ISBN: 978-0-367-47758-5 (pbk)
ISBN: 978-1-003-03642-5 (ebk)

DOI: 10.4324/9781003036425

Typeset in Sabon
by Taylor & Francis Books

For all those who resist inequality and social injustice

Contents

Contributors

Pauline Gardiner Barber is Professor (Emeritus) at Dalhousie University and specializes in global migration and the anthropology of labor. Her current research includes "Fast food, slow migrations: Canada's temporary foreign workers at home in the Philippines," a collaborative project with Catherine Bryan and two Philippine researchers. Funded by the Social Sciences and Humanities Research Council (SSHRC) of Canada, this transnational project tracks the mutually influential mobilities of capital and labor along the Philippines–Canada migration corridor and follows from previous SSHRC-funded Philippine research on the transnational consequences of Canada's "just-in-time" immigration restructuring.

Suzanne Bergeron is Professor Emerita of Women's Studies and Social Sciences at the University of Michigan Dearborn. Her research is focused on ways to foster diverse, noncapitalist economic practices within gender and development policy. She is currently a collaborating researcher with the United Nations Inter-Agency Task Force on the Social and Solidarity Economy, the Community Economies Research Network, the Revaluing Care in the Global Economy project and the Diverse Solidarity Economies Collective.

Catherine Bryan is an anthropologist and Associate Professor of Social Work at Dalhousie University. Her specialties include labor migration and immigration, transnational livelihoods, work and development, rural communities, social reproduction and feminist political economy. Her research funded by the Social Sciences and Humanities Research Council (SSHRC) of Canada has focused on the political economy of food in Canada, including investigations of immigrant fast food workers, seasonal agricultural workers and fish processing workers.

Kimberly A. Chang is Associate Professor Emerita of Cultural Psychology and Creative Nonfiction at Hampshire College. She is the founder of Memory-Works, a creative research and writing practice for individuals and communities who are trying to recover and reclaim histories that have been censored, silenced or erased. Her award-winning book, *Accomplice to Memory* (2018), combines memoir, historical fiction and documentary photographs to explore the hybrid possibilities of truth telling across generations and geographies. She is Prose Editor at *The Massachusetts Review*.

Edmé Domínguez Reyes served as an Associate Professor in Peace and Development Studies within the School of Global Studies at the University of Gothenburg before her retirement, having also held academic positions in her native country of Mexico, the US, and other parts of Europe. She has focused her research since the 1990s on gender analysis within the field of International Relations, with particular emphasis on gendered global political economy and democracy. Her main geographical area of study is Latin America, particularly Mexico, Central America and Bolivia.

Laura Dudley Jenkins is Political Science Professor and Women's, Gender and Sexuality Studies Faculty Affiliate at the University of Cincinnati's School of Public and International Affairs, where she co-founded the Feminist Comparative and International Politics concentration in the Political Science doctoral program. Her book, *Religious Freedom and Mass Conversion in India* (2019), won the American Political Science Association 2020 Hubert Morken Best Book prize.

Rahel Kunz (PhD, Political Science, University of Lucerne) is Senior Lecturer at the Institute of Political Studies at the University of Lausanne, Switzerland. Her research draws on feminist, poststructuralist and de-/postcolonial theories. She has published in *International Political Sociology, Journal of European Integration, Migration Studies, Politics & Gender, Review of International Political Economy* and *International Feminist Journal of Politics* and is the author of *The Political Economy of Global Remittances: Gender, Governmentality and Neoliberalism* (Routledge 2011).

L.H.M. Ling was, at the time of her untimely death in 2018, Professor in the Graduate Program in International Affairs at The New School in New York. Among her many books are *Postcolonial International Relations: Conquest and Desire between Asia and the Rest* (2002) and *The Dao of World Politics: Towards a Post-Westphalian, Worldist International Relations* (2014). She has been published in a host of journals, such as the *International Feminist Journal of Politics, Millennium, International Studies Review, Review of International Political Economy, International Studies Quarterly* and the *Journal of Peace Research*. She contributed to many edited volumes, including the first and second editions of this volume as well as the present one posthumously. She is remembered for her invaluable contributions to feminist postcolonial international relations thought, her tremendous creativity and drive, and the wondrous spirit she brought to all who knew her.

Rirhandu Mageza-Barthel recently served as Professor of Peace and Development Studies at the University of South Africa (UNISA). Her research focuses on the international relations of the Global South, particularly on gendered post-conflict transformation, sustainable development frameworks and African–Chinese relations. Among her publications, she authored the monograph *Mobilizing Transnational Gender Politics in Post-Genocide Rwanda* (2015) and is the co-editor of the volumes *Negotiating Normativity: Postcolonial Appropriations, Contestations and Transformations* (2016) and *Afrasian Transformations. Transregional Perspectives on Development Cooperation, Social Mobility and Cultural Change* (2020).

Marianne H. Marchand recently retired from the Universidad de las Américas Puebla, Mexico, where she held a chair in international relations and directed the Canadian Studies Program. She is currently an adjunct research professor at the Institute of Political Economy at Carleton University, Canada, after having held a visiting professorship there. In addition, she is widely recognized in the Americas for her scholarship on feminist international relations and is a member of the UNU-CRIS Hub México–CIDE, as well as academic editor of *Third World Quarterly*, one of the most important academic journals on issues related to the Global South.

Valentine M. Moghadam is a Professor of Sociology and International Affairs and former director of the International Affairs Program at Northeastern University, Boston, which she joined in January 2012. Previously she directed women's studies programs at Purdue University and Illinois State University and she was a section chief at UNESCO and a senior researcher at UNU/WIDER. Born in Iran, she is the author of many publications on politics, gender and the political economy of Middle East and North African countries.

Brenda Ramírez recently finished her MA degree in Sociocultural Anthropology at the Social Science and Humanities Institute of the Universidad Autónoma de Puebla, Mexico. Her MA thesis focuses on debt, migration and social reproduction in times of COVID-19. She co-authored "'Cambiando el chip': The gendered constellation of subjectivities of the financialisation of remittances in Mexico" in *Environment & Planning A: Economy and Space* (2022).

Michelle V. Rowley is Associate Professor in the Harriet Tubman Department of Women, Gender and Sexuality Studies, University of Maryland. She has also held a visiting appointment as a Benedict Distinguished Visiting Professor in the Women's and Gender Studies Program, Carleton College. Her publications address issues of gender and development, the politics of welfare and Caribbean women's reproductive health and well-being. She is presently completing a manuscript that examines queer representations of "home" in the English-speaking Caribbean.

Anne Sisson Runyan is Professor Emerita in the School of Public and International Affairs at the University of Cincinnati, USA. A recognized eminent scholar in the field of feminist international relations, she has published widely in the areas of feminist international political economy and peace and security studies, held multiple fellowships and a Fulbright Research Chair position, headed women's studies and politics departments, and served in leadership roles for the International Studies Association, the *International Feminist Journal of Politics* and the American Association of University Professors.

Gillian Youngs is an innovation expert with an international background as an academic researcher and leader. She has held professorial, senior management and visiting positions in UK and US universities, and presented and applied her feminist and digital economy research in Europe, Asia and Africa. She was a founding co-editor of the *International Feminist Journal of Politics* in 1999 and continues to serve on its International Advisory Council. Her recent work outside the academy has included high-level expert contributions on security, innovation and gender at the European Commission in relation to research funding programs.

Acknowledgments for the third edition

We began work on this third edition just before the COVID pandemic, which, along with other political and personal shocks, delayed its publication. But it was that tumultuous time, constituting the next shock after the Great Financial Crisis, the gendered contours of which we had just begun to chronicle in the second edition, that would further lay bare the vast gender and other inequalities and precarities plaguing the world's peoples and the planet. As spoken to in this volume, "recoveries" from global financial and health crises have been far from just and further crises already in the making have taken on new urgency in their aftermaths. These include climate and democracy crises, and the reemergence of great power conflicts, whether in the form of the Russian war on Ukraine or the Israeli war on Gaza, creating evermore military spending and humanitarian disasters. Just as the COVID crisis hit already vulnerable women and racialized peoples in the Global North and South particularly hard, the marked increase in climate change-induced disasters, (neo)authoritarianisms and increased militarization have considerable gendered and racialized dimensions that feminists continue to reveal. The introduction to this edition only briefly surveys these contemporary crises and some feminist thinking about them, while highlighting, through contributor chapters, the twin threats of persistent neoliberalism and rising neoauthoritarianism to women's empowerment, gender equality, and social and environmental justice struggles as well as varied resistances to unjust orders and relations in the global capitalist political economy.

We thank those contributors for their patience in getting this volume out and the insights their chapters reveal about ongoing restructurings in various sites. Indeed, no one volume can capture the extent of what we now refer to as global restructurings in the plural as complexities continue to mount as polities, economies, and gender identities and relations undergo contradictory restructurings. There remains continuity in the negative gendered impacts of ongoing expropriative, extractive and exploitative political economies, but there are also widening repertoires of resistances to challenge them.

Beyond the current contributors (and those who contributed to past editions as well), we also thank each other for producing together one more edition of this volume that colleagues and students around the world have found useful. Anne further thanks her former political science doctoral student, Murat

Yilmaz, who conducted style editing in the early life of the volume preparation and has since become an assistant professor of international relations at Kastamonu University in Turkey and with whom Anne continues to collaborate, along with her former doctoral students, Drs. Anwar Mhajne and Crystal Whetstone, on a sixth edition of *Global Gender Politics*. She especially thanks Stephen Bryant, her current political science doctoral student (and now doctoral candidate who is focusing his dissertation on women's and men's defections from ISIS), for completing style editing as the volume later came together and helping prepare the final manuscript for submission. These and other students who completed the feminist comparative and international politics doctoral concentration in political science that Anne instituted at the University of Cincinnati are populating the next generation of feminist international relations (IR) scholars. Funding and other institutional support over time from the School of Public and International Affairs, the College of Arts & Sciences, and the Taft Research Center at the University of Cincinnati enabled student support for this volume and Anne's collaborations with Marianne and the contributors to the volume.

Marianne would like to thank the many students (now alumni) who have studied with her and started the journey with her to "put feminist IR on the map in Mexico." Their critical engagements, support and queries have been a great source of reflection and continuing *amistades*. It is, therefore, that she would like to mention in particular her first PhD student in Mexico, Monica Trujillo, who has been one of the pillars and promoters of feminist IR and who sadly lost the struggle against COVID. It was through her efforts and those of many other alumni, including Rocio Osorno, Elena Ayala, Edmundo Meza, Marcela López-Vallejo and Adriana Sletza, that we finally were able to create one of the first sections or committees within the Asociación Mexicana de Estudios Internacionales, the Comité de Género, Interseccionalidad, Teorías Feministas y Queer. Finally, she would like to thank the Institute of Political Economy at Carleton University for the opportunity to spend a semester teaching and researching, which allowed her to dedicate time to finishing this third edition.

Anne and Marianne are also grateful to those who were a part of or gave feedback on various presentations we, and at times other contributors, made on parts of the volume in progress at International Studies Association and *International Feminist Journal of Politics* conferences and at the Institute of Political Economy at Carleton University. We particularly thank Hannah Rich at Routledge for her always helpful editorial assistance and patience all along the way as well as others at Routledge who assisted with copyediting and production.

Finally, while both Marianne and Anne have recently retired from their institutions, their scholarship continues apace, and their loved ones continue to provide the emotional and material support for them to continue it. Anne thanks her husband, Albert Kanters, for his past, ongoing and undying support of her work and life. Marianne thanks her partner, Héctor Pelaez, for his unconditional support during an especially trying period since the COVID crisis started, which meant having to deal with health, work and family issues.

Acknowledgments for the second edition

In the decade between the first and second editions of this volume, much has changed as global restructuring has worn on, which is why we agreed to produce this almost completely new snapshot of the phenomenon through gender lenses that attempts to capture the latest shifts in the sites of and resistances to it through fresh feminist sightings that come from contemporary postcolonial, postmodern, and queer scholarship. To accomplish this, we especially thank our many contributors to this volume, which contains one reprised piece, three new pieces by contributors to the first volume, and eight pieces by new contributors, including the preface. As before, these contributors come from a variety of disciplinary, interdisciplinary, institutional, and geographical locations and offer glimpses into restructuring processes on four continents (Africa, Asia, South America, and North America) and through analyses of a host of intergovernmental and nongovernmental policies and actions with implications for the most global to the most intimate relations. While the disciplinary backgrounds of our contributors are largely the social sciences, we note with particular pleasure that many of them hold positions in women's and gender studies departments, speaking to the growth and sophistication of globalization studies within feminist studies, which also accounts for even greater conceptual and methodological pluralism, including insights and analytical subjects, objects and methods associated with the humanities. We also thank many of these contributors for participating in several panels we organized at successive International Studies Association meetings through the Feminist Theory and Gender Studies Section in preparation for this volume.

On the manuscript production end, we are deeply indebted to Holly McEntyre, a graduate of the MA/JD joint degree program in Women's Studies and Law at the University of Cincinnati and Anne's research and graduate assistant for several years while completing her studies. Thanks to a fellowship and student assistance funds Anne received from the Taft Center at the University of Cincinnati to work on this volume, she had Holly's services. Holly admirably performed a phenomenal amount of tasks associated with completing the manuscript, ranging from administrative and clerical support to research and editing assistance. Anne is particularly grateful for not only her many competencies, but also her emotional support during the preparation of this volume.

We also thank Routledge staff, particularly Heidi Bagtazo, Editor of the Politics and International Studies division, who commissioned this second volume based on the strong reception to and impact of the first, as well as those who brought this volume to fruition from manuscript form.

Finally, we thank our respective departments and institutions for the sabbatical leave we both enjoyed while working on this volume; our partners, Hector and Al, and other family members for their support during its production, and each other for yet another collaboration among many that we hope will contribute to the ongoing struggle for social justice.

Acknowledgments for the first edition

This volume arose out of an international and interdisciplinary conference on "Gender and global restructuring: shifting sites and sightings," which we co-organized at the University of Amsterdam in May 1995 under the auspices of the Belle van Zuylen Institute for comparative and multicultural gender studies and the Research Center for International Political Economy (RECIPE). We are grateful to the generous funders of that conference, in particular the Belle van Zuylen Institute, the Faculty of Social Sciences at the University of Amsterdam, and the Nederlandse Organisatie voor Wetenschappelijk Onderzoek (NWO – The Dutch Organization for Scientific Research), for making the beginnings of this volume possible. In addition, we wish to thank Barbara van Balen, Sarah Richardson, and all the Dutch and international students (in particular, the members of the FAIR group) who helped us to organize the conference.

Since that conference, we have had the opportunity to share thoughts and ideas from the evolving manuscript with colleagues in academic and NGO settings (in Bad Böl, New York, San Diego, Vienna, Kansas, and back in Amsterdam) and with our students, who have over the years participated in our research seminars. The critical and constructive input of all these friends, colleagues, and students has sharpened our analysis and enabled us to develop our ideas more fully. For this support and input, we are very grateful.

Several of the contributors participated in the May 1995 Conference and the rest joined in the project as the volume took shape. Our greatest thanks go to the contributors for their insights, patience, and ongoing support for the project. We also wish to thank V. Spike Peterson, Christine Chin, Henk Overbeek, and Otto Holman for their very thoughtful and helpful reviews of the manuscript as well as Vicki Smith, Craig Fowlie, Fintan Power, Eve Daintith, and other Routledge staff in London for their assistance in bringing this volume to fruition.

We are particularly indebted to people who were vital to the production of the manuscript at our respective institutions: Marianne Franklin, editorial assistant for the RIPE Series in Global Political Economy, kept the project on track with Routledge, and at Wright State University, Connie Jacobs, administrative assistant to the Women's Studies Program, and work-study student Heidi Gerstenberger deserve tremendous credit for their extraordinary clerical support, without which we would have been hard-pressed to compile the manuscript. A faculty development grant from the College of Liberal Arts at Wright State also helped to defray manuscript production costs.

On more personal notes, we owe our deepest gratitude to our partners, Steven Stusek and Albert Adrian Kanters, and our families for all their emotional support. We also thank and celebrate each other for so joyfully engaging in this transcontinental collaboration, building a friendship in the process, and so diligently bringing the work to its conclusion. We can only hope that it will do justice to the many women and men who are progressively resisting and redirecting global restructuring, for whom it was written.

1 Introduction

Gender, global crises and global restructurings

Marianne H. Marchand and Anne Sisson Runyan

Introduction: Setting the stage for the current edition

The Global Financial Crisis (GFC) of 2008–2009 was a result of decades of neoliberal capitalist ideology and practices that privileged the amassing of financial capital over the production of goods producing gross inequalities between the rich and the rest; retreats of social safety nets and financial, labor and environmental regulations associated with welfare and developing states; and the feminization, or the flexibilization, casualization, informalization and privatization, of labor (Sassen, 2014; Peterson, 2003). The latter was brought about through shifts in productive and reproductive economies through reductions in wages and benefits particularly affecting male-dominated occupations (along with an increase in incarceration of unemployed, mostly racialized men), the growth of the service economy, and increasing reliance on "cheap" female labor, often provided by racialized and immigrant women, in service, manufacturing and privatized social reproductive occupations from childcare to healthcare (Sassen, 2014; Peterson, 2003). Since the GFC, the global landscape has been marked by many more major and minor transformations, challenges and crises. Although it is not our intention to name them all and discuss them in detail, we would like to highlight a few that may create, or already have created, new concerns about the global political economy (GPE) and its gendered dimensions as the backdrop for introducing this edition of the volume.

Taking center stage in the contemporary moment is the global climate crisis, which is much more visibly impacting lives around the world as weather patterns are disrupted in many ways. The increasing frequency and severity of hurricanes, floods, heat waves, wildfires and droughts are affecting planetary ecosystems, food systems, economies and habitats for humans and the more-than-human world, endangering the very existence of lifeworlds. However, the effects are not distributed equally across populations, countries and ecosystems, with the poor, and the already ravaged environments within which they live, being affected most significantly and disproportionately, particularly in the Global South where states have been rendered far less capable of implementing climate resilience and adaptability policies. From an intersectional feminist perspective, or one that takes into account the intersections among the structural inequalities of gender, race, class,

DOI: 10.4324/9781003036425-1

sexuality and nationality to produce complex social stratifications, the situation looks even bleaker: poor, indigenous and racialized women tend to be affected most (Trauger and Fluri, 2019) in their home countries and as climate refugees. Given the speed with which oceans are warming and icecaps are melting, even a (so far highly insufficient) reduction in the use of fossil fuels plus (so far very spotty) adaptability and resilience measures are probably not enough to turn the tide of global climate change. Rather, the gendered and racialized global neoliberal capitalist economic system driving extractivist, exploitative and polluting priorities that fall on the most vulnerable needs to be transformed to the core for creating a sustainable and more equitable global economy and planetary habitat.

The global climate crisis, which in itself can be seen as a crisis of care for the Earth, and the gendered and racialized social inequalities it lays bare, exacerbates the crisis of care for children, the elderly and the sick, also falling most on poor and working-class women, particularly of color, immigrant and in the Global South under ongoing neoliberal global restructurings. The privatization of social reproduction, with the imposition of austerities in welfare and developing states and the outsourcing of care by wealthier households to poor and working-class racialized and immigrant women has been going on for some time, with the global care chain, or the international division of reproductive labor in Parreñas's terms (2015), already quite visible by the 1990s. Feminists have long documented that such caregivers often work under exploitative working conditions and those who provide live-in care may find themselves faced with verbal and physical abuse, including sexual assault and domestic violence (Parreñas, 2015). But the crisis of care was further laid bare and widened by the global COVID crisis, which not only enforced privatized care, primarily by women, in locked-down homes where domestic violence rose, but also exposed how reliant underfunded healthcare systems are on poorly paid, yet classified as "essential," female labor, often of color and often immigrant. For poor and working-class women in the Global South, where protective equipment and vaccines were least available and food insecurity was heightened as global supply chains slowed significantly, their social reproductive work to sustain communities was critical but even more underresourced. Even for many middle-class couples in the Global North (and South), which the pandemic forced to work from home, the combination of providing care, including the need for increased educational support in the face of school closures and online learning, and working in the same domestic space put in sharp relief the need to rethink and reorganize social reproductive work and its relation to productive work. For feminists, the care crisis, which was especially pushed to the fore by the pandemic, is not about minor adjustments to or accommodations for "work–life balance" or just some minor increase in or minimal return to more public provisioning, but rather a profound overhaul of the productive–reproductive continuum and the gender dynamics of it.

As processes of privatization, marketization, financialization and casualization, which have played major roles in producing climate, care and health crises, are precaritizing more and more people in the GPE, there have been significant political repercussions as well. A notable rise in nationalist populism has been seen by some as a reaction of some of those being left behind economically (particularly working-class men) to cultural shifts, such as women's, racial, sexual and gender minority rights, and immigrant protections, that are turned into threats to an imagined national body politic and blamed on global cosmopolitan elites by nationalist populist politicians. While nationalist populist agendas on both the right and left gained steam in countering international trade agreements and neoliberal international financial institutions (IFIs), such as the International Monetary Fund (IMF), for eroding national control over economies, nationalist populists on the right further blame the United Nations (UN) and its international human rights agendas and agreements for undermining national identities. Different from resistances to the universalizing of Western commercial culture referred to as "macdonaldization" in the 1990s, we are now witnessing a rising illiberal political landscape where nationalist populist movements, politicians and parties most critical of progressive cultural shifts have been gaining ground. These movements and leaders in the Global North and South, with their anti-globalist and often anti-elitist discourse (despite the fact that elite figures and money have enabled these movements and their political representatives), have targeted human rights regimes in liberal democracies. In the US, these nationalist populist politics enabled Donald Trump to become president, resulting in full frontal attacks on women's reproductive, minority and migrant rights as well as diversity, equity and inclusion programs in workplaces and educational institutions, ranging from outlawing affirmative action nationwide to banning critical race curricula and the rights of trans children in schools in some states. There are also state efforts to ban teaching of climate change and even mention of it in state government information as well to make voting more difficult for the poor and people of color. These measures are part of what is being increasingly referred to as the "authoritarian playbook" practiced prior to Trump by such right-wing Global South leaders as Bolsonaro in Brazil, Modi in India and Duterte in the Philippines, and a possible second Trump term could result in even worse assaults on democracy and human rights. Across the Atlantic, first in Central Europe and now in Western and Southern Europe and the European Parliament, we see a similar phenomenon of right-wing parties on the rise and in power. The Brexit campaign in the United Kingdom (UK) was informed by nationalist sentiments, inspired by imaginaries of Britain's imperial past. Although some right-wing nationalist populist parties have lost recent elections (such as in Brazil and Poland), lost ground (such as in India) or are out of power (such as in the UK where Labor won the 2024 elections), nationalist populisms, which on the whole are against liberal democracies, universal human rights, migration and intersectional feminism at national and international levels, are now mainstreamed features of global political life.

The outbreak of the Russian war against Ukraine waged by Putin's authoritarian regime not only triggers reminiscences of nationalist imperial designs, adopting the central trope that the territory to be reconquered belongs historically to the aggressor, but also recalls geopolitical imaginaries of the Cold War, with its clear battlelines across Europe and other parts of the world. From an intersectional feminist perspective, this war is reinforcing a military-based hegemonic masculinity, at least in the two states involved. For instance, in Ukraine, women, children and the elderly were seen as vulnerable groups and allowed to flee the country, while able-bodied men between the ages of 18 and 60 were not. In Russia, any dissidence or call for an end to the war and for peace has been fiercely repressed. Yet, female family members of soldiers who died in the war have used their "feminized spaces" as mothers, wives or sisters to demand information about how their loved ones died. However, thus far any voices on both sides demanding peace have been crowded out. This has been visually underscored by photos that were taken of feeble negotiation attempts during the early days of the war and in which only men were sitting around the table. This war, too, has disrupted food supplies from Ukraine to parts of the Global South, increasing food insecurity, already severe from the pandemic, that again falls mostly on women and children there, while ratcheting up military buildup and spending by NATO allies of Ukraine and by Russia and its current allies of China, North Korea and Iran, with consequences for domestic spending for social welfare across all these political economies (some of which are also under economic sanctions imposed by the West as well as having already repressive social orders).

The extreme escalation of the Israeli war against Hamas is another example of voices for peace being crowded out, along with the destruction of human and nonhuman life, infrastructures and ecosystems. It was precisely in the context of the Palestinian–Israeli conflict that the Women in Black movement emerged in 1988 in the context of the first Intifada, calling for an end to the Israeli occupation. Yet, their historical and current peace with justice efforts have been completely silenced by the mainstream media, while Israeli protests more generally against the destruction of civilian life in Gaza as well as against the right-wing government there have also been treated as seditious rather than humanitarian. The worldwide humanitarian response to the situation in Gaza—with many young (and not so young) people, particularly on university campuses in many parts of the world, being "doxed" for demonstrating against the actions of Israel in Gaza—has raised the question of how critical perspectives are represented on social media and the internet in general, part of what has been referred to as the "virtual economy" (Peterson, 2003), which, in addition to virtual financial transactions that produced the havoc of the GFC, are currently wreaking havoc on sociopolitical identities and psychologies.

This is an increasingly important question as we are saturated by a mediated world, with a range of state and nonstate actors manipulating the information that we receive, through such practices as using bots, spreading conspiracy theories and calling unwelcome information fake news, while also reaping tremendous profits and gaining tremendous power through surveilling and manufacturing online and offline behavior. An example of this is how the COVID pandemic has triggered heated debates about vaccines, with anti-vaxxers rejecting vaccines developed following established scientific methods that have been developed and refined over centuries, with the effect of many unnecessarily dying of the disease once vaccines were available. In addition, the information we receive via social media is increasingly siloed through both algorithms and self-selection, resulting in a situation where we increasingly move within our own circles of like-minded people and are led to believe that the information we receive is the "truth" and that others outside of our circles are exposed to fake news.

The latest development in this mediated environment is artificial intelligence (AI) of which ChatGPT is only one example and, which like other AI products, scrapes the internet, regardless of intellectual and cultural copyrights, and applies algorithms to produce sanitized and often nonreferenced materials in answer to questions posed. One of us (Marchand) experimented with this tool by asking it for an intersectional and decolonial feminist analysis of the Israeli war on Hamas. The answer did list some relatively accurate, but nonreferenced and limited, representations of intersectional and decolonial feminisms and how those would critique patriarchy, colonialism and nationalism (but not capitalist relations) as contributing to the war. It also included reference to the politics of solidarity as a counter to the humanitarian disaster toward a just peace that centers human rights and security for all, including women (which was a more watered down and unnuanced conclusion that did not address particular social movements, their agendas or histories in the region).

However, it was not this generic answer but rather the proviso at the end that an intersectional, decolonial feminist approach was just one of many ways to analyze the case, warning that other perspectives must be weighed against it, which was most troubling. While seemingly suggestive of support for pluralist knowledge, such provisos did not occur when ChatGPT was asked about reproductive justice (constructed as a women's issue), thus, signaling that when it comes to war, and the particularly contentious case of Israel's war against Hamas, feminist approaches are more suspect. Although the experiment did not include asking for realist positions, for example, on the war, to see if those were treated as one among many perspectives, this experiment produced some worry about how critical approaches are treated more generally on ChatGPT and in AI more generally, filtering out, diluting or marginalizing positions uncomfortable for dominant perspectives and continuing a tilt toward them. Given AI, as a now extremely powerful tool in the virtual economy that is enriching those who control it, specifically men in STEM (science, technology, engineering and math) fields that have been particularly resistant to women's inclusion (see Youngs, this volume), we have to ask how knowledge is also being restructured in ways that benefit old hierarchies being reimposed in these times of right-wing ascendencies and new hierarchies based on novel and unregulated technologies that the neoliberal global economy assists in spreading, but in the process concentrates power even more.

The current edition in retrospect and prospect

As the foregoing backdrop suggests, this Introduction to this edition of *Gender and Global Restructurings: Sightings, Sites and Resistances* is concerned with a stocktaking of profound transformations, including economic, political and environmental crises, that have come to the fore since the GFC. In so doing it aims to revisit some of the issues and concepts that we first raised in the previous editions while indicating how contemporary feminist thinking can help to encompass and refine analysis of current features of global restructuring we highlighted earlier. Central to our retrospective endeavor is the question of whether the concept of global restructuring continues to help us in understanding and analyzing some of the profound transformations and crises that we have witnessed in the more than two decades since our first edition. In that edition, we hypothesized that it was better to think of processes associated with top-down, one-way and inevitable globalization at the time as global restructuring of socioeconomic, political and cultural life that was disjointed, non-encompassing and multidirectional, and, thus, open-ended in terms of the outcomes of conflicts between forces of domination and resistances to them. We also insisted on a more intersectional feminist lens to understand how global restructuring was simultaneously gendered, classed, raced and sexualized, and how intersectional identities and struggles challenged this process.

In the contemporary moment of evermore acute and varied global crises, we still see global restructuring as an apt characterization of ongoing and too often negative transformations, but we refer to it in this edition as global restructurings in the plural to better relay the complexities of competing, disjointed, multidirectional yet interconnected forces at work. The shift to thinking about global restructurings is also informed by further feminist theorizing about power relations and the GPE, which has increasingly engaged with other critical approaches to deepen intersectional analysis, including decolonial and postcolonial approaches, critical race studies and queer studies among others (Elias and Roberts, 2018).

It is also important to note that while our first edition applied feminist lenses and the concept of global restructuring to complicate globalization studies that were ascendant within the study of international political economy (IPE) in the 1990s in the immediate post-Cold War era, our second edition took into account the security turn in international relations (IR) more generally after the events of September 11, 2001. This led to a shift in feminist IR inquiry toward feminist security studies (FSS) to grapple with the subsequent war on terror and remilitarization. Although we made links between the rise in direct international militarized violence to the structural violence of neoliberal-cum-neoimperial restructurings of the global political economy, feminist international political economy (FIPE) inquiry more generally became less evident in the field of feminist international relations (FIR), at least until the global financial crisis of 2008–2009, followed by the next shock of the COVID crisis of 2020–2022, and now the climate crisis amidst also two new wars that are becoming more globalized. In recent years and in the face of these numerous crises, more FIR scholars have returned to breaking down the "conceptual" barriers that had arisen between FSS and FIPE. Elias and Roberts (2018, p. 9) are positive about this development as they argue that

> the silo-ing of feminist scholarship into areas that focus either on 'political economy' or 'security' (contested as these terms may be) greatly limits our ability to understand the complex nature of global politics as it is manifested from the macro to the micro scales.

As a result, more FSS scholars are applying political economy analyses to questions of war, peace and security, particularly in terms of the gendered economic and environmental conditions and infrastructures that have goaded armed conflict, been the result of it and are reproduced in so-called post-conflict contexts (Cohn and Duncanson, 2020), and FIPE scholars are seeing gendered violence, not as a division between direct and structural violence, but on a continuum in which international and domestic economic and militarized violence against women as well as violence against the environment are intertwined and require simultaneous and integrated struggles to produce more caring, green, nonviolent and just political economies (True and Tanyag, 2019).

Thus, this edition, both within this Introduction and in terms of the contributors' chapters to it, foregrounds the gendered violence of ongoing restructurings, particularly in the forms of the proliferations of virulent and even seemingly more benign forms of capitalism, from "expulsive," "cannibal," "disaster," "neoliberal," "neoauthoritarian," "racial," "homo," "gore" and "surveillance" (including AI) capitalisms to financial, development and philanthropic capitalisms that are deeply gendered as well as classed, raced and so on. At the same time, it also foregrounds particularly women's resistances, in various parts of the world and in differing socioeconomic and political locations, to these various forms of capitalist restructurings. Central to several contributions is challenging co-optations of the idea of "women's empowerment" by states and corporations under neoliberal capitalism to advance more radical understandings of what this should entail and how women resist neoliberal empowerment approaches, particularly at micro-levels. While the latest phases of gendered capitalist restructurings are indeed daunting, particularly in these times of deep ideological and political polarization (typically by gender, race, class, sexuality, religion and nationality) domestically and internationally that are productive of the present political, economic and environmental crises and disabling of meaningful responses to them by national and international institutional actors, it is now more often local and more micro-resistances and the cataloging of them that suggest rising noncooperation with top-down restructurings that are taking particularly virulent and authoritarian turns. Such micro-resistances also lay the basis for renewed larger-scale resistances to existential crises that are pitting neoliberal and neoauthoritarian capitalist forces and gendered, racialized and ecological violence against efforts to seek more democratic and social justice-informed restructuring from the bottom-up. Thus, the emphasis in this edition, as highlighted in several contributions, is on women's and feminist agency in resistance to neoliberal capitalist co-optation and neoauthoritarian capitalist repression of more inclusive, just and democratic thought and action toward alternative political economies.

The remainder of this introductory chapter more fully details how the concept of gender and global restructuring was addressed in previous volumes, followed by a section that addresses how the contemporary landscape of gender and global restructurings is being accompanied by advances in feminist scholarship that are deepening and widening feminist GPE scholarship. Following that is a discussion of the shift in the present moment from a focus on "globalization" to centering myriad forms of capitalism identified in feminist and other critical scholarship, underlining the value of seeing multiple and interconnecting types of violent capitalist restructurings that, however, can be and are being resisted when exposed. In the final sections, we provide an overview of the contributions to the present volume and their contributions to sightings and sites of capitalist restructurings and resistances to them, ending with a few concluding thoughts.

Revisiting past contexts and editions of *Gender and Global Restructuring*

In the first volume published in 2000, our objective was to analyze and unpack globalization from an intersectional feminist perspective. We argued that globalization is a term that is too vague to capture the profound transformations that were taking place. Instead, we suggested the use of the concept of global restructuring to address the following questions: "What are the gendered constructions of the new global political economy? How can we reconceptualize global space from a gender perspective?" (Marchand and Runyan, 2000, p. 2). We argued that these questions would reveal how global restructuring involved "the construction, reconstruction, and transformation of categories of knowing" and that such knowledge production also generated "new gender biases as well as reifying others" (Marchand and Runyan, 2000, p. 2). In addition to our concerns about knowledge production or what we called "sightings," we also turned our attention to specific gendered "sites" of global restructuring and the "resistances" against these transformations. To capture the range of ongoing transformations we argued that global restructuring better "reflects the notion that we are dealing with a set of multidimensional, multispeed, and disjuncted processes" (Marchand and Runyan, 2000, p. 7). By applying the concept of global restructuring, we intended to show that globalization was not a clear, overarching and unidirectional process, but rather that it was a "messy" process that was not easy to capture. Also, it was our contention, and continues to be, that the way in which the term globalization was often applied by some of its proponents and the mainstream media suggested it to be an intangible, universalist and irreversible process, something with which we profoundly disagree. In contrast, in the first edition, we used an intersectional feminist lens to reveal the highly variegated gendered, racialized and classed underpinnings of global restructuring/globalization that generated resistances by gendered, racialized and classed subjects.

Among the emergent trends we identified from the feminist GPE literature at the time were the feminization of the state, particularly with respect to its social welfare and regulatory apparatus, and significant parts of the economy in shifts to service work, expansion of casualized and informalized labor, reliance on cheapened migrant labor and the hypermasculinization of the finance economy as evidenced by the inordinate power of IFIs and transnational corporations (TNCs). This was aided by the rise of information and communications technology (ICT), to purvey and enforce neoliberal (or pro-market) ideology and practices. These practices included structural adjustment programs (SAPs) either imposed by the IMF on indebted Global South countries or adopted by Global North state leaders to cut state social welfare funding, increase exports and trade agreements, devalue currencies and quash labor organizing, while turning citizens with rights into mere consumers and/or exploited workers. These restructuring processes not only fell most heavily upon the poor and working-class, racialized minorities and majorities, and women within these categories, but also relied upon discursive constructions particularly of racialized, classed and/or migrant women, as the most compliant and "cheapest" labor to be tapped for capitalist growth through drawing them more fully into the formal and informal service and light manufacturing economies as home-based, sweatshop, sex and free trade/export-processing zone workers, but also as nannies and health care workers to replace the withdrawal (or relative lack) of state support for social reproduction. At the same time, certain men, such as those privileged by a manufacturing economy, were "falling down" and becoming more superfluous labor, while particularly racialized male labor stayed down. Most men and certainly few women could not achieve the new hegemonic masculinity of the financial sector of the global economy, which sought new forms of capitalist conquest but also had a softer side in promoting business management that emphasized teamwork and flexibility (Hooper, 2001). In subsequent years, this new hegemonic masculinity was referred to and embodied by "Davos man" invoking a masculinity tied to the World Economic Forum (Prügl, 2012). This hegemonic masculinity was, and continues to be, contrasted with other subordinate masculinities and femininities, which were articulated in the context of multiple gendered boundary renegotiations around the valorizations (or masculinizations) of the private, the international and the global realms, and the devalorizations (or feminizations) of the public, domestic and local domains.

The second edition of *Gender and Global Restructuring* (2011) was written and published in a very different context. The events of September 11, 2001, in particular, were generating a new geopolitical situation, which brought about a new "set" of global restructurings that we addressed in that volume. After many conversations, we concluded that the concept of global restructuring continued to be useful as it allowed us to capture the two developments of neoliberal globalization and neoimperial militarization, or the so-called twin towers or pillars of empire (Marchand and Runyan, 2011). By then as well, queer scholarship on globalization was developing and feminist postcolonial scholarship was becoming central; thus, we probed not only the gendered, racialized and classed nature of restructuring but also the heteronormative and (re)colonizing nature of it. It became evident that the hegemonic masculinity connected to the neoliberal globalization of the 1990s was being replaced by a militarized masculinity tied to the war on terror (WoT). This was also accompanied by the securitization and militarization of women, queers, and even feminism, particularly in the US, that operated to, for example, construct new nationalisms through contrasting supposed women's and queer freedoms in the West with their oppression in the Middle East, thus, justifying the WoT. At the same time, neoliberal restructuring was continuing apace, further privatizing care work and undermining labor rights and women's reproductive rights, but also, in line with securitization, hardening international borders against migrants who began to be constructed as terrorists. This left migrant labor even more vulnerable and, thus, even more exploitable to serve neoliberal interests. And while masculinist security actors regained preeminence in public discourse, policy and funding, global and national masculinist finance actors continued their hold on economies advocating even more austerities in part to divert resources to the WoT.

Yet, IFIs were also targeting women in the Global South with funded programs to make them conform to the discipline of the market. For instance, the World Bank promoted this strategy under the slogan "gender equality is smart economics." This marketization and concomitant financialization amounted to a deepening of neoliberal globalization, as it incorporated into the capitalist economy those who were unbanked and underbanked among others. IFIs even began to recognize and incorporate nonheteronormative, often female-headed households in the capitalist market to also make such women "more productive." Obviously, such inclusions did not occur on equal footing or under equal conditions, but rather tended to reinforce existing inequalities or generate new ones.

In addition, the increased militarization triggered by the events of 9/11 affected the possibilities of social movements and other groups to engage in resistance and opposition practices. On the one hand, the anti-globalization movement of the late 1990s and early 2000s morphed into the Global Justice Movement (GJM) that brought together congeries of social justice movements from around the world to produce analyses and manifestos that increasingly centered not only class-based, but race-, gender- and sexuality-based critiques of neoliberal and militarized restructuring (Eschle and Maiguashca, 2010). This also strengthened transnational feminist networks (TFNs) that allied around the goals of "peace, global justice, human rights, and environmentalism" (Moghadam, 2020, p. 179). On the other hand, the WoT tended to render dissent as bordering on terrorism, while later the shocks of the 2008–2009 GFC and the 2020–2022 COVID crises and their aftermaths served to disrupt the large-scale gatherings that the GJM held on regular bases in various parts of the world.

It was during the final stages of writing the second volume that the GFC broke out. This meant that we could not engage with its far-reaching implications through an intersectional feminist lens, although we were able to raise some initial concerns. In general terms, the GFC created new openings for intersectional feminist engagements with the GPE. For example, one unexpected effect of the GFC was that it seemingly provided new openings and spaces for women's inclusion and participation in the global financial sector. Even the international media raised this issue by challenging the toxic masculinized environment of global financial institutions (Prügl, 2012). Yet, this window of opportunity closed rather quickly, and it appears that 15 years later we are virtually back to the situation that gave rise to the GFC in 2008. Although the financial sector is now under tighter controls, in particular through the Basel Accords, signs of its inherent financial instability and uncertainty regularly pop up. The quick rise of cryptocurrencies has raised new concerns about financial stability, well-founded concerns given the size of the fraud Sam Bankman-Fried, the founder of FTX, committed and for which he was convicted.

Such accountabilities of the corporate class and the titans of the virtual economy are rare and will become even less likely with the ascendancy of right-wing forces that are bankrolled by wealthy elites, their think tanks and their dark money. Some have conservative social agendas, but all promote neoliberal agendas in the form of further deregulation or preventing regulation of their industries and of capital as well as tax cuts for the wealthy (Horton, 2022). While not only sustaining and increasing gross economic inequalities between the rich and the rest, such agendas also bode poorly for addressing the interrelated preeminent crises we identified earlier—climate, care, health, political, militarized violence and knowledge—in ways advocated by global justice, and particularly transnational feminist, movements informed by intersectional, decolonial, materialist, posthuman, indigenous, queer, critical masculinity and assemblage thought. We turn now to some of that thought that might assist in making more feminist sense of those crises through expanding and deepening critique of them.

Making better feminist sense of contemporary restructuring(s)

Building on the first two editions, in this volume we highlight some additional advances in feminist and other critical scholarship with which it engages to better analyze systems of power behind the multiple, intertwined contemporary crises, which we briefly outlined at the beginning of this chapter. The overwhelming complexities and speed of these crises require broad engagements of and advancements in critical thought, and this section points to some examples of how feminist thought has been informed and enlarged more recently in ways that promise to make better feminist sense of present crises. Here we briefly trace a few developments in feminist thought over the last two decades indicative of this trend: first, we take up how feminist scholarship has engaged with decolonial studies and critical race studies to deepen understandings of how current crises rest on intertwined intersectional and (neo)colonial power relations; second, we point to how feminists are recentering material relations and further developing thought on relations between the human and more-than-human worlds to expand critique of and resist interrelated human and environmental degradations; and third, we discuss how feminist scholarship is engaging with queer and masculinity studies to better challenge binaries and hierarchies that both right-wing and neoliberal forces seek to sustain or reimpose. We end the section with an example of how these strands are being brought together to produce more complex theorizing necessary for addressing the present complexity of restructurings.

By the 2000s, the concept of intersectionality, which was introduced in the early1990s by Kimberlé Crenshaw (1991), a leading theorist of feminist critical race studies, which holds that race and gender are structural forms of power that cannot be addressed separately from one another, started to "travel." In other words, it was adopted by feminists in other parts of the world and in the process has been transformed. For instance, decolonial feminist Maria Lugones brought Crenshaw's ideas about intersectionality in conversation with the concept of Aníbal Quijano's coloniality of power to posit the "coloniality of gender" (Lugones, 2014). For Rita Segato (2014), it is impossible to understand intersectionality without taking into consideration how gender discrimination and violence are interlinked with the discrimination and inequalities emerging from colonialism (see also Marchand and Ayala, forthcoming). In bringing the issue of coloniality, raised in decolonial feminist studies, into conversation with intersectionality, a deepening of our understanding of the grounded, complex realities lived by marginalized groups in the Global South and North has emerged. It has also underscored the need to revisit feminist knowledge production and provide openings for indigenous women's voices among others.

Feminist scholars have not only engaged in expanding and deepening our understanding about intersectionality in relation to coloniality, but have also taken a more critical stance toward the so-called linguistic or postmodern turn of the 1990s in feminist theory. Since the mid-2000s, feminist academics have been reconsidering the relationalities between culture, nature and the body. This reorientation is often referred to as feminist (new) materialism or posthumanism. This relatively new approach is particularly concerned with criticizing the human-centered world or the Anthropocene by introducing a decentering of the human in relation to other animate and sentient life forms and as well in relation to the technological world in order to challenge such binaries as human/nonhuman and biological/technological. Feminist new materialism, also referred to as material feminisms, emerged from the sciences. Roy and Subramaniam (2016) argue that feminist scholarship has primarily been produced in the humanities and social sciences, and in the process has marginalized the sciences, which is why "scholars working in the tradition of new feminist materialisms are fundamentally interested in producing different kinds of engagements with science, biology, and matter" (p. 26). They point out that it is not the intention of feminist materialism to discard the social and textual as they seek to build feminist bridges and transversal relations across the sciences, humanities and social sciences. They also remind us

> about the very material bodies of colonialism, in all their contradictory and violent histories. Postcolonial studies of science particularly illustrate how western scientific knowledge was not just a tool, mechanism, or logic, but developed alongside and was thus co-constituted with colonialism, and deeply invested and imbricated in colonial governance and expansion.
>
> (Roy and Subramaniam, 2016, p. 28)

Rosi Braidotti, who herself is situated in the humanities, defines the emergence of the critical posthumanities as being "driven by nomadic, embedded, embodied and technologically-mediated subjects [...] and by complex assemblages of human and non-human, planetary and cosmic, given and manufactured forces" (2019, p. 43). According to her, focusing on different lifeworlds implies analyses that address power relations and different types of exclusion or domination that entangle and go beyond the problematic category of the human.

Although in some tension with Western feminist posthumanism and arising from a critique of settler colonialism somewhat different from Latin American decolonial theorizing on the coloniality of power and gender, indigenous feminisms are advancing both posthuman and decolonial feminist studies through bringing to the fore alternative and regenerative cosmologies that do not just decenter the human, but center just relations between the more-than-human world and the human world as a prerequisite for just relations among humans (Simpson, 2017). As First Peoples whose material and spiritual relations with lands, waters, animals and plants have been torn asunder and whose lands, bodies, cultures and lives continue to be taken and destroyed under settler colonialism, indigenous peoples are not reducible to racial or ethnic categories used in intersectional thought, and their struggles for sovereignty, including indigenous women's sovereignty over their bodies and lives, are about making post-settler colonial worlds through restoring communal and just relations between humans and the more-than-human world and, thus, among humans (Tuck and Yang, 2012).

Together, these strains of feminist thought are developing capacities to reimagine subjects, subjectivities and relations that complicate and go beyond traditional categories of analysis to attempt to meet the challenges of disintegrating climates, bodies, polities, economies and social relations saturated by polarizing mediascapes and other technologies. They begin to point the way to encompass competing and allied forces, as interrelated constellations or assemblages, that constitute contemporary disjointed, multispeed and even contradictory restructurings that must be apprehended to challenge and redirect.

Other schools of thought with which feminist studies have engaged in conversations include queer studies and, to a lesser extent, critical masculinity studies, both of which to some extent also emerged out of feminist studies but advanced in their own ways. Queer studies have placed the concept of heteronormativity center stage and pointed at the heteronormative underpinnings of many, if not most, public policies. In the second edition of *Gender and Global Restructuring*, Amy Lind addressed how heteronormativity continues to inform development narratives, institutions and practices in the Global South and how these involve the "meaning and making of sexual subjectivities" (2011, p. 49). Homonormativity has also become a concern not only in relation to the homonationalism expected of queers during the WoT covered in the second edition, but also with respect to the neoliberalizing of queer subjectivities, similar to concerns about the neoliberalizing of feminism we addressed in past editions. This kind of neoliberalization refers to the emptying of radical demands for socioeconomic and political transformations from social movements as dissident identities are incorporated into capitalist relations. At the current moment, however, queer, and particularly trans subjects, are becoming especially vilified and outlawed (once again) by right-wing groups, in part because of the disruption to foundational binaries and hierarchies of families and nations they pose. This speaks to the necessity to push even further on those boundaries in feminist work.

While critical masculinity studies have received less attention in feminist theory, in part because feminist scholars have also addressed masculinities as part of their gender analyses, a recent development in critical masculinity studies suggests shifts that need to be made to better understand how hegemonic masculinity is operating now. Some authors argue that for hegemonic masculinity to maintain itself it has needed a realignment to produce "complex hybrid patterns of power" (Morris and Ratajczak, 2019, p. 1994). "Thus, the 'new man' may appropriate aspects of subordinated masculinity to make himself appear egalitarian and progressive, while continuing to accept and promulgate masculine privilege in hidden ways" (Morris and Ratajczak, 2019, p. 1994). According to Morris and Ratajczak (2019), this hybrid masculinity involves particularly elite men concealing their gender privileges. Although the rise of right-wing "strong man" politics suggests a reappearance of a hegemonic patriarchal ideal, the new man is more embodied by neoliberal corporate and other elites who appear to support various equality measures, but retain male (as well as class, race and so on) privilege to rule in more stealthy ways. The concept of complex, hybrid masculinities could also be applied to the ways in which right-wing movements and politicians are constructing men (particularly of dominant races, religions and so on) as victims of feminism and other progressive movements which are blamed for taking away their natural and rightful male privilege. In this way, even elite men can hide and deny their privilege by also constructing themselves as victims of changing social orders in which they might be held accountable.

An example of how many of the various aforementioned strains of thought are brought together is in the work of Jasbir Puar. In her well-known book *Terrorist Assemblages: Homonationalism in Queer Times* (2007), she addresses intersectionality, materiality and queer studies through the lens of assemblage theory. In particular, she contrasts intersectionality with assemblages, finding fault with the former for being too static and compartmentalized.

> As opposed to an intersectional model of identity, which presumes that components—race, class, gender, sexuality, nation, age, religion—are separable analytics and can thus be disassembled, an assemblage is more attuned to interwoven forces that merge and dissipate time, space, and body against linearity, coherency, and permanency.
>
> (Puar, 2007, p. 212)

In more recent work, however, Puar (2012) suggests that it is important to bridge intersectionality and its focus on identity-based politics with assemblage or "agencement" thinking that emphasize relations and energies among a range of bodies, actors and actants, both human and nonhuman. She concludes that both are necessary to analyze processes of disciplining and control:

> There are different conceptual problems posed by each; intersectionality attempts to comprehend political institutions and their attendant forms of social normativity and disciplinary administration, while assemblages, in an effort to reintroduce politics into the political, asks what is prior to and beyond what gets established. So one of the big payoffs for thinking through the intertwined relations of intersectionality and assemblages is that it can help us produce more roadmaps of precisely these not quite fully understood relations between discipline and control.
>
> (Puar, 2012, n.p.)

This has implications for how feminists might rethink how power is operating in dense webs that not only produce complex stratifications, but also create a kind of hall of mirrors that refract views of what is going on, making it ever more difficult to gain critical purchase. But understanding this helps to make more feminist sense of multiple and interrelated restructurings, productive of both crises and openings to resist them.

Having presented just a few developments in feminist thought that we think might be assisting in apprehending and resisting contemporary global crises, we now turn our gaze to more contemporary feminist and other critical critiques of the GPE, particularly in terms of a shift from "globalization" critiques to identifications and critiques of proliferating forms of capitalism as multiple yet interconnected forms of gendered, classed, racialized, homonormative and colonizing global restructurings.

From globalization to capitalist critique: Contemporary feminist analyses of proliferating forms of capitalist restructurings

The term "globalization" has increasingly fallen from favor, due initially to challenges to it by the largely leftist anti-globalization movement (what became known as the GJM) and more recently to the backlash to it by populist economic and ethnonationalists more often on the right, leading some to even posit we are in a post-globalization world in which states are eschewing interstate economic integration under a (neo)liberal capitalist order in favor of more mercantilist or protectionist, albeit still capitalist, policies. But as feminist political theorist Nancy Fraser (2022) argues, the major shift in critical thought on globalization has been to largely abandon this euphemism and to recenter analyses of capitalism itself. For her, the task in these times of multiple crises is to enlarge our apprehension of capitalism in orthodox Marxist accounts by understanding it as "multidimensional, encompassing not only the official economy, including finance, but also such 'non-economic' phenomena as global warming, 'care deficits,' and the hollowing out of public power at every scale" and "implicating multiple axes of inequality, including nationality/race-ethnicity, religion, sexuality, and class" (Fraser, 2022, p. 2). Relational feminist analyses of the GPE that interconnect institutional, material, symbolic and subjective realms of it (Peterson, 2003) have long understood this, as we argued in previous editions, but Fraser adopts the long understanding that economic relations are embedded in sociopolitical relations while taking this further in arguing that capitalism is a (global) societal system, albeit a highly variegated yet interconnected one, that "cannabilizes" the very inputs it relies on to accumulate wealth, such as nature and productive, reproductive and social reproductive labor (Fraser, 2022, p. 24). Capitalist accumulation rests on "free-riding" processes of dispossession via extraction (most associated with (neo)colonization of indigenous and racialized peoples), exploitation (of more often masculinized and race-privileged paid workers) and expropriation (of feminized and racialized unpaid work and natural resources), but in the process produces the very crises that threaten its functioning and acts "to incite a broad range of social struggles" (Fraser, 2022, p. 24).

Feminist political economist Saskia Sassen (2014, 2016) has observed similar trends in the nature of advanced capitalism, but focuses on how it expels what it no longer needs to consume. Writing in the wake of the GFC, she argues that advanced capitalism has become more characteristic of primitive accumulation, operating no longer to "incorporate" people and places into capitalist relations but rather to "expel" those unnecessary to or in the way of financial profits. For Sassen, expulsions take various forms, including:

> the growing numbers of the abjectly poor, of the displaced in poor countries who are warehoused in formal and informal refugee camps, of the minoritized and persecuted in rich countries who are warehoused in prisons, of workers whose bodies are destroyed on the job and rendered useless at far too young an age, of able-bodied surplus populations warehoused in ghettoes and slums. But I also include the fact that pieces of the biosphere are being expelled from their life space – and I insist that the tame language of climate change does not quite capture the fact, at ground level, of vast expanses of dead land and dead water.
>
> (Sassen, 2016, p. 89)

While "disaster capitalism," as Naomi Klein (2007) dubbed it, fed on the ruins left behind in the wake of "natural" (now understood as heavily "man-made") disasters by displacing the poor to expropriate and redevelop stricken areas for the rich, as such disasters proliferate, particularly in the Global South most subject now to climate change disasters, such areas may be rendered irretrievable for capitalist accumulation and, thus, they and the people in them may be more often simply expelled and left to die. The COVID crisis put this in sharp relief as marginalized populations, particularly by race, class and nationality, were least able to access life-saving healthcare and vaccines and most exposed as "essential workers" or as those who had no choice but to work for income, while lockdowns led to a dramatic rise in already pandemic levels of gender violence.

Thus, the "exes," as Fraser (2022) refers to them, that have constituted capitalism in greater or lesser degrees over time and place not only include extraction (via dispossession), exploitation and expropriation, but also expulsion. And together, these point to ever more and more widespread "necropolitical" capitalist forces at work that determine more often who and what is rendered expendable rather than who and what will be most incorporated in capitalist relations to be sustained for its purposes (until also used up).

Further enabling what Sassen (2014) refers to as the "savage sorting" between those extracted from and/or expelled and those not is the rise of neoauthoritarianism in North and South. Variously referred to as neoconservativism; the New, alt- or transnational Right; ethnonationalism; nationalist populism; or even neofascism, neoauthoritarianism is often depicted as a reaction to neoliberal globalization, which has been linked with the undermining of labor and environmental protection regulations, unionization, decent jobs and benefits, and public services, including social and health services. Deunionization and the casualization, flexibilization, informalization and, thus, the feminization of labor has made certain elements (such as so-called "angry white men" who have been affected economically and socially in shifts from manufacturing to service economies) susceptible to ethnonationalist anti-neoliberal globalization politics. As we have already pointed out, such politics rest on eschewing international trade agreements seen as outsourcing what were once good jobs, stopping immigration (depicted as stealing good jobs) and restoring (white) male privilege socially and economically. However, as we initially noted in the first edition, global restructuring sometimes also provides new openings for resistance. One contemporary example is how the new North American Trade Agreement, known as USMCA, CUSMA or T-MEC in the three respective countries, has provided opportunities for transnational labor organizing resulting in a collective agreement negotiated by the independent union at GM's plant in Silao, Mexico (DiCaro and Macdonald, 2022).

Despite such openings for resisting the feminization of labor in more progressive ways, feminist political theorist Wendy Brown argues that neoconservative responses are actually an extension of neoliberalism and its capital accumulation logics. In her book *In the Ruins of Neoliberalism* (2019), she expands upon how neoliberal logics have not only gutted public provisioning to such an extent that populations are made vulnerable to populist and anti-democratic appeals, but also have replaced public provisioning with privatized "familialization." The objective of familialization or the promotion of "family values" is to shift social obligations and provisioning from the state's responsibility to the familial unit around which neoconservatism and neoliberalism converge, the former for "moral" reasons and the latter for "economic" ones (Brown, 2019, p. 92). Hence, we see an actual alignment between patriarchal, racist, anti-immigrant and homo- and transphobic ethnonationalisms and neoliberal capital to further offload public provisioning at the expense of social reproduction in favor of private wealth accumulation. Such alignment also occurs through the kind of state intervention that neoconservatives, and particularly hypermasculinist architects of neoliberal authoritarianism within US right-wing think tanks (Horton, 2022) favor to enforce normative gender and sexual identities and relations as well as to harden border security to keep unwanted racialized im/migrants out. This occurs despite the fact that it is racialized female migrants who have been relied upon to provide cheap labor for social reproduction in the Global North and in global cities in the Global South (as focused on in Chang and Ling's chapter in this volume). Indeed, as theorists of "racial capitalism" (Gilmore, 2022) have long argued and Fraser (2022) has further taken up, capitalism has always been structurally racist as a regime that not only expropriated land and labor through (neo)colonization and slavery and continues to do so, including through criminalization and incarceration, but also puts racialized subjects at the bottom of exploited labor, which ethnonationalisms seek to sustain in part because labor among even nonracialized subjects is becoming more precaritized, particularly under financial capitalism, upping the ante to divide workers by race and nationality.

This state of affairs does not mean, however, that neoliberal capitalist efforts have ceased to try to draw more gendered and racialized subjects into capitalist relations, again ostensibly to improve their economic lot, but in practice often miring them in debt while also maintaining unequal social and geopolitical orders. Feminists, including contributors to this volume over time, have long critiqued "womenomics," which rests on the assumption that women not in the so-called productive labor force are an untapped resource for capitalist accumulation (despite their free reproductive labor on which such accumulation rests) and thus should be freed, in part by making patriarchal men more amenable to allowing women to work outside the home, to enter that labor force, whether through low-level jobs or micro-credit, as well as to enter the financial system by engaging in banking their savings. Such schemes do not typically, however, involve public provisioning for childcare, encourage shared reproductive labor or concerted efforts to end gender violence, and have not led women and other feminized workers into upward mobility, as enumerated in this volume by such contributors as Kunz and Ramírez and Barber and Bryan. Relatedly, long-standing feminist critiques have addressed "the business case for feminism" in which it is claimed that the best way to free women (not in the name of equality but rather to expand capitalist accumulation) is for them to enter into market relations. Contributions by Jenkins and Moghadam to this volume join these critiques that point to the realities of discrimination and debt, the depletion of social reproduction, pervasive sexual harassment and violence, and persistent high levels of unemployment, underemployment, exploitation and unsafe working environments for women in the formal (and informal) market. More recently, queer scholars have critiqued what Rao (2015) refers to as "homocapitalism," which is essentially "the business case" for queer rights adopted by such IFIs such as the World Bank, promoting them as a marker of modernity and on capitalist grounds of "efficiency and empowerment" in light of the enormous amount of economic loss from LGBTQIA+ discrimination.

For Rao, this move is not about queer emancipation, but rather the assimilation of queers (but more often race- and class-privileged ones) into the market, through such actions as pinkwashing, and to reduce queer struggles to participation in homonormative capitalism. While this butts up against neoauthoritarian anti-queer ideologies, the continued discrimination such ideologies support also keeps most queers in more marginalized positions in the capitalist economy through which to exploit their labor.

While many women, queers and racialized subjects continue to be relegated to the margins of the formal capitalist economy, they predominate in the much larger informal economy, also at the lower end. However, as Latin American feminist theorist Sayak Valencia (2018) argues, these processes extend way beyond the binary of the formal versus the informal economy. To understand the relations between extreme masculinist violence, the transnational drug trade, hyperconsumerism and neoliberal capitalism, particularly in border areas, she formulated the concept of "gore capitalism." Situating her analysis in the border town of Tijuana, Mexico, she uses gore capitalism to describe and analyze its multiple contradicting faces, using insights from the genre of gore films, necropolitics, decolonial feminism and queer studies, among others:

> We take the term "gore" from a genre of films characterized by extreme, brutal violence. Thus, 'gore capitalism' refers to the undisguised and unjustified bloodshed that is the price the Third World pays for adhering to the increasingly demanding logic of capitalism. It also refers to the many instances of dismembering and disembowelment, often tied up with organized crime, gender and the predatory uses of bodies. In general, this term posits these incredibly brutal kinds of violence as tools of necroempowerment.
>
> (Valencia, 2018, Introduction)

She emphasizes how resistances to and forces opposing the logic of contemporary capitalism have become extremely violent, or gore, and that "the destruction of the body becomes in itself the product or commodity; the only kind of accumulation possible now is through a body count, as death has become the most profitable business in existence" (Valencia, 2018, Introduction). Her multifaceted analysis takes us beyond Sassen's expulsions and Fraser's cannibal capitalism, by suggesting that, particularly in parts of the Global South, contemporary capitalism, in the desire it produces for consumption often unavailable to underclasses and particularly men in them, is generating a hypermasculinist underground, and significantly, economies that are ultraviolent and feed on and draw power and control from the spectacularization of that violence, particularly in the form of the display of the dismembered bodies of those who get in the way of the cartel economy.

New forms of violence and control are also coming from the heights of the ICT economy in the form of what economist Shoshana Zuboff (2019) calls "surveillance capitalism." Although neither a feminist nor a critical theorist of the GPE per se, Zuboff draws from Marxist thought to argue that beyond the extraction of land and labor characteristic of industrial capitalism, the new form of extractivism under advanced, postindustrial capitalism and activated through ICT corporations like Google, Facebook and so on is data extraction from our private lives, turning consumers into "users" whose private data is expropriated for commodification and behavioral modification for future profit (typically also at the expense of democracy through the manipulation of private data for authoritarian purposes), and employing far fewer people (who are primarily men), in more flexibilized ways, and from much more rarefied fields of data science across countries than in the industrial age. As noted earlier, the latest AI developments, including ChatGPT, not only extract from our private lives, making people dependent on search engines and social media to deliver their private lives to them, but also from our intellectual and creative products, scraping individual efforts online to turn them into corporate properties and ultimately, even in the views of the producers of AI, displacing entire occupations as well as endangering human and democratic controls over technology, including militarized forms of it. As one of our contributors, Gillian Youngs, notes in this edition, the overtly masculinized sectors of STEM, ICT and design are productive of these dark futures, necessitating not only the inclusion of more women but also a shift in what technology is for, advancing inclusion and social and ecological welfare versus exclusion and expropriation.

Hypermasculinity is particularly visible in neoauthoritarian, gore and surveillance capitalisms while also fundamental to the broader category of neoliberal capitalism and its endgame, cannibal capitalism, in their extraction and exploitation of women's reproductive labor. It is also instrumental to finance capitalism as a subset of, but central to, neoliberal capitalism. As we noted in our last edition and earlier here, much attention was given at the beginnings of the GFC to it being a testosterone-induced "man-made" crisis by unbridled risk-taking men at the top of the global finance industry and on stock trading floors of Wall Street and the London City. While we eschewed such biological determinist arguments, later feminist work on the symbolic meanings of this, such as in contributions to *Scandalous Economics: Gender and the Politics of Financial Crises* (2016), found that arguments were being made that if only "Lehman Brothers" had been "Lehman Sisters," the GFC might have been avoided (Prügl, 2016). Such talk of the more "prudent woman," however, did not change the fact that women were the most laid off in the financial sector "post-crisis" and hid the "ruthless" workings of finance capitalism itself (Prügl, 2016, p. 38). Indeed, as we argued in our last edition, empirical evidence just becoming available countered the notion that the GFC was mainly a "man-cession" most impacting working- and middle-class men. It was actually poor and working-class women as well as undocumented migrant men who bore the brunt of it in both the Global South and North, experiencing high rates of unemployment. Women were most affected by the withdrawal of social welfare and public services under the impositions of "austerity," and least supported by "recovery" efforts that went mostly to bailouts for the male-dominated financial and automobile manufacturing sectors and limited infrastructural projects employing primarily male workers to the detriment of re-expanding the public sector that would have produced more jobs and more jobs for women (Marchand and Runyan, 2011, pp. 247–248).

The COVID crisis did require massive infusions of public investments both for health care and to save small and more often large businesses, as well as to suspend payments on individual debt within the Global North and, occasionally, on Global South national debts to the IMF. As with the GFC, the COVID crisis opened a (small) window of opportunity to return to more Keynesian, state-supported economics, as well as debt repayment suspensions. And at least in the case of the US, infrastructure funding infusions passed under the Biden administration were reduced by Congress to physical infrastructure projects, albeit some toward greening the economy but still privileging male labor, and away from social welfare infrastructures in which women's labor is predominant. Thus, finance capital, whether private or public, remains masculinist in orientation and contributing to furthering the crisis of care.

A seemingly softer, more feminized form of neoliberal finance capitalism has also emerged in the midst of the longer trend of the retreat of the state from domestic public provisioning in the Global North and state-led development and humanitarian aid for Global South countries. "Philanthrocapitalism," embodied by the rise of private donor campaigns to alleviate human suffering primarily in the Global South, such as the (in)famous RED campaign led by rock star Bono to provide HIV/AIDS drugs, rests not only on the commodification of human suffering, but also deeply colonial relations, as discussed by Rowley in this edition (as well as in the second edition). Although private corporate donors abound in philanthrocapitalist projects to improve their "brand" as socially responsible, it is Western celebrities who build their own brand by appealing to individual Global North consumers, typically youth, to buy products like T-shirts made under questionable labor conditions typically in the Global South with the promise that (a fraction) of the proceeds from which will go to "charity," and, thus, to serve as "white saviors" of the downtrodden in the Global South in ways that "do not address or mitigate global inequalities endemic to consumer-based and free market-driven capitalism" (Trauger and Fluri, 2019, p. 40). Aside from philanthrocapitalism's incapacity to provide the kind of massive aid needed for the scope of human suffering or to effectuate the kinds of wealth redistributions globally to do so, it creates an illusion of care, while also propping up (neo)colonial relations, which are also highly gendered and racialized as marketing campaigns that often feature "third world women" or children as victims to be saved.

It is little wonder, then, that Global South feminist scholars and activists, such as Mageza-Barthel and Domínguez in their contributions to this edition, have turned to examining South–South alternatives to Western-based capitalist development and aid. Such work joins with the work of other scholars who have more recently revisited the 1950s Bandung gathering of Global South "non-aligned" countries for inspiration (Sud and Sánchez-Ancochea, 2022) and such works as Agathangelou and Ling's (2009) on "worldism," or a realignment to a more multipolar world in which alternative worldviews based more on mutual imbrication and interconnection can flourish and inform less unequal and violent political economies. While old and newer authoritarianisms remain rife within the Global South as well as the Global North making such alternatives difficult, Global South feminists have long allied, and continue to do so, to seek to make Global South states more accountable to alternative visions and actualizations of them. And certainly we have seen Global South coalescences and leadership with respect to combating climate change and seeking reparations for it and the crushing debts they have incurred as a result of extractivism and expropriation as well as indigenous populations within the Global South and North taking the lead on climate defense and restoration, informed and prior consent to any deleterious development projects on traditional indigenous lands throughout much of the world and even the prohibition of nuclear weapons (Runyan, 2022).

Thus, despite but also because of this array of multiple necropolitical capitalist restructurings, broad and interconnected social movements have been (re)activated to resist them, as the chapters by Domínguez and Mageza-Barthel in this volume illustrate. The GJM, while no longer as visible as it once was when regular gatherings were held for its adherents in various parts of the world since the early 2000s, did lay the basis for interconnecting struggles against economic, social, cultural and ecological oppressions tied to global capital resulting significantly from the work of TFNs that have comprised it (Moghadam, 2020). The challenge now, as intimated by Bergeron in this edition, is to find and widen the cracks within these myriad capitalist restructurings by exposing their consequences and contradictions and breaking their holds on imaginations that prevent alternatives. As feminist economists Gibson-Graham (1996) argued long ago, capitalism only sustains its hold when we see it as akin to "rape scripts" in which violent penetration seems inevitable for the presumed defenseless. For them, part of the work is to expose that the capitalist economy is actually dwarfed by more sustainable noncapitalist economic activity not necessarily colonized by capitalist logics (bartering, sharing, care work) that for many are part of everyday life. And as critical and feminist development economists Patel and Moore (2017) have argued, in order for us to cease imagining the end of world due to climate change more easily than the end of capitalism, it is time to see "capitalocentrism" as a root cause that is subject to change by a myriad of local arrangements and actions taking place around the world to produce more socially and ecologically just sociopolitical economies. What is needed to actually produce just, caring and regenerative systems is a restructuring of social and environmental relations, which must involve an integration of "a concept of justice that would consider justice for all people and for the planet, a multi-species justice, which, drawing from feminist theory, involves acknowledging, preventing, and responding to violence enacted against all kinds of beings" (Cohn and Duncanson, 2023, p. 32).

Contributions to sightings, sites and resistances in this volume

Perhaps more so than past editions, the contributor chapters to this volume cut across the themes of sightings, sites and resistances and thus are introduced here together in the order they appear in the volume. While some remain more oriented to theoretical advances (sightings) in understanding gendered global capitalist restructuring and others to bringing particular locations (sites) into view in the process, all address resistances to the proliferations of capitalist restructurings both theoretically and practically. While addressing (global) restructurings in their analyses, not all authors address or use the theoretical insights we have discussed in this Introduction. Rather, what the Introduction and authors' individual chapters showcase is that there are continuities as well as new approaches in feminist analyses of the GPE, which allow for rich debates and conversations to further our understandings of contemporary complexities and crises of the GPE. It is in this spirit that contributors were not asked to use or address any specific theoretical framework beyond addressing the three dimensions of sightings, sites and resistances through the prisms of their own research programs.

The contributions begin with a third reprise of Kimberly Chang and the late L.H.M. Ling's now classic "Globalization and its intimate other: Filipina domestic workers in Hong Kong" (Chapter 2), which still so powerfully reveals the underside of globalization, or Globalization 2. This is coded as feminized and racialized and is a direct result of Globalization 1, coded as masculinized and class- and race-privileged. But this time, the chapter is prefaced by Chang, who takes us into the experience of her co-authorship with Ling as an homage to her and the theoretical insights she brought to the case of Filipina domestic workers in Hong Kong that have stood the test of time in feminist theorizing on global restructuring. This site of global restructuring, repeated in so many other places where migrant domestic labor from the Global South continues to be relied upon and exploited in the Global North generally and global cities specifically, helped us to see not only how the forces of the capitalist global political economy, the remittance-hungry state and the heteronormative family congeal to entrap and exploit migrant domestic workers in the homes of the wealthy in a global city, but also how they engage in everyday resistances to their conditions. This resistance included gathering together in public space in rare times off from unrelenting labor to gain solidarity and engaging in non-normative sexuality to develop intimacies that are otherwise denied them by rapacious employers and family and state exhortations to remain heterosexually chaste. This landmark work set the stage for so much feminist work thereafter on global care chains, migrant domestic labor and everyday resistances.

Pauline Gardiner Barber and Catherine Bryan's "Labor here, consume there, accumulate everywhere: Improvisations of mobile capital and gendered labor along the Philippines–Canada migration corridor" (Chapter 3) takes us to new twists in migrant labor regimes under an endlessly adaptive capitalist system, moving beyond Barber's second edition chapter on migrant domestic work performed by Filipinas in Canada and the ways which they navigate their familial relationships at home from the diaspora, to focus on how feminized migrant labor from the Philippines is recruited for and treated in another sector of the Canadian economy, specifically the fast food industry and the premier Canadian icon of this, the Tim Hortons franchise. As was mentioned earlier, their chapter provides a detailed analysis of how exploitative racial capitalism operates and is embedded in complex intersecting migration regimes, corporate strategies and migrant aspirations. Tracking how female and male Philippine workers, many with university educations, are now swelling the ranks of counter attendant jobs in both urban and rural locations for a globalizing Tim Hortons, in part due to the promises this might lead to permanent residency in Canada, they find that ever-shifting Canadian immigration rules coupled with the ever-shifting needs of capital accumulation are more often ensuring that such workers remain trapped in temporary and unskilled status, too often resulting in downward mobility for their children. As the authors observe, Filipinas became preferred domestic workers in Canada due to assumptions about their compliant and child-friendly natures, while the latest preference for Filipino fast food workers rests on assumptions about not only their compliance, but also their willingness to work hard to please their Canadian consumers and employers. Thus, sustaining the feminization (and racialization) of Filipino workers, both female and male, continues to serve both the needs of capital and the Canadian state despite some shifts in the work such migrant labor performs.

Michelle Rowley's "'I still haven't found what I am looking for': Getting development out of the (RED)™?" (Chapter 4) also makes a reappearance, but in much-updated form. Theoretically reflecting on how philanthrocapitalism has evolved since the inception of rock star Bono's RED and ONE campaigns initially and still largely focused on "Africa" and its HIV-AIDS "problem," she points especially to the ongoing "seductive" quality of celebrity-driven humanitarianism, which creates the imaginary that markets can produce solidarity and relieve suffering. Moreover, she finds that this myth continues to be achieved through the "hypervisibility" of a homogenized "Africa," marked by a host of pathologies, and the appropriation of "Africans" by celebrities claiming to be in solidarity with them through shilling the stylized wares of the RED campaign marketed particularly to young consumers in the Global North. It is further achieved through the invisibility of laboring bodies in pain resulting from neocolonial and neoliberal capital, which ironically forms the backbone of the RED campaign that is even more reliant now on transnational corporate donors to combat HIV-AIDS and other infectious diseases, including COVID, which briefly became some focus of the One campaign. This does little however to disrupt the logics of ongoing under- and maldevelopment of African societies. Thus, Rowley returns to her reading of Malian filmmaker Sissako's film *Bamako* to make visible and audible the bodies and voices of those still struggling against crushing debts imposed by the IMF (despite a brief moratorium during COVID while African debt accrual continues to grow from a new source, China) and the resulting despair. This remains the centerpiece of her counter-reading of the claims to an "identity of care" made by philanthrocapitalists.

Rahel Kunz and Brenda Ramírez focus on the gendered financialization of development from another angle in their piece, "The gendered imperatives of the financialization of remittances in Mexico: Listening to the subjects-to-be-financialized" (Chapter 5). Just as Kunz revealed the disciplining pressures of neoliberal development forces on poor, rural Mexican women to become "productive" to supposedly unleash their economic potential as well as such women's resistances to market imperatives that rarely brought them increased incomes in her contribution to the second edition, she and Ramírez point to the latest efforts of neoliberal capital to get poor Mexican women to bank remittances from relatives who migrated to the US for work in order to promote a culture of saving and entrepreneurial investment. As such, this chapter is a clear example of a "business case" for feminism to the degree that it falls under the umbrella of "women's empowerment." What they found is that such Mexican women continue to prefer informal and collective savings and investment approaches among themselves rather than becoming entangled in formal, and too often corrupt, banking systems that can actually bleed them of credit and push them into indebtedness. Whether it is the making women productive strategy or the banking of unbanked women, such schemes are far from empowering of women. Rather it is how women resist such imperatives, including through self-exclusion from such schemes, that reveals their sense of empowerment.

While gendered neoliberal economic schemes for women's "empowerment" rarely if ever entail concomitant efforts for increasing women's political rights, the case of Tunisia, which Valentine M. Moghadam explores in "Restructuring, revolution, and women's elusive economic empowerment: The case of Tunisia" (Chapter 6) is an example in which some legal gains have been made for women's rights as a result of feminist legal activism, particularly since the Arab Spring when Tunisia appeared to be the one success story arising from it in terms of moving toward a path of democratization. However, the continued embrace of the liberalization of the Tunisian economy, coupled with continued conservative attitudes within the government and in civil society toward women's rights, the economic and social shocks of the COVID pandemic, and the rise of de-democratization in Tunisia by 2021, have translated into high degrees of unemployment and underemployment for even highly educated women and youth, particularly in the interior of the country, and inattention to supports for social reproduction, including childcare provision, that would better enable women to enter the skilled workforce. As Moghadam observes in this chapter, as she found in her second edition contribution that focused on the disconnect between the liberalization of North African economies and women's economic empowerment, the neoliberal global economy has proven time and again that it neither delivers democracy nor women's economic empowerment. While Tunisian women's struggles to gain inclusion in the skilled workforce have been led by labor and women's movements, not the result of some IFI "smart economics" approach, these movements have not been able to overcome so far the workings of neoliberal capitalist labor exclusion and exploitation nor the conservative cultural context.

Laura Dudley Jenkins's "'Empowerment' training for women workers in Bangladesh's garment factories: Corporate social (ir)responsibility (SIR)" (Chapter 7), a new contribution to this edition, reveals what "women's empowerment" really means in the era of so-called corporate social responsibility produced through "private–private" partnerships between transnational corporations like Walmart and international NGOs like CARE and legitimated by the UN Global Compact program. In her discourse analysis of three digital women's empowerment training programs for women workers in the ready-made garment industry in Bangladesh, notorious for the 2013 Rana Plaza factory fire in which at least one thousand largely women workers lost their lives when they were prevented by too many locked doors from escaping the flames and building collapse, she finds they are not about enabling women's workplace rights, but rather making women workers responsible for better dealing with the poor working and living conditions imposed on them. Whether it is admonishments to women to better position themselves for advancement in garment factory work by being compliant and efficient, to take better care of their menstrual hygiene (in the absence of sufficient menstrual supplies, bathrooms or bathing facilities) so as not to disrupt their work, or to get involved in digital banking to promote disciplined saving and expand the digital phone market, these training programs reinforce traditional gender roles and neoliberal market solutions while sidestepping corporate responsibility for workers' conditions, health and rights. Such are the results of the so-called business model for women's empowerment, but garment workers are not fooled by this approach as they continue to organize for better working conditions and lives.

Even in high-end occupations, such as those in the STEM fields, we still find a host of barriers to women's economic empowerment, according to Gillian Youngs's "Inclusive innovations: Feminist perspectives" (Chapter 8), which takes her focus in the second edition on gendered ICT in new directions. With much contemporary talk about technological innovation as being the new frontier and panacea for economic growth, she finds that what constitutes innovation remains mired in masculinist emphases on rear-guard technological fixes to what are at core sociopolitical crises. The still relative paucity of women in STEM fields, resulting from the usual litany of heterosexism, sexual harassment, inadequate childcare, inflexible working hours and cultures and so on, ensures that alternative approaches to innovation that actually start from human- and environmental-centered design models, thereby paying attention to underlying inequalities that technological fixes tend to reproduce and widen, are derailed. Such are the lessons from the COVID pandemic that no vaccine has resolved, and such are the lessons from market-driven green technological development that push for infrastructural changes in the built environment (and thereby privileging male-dominated jobs) without infrastructural changes in the sociopolitical environment called for by feminist green new deal models that emphasize innovation in social reproduction to produce both sustainability and equity.

Further possibilities for shifting from present neoliberal capitalist priorities that undermine equity, sustainability, and social, economic and environmental justice are gestured to in differing ways in the pieces by Rirhandu Mageza-Barthel, Edmé Domínguez Reyes and Suzanne Bergeron. The contributions by Mageza-Barthel and Domínguez analyze contemporary transnational feminist engagements in the context of South–South cooperation that pursue social justice in an increasingly multipolar global economy. In both cases, the authors provide the historical contexts from which these transnational feminist activities emerged. Mageza-Barthel's "Engagements with multipolarity: Sites and struggles of African–Chinese cooperation" (Chapter 9), another new contribution to this edition, harkens to the birth of the Non-Aligned Movement (NAM) at Bandung in the 1950s as paving the way toward a more multipolar world constituted ideally by South–South cooperation and solidarity informed by gender and social justice. While only recently has attention been given to rising Chinese investments in Africa as an alternative to dependence on Western development agencies and indebtedness to Western-led IFIs, Mageza-Barthel traces a much longer and more social justice-oriented history of African–Chinese relations forged between African (and particularly postapartheid South African) feminists and Chinese feminists. While women were largely absented from the Bandung conference, the spirit of South–South cooperation or "Third Worldism" it enlivened inspired women's movements across the Global South not only at the time, but also later on. South–South international feminism, particularly between African and Chinese women, took shape during the UN Decade for Women Conference in Nairobi in 1985 and the subsequent 1995 World Conference for Women in Beijing, and such exchanges have continued to some degree formally or informally since the rise of the Forum on China–Africa Cooperation (FOCAC) by the early 2000s. Although only one FOCAC Women's Forum has been held, FOCAC is "capitalist-friendly," and some African feminists are wary of China's current "hegemonic" designs, Mageza-Barthel suggests that there are possibilities immanent in African–Chinese feminist relations that can help reenvision a more just multipolar world.

South Africa and China are also part of the South–South cooperative framework of BRICS (originally consisting of the emerging market economies of Brazil, Russia, India, China and later South Africa, but since 2024 has expanded to include six more countries, namely, Argentina, Egypt, Ethiopia, Iran, Saudi Arabia and the United Arab Emirates, to form BRICS+). Given that one animation of BRICS was to seek a more multipolar world not exclusively governed by Western interests and in which the Global South has much more influence in world affairs to better meet its needs, transnational feminist economists and activists informed by feminist postcolonial analysis have formed BRICS Feminist Watch to analyze and monitor the BRICS bloc in terms of whether or not its development, trade and finance institutions and practices are gender-responsive. Although not based in the Global South, the Women in Development Europe network (now known as WIDE +) expanded its gender analysis and monitoring of EU development, trade and finance activities since the EU's expansion to include Central and Eastern Europe.

These two organizations are the focus of Edmé Domínguez's "Transnational feminist networks resisting economic restructuring: The cases of WIDE/WIDE+ and BRICS Feminist Watch" (Chapter 10), another new contribution to this edition. Even as such TFNs are supportive of Global South/non-Western alternatives to Western neoliberal capitalist hegemony, they know there is no assurance of gender-responsiveness in alternative banking and other financial development instruments and trade relations. Indeed, both organizations find that in the absence of strong feminist movements and/or in the presence of rising authoritarianism, whether within the EU or the original BRICS (now majority authoritarian countries within BRICS+), there is little to no gender-inclusiveness in their development, financial, and trade institutions and instruments. As problematic as this is, the efforts of such TFNs to expose this constitutes an important step toward necessary resistances to gender exclusionary unipolar and multipolar political economies. Yet, the efforts of these TFNs are directed at including issues of gender equity and social justice into contemporary economic policies and governance, but do not challenge the fundaments of the capitalist system, as more radical feminist political economists like Fraser and Sassen have done. Indirectly, these TFNs illustrate a dilemma faced by many transnational and local organizations and movements: either use dialogical strategies toward dominant neoliberal and authoritarian players and pressure them to address gender equity, social justice and climate issues, or disengage from global, regional and local governance structures and look for alternatives "outside the system." It is in the last contribution to this volume by Suzanne Bergeron that addresses this conundrum for feminist political economists/activists.

Suzanne Bergeron, whose work on the neoliberal and heteronormative governance by IFIs of female-headed household economies appeared in the second edition of this volume, takes a much different tack toward resistances in her entirely new contribution to this edition and serves as a provocative conclusion to it. She argues in "Moving past the co-optation narrative: Gender and development as a site of economic difference and ethical negotiation" (Chapter 11) that feminists are becoming entrapped in their own narratives about how neoliberal capitalism co-opts everything in its path, including feminism itself, making ultimately for no alternatives. Instead, she directs attention to the work of feminist economists J.K. Gibson-Graham and the Community Economies Collective (CEC) to catalog a host of diverse non-capitalist practices, and particularly those that enable social reproduction, which actually constitute the bulk economic activities worldwide, outstripping neoliberal capitalist practices that are only the tip of the iceberg of highly variegated economic practices, most of which do not serve neoliberal logics of maximizing accumulation and efficiency. She points to a range of examples, including the resistance of Mexican women to neoliberal pressures to bank remittances detailed by Kunz and Ramírez in this volume, as sites of ethical negotiations with neoliberal capital wherein women either adapt or abandon neoliberal capitalist practices in order to serve their own goals, such as solidarity-building and care-giving. Thus, while there have been and continue to be concerted and relentless attempts to engineer women's lives to be subservient to capital, to equate women's empowerment with neoliberal capitalist values, and to reduce feminism to "transnational business feminism" and "smart economics," there have always been and continue to be steadfast commitments to and a host of heretofore invisibilized practices for building care and solidarity economies. Recognizing this substantially opens actually many cracks in the seemingly impenetrable armor of neoliberal capitalism.

Concluding thoughts

Bergeron's concluding piece brings us full circle in the iterative life of this volume. As gestured to earlier here, our first edition highlighted J.K. Gibson-Graham's (1996) insight that global capitalist (aka globalization) scripts, whether enlisted by capitalist forces or their critics, end up reading like "rape scripts" in which there is no escape from inexorable and forced capitalist penetration. Our preferred use of the term "global restructuring" constituted a resistance to such scripts and opened space for contributors past and present to identify ways in which women and other marginalized others in the GPE have refused to succumb to neoliberal capitalist imperatives. Instead, we have seen through the lives, voices and struggles of gendered, racialized, classed and sexualized subjects in the GPE that restructuring, which we now refer to as restructurings, is never one way nor is it totalizing. There is no doubt that global restructurings "from above," and sometimes "from below" as Valencia (2018) suggests, have taken increasingly virulent and necropolitical turns over the past 25 years. This has occurred as neoliberal austerities have conjoined with neoconservative or neoauthoritarian forces to enforce them, as neoliberalism constituted the new imperialism characterized by "accumulation by dispossession" (Harvey, 2003) justified by wars on terror and as advanced capitalism no longer integrates but rather expels large swaths of people and renders the planet disposable. But in an odd, dialectical way, these extractions, exploitations and expulsions may also lead to the creation of new alternatives that do not fit this capitalist logic. For example, there have been successive transnational social movements, whether in the form of the Occupy movement, the World Social Forum as the nucleus of the Global Justice Movement, the globalized Black Lives Matter Movement, the more steady feature of TFNs, and the most recent rise of transnational and often indigenous climate justice defenders, which have repeatedly challenged global capitalism in its various forms (cannibal, racial, gore, philanthro, homo and so on), attesting to its dependence on gross inequalities and disposabilities. If, as Nancy Fraser (2022) has insisted, we understand capitalism not as an economic system but a societal one that expropriates and ravages the very inputs on which it depends—productive and social reproductive workers and the planet itself—then we can demand a restructuring not just of the global economy, but of global societal relations and well as human relations with the more-than-human world. And we can look to a host of everyday practices often engaged in by the most marginalized oriented toward human and planetary care, cooperation and solidarity. And as Naomi Klein (2023) has recently observed, this includes meeting the challenges posed by the current agents of chaos, disinformation and despair associated with the virtual economy with care for each other as we work to restructure socioeconomic, ecological and political life for collective flourishing.

References

Agathangelou, A.M. and Ling, L.H.M. (2009) *Transforming World Politics: From Empire to Multiple Worlds*. New York: Routledge.

Braidotti, R. (2019) "A theoretical framework for the critical posthumanities." *Theory, Culture &. Society*, 36(6), pp. 31–61.

Brown, W. (2019) *In the Ruins of Neoliberalism: The Rise of Antidemocratic Politics in the West*. New York: Columbia University Press.

Cohn, C. and Duncanson, C. (2020) "Whose recovery? IFI prescriptions for postwar states." *Review of International Political Economy*, 27(6), pp. 1214–1234.

Cohn, C. and Duncanson, C. (2023) "Critical feminist engagements with Green New Deals." *Feminist Economics*, 29(3), pp. 15–39.

Crenshaw, K. (1991) "Mapping the margins: Intersectionality, identity politics, and violence against women of color." *Stanford Law Review*, 43(6), pp. 1241–1299.

DiCaro, A. and Macdonald, L. (2022) "Union win at Mexican auto plant brings new hope for labour rights." UNIFOR, June 13. Available at https://www.unifor.org/news/all-news/union-win-mexican-auto-plant-brings-new-hope-labour-rights.

Elias, J. and Roberts, A. (2018) "Introduction: Situating gender scholarship in international political economy" in Elias, J. and Roberts, A. (eds.) *Handbook on the International Political Economy of Gender*. Cheltenham, UK: Edward Elgar Publishing, pp. 1–20.

Eschle, C. and Maiguashca, B. (2010) *Making Feminist Sense of the Global Justice Movement*. Lanham, MD: Rowman & Littlefield.

Fraser, N. (2022) *Cannibal Capitalism: How Our System Is Devouring Democracy, Care, and the Planet—and What We Can Do About It*. London: Verso.

Gibson-Graham, J.K. (1996) *The End of Capitalism (As We Knew It): A Feminist Critique of Political Economy*. Cambridge: Blackwell.

Gilmore, R.W. (2022) *Abolition Geography: Essays Towards Liberation*. New York: Verso Books.

Harvey, D. (2003) *The New Imperialism*. Oxford: Oxford University Press.

Hooper, C. (2001) *Manly States: Masculinities, International Relations, and Gender Politics*. New York: Columbia University Press.

Horton, L. (2022) *Men of Money: Elite Masculinities and the Neoliberal Project*. Lanham, MD: Rowman & Littlefield.

Hozic, A.A. and True, J. (eds.) (2016) *Scandalous Economics: Gender and the Politics of Financial Crises*. Oxford: Oxford University Press.

Klein, N. (2007) *The Shock Doctrine: The Rise of Disaster Capitalism*. New York: Metropolitan Books/Henry Holt and Company.

Klein, N. (2023) *Doppelganger: A Trip into the Mirror World*. New York: Farrar, Straus and Giroux.

Lind, A. (2011) "Querying globalization: Sexual subjectivities, development, and the governance of intimacy" in Marchand, M.H. and Runyan, A.S. (eds.) *Gender and Global Restructuring: Sightings, Sites and Resistances*, 2nd ed. New York: Routledge, pp. 48–65.

Lugones, M. (2014) "Colonialidad y género" in Espinosa Miñoso, Y., et al. (eds.) *Tejiendo de Otro Modo: Feminismo, Epistemología y Apuestas Decoloniales en Abya Yala*. Popayán: Editorial Universidad del Cauca, pp. 57–73.

Marchand, M.H. and Ayala Galí, E. (forthcoming) "Estudios feministas e interseccionalidad en las Relaciones Internacionales" in López-Vallejo, M., Lozano, A. and Cuadra, A. (eds.) *Metodología, Métodos y Relaciones Internacionales*. Mexico: Universidad de Guadalajara, Colegio de San Luís and Asociación Mexicana de Estudios Internacionales.

Marchand, M.H. and Runyan, A.S. (eds.) (2000) *Gender and Global Restructuring: Sightings, Sites and Resistances*. New York: Routledge.

Marchand, M.H. and Runyan, A.S. (eds.) (2011) *Gender and Global Restructuring: Sightings, Sites and Resistances*, 2nd ed. New York: Routledge.

Moghadam, V.M. (2020) *Globalization and Social Movements: The Populist Challenge and Democratic Alternatives*, 3rd ed. Lanham, MD: Rowman & Littlefield.

Morris, E.W. and Ratajczak, K. (2019) "Critical masculinity studies and research on violence against women: An assessment of past scholarship and future directions." *Violence against Women*, 25(16), pp. 1980–2006.

Parreñas, R. (2015) *Servants of Globalization: Migration and Domestic Work*, 2nd ed

Patel, R. and Moore, J. (2017) *The History of the World in Seven Cheap Things*. Oakland: University of California Press.

Peterson, V.S. (2003) *A Critical Rewriting of Global Political Economy: Integrating Reproductive, Productive, and Virtual Economies*. New York: Routledge.

Prügl, E. (2012) "'If Lehman Brothers had been Lehman Sisters…': Gender and myth in the aftermath of the financial crisis." *International Political Sociology*, 6, pp. 21–35.

Prügl, E. (2016) "'Lehman Brothers and sisters': Revisiting gender and myth after the financial crisis" in Hozic, A.A. and True, J. (eds.) *Scandalous Economics: Gender and the Politics of Financial Crises*. Oxford: Oxford University Press, pp. 21–40.

Puar, J.K. (2007) *Terrorist Assemblages: Homonationalism in Queer Times*. Durham, NC: Duke University Press.

Puar, J.K. (2012). "'I would rather be a cyborg than a goddess': Becoming-Intersectional in Assemblage Theory." *Philosophia*, 2(1), p. 49–66.

Rao, Rahul. (2015) "Global homocapitalism." *Radical Philosophy*, 194 (Nov/Dec), pp. 38–49.

Roy, D. and Subramaniam, B. (2016) "Matter in the shadows: Feminist new materialism and the practices of colonialism" in Pitts-Taylor, V. (ed.), *Mattering: Feminism, Science, and Materialism*. New York: New York University Press, pp. 23–42.

Runyan, A.S. (2022) "Indigenous women's resistances and the start and end of the nuclear fuel chain." *International Affairs*, 98(4), pp. 1149–1167.

Sassen, S. (2014) *Expulsions: Brutality and Complexity in the Global Economy*. Cambridge, MA: Belknap Press.

Sassen, S. (2016) "At the systemic edge: Expulsions." *European Review*, 24(2), pp. 89–104.

Segato, R. (2014) "Colonialidad y patriarcado moderno: expansión del frente estatal, modernización, y la vida de las mujeres" in Espinosa Miñoso, Y., et al. (eds.) *Tejiendo de Otro Modo: Feminismo, Epistemología y Apuestas Decoloniales en Abya Yala*. Popayán: Editorial Universidad del Cauca, pp. 75–92.

Simpson, L.B. (2017) *As We Have Always Done: Indigenous Freedom through Radical. Resistance*. Minneapolis: University of Minnesota Press.

Sud, N. and Sánchez-Ancochea, D. (2022) "Southern discomfort: Interrogating the category of the Global South." *Development and Change*, 53(6), pp. 1123–1150.

Trauger, A. and Fluri, J.L. (2019) *Engendering Development: Capitalism and Inequality in the Global Economy*. New York: Routledge.

True, J. and Tanyag, M. (2019) "Violence against women/violence in the world: Toward a feminist conceptualization of global violence" in Gentry, C.E., Shephard, L.J. and Sjoberg, L. (eds.) *Routledge Handbook of Gender and Security*. London: Routledge, pp. 15–26.

Tuck, E. and Yang, K.W. (2012) "Decolonization is not a metaphor." *Decolonization: Indigeneity, Education & Society*, 1(1), pp. 1–40.

Valencia, S. (2018) *Gore Capitalism* (translated by John Pluecker). Semiotext(e)/Intervention Series, no. 24. Boston: MIT Press.

Zuboff, S. (2019) *The Age of Surveillance Capitalism: The Fight for a Human Future at the New Frontier of Power*. New York: PublicAffairs.

Preface to "Globalization and its intimate other: Filipina domestic workers in Hong Kong" in remembrance of L.H.M. Ling

Kimberly A. Chang

"Globalization and its intimate other" was born out of a very different world than the one we inhabit today. As I write the Preface to this chapter 20 years after its first publication on the occasion of its reprint in the third edition of this volume, the most palpable difference is that my fellow author, mentor and friend, L.H.M. Ling—or Lily, as she was known to friends and colleagues—is no longer among us. Lily was the instigator behind this chapter, a consummate scholar, storyteller, critic and dreamer whose absence at this historical moment of global struggle against the pandemic and for racial justice is deeply felt. And yet, as this chapter makes its third appearance and I reflect on my conversations with Lily that generated it, I can't help but wonder: what has really changed?

To be specific, this chapter was born out of a series of late night/early morning phone calls between Lily and me during the mid-1990s, when I was in my first full-time teaching position at a brand new research university in Hong Kong and Lily was still at Syracuse (where she had been a member of my doctoral committee). It was a time of global expansion, interconnectivity, mobility and integration—or so the story goes. The internet was still in its infancy, so Lily and I communicated via that steadfast technology: the telephone. Hong Kong was in the throes of the countdown to its "handover" from Britain to China, accompanied by a brief hopeful flowering of democratic movements that now looks like too little, too late. And the so-called Asian financial crisis was looming unseen on the horizon.

During those heady years, I was juggling my newly acquired professional status with my equally new and demanding position as a mother while coming to terms with the only form of childcare available to me in Hong Kong: live-in domestic help. As part of my ex-pat package, I was provided with a three-story house with its own domestic servant quarters. At the same time, I had inherited a grant to do ethnographic research on domestic workers in Hong Kong and found myself spending my Sundays at a nearby shelter for migrant women from the Philippines and trying to write reflexively about this community on whom I depended and with whom I identified as a working mother (see Groves and Chang, 1999). Over the phone, I shared with Lily the internal conflict I felt as I moved between the high-powered universe of mostly male academics who had ambitiously dubbed themselves the "MIT of Asia" and the intimate world of

DOI: 10.4324/9781003036425-2

the migrant women who cooked, cleaned and cared for them and their families. Lily listened and immediately proposed, as she did with so many of her former students, that we collaborate on a piece of writing that would bring together my ethnographic stories of domestic work with her critical analysis of global restructuring.

Lily's invitation to collaborate illustrates not only her generosity as a mentor but also what a capacious thinker, writer and raconteur she was. Conversations with Lily always roamed large, moving seamlessly between a current research project and a dream last night, world politics and workplace power struggles, feminist theories and Eastern philosophies, and the latest Hollywood (or Bollywood) movie and a centuries-old Chinese folktale. Where others erected walls, Lily saw connections between disparate geographies, histories and cultural worlds—a survival skill learned as a diplomat's child who was constantly on the move. To connect these worlds, Lily drew on the power of a good story and she was especially skillful at drawing one out of you, asking exactly the right questions to enable you to narrate the characters, plot and moral of your story. She also loved a good theory; the bigger, the better in its capacity to shed light on the structures of power that shape the conflicts and choices of everyday life. For Lily, story and theory were two sides of the same coin, and both were necessary for grasping the contradictory realities of globalization.

Lily was quick to see in my stories of ex-pat academics and migrant workers not simply the work/family conflict of Western liberal feminism but a larger catch-22 that was raced and classed as well as gendered—and decidedly global in its scope. If my stories showed domestic workers struggling to negotiate the terms of their "service" in the confines of their employer's household, Lily's theorizing about the relation between "technomuscular capitalism" and "the regime of labor intimacy" provided the connective tissue for understanding the structural inequities that produced the painful choices of those caught in between these twin globalizing processes. At the same time, Lily heard in the intimate tales of domestic service a counternarrative to the dominant debates on globalization: one based not on false choices between tradition vs. modernity, East vs. West, or local vs. global, but on daily engagement with and negotiation across differences and hybridities—much as Lily lived her life.

Rereading our chapter today in the midst of a global pandemic is both disquieting and instructive. On the surface, state responses to the pandemic in the form of travel bans, border closures and workplace shutdowns contrast with the mobility and integration of neoliberal global restructuring in the 1990s. Yet even as the world has ground to a halt, with a devastating and unprecedented loss of lives and livelihoods, markets have bounced back, and corporations are adapting to new remote realities. While some enjoy the safety and privilege of Zooming into work from home, others deemed "essential" face the daily intimacies and precarities of service work and caregiving in the midst of a highly contagious and lethal virus—exposing the uneven impact of this global health crisis. Moral dilemmas abound, particularly for those engaged in feminized labor (healthcare, teaching, parenting and all forms of caregiving) who face impossible choices between not only work and family but also their jobs and their lives. Case counts and death tolls bring into sharp focus the way that COVID-19 discriminates along racial and class lines. The rise of anti-Asian, anti-Black and anti-immigrant rhetoric and violence, coupled with claims by the White right for the "freedom" to go unmasked, highlight the racist ideologies that accompany the spread of the virus. Meanwhile, in global cities from Hong Kong to Seattle to Paris, as the pandemic enters its second wave, governments are not only policing their borders but waging war on their own citizens. The pandemic, it seems, has made the brutality of the technomuscular state and the exploitation of labor intimacy all the more visible.

At this moment of necessary and imminent change, I try to imagine the conversation Lily and I might have if she were still alive. Regrettably, over the last decade, our professional lives took us in different directions, and thus, news of Lily's sudden and untimely death came to me late and as a great shock. The last time we spoke—Lily in New York City and I in Western Massachusetts—we discovered that both of us had turned to creative forms of writing in order to fully render the hybrid subjects of our work, and we exchanged short stories. Lily's was titled "Romance," the story of an educated young woman in India who is determined to pursue her passion for writing in the face of family pressure for an arranged marriage. The writing is vivid and visceral, evoking the tension between where the world is taking her and where she aspires to go (with thanks to Arthur Kleinman, 2006, for naming this fundamental human dilemma). This theme, I recognize now, was a constant in Lily's work, one which she explored via increasingly creative sources and forms—plays, poetry, fiction, film, food, fashion—as an alternative means of *imagining world politics*. In her recent book bearing this title (Ling, 2014a), Lily tells the Daoist fable of Sihar and Shenya and the dialectical relationship between yang and yin as a corrective to the dichotomies, hierarchies and epistemic violence of Eurocentric, masculinist international relations theory and practice. We need stories like this, Lily writes in the preface, to show the linkages between the familiar and the alien, the present and the past, self and other—and to expand our imagination about what is possible. We need artistic expression; she goes on to say, "to inhabit change while appreciating its disruptive stimulations" (Ling, 2014a, p. xxi).

I imagine talking with Lily about this book and its twin, *The Dao of World Politics* (Ling, 2014b), asking how she came to write one as a fable for a general audience and the other as an academic text. She tells me that she just bought my hybrid book, *Accomplice to Memory* (Zhang, 2017), and appreciates the fact that I published it under my Chinese name. I tell her I'm excited by her most recent piece (Ling, 2019) on "epistemic compassion," the connections she makes between the ethos of the ancient Silk Roads, Dubois's double consciousness, and China's current Belt and Road Initiative. I want to know how to find that kind of compassion in between worlds. We talk about our mothers, our students, the future of Hong Kong and the not-so-cold war brewing between the US and China. We take heart in the myriad movements for democracy, human rights and racial justice that are happening on the streets around the world, the shared language of the protestors, the symbolism of "I can't breathe" and what it means to "be water." She reminds me that this is a Daoist concept, that water never sees the world from a god's-eye-view, but rather from the multiple and changing perspectives of the puddle, the ditch, the brook, the canal, the reservoir—that water is always moving, filling, spilling, shaping, disrupting and transforming with its surroundings. I thank her for this reminder. We marvel at the separate yet parallel paths our lives have taken, like two rivers that will eventually empty into the same sea, and regret that we did not come together to collaborate more.

Be water.

2 Globalization and its intimate other

Filipina domestic workers in Hong Kong

Kimberly A. Chang and L.H.M. Ling

Introduction

At least two processes of globalization or global restructuring operate in the world political economy today. One reflects a glitzy, Internet-surfing, structurally integrated world of global finance, production, trade and telecommunications. Populated primarily by men at its top rungs of decision-making, this global restructuring valorizes all those norms and practices usually associated with Western capitalist masculinity—"deregulation," "privatization," "strategic alliances," "core regions," "deadlands" —but masked as global or universal. Like the colonial rhetoric of old, it claims to subsume all local cultures under a global umbrella of aggressive market competition—only now, with technology driving the latest stage of capitalism. We refer to this global restructuring as "technomuscular" capitalism (TMC).[1]

There is a second process of global restructuring. It is more explicitly sexualized, racialized and class-based than TMC and concentrates on low-wage, low-skilled menial services provided by mostly female migrant workers. They perform intimate household services, e.g., caring for the young and elderly, cleaning the house, washing clothes, preparing food and generally providing domestic comfort and care. This service economy involves other intimacies as well: leaving home, living among strangers, facing sexual harassment and abuse and making moral choices. We refer to this second global restructuring as a "regime of labor intimacy" (RLI). It is, in every sense, an intimate other to TMC.

Filipina migrant workers in Hong Kong stand at the nexus of these two globalization processes.[2] They inhabit the RLI needed and created by TMC. These women work at low-wage, low- to semi-skilled jobs as nannies, nurses, maids, entertainers and/or hostesses to the upwardly mobile, technically linked, high-salaried cosmopolitans of TMC. While they can earn up to six times what they would make at home, Filipina domestic workers often find themselves incarcerated within this regime of "labor intimacy." Sending and receiving states promise them wealth and mobility through domestic work but deliver a sentence of sexualized, racialized service instead. In this way, the twin processes of globalization exacerbate a growing gap between cosmopolitans and those who toil in the intimacy of their homes.

DOI: 10.4324/9781003036425-3

In this chapter, we ask: Why are certain segments of the world population geared toward the high-tech, high-wage world of TMC, while others are assigned to a low-tech, low-wage RLI? How do these different positionings within a globalized political economy affect subjectivity in general and that of the subaltern woman, in particular? And what implications can we draw about the nature of global restructuring as it polarizes TMC from labor intimacy even while sustaining both?

We rely on ethnographic fieldwork conducted by Kimberly Chang and Julian Groves (2000) on Filipina domestic workers in Hong Kong from 1992 to 1997. Their research includes various media sources on the Filipina migrant community from both the Hong Kong press (such as the *Hong Kong Standard*) and Filipino publications (such as *FEER*). One such source, *Tinig Filipino*, is published by and for the Filipino migrant community overseas. We conclude with the implications of both global restructuring processes for understanding our contemporary world order.

Global restructuring I: Technomuscular capitalism (TMC)

Studies of global restructuring typically reflect two normative stances: a liberal internationalism that accepts "globalization" as a contemporary market response to "internationalized" consumer and producer demands and a critical reassessment of global restructuring as historically continuous, ideologically hegemonic and materially impoverishing for the majority of the world. Liberals cite the canons of *laissez-faire* neoclassical economics to promote global restructuring and generally focus on policy prescriptions to adjust to newfound opportunities (e.g., capital gains) as well as challenges (e.g., unemployment). Critics of global restructuring reflect a more varied theoretical background, e.g., Gramscian international political economy, world-system theory, classical Marxism and regulation theory. They focus primarily on the structural inequities and/or inherent instabilities that arise from global restructuring, such as the emergence of global elites, a capitalist "world hegemony" and regressive structural adjustment policies (SAPs). Instead of public policy, critics assess the nature of our global political economy and its future scenarios. For example, they speculate on the outbreak of counterhegemonic movements at various localities (Gramscian globalists), systemic consequences to deepening inequalities in the center-periphery relations (world-system theorists), capitalism's "internal contradictions" (classical Marxists) or alternative "regimes of accumulation" to late-modern capitalism (regulation theorists).

Despite these differences, both liberals and critics agree on the subject matter itself, e.g., "globalization's" characteristics, impact, ideology and culture.

Identifying features of global restructuring

"Globalization" studies conventionally refer to unprecedented levels of integration in finance, production, trade, telecommunications and the media on a worldwide scale.[3] As such, "globalization" differs from "internationalization," which suggests only "the geographic spread of economic activities across national boundaries" (Dicken, 1992, p. 1). Some authors date the rise of global restructuring to the heyday of "casino capitalism" (Strange, 1986) or "hyperliberalism" (Cox, 1987) in the 1980s, when the Reagan–Thatcher–Kohl triad of industrialized economies deregulated capital and taxation. Others trace it to the 1970s when world capital markets broke from the nation-based Bretton Woods system (Kapstein, 1996). Whatever the periodization, global restructuring signals an era of extraordinary collaboration across states, between firms and also between states and firms (Dicken, 1994). Integrated media and marketing networks also globalize the production of images, ideas and consumption patterns (Leslie, 1995). Some find a structural convergence across multinational (or better, transnational) corporations that transcend traditional boundaries in production, finance and distribution (Reich, 1992; Berger, 1996). These circuits of capital and institutions contribute to the rise of "core regions" in a new, post-Cold War geopolitical order (Agnew and Corbridge, 1995). "Global cities" (Sassen, 1991) like New York, London, Tokyo and Hong Kong, among others, now have more in common with one another than with their respective local municipalities. Similarly, "deadlands" of economic development afflict regions located in the First World as much as they do in the former Second or Third Worlds. This new, transnationalized geopolitical order supersedes and obsolesces the state-led, territory-bound one of Cold War politics and superpower rivalry (Agnew and Corbridge, 1995).

The role of the state

Liberals and critics alike view global restructuring as a fundamental challenge to the traditional functions, if not the viability, of the state.[4] Some liberals argue that states must accept their reduced role under the new reality of global competition. The state's sole responsibility is to educate the consuming public with better information. Even the liberal capitalist state in the West, caution democratic theorists, needs to revise its understanding of sovereignty, democracy and political community to survive under global restructuring (Barber, 1996; Held and McGrew, 1993). Otherwise, a crisis of politics and economics may emerge, stoked by post-Cold War nationalism in the face of the new "world empires"—multinational corporations (Barnet and Cavanagh, 1994)—and their dire consequences for unemployment/underemployment (Kapstein, 1996).

Critics of global restructuring admit that the state is "hollowing out" in a distinctive way, e.g., it is becoming increasingly obsolete as "more and more economic, social, and cultural activity is going to take place across (rather than within) national frontiers" (Thrift, 1992, p. 6). Gramscian globalists label this process an "internationalizing of the state." That is, states turn inside-out to accommodate the external exigencies of globalized production (Cox, 1987). According to some, this will lead to greater instability between a territorially based interstate system and a global economy that undermines it daily (Gill, 1992).

A transnationalized ideology of liberal capitalism

Liberal capitalism, almost all agree, is spreading to both the "heartland" and "outposts" of the world economy. Liberal internationalists laud globalization as a triumph of self-interest matched with rationality. Francis Fukuyama (1989) remains the most blatant advocate of this perspective.

Critics, especially Gramscian globalists, castigate Western liberal capitalism as oppressive, invidious and hegemonic. Not only does it ensure the dominance of certain capitalist production processes and relations, but it also perpetuates a world-order ideology that validates the supremacy of leading states and their dominant social classes (Gill, 1995; Cox, 1987). With its seductive profits and privileges, the world hegemony of liberal capitalism sets up specific relations of production. Many fear that this increasing interconnectedness among global elites may widen gaps between the rich and the poor, thereby further destabilizing the global political economy (Marshall, 1996; Agnew and Corbridge, 1995; Dicken, 1992). For this reason, Gramscian globalists forecast the possibility of multiple counterhegemonic movements. These will lay the foundation, they believe, for a new, emancipatory transnational historic bloc that will transform the capitalist world hegemony.

Global society/culture/persons

All agree that globalization transforms familiar forms of social organization and cultural meaning. Liberals emphasize the "bridging mechanisms" of a new revolutionary class emerging under globalization—culture-straddling, globe-spanning cosmopolitans. Ulf Hannerz (1990, p. 239) defines cosmopolitanism as "an orientation, a willingness to engage with the Other. It is an intellectual and aesthetic stance of openness toward divergent cultural experiences, a search for contrasts rather than uniformity." For this reason, Hannerz disqualifies expatriates and migrants as cosmopolitan, for, he explains, they retain an indigenous cultural identity even while living/working overseas.

Critics, in contrast, view these late-/postmodern cosmopolitans as another in a long line of capitalist elites. Gramscian globalists theorize that cosmopolitans operate as a "global historic bloc." They form cross-national, cross-cultural "global classes" that uphold "mutual interests and ideological perspectives" that institutionalize a "common criteria of interpretation ... and common goals anchored in the idea of an open world economy" (Cox, 1993, p. 254). This global historic bloc includes the "affluent minorities in the OECD and ... the urban elites and new middle classes in the Third World" (Gill, 1995, p. 405).

Subjectivity under late modernity

Given their concern with elites, both liberals and critics view global restructuring in terms of the cosmopolitan and his subjectivity. Scott Lash and John Urry (1994) extend liberal optimism to the late-modern subject by characterizing it as "reflexive individualism." The late-modern subject, they write, "deepens" by "open(ing) up many positive possibilities for social relations—for intimate relations, for friendship, for work relations, for leisure, and for consumption" (Lash and Urry, 1994, p. 31). Global restructuring, they claim, produces not only *objects* but also *signs* that traverse rapidly and easily across communication networks (Lash and Urry, 1994, p. 5).

David Harvey (1989) voices concern rather than celebration for the late-modern subject. He identifies a late-modern "fragmentation" due to time-space compression under globalized, flexible production methods. This modern treatment of time and space as coherent and linear—e.g., "annihilation of space by time (Becoming)"—now faces obsolescence from a postmodern sensibility where time and space are simultaneous, disjointed, and multiple, e.g., "spatialization of time (Being)" (Harvey, 1989, p. 261). This induces a postmodern response, according to Harvey (1989, p. 350), of withdrawal "into a kind of shell-shocked, blasé, or exhausted silence" that convinces the late-modern subject "to bow down before the overwhelming sense of how vast, intractable, and outside any individual or even collective control everything is."

Globalization as colonial rhetoric

These renditions of global restructuring, while informative and important, exhibit what David Spurr (1993) calls the "rhetoric of empire." By this, he means a discursive pattern of image-making, referencing, cataloging and general reality-framing that stems from the Western colonial enterprise originating from the sixteenth century and lasting to the present.

Both liberals and critics of global restructuring partake in this colonizing rhetoric. To begin with, they survey the world with a god's-eye-view. Buttressed with scientific objectivity and rational argumentation, they ascertain for the rest of us what global restructuring is, who it affects, where it is going and why. This perspective, more likely than not, reflects a common configuration of race/gender/class/age/location, e.g., older White masculinized cosmopolitans working in or near global cities. One may protest: the nature of the subject—global restructuring—requires a god's-eye-view! But, what Spurr critiques—and what ails "globalization" studies—is that the colonial gaze unreflexively focuses on only a small segment of the world at the expense of its vast majority.

Take, for example, how "globalization" studies cast the relationship between global and local forces. Liberals outrightly embrace one-way penetration of the local by the global. Not only does the global provide greater "modernity," "progress," "democracy" (even "history"!), they assert, but that is what the global *should* do to the local. Critics disagree, at least theoretically. Gramscian globalists, for example, may recognize that "different master (global) narratives" may fuse with "local vernaculars (e.g., separatism, folklorism, local sacred beliefs)" to produce a heterogeneous "global culture" ("Editorial," 1994, p. 4). In the end, we learn little of how a transnationalized ideology like liberal capitalism *interacts* with and subsequently *constructs* a local ideological context and its subject. What Gramscian globalists tell us instead is how liberal capitalism triumphs over and annihilates the local (Ling, 1996b).

This one-sided rendition of global restructuring reflects an underlying classification scheme: e.g., history-making capitalist economies vs. history-lagging noncapitalist ones; wealthy centers vs. exploited peripheries; transnational firms vs. territorially bound states; globe-straddling cosmopolitans vs. locally bound parochials. Thus, the world is divided into dichotomous categories that reproduce the West/rest, self/Other rationales of an older colonial tradition. Additionally, the global and the local are placed in irreconcilable oppositions, thereby compelling a (false) choice between one or the other. This distracts attention from those processes of interaction, appropriation, synthesis, hybridity and transformation that course through global and local forces. Some coin a trendy phrase, "glocalization" (see Karam, 2000), to refer to this phenomenon, but it remains (as yet) undertheorized and underspecified.

"Globalization" studies also train our intellectual sights on macro-corporate entities such as finance, production, trade, telecommunications, media, drug cartels and the Mafia. Liberals and critics alike fixate on their "structural integration," "corporate strategies," "logic of collective action" and "economic vs. state power." Those who populate this global economy become abstracted into consumers, producers, citizens, elites or cosmopolitans. These same liberals and critics presume that "categories of capitalism" and their *laissez-faire* principles apply universally across culture, race or gender. In so doing, they mask normative and ideological presuppositions regarding "who is 'wealthy' and who is 'poor,' who is 'advanced' and who is 'behind,' who is 'rational' and who is 'irrational,' who is 'peaceful' and who is 'violent'" (Murphy and Rojas de Ferro, 1995, p. 63). What results is an unreflective reproduction of the values, norms, institutions and practices of those who have always been on top.

Not surprisingly, the few probes that we have on subjectivity under late-modern capitalism are also idealized. As we have already mentioned, the "globalization" literature privileges one type of subjectivity—Westernized, masculinized and industrialized—over other possible configurations. In both liberal and critical scenarios, the late-modern subject confronts a high-tech, postmodern world in which traditional forms of social organization (e.g., the nation-state) no longer hold.

This presumption stems from the literature's constant affirmation of liberal capitalism as globalization's defining ideology. Whether celebrating or castigating it, the literature sets liberal capitalism—which essentially upholds Western-style capitalism—as the organizing rationale behind the world political economy. In so doing, "globalization" studies implicitly place the industrialized West at the geopolitical–economic center of the world, with "the rest" as its reactionary appendage.[5]

Such discursive moves eradicate the subaltern.[6] Though subalterns may constitute the majority of the world's population, its labor force and consumption market, they are omitted from consideration when surveyed from a god's-eye-view. It discounts, in short, all those who are not Westernized, capitalized and masculinized living in global cities as consumers, producers, citizens, elites or cosmopolitans. At the same time, we lose sight of what it means to live, work, play and die in a globalized but varied economy—and how all these may differ for different groups. Here, Gayatri Chakravorty Spivak (1988) rightly charges, the subaltern woman suffers especially. She is "invisibilized" and silenced by two crushing discourses: a masculinist discourse of imperialism and an equally masculinist reactionary anti-imperialism. Consequently, the subaltern woman and other feminized subjects have no language, rhetoric, discourse or even voice to express their subjectivities. As we will demonstrate in the remainder of this chapter, they are perhaps the most globalized subjects of all.

A growing body of feminist scholarship aims to "re-visibilize" and re-articulate women under various processes of global change (Safa, 1981; Nash and Fernandez-Kelly, 1983; Sen and Grown, 1987; Ward, 1990; Marchand, 1996). Though primarily concerned with global restructuring rather than "globalization," this literature explicitly recognizes gender as a fundamental dimension along which all social processes and practices are organized, experienced and rendered meaningful. Thus, the subjects of these studies are not disembodied persons who transverse across time and space but corporeal women and men whose choices and movements reflect their gendered, racialized and class-based identities in the worlds they inhabit.

Throughout, feminist analyses of "everyday resistance" recur, returning both the subject and agency to our understanding of global restructuring. In underscoring women's responses, though, many such studies underestimate the impact of macro-structures in limiting women's choices. This tendency to "romanticize resistance" (Abu-Lughod, 1990, p. 42) ignores the complex structures of power in which acts of resistance are embedded (see Groves and Chang, 1999). Not only is this historically inaccurate, but it obscures the very problem that initially motivated these studies.

Global restructuring II: A regime of labor intimacy (RLI)

In this chapter, we seek to learn from these insights while redressing their weaknesses. To *de-colonize* global restructuring, we retain the focus on corporeal agency found in feminist literature. This requires viewing global restructuring from below, in person, and located at a specific geopolitical–cultural site. We also look at noncorporate, though no less organized, forms of working and living in the global political economy. This "re-sighting" helps us examine the full complement of global life from its macro-structural aspects (like the gendered, racialized state) to its micro-subjective impact (such as on the subaltern woman). At the same time, we aim to avoid romanticizing or individualizing subjectivity by placing it within larger structures that operate in the global political economy. Through ethnographic research, we decipher what Murphy and Rojas de Ferro (1995) refer to as the "circulation of meanings" or "regimes of representation" that shape history and embed structures of power. This means redefining what constitutes global culture/society/persons. It also requires taking seriously how corporeal subjects themselves make sense of their globalizing world. From this basis, we may trace how contending ideologies may intertwine or coexist in a late-modern subjectivity, thereby extending a different definition to cosmopolitanism and cosmopolitans.

More specifically, we examine global restructuring from a gendered and racialized perspective. By this, we refer to the recognition that all social processes, practices, meaning structures and institutions (like the state) assign and reflect historically constructed notions of "masculinity" and "femininity" that are also class-based, racially specific and culturally defined. Typically, this gendering process reflects a patriarchal power structure that glorifies men, masculinity and manhood and denigrates women, femininity and womanhood. These constructions of gender differences entail more than biological differences. They may apply to whole groups of people regardless of sex. Both male and female cosmopolitans of TMC, for example, take on "masculinized" traits of high-tech mobility, autonomy and challenging opportunities in comparison to their "feminized" counterparts in the RLI, who must contend with low-wage menial labor, enforced intimacy and incarcerating daily routines. As a case in point, we focus on Filipina domestic workers in Hong Kong.

A globalized service economy

TMC's "structural adjustment" policies of the 1970s–1980s account for today's "global feminization" of labor intimacy.[7] These policies forced governmental retrenchments into anti-unionism, subcontracting and resorting to temporary or contract workers. This led to the development of three major categories of workers in the Philippines: women, overseas contract workers and child workers.[8] Women were more cost-effective to hire, but they also became the first ones fired. A worldwide "skill polarization" emerged, with some workers representing "an elite of technically skilled, high-status specialist workers possessing higher-level institutional qualifications" (such as financial analysts), while others constituted "a larger mass of technically semi-skilled production and subsidiary workers requiring minor training" such as assembly line workers (Standing, 1989, p. 1079). As states further deregulated labor to enhance flexible accumulation under global restructuring, many workers saw overseas employment as their only hope.[9] In 1992, 2.5 million people, or 8 percent of the Filipino workforce, sought contract work overseas (*FEER*, 2 April 1992, p. 22).

These economic forces, combined with a historical racialization and sexualization of work, channeled massive numbers of Filipinos to venture overseas for income in the RLI. In the mid-1980s, nearly half of Filipino contract workers overseas were women (Eviota, 1992). First, they worked as "medical workers, secretaries, clerks and teachers, then eventually as domestic help and sex workers" (Rosca, 1995, p. 526). In 1984, 84 percent of Filipina migrants went to the Middle East; by 1987, they started to shift to the capital-surplus countries of East Asia, such as Hong Kong, Singapore and Japan (Heyzer, 1989, p. 1116).[10]

Filipina migrants are usually the sole supporters of landless parents and/or unemployed husbands, as well as children. A large proportion are college-educated but were unable to find work at home in the fields for which they were trained. Migrant workers from the Philippines average 6.9 years of work abroad; 18 percent have had some college education and 36.8 percent have earned a college degree (*FEER*, 8 March 1990, pp. 32–33). Domestic work overseas can bring Filipinas six times what they earned in the Philippines (Eviota, 1992).

While overseas pay may be high, Filipina migrants often find themselves incarcerated within an RLI. They discover that the larger community often links their domestic work with sexualized service (Chang and Groves, 2000). Pseudo-employment agencies and other illegal underground networks recruit an undetermined number of Filipinas under the guise of domestic service or "entertainment jobs" only to put them to work as prostitutes in bars or brothels (*FEER*, 14 October 1993, pp. 38–39; Eviota, 1992). Still, other women turn to prostitution when domestic contracts are prematurely terminated and/or crippling debts are owed to recruitment agencies in the Philippines. Indeed, the governments of both the Philippines and receiving countries—particularly in Asia, where the sex trade is most rampant—are complicit in promoting such forms of sexual exploitation, particularly with their failure to regulate recruitment agencies or enact legislation to protect (rather than limit) the rights of domestic workers.

The complicit, patriarchal state

The state may be "hollowing out" under TMC, but it enjoys a renewed vigor in the RLI. The state actively structures, facilitates and sustains a globalized service economy. The Philippines government, for example, supervises, regulates, transports and taxes its overseas contract workers with various state agencies organized under the Department of Labor. In the 1970s, the Marcos government initiated overseas contract work as a developmental strategy to enhance economic competitiveness. A decade later, it utilized overseas employment to manage a spiraling external debt (Jose, 1991; Standing, 1989).[11] The state initially decreed that all migrant workers must remit at least half of their monthly salary through authorized government channels. But, a grassroots organization of migrant workers, United Filipinos Against Forced Remittance, defeated this legislation in 1984.[12] Now, the government seeks to charge migrant workers for "health care" (Rosca, 1995).

Despite recent protests over the treatment of Filipina domestic workers overseas, the state continues to market overseas contract work as part of a national development policy. President Fidel Ramos refers to Filipina migrant workers as "a vital export commodity (for) the Philippines' own economic strategy" (Rosca, 1995, p. 524). In 1991, remittances to the Philippines from overseas contract workers amounted to approximately 12 percent of its gross national product (GNP) (*FEER*, 22 August 1991, p. 56). In 1992, overseas remittances accounted for 25 percent of the country's foreign-exchange earnings (*FEER*, 2 April 1992, p. 22).

Reliance on overseas remittances is complemented by the Philippine government's development policy at home. This development policy for the new century, Philippines 2000, centers on efforts to woo foreign investors with attractive deals—which often include women—at the expense of social, economic and environmental deterioration within the country (Eviota, 1992). Increasingly, "development" and "sex tourism" have become mutually reinforcing sources of hard currency. Even with the closure of US military bases, "bikini bars" remain a lucrative feature of the tourism and business landscape in the Philippines. In addition, with the growth of the bride trade and the exportation of female "entertainers" to Japan and other Asian countries, the "services" of Filipinas are increasingly available abroad.[13]

Receiving states are equally complicit. In Hong Kong, immigration policies subject Filipina domestic workers to effective indentured servitude by legally binding them to full-time, live-in work for one employer without specifying the conditions of their service. Authorities in both Singapore and Hong Kong restrict Filipinas from changing employers and types of employment and even having the right to terminate their jobs for two years (Heyzer, 1989, p. 1116). In Singapore, maids must undergo a mandatory six-month pregnancy check to determine their "employability" (Heyzer, 1989, p. 1116). State authorities in Japan often turn a blind eye to the illegal but lucrative recruitment of Filipinas to serve as its "hostesses" and "entertainers" (*FEER*, 14 October 1993, p. 39).

The state's complicity in this RLI is not a recent adaptation to globalizing trends. It reflects a long-standing ideology of sexualized, racialized service for certain sectors and members of the world political economy.

Transnational ideology of racialized, sexualized service

As TMC spouts the transnational ideology of universalism and liberalism to promote capital mobility, technological development and flexible production, the RLI operates on a symbiotic ideology of racism/sexism to institutionalize its globalized service economy. The deterritorialization of capital under TMC helps to mystify both transnational ideologies of liberalism and sexualized, racialized service. The former becomes a shining standard bearer to all that is possible, while the latter remains hidden and illegitimate despite the virtual incarceration of, in particular, female migrants into sexualized service with all its abuses, exploitation and possibility of life-threatening disease.[14]

Indeed, the global economy casts Filipinas and other Asian women as the very embodiment of "service" (Ling, 1996a, 1997). The stereotype of the Filipina as sexually subservient is rooted in a history of colonialism, sexism and poverty. As already mentioned, "sex tourism" has underwritten the Philippines' debt-ridden economy for decades. Exceptionally, the Aquino government sought to clean up this "service economy"—especially its offshoot into sex tourism—as part of a larger campaign to restore national dignity. But, such efforts failed because they ignored the entrenchment of this service economy in an international political economy that limits options for Filipinas and provides wealthy Western and increasingly Asian businessmen with the economic power to purchase and trade women as sexual commodities (Enloe, 1989). The commodification of Filipinas now takes on the form of a "maid trade" (Chang and Groves, 2000).

In Hong Kong, as the Filipina community has grown and become more visible, their presence has created a public debate about domestic workers that has been framed largely in terms of women's sexuality (Chang and Groves, 2000). Complaints about their occupation of public space, neglect of duties or illegal activities condemn this all-female community in moral terms. The Filipinas, many imply, offer more than domestic services in exchange for money. Filipinas are held as "morally suspect" (Constable, 1996) by many local residents and employers, who presume that the women have an ulterior motive in going abroad: "to find a man and obtain financial security" (Constable, 1996, p. 466). Such debates often take place in newspaper editorials where Filipina domestic workers are accused of neglecting children, seducing husbands and moonlighting as prostitutes. Indeed, the media are full of such allusions to women's sexuality and its economic significance, from suggestive newspaper headlines such as "Maids too much of a distraction for employers" (*Hong Kong Standard*, 12 May 1997) to more sensationalist captions such as "Maid turned to prostitution" (*South China Morning Post*, 12 May 1983). This sexualized image of the Filipina pervades public discourse in Hong Kong, casting domestic workers into the morally dubious category of laborers associated with the sex industry. Filipina domestics are thus judged and held accountable, not for the "intimate labor" that they provide for the families of Hong Kong but as women who leave their own families to sell their services abroad for economic gain.

The image of the Filipina woman as a "prostitute" is also highly racialized in Hong Kong. One local writer, for example, devoted a whole chapter in his book *The Great Hong Kong Sex Novel* to the sexual escapades of Filipina domestic workers as seen through the eyes of two Western businessmen. Titled "Filipina Mon Amour," the chapter depicts Filipina women as "little brown Eskimos" who perform sex with great "tropical ardor" (Adams, 1993, pp. 73, 83). Such images hark back to the days of sex tourism in the Philippines, yet are revived in Hong Kong, which is still marketed as one of Asia's ports of "entertainment" for foreign enlisted men— and increasingly businessmen. In one newspaper editorial, an employer complained that his maid entertained foreign men in his house while he was away and frequented bars in the red-light district of Hong Kong:

> The main reason why Chinese employers do not like their maid staying away overnight is because they know all too well how it is being spent! Just drop by any Wanchai bar and you will see Filipinas walking off arm in arm with sailors. Many of them don't even bother to get into the bars but wait outside to be picked up.
>
> (W.C. Lau, "Sensible to pay return air fare to Philippines," letter to the editor, *South China Morning Post*, 24 June 1985, p. 22)

As this quotation suggests, the mere association with a foreign man is enough to impose upon a Filipina woman the label of "prostitute."

At the same time, migrant workers themselves succumb to the honeyed rhetoric of transnational liberalism. Many see overseas employment as a means of bootstrapping from intimate labor to TMC: "A lowly job overseas with good pay is better than working as a professional with a low salary in the Philippines" (*FEER*, 8 March 1990, p. 32). Once abroad, however, they find a very different outcome:

> In the Philippines, it's really difficult for even university graduates to get work, and even then, the pay is bad. I thought that if I worked here for one or two years, I could save enough to go home and start a business. But by the time I pay my debts here (in Japan), I will have saved almost nothing.
> (*FEER*, 14 October 1993, p. 9)

In response to liberalism's empty promises, Filipina domestic workers often retrench into a romanticized conservatism of God, family and country.

Cultural reification: God, family and country

In Hong Kong, many Filipina domestic workers resist their racialization and sexualization by redefining service in terms of devotion to God, family and country.[15] They regularly center social activities around religious organizations (usually affiliated with the local Catholic Church), which enforce extensive rules, both formal and informal, on where to go, what to do, when to do it and with whom. Penalties for breaking the rules include fines, ostracism and even expulsion from the group. These organizations emphasize religious or cultural activities such as singing church hymns or Filipino folk dances to ward off society's association of Filipinas with prostitution, e.g., singing karaoke songs and disco dancing in places of ill repute. In the process of redefining service, many Filipinas mythologize a "traditional culture" that does not necessarily reflect life as it is in the Philippines (Chang and Groves, 2000).

Some Filipinas draw upon their religious faith to define themselves as servants of the Lord rather than the physical world of men. They describe this service to God and the church as cleansing, filling them with a sense of "righteousness" and "completeness" that comes only once a week on Sundays. Articles in *Tinig Filipino* speak directly to the women's faith as a means of redefining sexual service. In one issue, the editor imagined a "love letter" written by God to Filipina overseas contract workers, who are described as the "Chosen People to be Helpers of the World" (L.R. Layosa, "Into Thy Hands," *Tinig Filipino*, April 1994, p. 6). In this letter, God urges Filipina, domestic workers to embrace their work as servants, bringing to it their "true Christian values, your resilient, cheerful, persevering and helpful qualities," and "humble ways." As one woman put it: "I am not only here to earn money, I am here used by God as an instrument to show special light to my employers." In this way, the notion of service is cleansed of its sexual overtones and becomes an almost sacred activity, giving the women a sense of moral identity and purpose (Chang and Groves, 2000).

Many Filipinas also embrace their identities as wives, mothers and daughters to counter the sexualized image of the service provider. They invoke their marital or family status to ward off sexual advances from male employers, e.g., they are "not available" because they must "sacrifice for the family first." Public events also advance this theme of sacrifice for and devotion to migrant families. Articles in *Tinig Filipino* frequently flag traditional family values as a means of resisting the temptations of Hong Kong—e.g., illegal part-time work, "loan sharks," spending on oneself instead of sending remittances back home, extramarital or illicit affairs and so on. For example, one article emphasizes various kinds of "patience," including "patience with desire" such as "buying a house, saving money, marrying, etc." (M.E. Loria, "Adjustments to the local situation," *Tinig Filipino*, April 1994, p. 25) as a way of serving one's family rather than oneself.

Finally, some maids seek refuge in a refurbished national identity. Articles in *Tinig Filipino* repeatedly remind the women of their role as "economic heroes" of the Philippines:

> Through your good works in those places where you are temporarily working, you will become instruments in the economic improvement or progress of your "sick" nation through the dollars you send back home. In the future, through your perseverance and hard work, your children and your children's children will be the ones to benefit from your nation's progress.
>
> (L.R. Layosa, "Into Thy Hands," *Tinig Filipino*, April 1994, p. 6)

Such articles portray the women as active participants in the economic destiny of the Philippines, as opposed to sexual commodities. Other articles redefine Filipinas as "helpers of the world" rather than the "world's cleaners" (M. de Torres, "The Filipino: world class," *Tinig Filipino*, March 1994, p. 15). Service, in this sense, takes on a strong nationalistic overtone. For example, in the letter from God, the editor urges maids not only to educate their employers' children but to "Filipinize" them (L.R. Layosa, "Into Thy Hands," *Tinig Filipino*, April 1994, p. 6).

While this retrenchment into God, family and country provides a moral identity, it also creates painful moral dilemmas for Filipinas. Cultural and religious values offer a haven from the transnational ideology of sexualized, racialized service. But, they also become controlling and oppressive, depriving the Filipina woman of the autonomy and independence that liberal capitalism insists is hers. Yet, if she fails to live up to the moral standards of her community, she risks being labeled as "loose" or promiscuous. Thus, the two processes of global restructuring—TMC and labor intimacy—catch the Filipina migrant worker in between: tradition or modernity, virtue or independence, sainthood or sin. Recognizing the impossibility of such choices ("I'm no saint! You have to be naughty sometimes!"), some women choose to loosen or even break their ties with their community—often at great personal cost. Still others choose another alternative: "tomboyism."

Sexual alternative: Tomboyism

Given such intense scrutiny of their sexuality by their immediate environment as well as the global economy at large, some Filipina migrant workers opt out through a homosexual identity they call "tomboyism."[16] Tomboys wear men's clothing, have short hair, behave in a conventionally masculine manner and have liaisons or affairs with other Filipinas. Some claim that outfitting as a tomboy prevents them from being perceived as "cheap." It also saves from sexual harassment from men while offering some protection to other Filipinas. As one woman put it: "Any friend can protect you, but the protection of a tomboy is different." A tomboy, for example, replaced the former president of the Filipina shelter in Hong Kong when the latter was caught having an affair with her male employer. Indeed, many tomboys hold positions of power and responsibility within the Filipino community, where their image as "strong" and "faithful" women challenges the stereotype of Filipinas as sexually subservient or promiscuous.

The migrant community tolerates tomboyism, despite the Catholic Church's injunction against homosexuality, precisely because it relieves Filipinas from their intense sexualization while overseas. Some women even speak of lesbianism as a show of devotion to their families. Tomboys are seen to offer a "safe outlet" for women: a means of enjoying the romance and intimacy of a relationship while at the same time preserving marital vows. The women thus construct lesbianism as a form of fidelity rather than promiscuity. Most importantly, a relationship with a tomboy would not disrupt family life since there is no risk of pregnancy. One article in *Tinig Filipino*, for example, describes tomboys as "gorgeous, faithful, sympathetic" and so forth. These are words from women who are too afraid of flushing their fetus in the toilet: "With a lesbian, I'm safe" (L. Eronico, "The Modern Romeos in the Making," *Tinig Filipino*, March 1994, p. 10).

Conclusion

The moral dilemmas of Filipina domestic workers in Hong Kong stem from their placement between two processes of global restructuring: labor intimacy and TMC. An examination of their internal dialectics provides a more comprehensive understanding of our late-modern global economy (see Table 2.1).

1 Labor intimacy results from and sustains TMC. Gross wage inequities increasingly casualize and informalize labor so that some workers have more means to hire others who need more economic compensation. Migrant workers toiling in the household also release cosmopolitans from time-consuming, mind-numbing, nonrewarding chores so that they may pursue their "casino capitalism," "technology districts," "strategic alliances," "global cities" and "trilateral economies." Thus, the cycle of wage inflation and labor domestication continues.

2 The state may be released from traditional duties of sovereignty or community to further the "flexible production" or "mobile capital" of TMC. But this reserves the state's resources to continue its historical institutionalization of racist, sexist and classist policies in the RLI.[17] As migration within East Asia shows, such state power parallels that of firms in its global reach.
3 A transnational ideology of sexualized, racialized service privatizes and mutes the contradictions of transnational liberalism. In this way, liberal internationalists may promote the public rhetoric of wealth, opportunity and mobility even as a majority of the world's population struggles with poverty, exploitation and structural incarceration. As demonstrated by Filipina domestic workers in Hong Kong, sometimes local resistance to global restructuring takes on the form of reifying those very pillars of society and state that are most conservative, patriarchal and hegemonic.
4 The cultural retrenchment and paralyzing moral dilemmas found in the RLI provide a stable pool of labor for the late-modern cosmopolitans of TMC to experiment with their time-space compression and/or reflexive individualism. Little chance exists, then, of local counterhegemonies overhauling the capitalist world hegemony. Most likely, systemic changes or transformations will arise from the interstices of local–global interaction and the constituent-specific negotiations that they reflect.

This case study on Filipina migrant workers in Hong Kong broadens our understanding of subjectivity and cosmopolitanism under late-modern capitalism. It demonstrates that geographical mobility does not necessarily translate into a psychological or emotional detachment. Indeed, our case study underscores that recourse to "reflexive individualism" or "blasé withdrawal" highly

Table 2.1 Schematic representation of technomuscular capitalism (TMC) and regime of labor intimacy (RLI)

Category	*TMC*	*RLI*
Identifying features	Integration of technology, trade, production and communications facilitated by globalized financial networks	Exportation of low-wage, low-to-medium skilled workers to service "intimate" jobs in cosmopolitan homes
The role of the state	Internationalized or "hollowed out"	Complicit, patriarchal, vigorous
Transnationalized ideology	Liberal capitalism	Sexualized, racialized service
Nature of global society, culture, persons	Global elites, or cosmopolitans, postmodern individualism, or "shell-shocked" withdrawal	Cultural reification: God, family, and country, crossing sexual boundaries, moral dilemmas

correlates with relative power disparities in the global political economy. A middle-aged, middle-income, masculinized professional without household duties may feel free to "reinvent" himself or herself to "join new communities." But the scope of such choice for a middle-aged, low-income, feminized domestic worker facing a barrage of sexual and racial discrimination is much smaller. Though choices do exist, they take very different and unanticipated forms. Some migrant workers choose to reify their indigenous culture; others seek subterfuge in an alternative sexuality.

In shifting from a (neo)colonial, masculinist god's-eye-view to the perspective of a subaltern woman from a specific location, we also change our notion of what constitutes global and globalism. Hannerz's high-style multiculturalism still applies, but another kind of cosmopolitanism/globalism comes into sight as well. It also requires competence, mastery, autonomy, self-made-ness and intellectual acumen. But, it has less to do with abstract, evaluative qualities like intellectualism or aesthetics than with a pragmatic outlook that aims to engage with, fit in, sort through and negotiate across differences. Less idealized, it is instead embodied in the daily demands of global life: caring for young and elderly people who are not from one's own culture or country, cleaning their houses, washing their clothes, preparing their food, living a life where local knowledge, tastes, habits and customs blur ceaselessly with global ones. This "pragmatic globalism" recognizes contending ideologies (sometimes incommensurate ontologies) where they exist (e.g., work vs. family, devotion vs. service, saint vs. whore, Catholicism vs. homosexuality, Tagalog vs. English) but ultimately seeks to work them out such that they emerge as reformed, transmuted parts of oneself, not a quaint custom or exotic locale that can be "exited" at will. Thus, pragmatic globalism does not force a selection between false choices: modernity vs. tradition, contrast vs. uniformity, globalism vs. localism, reflexivity vs. withdrawal. Rather, it aspires for an overall sanity that endures through all the conflicts and contradictions that beset our daily, global life.

Notes

1 We borrow the description of "techno-muscularity" from Elaine Boose's identification of American self-perceptions during the Vietnam War (1993, pp. 67–106).

2 Since the mid-1980s, Hong Kong has become the second largest destination (next to the Middle East) for Filipina migrant workers. From 1975 to 1991, the number of Filipina domestic workers in Hong Kong jumped from 1,000 to nearly 66,000 (Asia-Pacific Mission for Migrant Filipinos, 1991). By the late 1990s, new arrivals were estimated at a rate of 80 per day, bringing the Filipina population to over 130,000, making it the largest non-Chinese community in Hong Kong (Constable, 1997).

3 Paul Welfens (1989, p. 273) notes, for example, that "85 percent of international trade in technology is concentrated among companies from just ten market-economy, industrial countries – and that these are all among the top fifteen countries for direct investment."

4 A caveat: debates about the demise of the state under global restructuring are far from settled. Stephen Krasner (1994), for instance, reiterates that states remain what they have always been: rational, self-interested, unitary and the most important actors in international relations. Thus a state-centric analysis still offers the most

parsimonious elegance for predictive theory while, at the same time, explaining radical changes in the world political economy. The Economist (7 October 1995, pp. 15–6) agrees that the powerless state is a "myth." For evidence, it refers to continued high levels of public spending in states that are supposed to be the most globalized. For a critique of this line of reasoning, see Strange (1994).

5 This literature identifies Japan as an industrialized economy but not a member of the geopolitical club.

6 The concept of subalternity builds on earlier notions of the comprador, that is, a class or grouping of people structurally placed to serve the governing needs of another. But where comprador connotes a commercial relationship, subaltern suggests a political one.

7 Here, "feminization" refers to a process of physical embodiment as well as social construction. That is, more women are working in certain sectors of the global economy. These are usually low-wage, low-skilled and low-mobility workers. At the same time, the global economy assigns to both women and men who work on its lower rungs traits historically identified as "feminine," e.g., backwardness, irrationality, passivity and victimhood.

8 In 1985, there were 5–7 million Filipino working children within the 5–14 year age group, mostly in rural areas (Ofreneo, 1993, p. 255).

9 For example, the Philippines government in the 1980s removed most enterprises from coverage by various labor laws to reduce production costs for multinational corporations (Standing, 1989).

10 Surveys on Filipina migrant workers indicated the following figures: 20,000 in Greece; 40,000 in England; 50,000–100,000 in Hong Kong; 60,000 in Spain; 75,000 in Singapore; 80,000 in Italy; and 750,000 in the Middle East (Rosca, 1995; Asia-Pacific Mission for Migrant Filipinos, 1991).

11 In 1974, the Philippines' external debt amounted to $3.75 billion; by 1990, it had risen to $28 billion with an 8.6 percent unemployment rate (FEER, 8 March 1990, pp. 32–33).

12 In 1990, for instance, overseas contract workers remitted $856 million through official channels and another $3 billion through private channels (FEER, 8 March 1990, pp. 32–33).

13 Ninotchka Rosca (1995, p. 524) reports that over 75,000 Filipinas work in the Japanese sex industry.

14 According to Rosca (1995, p. 524), between 30,000 and 50,000 Filipinos around the US bases in the Philippines have contracted HIV.

15 This section of the chapter draws directly from Chang and Groves (2000).

16 "Coming out" is common for migrants who may cross sexual borders along with national ones (Espin, 1994).

17 This dual strategy is apparent in the US Congress, for example, where many conservatives call for less governmental regulation of the "private," corporate sector while advocating more for the "public," civic sector such as immigration, welfare, education and reproductive rights for women.

References for Preface and Chapter

Abu-Lughod, L. (1990) "The romance of resistance: Tracing transformations of power through Bedouin women," *American Ethnologist*, 17, pp. 41–55.

Adams, G. (1993) *The Great Hong Kong Sex Novel.* Hong Kong: AIP Publications.

Agnew, J. and Corbridge, S. (1995) *Mastering Space: Hegemony, Territory, and International Political Economy.* London: Routledge.

Barber, B. (1996) *Jihad vs. McWorld.* New York: Ballantine Books.

Barnet, R.S. and Cavanagh, J. (1994) *Global Dreams: Imperial Corporations and the New World Order*. New York: Simon and Schuster.

Berger, M. (1996) "Yellow mythologies: The East Asian miracle and post-Cold War capitalism," *Positions*, 4(1), pp. 90–126.

Boose, E. (1993) "Techno-muscularity and the 'Boy-Eternal': From the quagmire to the Gulf," in Cooke, M. and Woollacott, A. (eds.) *Gendering War Talk*. Princeton, NJ: Princeton University Press, pp. 67–106.

Chang, K.A. and Groves, J.M. (2000) "Neither 'saints' nor 'prostitutes': Sexual discourse in the Filipina domestic worker community in Hong Kong," *Women's Studies International Forum*, 23(1), pp. 73–87.

Constable, N. (1996) "Jealousy, chastity, and abuse: Chinese maids and foreign helpers in Hong Kong," *Modern China*, 22(4), pp. 448–479.

Constable, N. (1997) *Maid to Order in Hong Kong: Stories of Filipina Workers*. Ithaca, NY: Cornell University Press.

Cox, R.W. (1987) *Production, Power, and World Order*. New York: Columbia University Press.

Cox, R.W. (1993) "Structural issues of global governance: implications for Europe," in Gill, S. (ed.) *Gramsci, Historical Materialism, and International Relations*. Cambridge: Cambridge University Press.

Dicken, P. (1992) *Global Shift*. London: Guilford Press.

Dicken, P. (1994) "Global-local tensions: Firms and states in the global space-economy," *Economic Geography*, 70(2), pp. 101–127.

"Editorial: Forum for heterodox international political economy." (1994) *Review of International Political Economy*, 1(1), pp. 1–12.

Enloe, C. (1989) *Bananas, Beaches, and Bases: Making Feminist Sense of International Relations*. Berkeley, CA: University of California Press.

Espin, M. (1994) "*Crossing borders and boundaries: The life narratives of immigrant lesbians*," paper presented at the 102nd Annual Convention of the American Psychological Association, Los Angeles, CA, August.

Eviota, E.U. (1992) *The Political Economy of Gender: Women and the Sexual Division of Labor in the Philippines*. London: Zed Books.

Fukuyama, F. (1989) "The end of history?," *The National Interest*, 16, pp. 3–18.

Gill, S. (1992) "Economic globalization and the internationalization of authority: limits and contradictions," *Geoforum*, 23(3), pp. 269–283.

Gill, S. (1995) "Globalization, market civilization, and disciplinary neoliberalism," *Millennium*, 24(3), pp. 399–423.

Groves, J.M. and Chang K.A. (1999) "Romancing resistance and resisting romance: Ethnography and the construction of power in the Filipina domestic worker community in Hong Kong," *Journal of Contemporary Ethnography*, 28(3), pp. 235–265.

Hannerz, U. (1990). "Cosmopolitans and locals in world culture," in Featherstone, M. (ed.) *Global Culture: Nationalism, Globalization, and Modernity*. London: Sage.

Harvey, D. (1989) *The Condition of Postmodernity: An Enquiry into the Origins of Cultural Change*. Oxford: Blackwell.

Held, D. and McGrew, A.G. (1993) "Globalization and the liberal democratic state," *Government and Opposition*, 28, pp. 261–288.

Heyzer, N. (1989) "Asian women wage-earners: their situation and possibilities for donor intervention," *World Development*, 17(7), pp. 1109–1123.

Jose, V. (1991) "Philippine external debt problem: The Marcos years," *Journal of Contemporary Asia*, 21(2), pp. 222–245.

Kapstein, E.B. (1996) "Workers and the world economy," *Foreign Affairs*, 75 (May/June), pp. 16–37.

Karam, A.M. (2000). "Feminisms and Islamisms in Egypt: Between globalization and postmodernism," in Marchand, M.H. and Runyan, A.S. (eds.) *Gender and Global Restructuring: Sightings, Sites, and Resistances*. London and New York: Routledge.

Kleinman, A. (2006) *What Really Matters: Living a Moral Life Amidst Uncertainty and Danger*. New York, NY: Oxford University Press.

Krasner, S.D. (1994) "International political economy: Abiding discord," *Review of International Political Economy*, 1(1), pp. 13–20.

Lash, S. and Urry, J. (1994) *Economies of Signs and Spaces*. London: Sage Publications.

Leslie, D.A. (1995) "Global scan: The globalization of advertising agencies, concepts, and campaigns," *Economic Geography*, 71(4), pp. 402–426.

Ling, L.H.M. (1996a) "Democratization under internationalization: Media reconstructions of gender identity in Shanghai," *Democratization*, 3(2), pp. 140–157.

Ling, L.H.M. (1996b) "Hegemony and the internationalizing state: A postcolonial analysis of China's integration into Asian corporatism," *Review of International Political Economy*, 3(1), pp. 1–26.

Ling, L.H.M. (1997) "*The other side of globalization: Hypermasculine developmentalism and media constructions of gender identity in East Asia*," paper presented at the ISA Meeting, Toronto, Ontario, March 18–22.

Ling, L.H.M. (2014a) *Imagining World Politics: Sihar & Shenya, a Fable for our Times*. New York, NY: Routledge.

Ling, L.H.M. (2014b) *The Dao of World Politics: Towards a Post-Westphalian, Worldist International Relations*. London: Routledge.

Ling, L.H.M. (2019) "Three-ness: healing world politics with epistemic compassion," *Politics*, 39(1), pp. 35–49.

Marchand, M.H. (1996) "Reconceptualizing 'gender and development' in an era of 'globalization'," *Millennium*, 25(3), pp. 577–604.

Marshall, D.D. (1996) "Understanding late-twentieth-century capitalism: Reassessing the globalization theme," *Government and Opposition*, 31 (Spring), pp. 193–215.

Murphy, C.N. and Rojas de Ferro, C. (1995) "The power of representation in international political economy: Introduction," *Review of International Political Economy*, 2 (1), pp. 63–69.

Nash, J. and Fernandez-Kelly, M.P. (eds.) (1983) *Women, Men, and the International Division of Labor*. Albany, NY: State University of New York Press.

Ofreneo, R.E. (1993). "Structural adjustment and labor market responses in the Philippines," in Muqtada, M. and Hildiman, A. (eds.) *Labor Markets and Human Resource Planning in Asia: Perspectives and Evidence*. Geneva: ILO.

Reich, R. (1992) *The Work of Nations*. New York: Vintage Books.

Rosca, N. (1995) "The Philippines' shameful export," *The Nation*, April 17, p. 522.

Safa, H.I. (1981) "Runaway shops and female employment: The search for cheap labor," *Signs: Journal of Women and Culture in Society*, 7, pp. 418–433.

Sassen, S. (1991) *The Global City: New York, London, Tokyo*. Princeton, NJ: Princeton University Press.

Sen, G. and Grown, C. (1987) *Development, Crises, and Alternative Visions: Third World Women's Perspectives*. New York: Monthly Review Press.

Spivak, G.C. (1988). "Can the subaltern speak?," in Nelson, C. and Grossberg, L. (eds.) *Marxism and the Interpretation of Culture*. Chicago, IL: University of Illinois Press.

Spurr, D. (1993) *The Rhetoric of Empire*. Durham, NC: Duke University Press.

Standing, G. (1989) "Global feminization through flexible labor," *World Development*, 17(7), pp. 1077–1095.

Strange, S. (1986) *Casino Capitalism*. Oxford: Blackwell.

Strange, S. (1994) "Wake up, Krasner! The world has changed," *Review of International Political Economy*, 2, pp. 209–220.

Thrift, N. (1992) "Muddling through: World orders and globalization," *The Professional Geographer*, 44, pp. 3–7.

Ward, K. (ed.) (1990) *Women Workers and Global Restructuring*. Ithaca, NY: Cornell University Press.

Welfens, P.J.J. (1989) "The globalization of markets and regional integration," *Intereconomics*, (November/December), pp. 273–281.

Zhang, Q.M. (2017) *Accomplice to Memory*. Los Angeles, CA: Kaya Press.

3 Labor here, consume there, accumulate everywhere

Improvisations of mobile capital and gendered labor along the Philippines–Canada migration corridor

Pauline Gardiner Barber and Catherine Bryan

Introduction: Spatial entanglements of capital and mobile workers

Despite decades of distraction when Marxist-inspired scholarship was disparaged, feminist political economists have continued studying how gendered global labor markets contribute to capitalist accumulation. With a feminist political economy lens, this chapter explores the recent history of the rapid transformations of gendered social reproduction in Philippine communities as workers, women and men, migrate abroad. The emphasis is on how workers create and then modify plans as they seek entry into gendered global labor markets and contribute to capitalist accumulation scenarios. Typifying Eric Wolf's (1982) proposition, the chapter explores how the modalities of capital and labor press both into patterns of global movement, creating new frontiers of accumulation, disrupting local livelihoods to then dispossess select populations, some of whom become mobile, adding to various pools of surplus labor. As Bauman (1998) and critics of globalization have observed, yet others are condemned to immobility without the means to migrate, but we focus here on mobile workers who remained connected to the people and places they call home; the ever-shifting gendered geometries of space, time and social/power relations that exemplify the spatial stretching that Massey (1994) outlined in her early work. Since capitalism is infinitely creative and not at all monolithic with predetermined outcomes, it remains imperative to investigate how the spatial entanglements of mobile capital, gendered labor and associated temporalities are socially and historically constituted in particular places. Disentangling the complexities of contemporary capitalism is especially challenging when accumulation frontiers involve mobile capital and labor following similar transnational trajectories of movement, albeit in a different temporal sequence. Capital-friendly facilitating states further complicate cross-border mobilities, as is illustrated here through the case of Philippines–Canada migration.

Drawing from ethnographic research exploring the transnational repercussions of Canada's long-term reliance on migrant Filipino workers, initially in care work and more recently in food services, this chapter examines the entanglement

DOI: 10.4324/9781003036425-4

of mobile capital in labor regimes channeling migrant workers between the Philippines and Canada.[1] The main proposition ordering the chapter is that migration inevitably relies upon improvisations across three registers. First are the migrants, each with their personal vision of a projected future, typically a future that includes other family members. Second come neoliberal states, unpredictable in the opening (for migrating citizen departures) and closing (to noncitizens) of national borders. Third is capital in various forms, relentlessly mobile, colluding with states to profit from the expansive mobilities of downgraded labor. Since migrants' improvisations require considerable financial and personal costs, expended prior to, during and subsequent to their journeys, the improvisations of capital and states are particularly harsh for the disruptions caused by too well-thought-out migration plans.

Exemplifying a geographically stretched accumulation frontier, the complexities of mobile global capital seen in the Philippines–Canada labor migration corridor have seen increasingly well-prepared yet disposable migrants (first mostly women, then women and men) become precariously implanted, sequentially in terms of policy priorities targeted toward the two specific sectors in question. From the mid-1970s until 2008, when Canada's immigration policy restructuring became fixated on global talent and rapid adjustment to labor market priorities, Filipinos, many with tertiary-level training, including in nursing colleges, entered Canada on temporary live-in care work visas. Such visas were of interest because they offered a clear pathway to permanent residence for the applicant, and later, allowed for eligible family members to enter Canada under the family reunification program. The majority of those receiving care worker visas (90 percent) were women working as "nannies" and as personal care workers for the elderly.

Commencing in 2008, the arrival of Filipinos in Canada rapidly increased under the nationally expanded federal Temporary Foreign Worker Programme (TFWP) operating in tandem with the federal government's delegation of immigrant selection processes to all provincial and territorial nomination programs (PTNPs or PNPS) that had not previously participated in immigrant selection, as had been the case for Manitoba and Quebec (Carter, 2009). Under this initiative, motivated by economic and demographic agendas, provinces and territories were encouraged to design specialized immigration streams. Visa programs proliferated, some of which opened new pathways to permanency, even for people with temporary work visas. With remarkable resourcefulness in their improvisations, Philippine migrants then entered Canadian provinces, coast to coast, in significant numbers to work in the food service industry.[2] By 2010 and for several years thereafter, the Philippines was the top source country for migrants entering Canada across all visa streams, both permanent (including family reunification for previously landed live-in care workers) and temporary, a situation which set the scene for the following discussion of labor and capital mobilities. Significantly, women's social reproductive labor, supporting left-behind family members through remittances while performing care work in the households of their Canadian employers and/or in institutions providing elder care, provides the foundation for the Philippine migration corridor and the capital that seizes advantage from such movement. The subsequent arrival of Filipinos on temporary work visas in food services is also best understood as a feminized labor stream, given the service dimensions of such work and its articulation with socially reproductive labor (Bryan, 2017).

The ethnographic substance of the chapter explores how political and economic decisions reverberate in the livelihood decisions of migrants, actual and potential. Several representative "cases" illustrate how workers gain skills and become globally mobile as they track employment opportunities offered by mobile capital. Sometimes, forced to expand their skill repertoire, migrants must contend with the capriciousness of capital-privileging state policies that open and close borders to certain kinds of workers, typically devaluing their skills. Hence, the mobilities of workers—their migration journeys and the labor markets they populate—well illustrate the fluid spatial and temporal entanglements of capital accumulation on a global scale. The multiple precarities migrant workers confront are not limited to the hardships of employment and sometimes corrupt actors in migration industries. In many countries, along with lengthy separations from loved ones, they also contend with the lack of employment protections, including adequate healthcare.

The chapter is organized into four sections. First, there is a review of the Philippines–Canada migration corridor and the rationales underscoring the rapidly changing labor import and export policies that orchestrate the relationship between these two countries. The second section briefly explores the arrival in Canada of Filipino nurses and care workers, a subject that has been well rehearsed in numerous studies, including Barber's chapter in the second edition of *Gender and Global Restructuring* (Barber, 2011). Discussion in section three then concentrates on a more recent case study of one major Canadian/global corporation to reveal how the gender and generational layering of earlier Filipino arrivals and, for temporary workers, reluctant departures enabled the complex nexus of mobilities whereby Filipinos, in both countries, came to serve as producers and consumers for an iconic Canadian company: Tim Hortons, purveyor of coffee and specialty donuts. Named after a famous Canadian ice hockey star, the company has long ceased to be Canadian per se and is now owned by an expansive global corporation that recently announced plans to increase its presence in several countries, including China where the first outlet opened in 2019 (Lewis, 2019). Prior to launching in the Philippines, in early 2017, the brand was aggressively marketed as Canadian in television advertisements in both countries, each campaign sentimentally oriented to Filipinos in the diaspora (for Canadian-based Filipino audiences) and with Philippine cultural idioms (for migrant returnees familiar with the brand but currently resident in the Philippines). Hence, we come to the mobilities of capital and labor that serve to illustrate (and update with the inclusion of capital) gender and global restructuring dynamics along the Philippines–Canada migration corridor.

Finally, section four serves as both a conclusion and a postscript to reflect upon how the COVID-19 pandemic of 2020 disproportionately affects migrant workers in global labor markets, as well as the remittance-dependent households they support. The plans of migrants-in-waiting living in the Philippines were yet again disrupted. Concluding remarks touch upon how the 2020 pandemic further exposed major flaws in Philippine development policy's reliance on gendered labor export and remittances dating back to the 1970s. In Canada, the pandemic exposed the ongoing vulnerability of racialized migrants from the Philippines with precarious feminized jobs and citizenship status, working in health care and associated occupations such as care work.

The Philippines–Canada migration corridor

The Philippines–Canada migration corridor is shaped by the shifting neoliberal policies of both states (Bello, 2004; Satzewich, 2016) and entails a *two-way* exchange of labor and capital. For the Philippines, the contributions of migrants to the national economy through remittances have been a significant labor export policy driver, and the explicit linking of migration as a solution to the trade gap, foreign earnings and domestic/household consumption has been a constant feature of Philippine political economy since Barber first began fieldwork in the Philippines in the early 1990s (Barber, 1996, 2004). In a familiar annual refrain, the *Philippine Star* reported 2019 remittances, citing a senior ING Bank Manila economist to summarize the then status quo before the COVID-19 global pandemic[3]:

> Remittances provide a steady stream of foreign exchange to help augment the widening trade gap to limit the current account deficit. Together with business process outsourcing receipts, OFW [overseas foreign workers] remittance flows also augment domestic wages, translating to potent purchasing power to fund household consumption and even capital formation.
> (Agcaoili, 2020)

Exceeding projections for 2019, personal remittances (cash and noncash items) were yet again reported at record levels, increasing by 3.9 percent for a total of $33.47 billion, up from $32.21 billion in 2018, accounting for a 9.3 percent overall boost to the gross domestic product (GDP). At $30.13 billion, cash remittances comprise a significant proportion of the recorded transfers (Agcaoili, 2020). From the perspective of remitting Filipinos, the more immediate concern has clearly been augmenting household livelihoods, where our research indicates expenditures vary in accordance with class, gender and generational projects. Migration scholars studying both the Philippines and the destinations that benefit from its labor export policies have well described the multidirectional gendered effects of remittances from globally situated Filipinos, most of whom work regionally on overseas contracts. Examples include Chin's (1998) study of female domestic workers in Malaysia; Constable's ongoing work with similar groups in Hong Kong (1997, 2014); Fajardo's (2011) innovative project on migrant seafarers' masculinities; and McKay's (2012) detailed discussion of the continual setbacks, departures and returns of globally connected contract workers from one migrant-sending Philippine village. Empirically, we also know a good deal about the precarious positioning of Filipino and other temporary workers in Canadian labor markets (Goldring and Landolt, 2011; Tungohan, 2017), the settlement struggles of those previously employed as migrant care workers (Bonifacio, 2013), and the human rights issues associated with the TFWP and its privileging of economic priorities (Nakache and Kinoshita, 2010).

As a major global labor export nation with a current population of just over 108 million (World Bank, 2020), the Philippines has seen major increases in the total annual number of land- and sea-based overseas workers to the point where an estimated 2.2 million people in over 200 countries were deployed in 2019 (Philippine Statistics Authority, 2020). The statistics, destinations and occupations reveal the wide-ranging skills Filipinos bring to global markets, indicating their resolve to earn and remit wages unavailable at comparable levels in the Philippines. By gender, the 2019 estimates show a higher number of women deployed (56 percent), with the largest proportion of migrants falling between 30 and 34 years old, although women tend to be younger compared to their male counterparts, 7 percent of them ranging from 15 to 24 years old, while 46.9 percent were 25 to 34 years old. The largest grouping of workers are in what are described as elementary occupations (39.6 percent), but 18 percent work in services and sales, followed by plant and machine operators at 12.2 percent, with technicians and associate professionals at 8.7 percent. Some 8.5 percent are professionals, with the remaining 8.1 percent represented in craft and related trades (Philippine Statistics Authority, 2020).[4]

In sum, globally, migrants are overwhelmingly hired to work in racialized, stratified and mostly gendered labor streams because they offer various levels of in-demand skills, with the top destinations being in the Middle East (Saudi Arabia and the United Arab Emirates), followed by Hong Kong and Taiwan. Canadian visas are more difficult and costly to obtain when various pre-migration plans are accounted for. Moreover, Canadian labor markets attract better-resourced Filipinos interested in permanent migration, a choice that significantly narrows the options for would-be migrants. The range of countries where Filipinos reside permanently is significantly reduced compared with their global labor market participation. As of 2018, by far the highest percentage of registered overseas Filipinos were in the US (60.54 percent), followed by Canada (20.12 percent).[5]

The social reproduction of Philippine migration

The process of Philippine labor export accelerated under the Marcos regime (1965–1986) as the dictator encouraged migration as a strategy to defuse political unrest stemming from state violence, high unemployment and poverty.

Despite pledges to develop bilateral arrangements affording better protections for Filipino overseas workers, the subsequent presidency of Corazon Aquino (1986–1992) saw intensified commitment to overseas migration on the part of Filipinos concerned with augmenting household livelihoods in an economy severely distorted by colonialism and decades of political corruption (Gonzalez, 1998). State-brokered migration, with the politically inspired narrative of the migrant hero, was developed during the Ramos administration (1992–1998) as an incentive to further encourage migrant departures (Guevarra, 2010; Rodriguez, 2010). During his re-election campaign, which occurred during the volatile period when Barber first began long-term research on Philippine gendered migration, Ramos had to contend with widespread anti-migration protests in response to the maltreatment of women overseas workers, including the two legendary cases in 1994 of Flor Contemplaçion executed in Singapore and Sara Balibagan flogged and jailed in the United Arab Emirates. The Ramos administration's response was to explicitly normalize labor export. Migration industries came under new regulations, departing migrants were subject to tighter border scrutiny of employment papers and more provision was made for left-behind families and returning migrants. Since Ramos's successful pledge to increase (to over one million persons per year) and regularize labor export, migration has remained contentious domestically and in the labor diaspora (Francisco and Rodriguez, 2014).

As gendered migration became more culturally acceptable (Barber 2011) and was further bolstered by the activities of subsequent administrations, many potential migrants' aspirations have shifted from the daily survival of immediate kin to generational concerns, such as educating the next generation perhaps for migration or under the worst-case scenario, lesser paid back-up middle-class jobs in the Philippines where there are high rates of youth unemployment. One recent study shows that state-deployed migrants have become more youthful and better educated. In 2010, 29 percent of younger migrants had four-year college degrees and 16.6 percent were enrolled in a college course prior to deployment (Battistella and Liao, 2013). "Migration management" by the Philippine state is considered exemplary in comparison to similar labor export nations in the region (Geiger and Pécoud, 2010; Barber and Bryan, 2017). Administrative protocols include the regulation and licensing of the recruitment sector, the monitoring of overseas employment contracts, liaisons with agencies and employers from destination countries (an explicit form of state brokerage) and strict border control of migrant departures. In this regard, there is a requirement that all contract workers attend pre-departure training sessions at the Philippines Overseas Employment Agency (POEA) prior to obtaining exit visas. While potential migrants continue to leave without state authorization, for example, by claiming they travel as tourists, many suspected of seeking unregulated employment abroad are prevented from leaving if they fail to produce legitimate tourist narratives and documents. Our data indicates that some migrants without approved employer documents may attempt to exit the country numerous times, sometimes with success. Such unrecorded departures are factored into the overall estimates of overseas workers, an acknowledgment that border regulation can mitigate but not prevent migrant desperation and risk-taking in their entry into global labor markets.

The link between remittance spending and educating the next generation of migrants, what can be referred to as the social reproduction of migration, warrants further comment. Not only do migrant remittances place a high priority on educating the next generation, but Philippine migration management extends into the educational sector in a contradictory fashion and is implicated in how the state intervenes (or not) in the educational sector. Tertiary education enhances the migration potential for more youthful migrants (as noted earlier); it also increases the overall costs for potential migrants while increasing the financial risk from an oversupply of certain types of skilled workers in global labor markets. Relatedly, migrant education has allowed for the introduction of poor-quality educational programming. Nursing provides one well-known example of how global demand led to the proliferation of Philippine nursing schools of vastly uneven quality, a situation that had negative repercussions for well-qualified registered nurses seeking overseas employment (Barber, 2013; Nourpanah, 2019; Valiani, 2012).[6]

Encouraged by labor export policies, migration industries have continued to flourish. On any given day, the POEA website lists recruitment agencies under sanction, indicating the challenges involved with the regulation and licensing of the recruitment sector. Similarly, proliferating educational institutions comprise a vital migration industry. For those who can afford them, institutions of uneven quality offer new credentials in sync not only with global market trends but also migration management agendas, for example, along the Philippines–Canada corridor. Adaptive to market demand, institutions are class diversified with numerous private institutions catering to specific markets, most recently and relevant to Canada's more complex immigration system, the hotel and restaurant management (HRM) trades. Notably, the state allows private school associations to self-regulate. As Ortiga (2018) notes, the link between educational institutions and labor export represents "early state brokerage," a manifestation of Philippine neoliberalism. Many working-class students in HRM courses have never stayed in hotels, and only those from more elite institutions can aspire to work in globally branded hotels. Graduates from HRM courses are among the many who enter Canada as temporary foreign workers (TFWs).

Destination Canada

Migrants seeking positions in Canada acquire education in differently classed institutions as they assess possibilities and adapt to changing policy scenarios. Prior to the expansion of the TFWP, the primary pathway for Filipinos was through the now-reformed live-in caregiver program (Bonifacio, 2013), sometimes involving step-migration through several labor markets (Barber, 2011; Paul, 2017). Filipinos, primarily women, have long entered Canada with uneven nursing qualifications, often to work as caregivers, sometimes as personal care assistants, but are seldom hired directly as registered nurses (Nourpanah, 2019;

Pratt, 1999, 2004; Stasiulis and Bakan, 2005). Through their Canadian presence and economic remittances for family livelihoods and debt repayment (Asis, 2015; Baggio, 2010; Gresham, Smit and Smith, 2015), and through family reunification strategies (Kelly, 2014), they have helped forge the Philippines–Canada migration corridor as a transnational relational and culturally performative space of class identity (Kelly, 2012).[7] Indeed, as Semyonov and Gorodzeisky (2008) show in a study spanning 1999–2000 and covering 2,346 remittance-receiving households, respondents reported being better off, objectively and subjectively. And, since remittance spending includes the purchase of food, clothing and, significantly for our purposes here, education, the Semyonov study provides early statistical evidence confirming ethnographic data from global migrants of the seeming class improvement possibilities generated by migration; migration is increasingly linked to a cultural understanding of being middle-class (Barber, 2004).

From caring to fast food along the Philippine migration corridor

Despite migration's class mobility possibilities, seen in the social reproduction projects of second and even third-generation family members, the expansive literature on global Philippine migration, with few exceptions, has generally described migrants in relatively low-skilled employment, albeit sometimes with higher credentials than demanded of their positions; as in the case of nurses as caregivers (Aguilar, 2014; Pido, 2017). Because of this feature of their migrations, Filipinos have been depicted as exploited global workers, subjected to recolonizing discourses of underdevelopment (Constable, 1997; McKay, 2012; Parreñas, 2001). Moreover, within Canada and beyond, an archetypical Filipino migrant emerged, anchored in a racialized colonial discourse (De Leon 2014): the reliable, gentle, child-friendly, female nanny, sufficiently well-educated, high functioning in English and other European languages (Parreñas, 2008; Stenum, 2008; Polanco, 2016; Zontini, 2010).

Arguably, from media accounts, this stereotype, at least in Canada, has been replaced with the youthful, resilient, hardworking, eager-to-please fast food server, *female or male* (Barber, 2018). Following Canada's National Occupational Classification (NOC), fast food service (as counter attendants) is considered un- or low-skilled, and therefore a form of employment for retirees or young people newly entering the workforce.[8] The populating of the national fast food sector by Filipinos might suggest these workers, too, are unskilled. However, a closer examination of the migration pathways of Filipinos entering Canadian fast food employment reveals this to be incorrect. Despite their racialized identities in Canada, Canada's temporary food service workers are typically not who they seem to be. Many, including all of the 45 migrants-in-waiting we interviewed as they were seeking deployment to Canada between 2014 and 2019, had university degrees, many in hotel and restaurant management, and most had experience working as managers or shift supervisors in Manila establishments, which qualified them for a NOC code designated as skilled.[9] Still, they were seeking employment as temporary counter attendants. Here again, Canada's immigration reform, with its expansive visa programming and the prioritizing of skill, is responsible for a further iteration of Philippine migration pathways into Canada whereby migrants continue to deliberately deskill, hoping to upskill. The most common cultural idiom we heard from them as they expressed their desire to "please" their Canadian employer was "God willing."

In 2017, for the third year in a row, the Philippines was Canada's second source country for permanent residents, with 40,857 entrants, sitting above China at 30,279 and below India at 51,651 (Government of Canada, 2018). Some entrants had transitioned from temporary to permanent status, most especially those who entered with the caregiver visa, which has always offered a pathway to permanency once certain conditions of live-in employment were met. This has not necessarily been the case for other TFWs who entered as fast food workers under provincial programs where transition to permanency has sometimes been possible. As explained later, some employers promote counter attendants to become supervisors or managers, an upskilling move that allows for a pathway to permanency. However, many who anticipated such a transition and who entered as temporary fast food workers were unable to achieve their goal of permanent residence (Immigration consultant, interview, Manila, 2018). Meanwhile, between 2015 and 2017, visas for Philippine temporary workers hovered between fourth and fifth rankings across Canada, mainly because of modified visa requirements, including the removal of the live-in component of the caregiver visa and a new lottery system for their permanent visas (Government of Canada, 2019). This represents fewer admissions from five years earlier when the Philippines was the top source country across all visa programs, permanent and temporary (Alboim and Cohl, 2012). Nonetheless, Canada remains popular as a destination for permanent migration, with many seeking advantage from the constantly changing priorities of provincial programs.

Canada's just-in-time immigration restructuring

To backtrack a little before discussing the Tim Hortons case, more detail about Canada's policy reform is necessary.[10] In 2010, the Harper conservative government (2006–2015) introduced an omnibus budget bill with various controversial social and economic policies, including major changes to Canada's long-standing immigration program, which for decades had allowed approximately 250,000 new immigrants and refugees into the country per year. Restructuring shifted the processing of applications from a predictable first-in, first-out queue for economic class applicants to a market-driven model promoted as "modernizing" the system to allow Canada to be more selective and competitive in the global quest for skilled labor while also rapidly feeding the labor market shortages with temporary workers (Barber, 2013). In January 2015, a further reference to the fetishized approach to time saw the introduction of a new web-based Immigration Refugees and Citizenship Canada (IRCC) portal called Express Entry (EE).[11] This adaptation allowed employers to access a "pool" of digitally pre-screened applicants who had filed for permanent residency guided by new parameters that valorized younger applicants within skilled NOC categories and awarded points for those who had received a job offer and/or had Canadian experience. In the initial EE draws, the majority of successful applicants were Filipinos already living and working in Canada and able to achieve appropriate NOC scores based on their qualifications. Key here is the employment offer and having Canadian experience.

The neoliberal pressure on urgency in addressing the insatiable and fickle needs of labor markets reflects what Harvey (1989) described as spatial-temporal fixing. Such fixes continue in the prodding of Canada's multilevel policy mechanisms, including migrant streaming through various visa categories, high-skilled and suitable for permanent entrance, ergo citizenship, and the disposable low-skilled, forced into temporary work contracts. Ostensibly to address the backlog of applications in the immigration queue, a moratorium on the processing of new applications was implemented in 2012 and held in place until May 2013. Many applications that had been in process for up to six years were canceled, with visa costs eventually refunded. The moratorium was devastating for the 280,000 Filipino migrants-in-waiting who had filed applications for Canada under the provisions of the highly regarded points system, which while it favored skill and education, carried no expectation that migrants match particular occupations or settlement patterns. Taken together, EE and PTNPs did both.

In effect, the dislodging of the immigration queue was replaced with just-in-time flexibility, supposedly adaptive to market needs (Barber, 2013). Migrant advocates reported during interviews at that time that despite embassy claims about the ordered approach to processing backlogged files, there were irregularities. Some who had filed applications spoke about files being returned, while friends with similar qualifications who filed on the same date had their applications processed. Staff at one reputable recruitment agency reported that some who would have been approved for entry into Canada had resorted to temporary contracts in less desirable countries. Meanwhile, many who hoped to wait out the moratorium were disappointed by the implementation of a new skilled visa quota system targeting specific jobs, initially mainly in health professions. Economistic concerns over labor markets trumped any other priorities, including demographic concerns in Canadian regional political economies. PTNPs became a means to address such concerns, hence their variability in specifications for nominees for permanent residency.

Harper's immigration policy reforms were calculated to allow employers ready access to a cheaper, potentially more reliable and employer-dependent labor force. Such reforms, in combination with national and provincial labor and employment policy can be read as capital-biased class policies favoring those with capital through the provision of cheaper and more vulnerable temporary labor. Ultimately, the presence of reliable (yet precariously implanted) "foreign workers" created friction between some local workers and targeted temporary workers despite the seeming popularity of Filipino Tim Hortons counter attendants across the Canadian landscape (MacDonald, 2014). Media reports suggest popularity arose in part because Filipinos had acquired a national stereotype as cheerful yet compliant workers, and in the case of rural Canada, they maintained their supposed sunny cultural disposition despite displacement from their tropical home and emplacement in Canada's frigid landscapes. As discussed in the next section on Tim Hortons, research suggests something more sinister might have contributed to Filipinos' strong work ethic. Working hard to please one's employer to secure a pathway to permanency remains one mechanism of exploitation available to TFW employers. Contract workers are able to use an employer's offer of a regular job to gain traction in securing a permanent entry visa either federally through EE or through a particular PTNP (Bryan, 2019; Polanco, 2016).

However, the increased presence of temporary workers stirred public debates about their role in the Canadian economy, culminating in 2014 in a further shorter moratorium on TFW hiring in food services. This was followed by a couple of local workers (one young male and one older woman) in fast food establishments in different provinces who complained to the media that they were dislodged from shifts because employers wanted to take full advantage of their TFWs, given their investment in recruitment and travel costs (mandated employer expenses). Migrant workers are also more profitable to employers than local residents in situations where employers provide TFWs with overpriced rental accommodation deducted from salaries, as was common in some smaller communities on the prairies (Bonifacio, 2013). When the 2014 moratorium was lifted, tighter restrictions were placed on the recruitment of TFWs to areas with higher rates of unemployment. Proposed new measures included increased employer processing fees and caps on migrants hired and hours worked. In effect, the Harper conservatives sought to press locally unemployed and/or Canadian seasonal workers to become more mobile for work in industries that relied upon TFWs. Such efforts to compel local workers into low-wage jobs in competition with TFWs met with resistance and were dropped.

To summarize, more than the shifting interests of Filipino migrants-in-waiting, the changing profile of Canada's temporary labor force reflects successive policy reforms to curtail what many decried as employer abuse of the program (May 2016). However, Tim Hortons remained one of the top Canadian employers receiving Filipinos on temporary work permits, which were subjected to several moratoriums followed by the imposition of the "cumulative duration rule," known as the "4-in, 4-out rule," in effect from 2011 to 2016. This ruling prevented TFW contract renewals, meaning low-skilled workers had to exit Canada after four years and remain out for four more years. Too late for many who arrived during this period, the newly elected Trudeau government overturned the four-year rule in 2016. From 2008, in tandem with federal restrictions and approvals, the expanded PTNPs have served to stream migrants away from core cities (Toronto, Vancouver, Montreal) into regional labor markets (Government of Canada, 2014). Policy shifts in successive rounds of immigration reform under both regimes have created havoc for Filipino migrants-in-waiting seeking permanent status who have invested hard-earned resources in applying for carefully selected visas. Despite policy unpredictability over the last decade, research shows Filipinos continue to familiarize themselves with the new system, including the EE portal and revised provincial programs.

Tim Hortons

Improvisations of mobile capital

We now turn to a new generation of Filipinos and how their lives connect with previous generations whose social reproduction strategies link them to Tim Hortons, a major beneficiary of mobile Filipino labor in Canada and now the Philippines (Bryan, 2017). Tim Hortons is Canada's largest quick-service restaurant chain and, despite some challenges, remains one of the country's most popular coffee shops. Since opening in Ontario in 1964, the chain has expanded to 4,500 locations across the country where it occupies an iconic position within Canada's social and cultural landscape. Sociologist Patricia Cormack proposes that Tim Hortons exploits "the ambiguities and contradictions within the project of Canadian identity" (2008, p. 370). Dependable and accessible in *everyday, ordinary* Canadian life, the brand is featured in political campaigns and amplifies key cultural idioms—ice hockey and donuts—ensuring a reputation as "Canada's coffee shop." The brand's "Canadianness" is, however, illusory. Following its acquisition in 2014 by Restaurant Brands International (RBI), the brand has expanded into Europe, Asia and the Middle East. Unlike Canada, where restaurants are owned by individual franchisees, typically with one to three outlets, Tim Hortons Philippines is owned by one master franchisor. In 2017, when the brand launched in the Philippines, Canadian TV ads also symbolized the multilayered connections of migration journeys and tearful family reunions set, realistically, in a Tim Hortons Philippine café, all images with particular poignancy for those familiar with the brand and Filipinos' migration journeys along the well-worn migration corridor to Canada.

Indicative of the tensions surrounding the global mobilities of capital and labor and class and consumption are the controversies confronted by Tim Hortons in Canada since RBI's acquisition (Luckhardt, 2014; Sturgeon, 2014). Canadian consumers, franchisees and media commentators all expressed concern over cost-cutting measures, inspiring the latter group to organize under the banner of the Great White North Franchisee Association (GWNFA) (Hunter, 2018). Meanwhile, workers organized against employment conditions, and media commentators joined GWNFA to question RBI's vision for an upscaled Canadian Tim Hortons (CBC Radio, 2018; Mintz, 2019). Ironically, Tim Hortons Philippines models the upscaled, newly classed, contemporary urban space that Canadians appear to be resisting in favor of the familiar, sometimes shabby, working-class outlets spread across the land. Indeed, the prioritization of Canadian "ordinariness" works to obscure foreign ownership and, in more recent years, the company's reliance on the availability of precarious, temporary migrant labor.

After Tim Hortons was owned by the Ohio-based Wendy's International between 1995 and 2006 and was returned to Canadian ownership on August 26, 2014, a $12.5 billion merger resulted in RBI, run by Burger King's Brazilian owner 3G Capital. To secure the deal, Burger King agreed that the company's combined headquarters remain in Ontario, and yet, criticism over 3G Capital's acquisition was far-ranging, focused primarily on the corporation's "ruthlessness" in extracting as much value as possible from acquired companies (Gilpin, cited in Luckhardt, 2014). Most of the Canadian franchisees, as small business owners, depend on Tim Hortons for a range of supplies and services, ranging from donuts to real estate. While lamenting the loss of Tim Hortons's Canadianness, GWNFA franchisees dramatically underplayed the layers of exploitation in how Canadian franchisees recruit and set to work precarious international labor to maximize profit. Already embedded in the Tim Hortons commodity served by TFWs is a particular form of surplus value, cultivated through a migration scenario in which labor is rendered vulnerable to the excessive demands of capital, making them more attractive relative to less vulnerable local resident populations, who are far less willing to take these minimum wage jobs.

3G's objective of globalizing Canada's coffee shop was effectively accomplished. By 2019, two years after its arrival in the Philippines, over 100 stores had opened across the archipelago (HQ Manila, interview, May 2019). While Canadian franchisees struggle to afford the renovations demanded of them by 3G, the restaurants in Manila already conform to the company's vision of the new affluent but affordable Tim Hortons—an outcome of timing but also possibly that the "master franchisee," a member of the Philippine elite, aligns him more closely with 3G Capital than with small owner-operators in Canada.

Improvisations of mobile workers

Tim Hortons's upscale Manila cafés are modern with clean lines and pleasant lighting, selling location-specific merchandise alongside the familiar breakfast sandwiches and donuts (made with dough shipped from Canada). Many cafés are located in business districts where new high-rise condominiums and office locations house the flourishing new call center industry and young, upwardly mobile professionals. In other words, Tim Hortons Philippines is differently classed than in Canada. Important for the argument here, the class profile of Tim Hortons Philippines is further elevated by its association with the country's middle-class *Balikbayan* economy[12]—a consequence of the state's long-standing promotion of labor migration and subsequent practices of remittance-sending and transnational social reproduction wherein daily and intergenerational survival, but more accurately (particularly for those who emigrate), upward mobility and class projects may be realized. Significantly, for those in Canada, this intergenerational process begins with women's commodified care labor.

Related to its class profile, Tim Hortons Philippines is overtly branded Canadian. On a busy Manila intersection, in April 2019, a newly opened Tim Hortons beckoned customers with red and white balloons, the colors of the

Canadian flag. "Welcome to Canada" was inscribed in red on the café's door. Inside, walls are decorated with a stylized map of Canada's topography overlaid with red text: "we believe in togetherness; we make neighbours of strangers; we create common ground; we seek to share the best of Canada with your community." This 2019 version of welcoming Filipinos into a symbolically Canadian space reiterates earlier versions of this theme encountered in several previous field trips where the virtues of Canadian employment were being promoted. For example, in 2013 in Iloilo city, a large poster slung outside a recruitment office read, "Canada welcomes you." Two years later, in a Manila office, in small meeting rooms used for client briefings, mannequins wearing the Tim Hortons counter attendant uniforms faced walls displaying Canadian maps, currency and provincial iconography. To attend an information session about Canada's immigration options in such spaces is to be exposed to a positive version of Canadian employment in the food services industry.

In one such office in 2014, Barber interviewed six women and six men, all in their early 30s. The migrants-in-waiting had elected to pay for French lessons while waiting for their Quebec employer to send airfares. The franchisee had selected them as TFW's through a Skype interview coordinated by the recruiter. Since the Quebec customers were seasonal forestry workers, the employer was waiting for the arrival of spring weather to increase her customer base. Although the visas stated the recruits were to be unskilled counter attendants, all were then currently employed as food service managers and held HRM university credentials. That Canadian policy allowed for upskilling through promotion to shift supervisors or managers and, thereby, possible candidacy for permanent resident status had been communicated to the recruits. Over lunch, they eagerly asked about Canada and expressed hope that their employer would like them sufficiently to issue the desired promotion. Here, we see a scenario where migrants are set in competition with their compatriot cohort, laying the groundwork for a compliant, exploitable employer–employee relationship. As things turned out, migrant arrivals were staggered, with some having to undergo the costly renewal of various documents because their visas expired prior to deployment. In this instance, migrant precarity was not gender-specific, and unlike previous generations of women caregivers, none of the participants in the French class had children, although most were leaving partners behind who would only be able to join them several years hence, should they achieve promotion and permanent job offers. All spoke of projected Canadian futures, revealing how Tim Hortons's accumulation strategies profit from the Canadian dreams of Filipino workers *and* from middle-class consumers.

Conclusion in the time of COVID-19

Probing beyond statistics, this chapter's analysis of the improvisations of capital and labor along the Philippines–Canada migration corridor explores the experiences over time of many well-qualified migrants arriving in Canada as temporary workers with different skill sets traveling under different visa programs. Many Filipinos drawn to Canadian futures have sought transfer to permanency through targeted federal and/or provincial immigration programs (Lu and Hou, 2017). Recently accelerated policy changes have prevented or delayed this transition for many, but to what effect? One tentative hypothesis suggests that migrant returnees and underemployed migrants-in-waiting in the Philippines are pressed into precarity, unable to realize the benefits of their tertiary education. Further, in a study of intergenerational social mobility, Kelly (2014) found that children of immigrants from the Philippines represent a "double anomaly" in the Canadian landscape in that they are less likely to hold a degree than either their parents or their peers in other racialized immigrant groups. Despite the educational credentials of their parents, the youth in Kelly's study experienced familial financial hardship as their parents worked long hours in multiple jobs. This represents a violation of the Canadian dream so cleverly manipulated in the case of globalizing Tim Hortons with its mobile capital and state-facilitated exploitative labor mobilization strategies.

Here, we come to a major contradiction along the Philippines–Canada migration corridor. Recall that there is increasing evidence of educational attainment, funded through remittances, in the social reproduction of migration in the Philippines. Once in Canada, the rewards from that valorization of education may remain unrealized, if not overturned, because of the exploitative nature of the migratory framework. Changes to the live-in caregiver program have yet to mitigate the harsh realities and dispossessed futures being confronted by Filipino families in Canada who contend with a history of long-term familial disruption.[13] Beyond the caregivers, other well-qualified TFW visa holders, including those with HRM experience, continue to enter unskilled visa streams in search of their own dream of Canadian family life, representing a further cohort of Filipinos subjected to Canadian policy vagaries and family disruptions. But there is activism in this regard.

Currently, in Canada, there is a large political movement headed by the Migrant Rights Network, a broad coalition of migrant groups, including those who have long worked with care workers, advocating an end to all temporary work visas. The dire circumstances of temporary visa holders in Canada have yet again been exposed during the COVID-19 global pandemic, leading to increased pressure on IRCC to transfer all temporary workers to permanent residency. In October 2020, Migrant Rights released a report based on a survey detailing alleged abuses suffered by hundreds of Canada's women domestic workers during the pandemic (CBC News, 2020a). Abuses include job loss and ongoing problems in accessing Canada's COVID-19 Emergency Response Benefit (CERB) available to workers laid off during the pandemic. Additionally, in an all too familiar call, rehearsed in numerous global studies over the years, workers spoke of new restrictions on their mobility, being confined to employers' homes and not being paid for additional hours worked. Migrant Rights concluded that conditions for migrant domestic workers had worsened during the pandemic, exposing the racism and sexism underpinning their contracts. In response, Canada's Chief Public Health Officer, Dr. Theresa Tam, agreed, noting that migrant workers have been disproportionately affected by the COVID-19 pandemic. She concluded: "The virus didn't create new inequities in our society; it exposed them and underscored the impacts of the social policies on our health status." In response, the Offices of Immigration and Employment pledged to "reimagine" the TFW program, specifically to "how to better protect workers—and that includes considering new pathways to permanent residence" (CBC News, 2020a). In April 2021, we await those *reimaginings* as COVID cases intensify across the country, and frontline healthcare workers, for example, caring for seniors in public and private long-term care, disproportionately staffed by Filipinas (nurses and personal care workers) are yet again placed at risk (CBC News, 2020b). Filipino workers (and other migrants) living in Canada are eagerly awaiting details of policy reform, which never seems to work to their advantage.[14]

Meanwhile, in the Philippines, Tim Hortons December 2020 ads read "Good tidings and treats. We are here for you!" which suggests that despite the pandemic ravaging poor Philippine communities, the coffee chain aspires to "business as usual," in keeping with its middle-class profile. But COVID-19 is not "business as usual" for Filipino global migrant workers, nor, in the case of Tim Hortons, their customers. Both groups are reliant upon migrant labor's remittances, and the logic of capital marking them as designated essential workers serving others.[15]

The pandemic was brutal to Filipino global migrants, the households who depend on them and the national economy. As of April 2020, some 300,000 overseas workers experienced immediate impacts, including displacement from sectors such as leisure, hospitality (hotels and restaurants) and retail. Many others received shorter hours and lower wages. Tens of thousands of seafarers were stranded overseas, including in Canadian ports, while working on extended contracts, unable to be repatriated because of travel restrictions and/or the tardiness of employers. Meanwhile, demand for nurses to be deployed increased, but overall overseas deployments have dropped significantly. For those many thousands who were repatriated, there are reintegration and employment challenges (Asis, 2020). And, of course, there is the unreliable, if not unknowable, statistic of deaths directly attributable to COVID.[16] Again, Philippine reliance on labor export exposes the potentially disastrous consequences for migrants and those that depend upon them while it underscores the instabilities of the facilitating neoliberal national political economies.[17]

A further lesson to be drawn from this chapter's analysis of the accumulation strategies dependent upon mobile capital and labor, the intersections and disruptions, along the Philippines–Canada migration corridor is that of the gendered social reproduction of migration. As feminized migration took hold, women's remittances, for our purposes here, from Canadian deployment, initially in care professions and more recently in feminized HRM and associated service work, aided in educating several further generations of migrants, many of whom struggled to obtain employment commensurate with their qualifications and, therefore, the promise of the better (middle-class) life to which they aspire. This occurs despite the consumption pressures applied to them as described in this case study of one global corporation, Tim Hortons, which mobilizes brand Canada as a destination and identity while profiting from the mobilities (and deskilling) of precariously employed Filipino labor in both countries.

Notes

1 A similar discussion of Philippines–Canada migration and the transnational circuits of capital and labor exemplified in the Tim Hortons example is contained in Barber (2022).
2 A Canadian recruitment agency reported that between 2010 and 2020, a total of 4,286 food counter workers, both attendants and supervisors, arrived as TFWs to work at Tim Hortons (Virtual interview, April 2021).
3 A 2020 webinar on the economic impact of COVID-19 for overseas Filipinos reported massive increases in deployed workers: 36,035 in 1975; 1.8 million in 2013–2015 to 2,112,331 in 2016; and 1,992,746 in 2017 (Asis, 2020).
4 Deskilling aside, migrants are not defined by labor market slots. Migrant agency includes entrepreneurship (Milgram, 2019).
5 Japan, Australia, Italy, the UK, New Zealand, Germany, South Korea and Spain complete the list of the top ten Filipino diaspora populations, all of which are relatively modest in size; 151,158 in Japan to 15,721 in Spain (Commission on Filipinos Overseas, 2018).
6 Prior to 2016, the Philippines was the last country in Asia with a ten-year basic education system (Grageda, 2016). Because of this, qualified registered nurses were required to complete expensive additional training in certain countries, including the US, UK and Canada. Commencing in 2012, curriculum reform, labeled K–12 (Kindergarten to Grade 12), mandated two more years of education, a strategy complementary to neoliberal policies promoting remittances as national development (Acacio, 2008; Rodriguez, 2010).
7 As Kelly (2012) explains, in migration scholarship, the spatiality of class needs to be understood, not just in terms of social position and processes, but also in terms of performance and politics, that is, for its cultural dimensions and how these are constituted through migration.
8 In this regard, food counter attendant positions may be seen to represent feminized work involving male migrants in service work's emotional labor (Hochschild, 1983) relative to better paid, more traditionally male-defined jobs such as trades, seafaring and engineering. Under Canada's NOC codes, these broad categories, which call for more training, are higher-ranked skill designations separated from more physical work and labor, typically unskilled.
9 The Canadian recruiter estimated the gender breakdown of deployed Tim Hortons's TFWs as 80 percent female because "most employers prefer females" with male workers preferred for night shifts. Further, unmarried workers offer employers greater flexibility for shift work (Virtual interview, April 2021).
10 The Social Sciences and Humanities Research Council of Canada (SSHRC) funded Barber's project "Just-in-time immigration: Philippine translations of Canada's Immigration Program" (2015–2019). Catherine Bryan, as a doctoral and post-doctoral researcher, collaborated in field research and various writing projects. Together we were awarded a new SSHRC project "Fast Food, slow migration: Canada's temporary workers at home in the Philippines" (2020–2025).
11 Citizenship and Immigration Canada (CIC) was rebranded IRCC in 2015, after the Trudeau government took office, signaling a more humanitarian approach to refugee policy.
12 So-called in reference to the cultural practice of migrants returning to the Philippines with large boxes packed with gifts and goods for distribution to kin and community.

13 In February 2019, IRCC announced further changes to the caregiver program would be piloted to replace expiring and "ineffective" pilots implemented in 2017. The two new five-year pilots allow caregivers to come together with family while still allowing a pathway to permanency based on an assessment completed prior to arrival (Government of Canada, 2019).

14 On April 14, 2021, IRCC announced new measures to allow 20,000 TFWs in health care (doctors, nurses, home support workers, housekeepers and "other assisting occupations"), 30,000 in other essential occupations and 40,000 graduated international students to apply to become permanent residents provided they passed a language test and currently have valid visas. Family reunification will follow from successful applications (Government of Canada, 2021a).

15 In an interesting reversal of "fate," in mid-April 2021, as a result of a shutdown of flights from the Philippines, some Filipina domestic workers in Hong Kong stood to experience a more competitive labor market with projected salary increases for locally (Hong Kong) based workers. The flight ban was in response to 16 N501Y mutated cases found in Philippine migrant worker arrivals over a seven-day period (Cheung, 2021).

16 The Department of Foreign Affairs (DFA) reported that COVID was the top cause of death among overseas Filipino workers from 2012 to 2023 (Abad, 2023), but not all COVID-related deaths were identified as such.

17 By way of example, on April 15, 2021, IRCC issued a news release stating plans to "prioritize" 6,000 caregiver applications by the end of the year; 1,500 by June 30 (Government of Canada, 2021b). Caregivers are described as "front-line heroes" waiting to be reunited with their families, which becomes possible once permanent residency is approved. However, COVID has taken a major toll on Canadian women's labor force participation, so the new measures are also politically expedient. Moreover, IRCC notes that as of March 3, 2021, there were 12,000 applications stalled in the processing inventory. Again, IRCC appeared to be responding to pressure to meet immigration quotas for 2021 while ensuring an essential labor supply.

References

Abad, M. (2023) "Death among Filipinos abroad in last 10 years – DFA." Available at https://www.rappler.com/nation/overseas-filipinos/dfa-report-house-hearing-top-cause-death-filipinos-abroad-2013-2023/.

Acacio, K. (2008) "Managing labor migration: Philippine state policy and international migration flows, 1969–2000." *Asia Pacific Migration Journal* 17(2), pp. 103–132.

Agcaoili, L. (2020) "Remittances hit record highs in 2019." *Philippine Star*. Available at https://www.philstar.com/business/2020/02/18/1993922/remittances-hit-record-highs-2019.

Aguilar, F. (2014) *Migration Revolution: Philippine Nationhood and Class Relations in a Globalized Village*. Quezon City: Ateneo de Manila University Press.

Alboim, N. and Cohl, K. (2012) "Shaping the future: Canada's rapidly changing immigration policies." Maytree. Available at https://maytree.com/wp-content/uploads/shaing-the-future.pdf.

Asis, M. (2015) "'All in the family': Remittances, gender and public policies in the Philippines," in T. Van Naerssen, L. Smith, T. Davids and M. Marchand (eds) *Women, Gender, Remittances and Development in the Global South*. Aldershot: Ashgate.

Asis, M. (2020) Rethinking the future of labor migration. After repatriation: Hanap-buhay, hanap pag-asa. *Migration Outlook Webinar Series*, Manila: Scalabrini Migration Centre, July 17. Available at smc@smc.org.ph.

Baggio, F. (ed.) (2010) *Brick by Brick: Building Cooperation between Migrants' Associations in Italy and Spain.* Manila: Scalabrini Migration Center.

Barber, P.G. (1996) "Modes of resistance: gendered responses to global impositions in coastal Philippines," *Asia Pacific Viewpoint* 37(2), pp. 181–194.

Barber, P.G. (2004) "Contradictions of class and consumption when the commodity is labor," *Anthropologica* 46(2), pp. 213–218.

Barber, P.G. (2008) "The ideal immigrant? Gendered class subjects in Philippine-Canada migration," *Third World Quarterly* 29(7), pp. 1265–1285.

Barber, P.G. (2011) "Women's work unbound: Philippine development and global restructuring," in Marchand, M.H and Runyan, A.S. (eds.), *Gender and Global Restructuring: Sightings, Sites and Resistances*, 2nd ed. London and New York: Routledge.

Barber, P.G. (2013) "'Grateful' subjects: Class and capital at the border in Philippine-Canada migration," *Dialectical Anthropology* 37(3–4), pp. 383–400.

Barber, P.G. (2018) "The entanglements of neoliberal temporalities and class politics in Philippine migration to Canada," in Barber, P.G. and Lem, W. (eds.), *Migration, Temporality, and Capitalism: Entangled Mobilities across Global Spaces.* New York and London: Palgrave Macmillan.

Barber, P.G. (2022) "Going global, Philippine migrant encounters with mobile capital," in Kasmir, S. and Gill, L. (eds.), *The Routledge Handbook of the Anthropology of Labor.* London and New York: Routledge.

Barber, P.G. and Bryan, C. (2017) "International organization for migration in the field: 'Walking the talk' of global migration management in Manila," *Journal of Ethnic and Migration Studies.* doi:10.1080/1369183X.2017.1354068.

Battistella, G. and Liao, K. A. (2013) *Youth Migration from the Philippines: Brain Drain and Brain Waste.* UNICEF Philippines and Scalabrini Migration Center. Available at http://mdgfund.org/sites/default/files/Youth-Migration-Philippines-Brain-Drain-Brain-Waste.pdf.

Bauman, Z. (1998) *Globalization: The Human Consequences.* New York: Columbia University Press.

Bello, W. (2004) *The Anti-Development State: The Political Economy of Permanent Crisis in the Philippines.* Quezon City: University of the Philippines Diliman.

Bonifacio, G. (2013) *Pinay on the Prairies: Filipino Women and Transnational Identities.* Vancouver/Toronto: UBC Press.

Bryan, C. (2017) "Understanding service work as reproductive labour: A feminist political economy of Filipino migrant hotel workers in rural Manitoba," in Bonifacio, G. (ed.), *Gender, Feminism and Global Cross-cultural Connections: International and Interdisciplinary Perspectives.* Castle Hill, AUS: Emerald Press.

Bryan, C. (2019) "Labor, population, and precarity: Temporary foreign workers transition to permanent residency in rural Manitoba," *Studies in Political Economy* 100(3), pp. 252–269.

Carter, T. (2009) *An Evaluation of the Manitoba Provincial Nominee Program.* Winnipeg: Manitoba Labor and Immigration, Immigration Division.

CBC News. (2020a) "Exploitation of migrant care workers has increased since COVID-19 struck, report says." Available at https://www.cbc.ca/news/canada/report-migrant-care-workers-exploitation-pandemic-1.5779915.

CBC News. (2020b) "How Filipino-Canadian care aides are disproportionately affected by the COVID-19 pandemic." Available at https://www.cbc.ca/news/canada/british-columbia/covid-19-filipino-care-aides-affected-1.5589603.

CBC Radio. (2018) "Should unions organize low-wage and temporary workers?" Available at https://www.cbc.ca/radio/checkup/should-unions-organize-low-wage-and-temporary-workers-1.4484733.

Cheung, E. (2021) "Hong Kong coronavirus: 5 new cases confirmed; flight ban could send pay skyward for locally hired domestic workers, agency bosses say." Available at https://www.scmp.com/news/hong-kong/health-environment/article/3129444/hong-kong-coronavirus-flight-ban-could-send-pay.

Chin, C. (1998) *In Service and Servitude: Foreign Female Domestic Workers and the Malaysian "Modernity" Project*. New York: Columbia University Press.

Commission on Filipinos Overseas. (2018) *Stock Estimate of Filipinos Overseas: Number of Registered Filipino Emigrants by Major Country of Destination*. Available at https://cfo.gov.ph/statistics-2/.

Constable, N. (1997) *Maid to Order in Hong Kong: Stories of Filipina Workers*. Ithaca: Cornell University Press.

Constable, N. (2014) *Born out of Place: Migrant Mothers and the Politics of International Labor*. Berkeley: University of California Press.

Cormack, P. (2008) "True stories' of Canada: Tim Hortons and the branding of national identity," *Cultural Sociology* 2, (3), pp. 369–384.

CTV News. (2014) "Double-doubles and Timbits: Tim Hortons a big part of Canadian identity." Available at https://www.ctvnews.ca/business/double-doubles-and-timbits-tim-hortons-a-big-part-of-canadian-identity-1.1980361.

De Leon, C. (2014) "Family separation and reunification among former Filipina migrant domestic workers and their adult daughters in two Canadian cities," in Romera, M., Preston, V. and Giles, W. (eds.), *When Carework Goes Global: Locating the Social Relations of Domestic Work*. Aldershot: Ashgate Publishing.

Fajardo, K. (2011) *Filipino Crosscurrents: Oceanographies of Seafaring Masculinities and Globalization*. Minneapolis: University of Minnesota Press.

Francisco, V. and Rodriguez, R. (2014) "Countertopographies of migrant women: Transnational families, space, and labor as solidarity," *WorkingUSA: The Journal of Labor and Society* 17, pp. 357–372.

Geiger, M. and Pécoud, A. (2010) *The Politics of International Migration Management*. New York & London: Palgrave MacMillan.

Global News. (2015) "Tim Hortons confirms it cut 350 people in layoffs this week." Available at https://globalnews.ca/news/1801314/tim-hortons-cut-350-people-in-layoffs-this-week/.

Goldring, L. and Landolt, P. (2011) "Caught in the work-citizenship matrix: The lasting effects of precarious legal status on work for Toronto immigrants," *Globalizations* 8(3), pp. 325–341.

Gonzalez, J. (1998) *Philippine Labor Migration: Critical Dimensions of Public Policy*. Manila: De La Salle Press (ISEAS).

Government of Canada. (2014) *Overhauling the Temporary Foreign Worker Programme. Putting Canadians First*, WP-191–106–14E. Ottawa: Government of Canada.

Government of Canada. (2018) "Permanent resident data as of March 31, 2018. Table 1: permanent residents admitted in 2017 by top 10 source countries." Available at https://www.canada.ca/en/immigration-refugees-citizenship/corporate/publications-manuals/annual-report-parliament-immigration-2018/report.html.

Government of Canada. (2019) "Caregivers will now have access to new pathways to permanent residence." Available at https://www.canada.ca/en/immigration-refugees-citizenship/news/2019/02/caregivers-will-now-have-access-to-new-pathways-to-permanent-residence.

Government of Canada. (2021a) "New pathway to permanent residency for over 90,000 essential temporary workers and international graduates." Available at https://www.canada.ca/en/immigration-refugees-citizenship/news/2021/04/new-pathway-to-permanent-residency-for-over-90000-essential-temporary-workers-and-international-graduates.html.

Government of Canada. (2021b) "Minister Mendicino launches plan to accelerate caregiver application processing." Available at https://www.canada.ca/en/immigration-refugees-citizenship/news/2021/04/minister-mendicino-launches-plan-to-accelerate-caregiver-application-processing.html.

Grageda, H. (2016) "Despite opposition, K-12 education reform moves forward in the Philippines." Available at https://asiafoundation.org/2016/08/24/despite-opposition-k-12-education-reform-moves-forward-philippines/.

Gresham, P., Smit, M. and Smith L. (2015) " Gender dimensions of the 'national script' on migration and remittances in the Philippines," in Van Naerssen, T., Smith, L., Davids, T., and Marchand, M. (eds.), *Women, Gender, Remittances, and Development in the Global South*. Aldershot: Ashgate.

Guevarra, A. (2010) *Marketing Dream, Manufacturing Heroes: The Transnational Labor Brokering of Filipino Workers*. New Brunswick: Rutgers University Press.

Harvey, D. (1989) *The Condition of Postmodernity: An Enquiry into the Origins of Cultural Change*. Oxford: Blackwell.

Hochschild, A. (1983) *The Managed Heart: Commercialization of Human Feeling*. Berkeley: University of California Press.

Hunter, B. (2018) "Coffee calamity: Tim Hortons parent, franchise owners in civil war." Available at https://torontosun.com/news/national/coffee-calamity-tim-hortons-parent-franchise-owners-in-civil-war.

Kelly, P. (2012) "Migration, transnationalism, and the spaces of class identity," *Philippine Studies: Historical and Ethnographic Viewpoints* 60(2), pp. 153–186. Quezon City: Ateneo de Manila University.

Kelly, P. (2014) *Understanding Intergenerational Social Mobility: Filipino Youth in Canada*, IRPP Study 45. Montreal: Institute for Research on Public Policy.

Lewis, M. (2019) "Tim Hortons takes on the world." Available at https://www.thestar.com/business/2019/05/15/tim-hortons-takes-on-the-world.html?rf.

Lu, Y. and Hou F. (2017) *Transition from Temporary Foreign Workers to Permanent Residents, 1990 to 2014*, Analytical Studies Branch Research Paper Series 11F0019M – 389. Ottawa: Statistics Canada.

Luckhardt, N. (2014) *Trouble Is Brewing: Why the Tim Hortons Takeover Is a Bad Deal for Canadians*. Canadian Centre for Policy Alternatives. Available at https://www.policyalternatives.ca/publications/reports/trouble-brewing.

MacDonald, M. (2014) "True blue," *The Walrus* 11(4), p. 41, https://thewalrus.ca/true-blue/.

Massey, D. (1994) *Space, Place, and Gender*. Cambridge: Polity Press.

May, B. (2016) *Temporary Foreign Worker Program: Report of the Standing Committee on Human Resources, Skills and Social Development and the Status of Persons with Disabilities*, 42nd Parliament, 1st Session, September. Ottawa: House of Commons.

McKay, D. (2012) *Global Filipinos: Migrants' Lives in the Virtual Village*. Bloomington and Indianapolis: Indiana University Press.

Milgram, L. (2019) "Gift-commodity entanglements: (in)formalizing regulation in a transnational Philippine market trade," *Anthropologica*, 61(1), pp. 51–63.

Mintz, C. (2019) "How Tim Hortons lost its way." Available at https://www.macleans.ca/opinion/how-tim-hortons-lost-its-way/.

Nakache, D. and Kinoshita, P. (2010) *The Canadian Temporary Foreign Worker Program: Do Short-Term Economic Needs Prevail over Human Rights Concerns?* IRPP Study, 5. Montreal Institute for Research on Public Policy.

Nourpanah, S. (2019) "Drive-by education: The role of vocational courses in the migration projects of foreign nurses in Canada," *Journal of International Migration and Integration*, 20(4), pp. 995–1011.

Ortiga, Y. (2018) "Education as early stage brokerage: Cooling out aspiring migrants for the global hotel industry," *Pacific Affairs* 91 (4), p. 717–738.

Parreñas, R. (2001) *Servants of Globalization: Women, Migration and Domestic Work*. Palo Alto: Stanford University Press.

Parreñas, R. (2008) *The Forces of Domesticity: Filipina Migrants and Globalization*. New York: New York University Press.

Paul, A. (2017) *Multinational Maids: Stepwise Migration in a Global Labor Market*. Cambridge, UK: Cambridge University Press.

Philippine Statistics Authority. (2020) "Total number of OFWs estimated at 2.2 million," Reference No. 2020–2099. Available at https://psa.gov.ph/content/total-number-ofws-estimated-22-million.

Pido, E. (2017) *Migrant Returns: Manila, Development, and Transnational Connectivity*. Durham and London: Duke University Press.

Polanco, G. (2016) "Consent behind the counter: Aspiring citizens and labor control under precarious (im)migration schemes," *Third World Quarterly* 37(8), pp. 1–19.

Pratt, G. (1999) "From registered nurse to registered nanny: Discursive geographies of Filipina domestic workers in Vancouver B.C.," *Economic Geography* 75(3), pp. 215–236.

Pratt, G. (2004) *Working Feminism*. Philadelphia: Temple University Press.

Rodriguez, R. (2010) *Migrants for Export: How the Philippine State Brokers Labor to the World*. Minneapolis: University of Minnesota Press.

Satzewich, V. (2016) *Points of Entry: How Canada's Immigration Officials Decide Who Gets In*. Vancouver: UBC Press.

Semyonov, M. and Gorodzeisky, A. (2008) "Labor migration, remittances and economic well-being of households in the Philippines," *Population Research and Policy Review* 27, pp. 619–637.

Stasiulis, D. and Bakan, A. (2005) *Negotiating Citizenship: Migrant Women in Canada and the Global System*. Toronto: University of Toronto Press.

Stenum, H. (2008) *Au Pair in Denmark: Cheap Labor or Cultural Exchange – A Study of the Au Pair Programme in Denmark with Special Focus on Filipino Migrants*. Copenhagen: FOA – Trade and Labor.

Strauss, M. (2017) "Tim Hortons franchisee feud heats up," *Globe and Mail*, September 22, Section B1.

Sturgeon, J. (2014) "Goodbye Tim Hortons, hello…Restaurant Brands International." Available at https://globalnews.ca/news/1718748/goodbye-tim-hortons-hello-restaurant-brands-international/.

Tungohan, E. (2017) "Temporary foreign workers in Canada: Reconstructing 'belonging' and remaking 'citizenship'," *Social and Legal Studies*, https://doi.org/10.1177%2F0964663917746483.

Valiani, S. (2012) *Rethinking Unequal Exchange: The Global Integration of Nursing Labor Markets*. Toronto: University of Toronto Press.

Wolf, E. (1982) *Europe and the People without History*. Berkeley: University of California Press.

World Bank (2020) *Population Totals*. Available at https://data.worldbank.org/indicator/SP.POP.TOTL.

Zontini, E. (2010) "Gender and resisting fortress Europe in Italy and Spain," in Lem, W. and Barber, P.G. (eds.), *Class, Contention and a World in Motion*. New York: Berghahn Books.

4 "I still haven't found what I'm looking for"

Getting development out of the (RED)^{TM}?

Michelle V. Rowley

Introduction

Shirley Temple Black, Audrey Hepburn, Angelina Jolie, Don Cheadle, Oprah or collective constellations such as Bob Geldorf and Midge Ure's 1985 *Live Aid Concert* and later, their 2005 *Live 8*; these all sit within an ever-expanding pantheon of celebrity-driven humanitarianism (Cooper, 2008, p. 3). Aided and abetted by an imprimatur of "development," these models of celebrity-driven humanitarianism have, at different points, burst through the seams of our leisure media consumption, bringing us into a visual relationship with a diverse slate of issues that include global poverty, HIV/AIDS, world hunger, war and genocide. Each of these examples has, in some way, leveraged cultural capital to garner attention to human misery, particularly in the Global South, offering Western charitable giving as a form of amelioration. The spatial politics and rhetoric that shape this relationship between the Global South and Western charitable giving are dynamic. On the one hand, the examples that I offer above enacted a performance of care to a Global South that was rendered as geographically specific ("Africa"), immediately recognizable to the Western eye (through the visually emblematic "emaciated child"), but, and most important, far away from Western realities ("us"). On the other hand, more contemporary celebrity humanitarianism manifestations are strikingly different from these antecedents, albeit with similar endpoints. These giving relationships, which I take up in this chapter as examples of philanthrocapitalism, are defined by a performance of a/proximal care, taking a/proximal care as a veneer of global affinities that are governed by a specter of empathy that we as individual consumer-donors enact through our practices of brand consumption (e.g., RED). At the very core, philanthrocapitalism holds the presumption that "capitalism itself can be naturally philanthropic ... which tends to benefit everyone, sooner or later, through new products, higher quality, and lower prices" (McGoey, 2015, p. 7; Bishop and Green, 2008, p. 194). In this model, it is culture, consumption and commerce, not celebrity ambassadors, that cross borders. It is culture, consumption and commerce that persuade the consumer-donor that she can not only make *direct* humanitarian aid interventions but simultaneously be an agent of a form of participatory economic development.[1] Yet, despite their performed differences, our contemporary instantiation of consumption-based

DOI: 10.4324/9781003036425-5

humanitarianism, like its antecedents, continues to be anchored in the reliance on "there" and "them," where the laboring body feels near but not too near.

This revised chapter examines the narratives and attendant inequities that shape consumer-donor models of celebrity-driven humanitarianism.[2] I interrogate how race, gender and geopolitics are deployed as categories of seduction in the (RED) TM campaign, aimed explicitly at wooing us to believe in capitalism's power to produce global solidarity and solve rather than exacerbate inequity. I analyze the global political economy and the emerging symbolic economy that have become integral to the glamorization of philanthropy within development campaigns such as the (RED) campaign. In the analysis that follows, I interrogate how race, masculinity, femininity and geopolitics manifest and are variably deployed as categories of seduction in the (RED) campaign. Aid discourses, I suggest (and challenge), rely heavily on these analytical categories to produce a sense of consumer-donor citizenship, a global citizenship that is committed first and foremost to the belief that markets can produce global solidarity and solve human suffering. Finally, I challenge the repetitive emergence of "Africa" as a trope within the practice of "philanthropy as development" through a reading of Abderrahmane Sissako's film *Bamako* (2006). I draw on Sissako for the ways in which his work does not allow us to rest easy with quick dismissals of "complicity or complacency" in relation to the imperial impulses of globalization and discourses of "aid." I juxtapose my analysis of celebrity-driven "philanthropy as development" campaigns against this artist's work to foreground the paternalism inherent in these projects as directed to the African continent and as it extends to their target consumer-donor base: the US (and most typically female) consumer, and where they intersect, college students.

In similarly problematic ways, such students (often with "well-meaning," "progressive" agendas) are coming to identify consumption as the appropriate response to global poverty and disease: buy (RED), support ONE, since (RED) and ONE afford at least a psychic (as opposed to experiential or firsthand visual) awareness of global inequity. This increasing psychic awareness that the campaigns have brought to the campuses of some 1,300 universities and colleges has produced a profound sense of accomplishment among the organizers of the two campaigns. Take, for example, Bono's admiration of, if not reliance on, his college-based constituency is evident:

> Those college kids are redefining their country through the prism of the fight against poverty. Issues like that afford a chance to America to re-describe itself to the world. But they also afford America a chance to re-describe itself to its citizens. That's what's going on.
>
> (DeCurtis, 2007, p. 62)

This perceived sense of student politicization arguably popularizes and democratizes the field of development through an amorphous network of scattered, individual, global consumers whose giving and charitable subjectivity is (re) produced through hypervisible and racialized laboring bodies in pain.[3]

Profit philanthropy sites: The new haute couture of development

In the world of celebrity-driven humanitarianism, 2006 was monumental. Philanthropist Bobby Shriver and rock star Bono (aka Paul David Hewson) launched the (RED)^{TM} campaign, which ushered in a form of celebrity-driven humanitarianism that was, in comparison to all precedent, fundamentally different. Shriver and Bono's approach to aid sidestepped an already receding and unstable state-to-state/state-to-international donor model of aid and development. They supplanted these traditional models with an intricate, multitiered, transnational network of corporate actors, individual consumer-donors and putatively harmed bodies, all connected by two things: paraphernalia (product/profit nexus) and messaging (product/person). In other words, the product, branded right, would produce profit and new subjective and material possibilities for the consumer-donor and the global "Other" alike.[4] Shriver and Bono's careful scaffolding of material and messaging infrastructure is what marks the (RED) campaign as emblematic of philanthrocapitalism—the marketing hype that accompanied its launch, its range of corporate "allies," its broad-based deployment of known celebrities alongside its iconographic branding of Bono himself, its international reach, its ability to capture the minds of individual consumer-donors and now, over 15 years later, its longevity. Shriver and Bono had successfully ushered in a streamlined and sleek infrastructure of corporatized celebrity humanitarianism, packaged, marketed and tied in a red bow; their intended consumer-donor at the ready to unwrap it.

In the collision of culture, affect, aid and consumption, Bono's mega-personality stands above the rest, prompting William F. Cooper (2008) to coin the term "Bonoization" as a means of underscoring the extent to which Bono has emerged as the "archetypal" instantiation of celebrity influence. Cooper places emphasis on the profound levels of influence and credibility that Bono exudes as a result of his iconic, rock-star status and signature fashion sense; his communication skills and manipulation of political structures and actors; his moral credibility through an invocation of Catholicism and other world religions; and the ambiguity of his Irish identity, which posits both a "First World" *and* colonized sensibility (Cooper, 2008, pp. 36–48; Mugubane, 2008; Browne, 2013, p. 50).

Bono's unquestionable political reach runs the gamut from high political and economic officeholders to the gurus of popular culture. Through these relationships, he blends and mixes these spheres in ways that make popular culture of unparalleled importance to global political events through popularizing policy-related matters. In a *Rolling Stone* interview conducted with music critic Anthony DeCurtis during the final year of the George W. Bush administration, Bono punctuates his skepticism about the capacity of a US-driven model of democracy to bring about peace in the Middle East with repeated references to his access to powerful global leaders (then-US President Bush, then-World Bank President Paul Wolfowitz and past and present Republican strategist Karl Rove) and the terms of familiarity by which he addresses them (e.g., the use of

"Condi" to refer to then-US Secretary of State Condoleezza Rice) (DeCurtis, 2007, p. 61). An overview of a Bono photo gallery often leaves the observer wondering, who needs whom more?[5] Is it Bono's need for access to formal political leverage or the need of formal political actors for access to Bono's "brand" of personal/popular politics?

Bono's expressions of political sentiment in a cultural vanguard such as *Rolling Stone* highlight his iconic merging of cultural, political and economic spheres, but his credibility is not merely one of political access. His fluency in development rhetoric, his association with economist Jeffery Sachs and, by extension, Sachs's declared commitment to aid have accorded significant credibility to his advocacy for and invocation of global aid politics. For his humanitarian work alongside Bill and Melinda Gates, Bono graced the covers of *Time* magazine in 2002 and 2005, and, in 2006, he again entered the ranks of *Time*'s "100 Most Influential People."[6] The multisite launch of Bono's antiretroviral drugs for African HIV/AIDS sufferers (RED) Campaign included venues such as the World Economic Forum (2006) for its initial announcement; a March 2006 UK launch; and a US shopping frenzy launched along Chicago's Magnificent Mile with talk show magnate Oprah (October 2006)—the latter ending with a meeting between Bono and then-President Bush. These highly orchestrated deployments of Bono's celebrity persona through political access and cachet are disguised by his casual style. Bono's blending of the political with the popular reconfigures the issues that have come to matter in the teaching of development studies and the popularization of the domain, as it were. Interestingly, these reconfigurations can be so muddled that what we sacrifice is transparency (Escobar, 1995, p. 205).

Despite his assertion otherwise, Cooper's analysis of Bono's work rests disproportionately at the level of the individual, a cult of personality, as it were. I want to consider a more systemic and global analysis of Cooper's discussion of Bonoization—through an interrogation of Bonoization as an embodied and metaphoric, mobile manifestation of philanthrocapitalism. In addition to these unparalleled personality-based resources, Bonoization notates Bono as both actor *and* institution. The Bonoization of philanthrocapitalism is possible precisely because they both embrace the same logic and deploy very similar practices and grammar associated with globalization; it relies on but now exceeds his personhood. Much of Bono's activity as an actor and institution coalesces around his ONE and (RED) campaigns. In the initial publication in the second edition of *Gender and Global Restructuring* (2011) of this now updated piece for the third edition, the campaign vowed to halve the number of the world's poor by the year 2015 and to raise funds to provide antiretroviral medication for people in "Africa."[7] Among Bono's then successes was a petition in support of debt forgiveness, signed by 21.2 million people globally (Cooper, 2008, p. 43). In addition to the eradication of poverty, ONE's vision continues to include reducing infant and maternal mortality among the world's poorest and reversing the spread of diseases that are particularly virulent on the African continent (e.g., HIV/AIDS, malaria and tuberculosis) and were most targeted there by the ONE campaign prior to the COVID-19 pandemic. Fourteen years after its launch, the campaign, in conjunction with its partner brands, had raised approximately $650 million across eight different countries and continues in its work toward an "AIDS-Free Generation." By 2021, ONE and its (RED) Campaign were drawing attention to the lack of access to COVID-19 vaccinations in Africa, adding the pandemic to its fundraising efforts to tackle preventable diseases on the continent, but still, most centrally, AIDS.[8] Above all else, as a global actor, Bono has for almost two decades offered a script by which the North can perform an identity of care.

The (RED) campaign continues to work in concert with a constellation of megabrands, such as Gap Inc., Giorgio Armani, Converse, Nike, Apple, American Express (UK), Hallmark, Dell, Starbucks and Windows.[9] The Global Fund continues to serve as its trustee, and the campaign promotes itself as a commercial initiative that primarily aims to raise funds to fight the AIDS pandemic in "Africa" (which, as of 2010, referred to Swaziland, Rwanda and Ghana, but by 2020 had been extended to include Kenya, Lesotho, South Africa, Eswatini, Tanzania and Zambia) by providing antiretroviral medication. When designated (RED) products are purchased, between 5 and 40 percent of the profits are donated to the Global Fund. It aims, therefore, to create awareness and facilitate a "sustainable flow of private sector money … to fight the AIDS pandemic in Africa." (RED)'s manifesto is clear: it is not a charity, it is a "business model."[10]

Unlike traditional modes of philanthropy, (RED)'s multimillion-dollar marketing strategy promotes a range of highly stylized products. Its product selection includes toys for the technologically savvy and fashion for both high-end sophisticates and middle-tier cosmopolitan chic. Through very strategic advertising placement, the marketing power of (RED) is exponentially enhanced by the cachet, brand recognizability and the deployment of a high-powered list of celebrities by its corporate partners.[11] (RED)'s model of philanthropy is unique by virtue of its own brand recognizability, as separate from its corporate partners—an unusually collaborative corporate structure, wherein already-established brands have attached *their identity* to the (RED) philosophy—and in its potential for becoming a philanthropic monopoly, because of its malleable boundaries, which allow for an expanding base of new corporate members. The resulting synergy is a curious inversion of accepted notions of sustainability in development, positing in its place notions of consumption meeting the wants of future generations without compromising the profits of the present.[12]

(RED)'s branding process comes to suggest more than a commodity. Rather, it deploys a tried and trusted marketing strategy; it offers a relationship, an experience and an identity to global consumers (Klein, 2000). Adherence to fashion might be seen as an individualized pursuit in response to social and cultural trends; (RED) builds on the individual display and maintenance of social status that fashion makes possible. In addition to the maintenance of social status, (RED) also interpolates fashion and lifestyle into a range of "glocalized" expressions of political economy.[13]

However, the connection between consumer identity formation and product alliance is premised on an additional set of neoliberal assumptions. (RED) depends on and promotes a steady belief in the inevitability and "naturalness" of the market. The naturalization of consumption itself requires a "modernist model of human nature (read: elite male nature) as competitive, self-interested and acquisitive" (Peterson, 2003, p. 143). (RED) manages to keep its brand equity by maintaining a finely-tuned balance between the acquisitive, self-interested aspect of neoliberal consumption and the redemptive, as reflected in its manifesto: "As first world consumers, we have tremendous power, what we collectively choose to buy, or not buy, can change the course of life and history on this planet."[14] In the foreground are the redemptive possibilities of economic fundamentalism, framed by the steady juxtaposition of consumption and redemption as the preferred mode of addressing global disparity. The narrative progression of the (RED) manifesto places custodial responsibility for (RED) in the hands of the consumer and, by extension, brown and black bodies in pain.

> You have a choice ... If you buy a (RED) product ... At no cost to you, a (RED) company will give some of its profits ... to our brothers and sisters dying of AIDS in Africa ... we believe that when customers are offered this choice ... they will choose (RED) ... And more lives will be saved. You buy (RED) stuff. We get the money, buy the pills ... If they don't get the pills. They die ... All you have to do is upgrade your choice.
>
> ((RED)™ Manifesto)

The narrative structure is telling; antiretroviral medication is a by-product and secondary to profit generation. In order to achieve this, the narrative invokes an empathetic relationship between the consumer and the product, whereby responsibility for the corporate soul is placed squarely in the hands of the consumer (Klein, 2000, p. 23). The interplay between commodification, consumption and concern is always at work in a textual analysis of the (RED) and ONE website, culminating in a kind of Orwellian interchange between the product and the person.[15]

One of the many descriptors attached to discussions of globalization is the encroaching deterritorialization of the world. This idea, when summoned, suggests an increasing interconnectedness between markets and geographies, as well as the permeability of national boundaries. However, one of the contradictions of our supposed "global village" is a persistent and rigid separation between the spheres of consumption and production. Integral to the pleasures of consumption is that we do not see the laboring or ailing bodies that make consumption possible.

The erasure of both laboring and suffering bodies becomes necessary if the brand is to signify the problem and the solution. Throughout this discussion, I have been pointing to the fact that development as *haute couture* brings us into a psychic—rather than an experiential or firsthand visual—relationship with global crises, inequity and suffering. This reference to the psychic is one that highlights the ways in which "Africa" functions as an imaginary—an imaginary that makes it become a psychic spectacle, that which is made hypervisible through renderings, imaginations and projections. In other words, we see without the need to engage because what we see is rendered for us through the brand. And what fantastical renderings they are! There is the rendering of the continent as a country: "in Africa"—the recurring pathologization and homogenization of an entire continent under the sign of HIV/AIDS. There is the rendering of a smiling Maasai warrior as the emblematic representation of the "African" being helped, despite the fact that the Maasai populate Kenya and Tanzania (East Africa), while the Global Fund presently works in three non-Maasai territories.[16] At very few points in (RED)'s marketing arsenal, do we see the ailing bodies for whom the brands are reputedly in service. These bodies are never tied to the brand; indeed, the very success of the brand as chic metropolitan sophistication dictates and demands their absence.[17]

The imbrication of (RED) in a profit-seeking agenda brings it into direct conflict with its own ethics of care for those who reside in the Global South. In keeping with a growing emphasis on corporate social responsibility (CSR) many of (RED)'s corporate partners have well-documented CSR policies, most notable being those of Gap Inc.[18] Gap Inc. began its social responsibility reporting in 2004. Among the highlights of its report are increased factory inspection, use of organic cotton, contributing US$525 million to the Global Fund by 2007, and the notation that "social responsibility can provide new ways to engage our customers" (*Gap Inc. 2005-2006 Social Responsibility Report Fact Sheet*). Still, as will be the case in competitive, exploitative global markets, the seduction of "cheap" labor has, on many occasions, placed Gap Inc. on the defensive, for example, in response to charges of its use of child labor in India.[19]

The COVID-19 pandemic and ensuing inflation presented models such as (RED) with a dilemma. In the face of an ever-shrinking North American middle class, where disposable incomes have been further decimated, it has had to grapple with shifting calculations among weakened North American pockets, political pressures to keep jobs and dollars within the US, and a target population that is even more deeply committed to buying goods cheaply. How do models such as (RED) now fare? For whom, then, should the consumer-donor care for when facing personal conditions of precarity? Should she care for the ailing bodies who are "helped" by her consumption? Should she care for the laboring bodies who have contributed, often to their detriment, to what she consumes? Should she now care for her weakened purchasing power even when it far exceeds those made invisible? These tensions and contradictory flows of global capital and ethical intent remain unresolved.

By the campaign's own assessment, (RED) had, in a little over a year of its initial operation, contributed US$50 million to the Global Fund. There is, of course, something that remains strikingly persuasive in Bono's (2007) early assessment of the HIV/AIDS pandemic:

> This is an emergency—normal rules don't apply. There are no easy good or bad guys. Do you think an African mother cares if the drugs keeping her child alive are thanks to an iPod or a church plate? Or a Democrat or a Republican? I don't think that mother gives a damn about where that 20-cent pill comes from, so why should we. It can lead to some uncomfortable bedfellows, but sometimes, less sleep means you are more awake.

My concern is not with these moral inconsistencies but rather the lack of systemic interconnections made among a series of unreliable dependencies—a reliance on consumption in the North juxtaposed against reduced disposable income that has been hitched to alleviating poor health indicators in the Global South based on deployment of these very vulnerable networks for profit.[20] In other words, the pandemic further revealed our circular imbrication in each other's health and poverty.

The links between fashion and territorial crises are pernicious and precarious. In the world of marketing, "product abandonment" signals the point at which profit-motivated decisions are made about the continuance of a product. Abandonment can occur as a result of weak performance or in response to the need for new and "more promising" product generation (Gruenwald, 1997). It is an efficiency approach that prioritizes financial security, marketing strategy, cost, value and scope of the product (Hamelman and Maze, 1972). Social costs are rarely, if ever, seen as an accounting variable. The questions that logically follow are: What becomes of the crisis when the fashion is no longer marketable? Who is saved when the instrumentalized use of the sign "Africa" as a fashion icon becomes abandoned once again?

Economically mi(red): Getting Africa out of the (RED)

Bono and Shriver's (RED) has since been lauded as offering a new and sustainable model of corporate engagement (Asongu, 2007). But what does "sustainable" mean in the context of philanthrocapitalism? As these "humanitarian" campaigns draw more heavily on free-market logics and distributive practices, what new and problematic intimacies might we have to confront as people are positioned within these economic circuits? And, given that "Africa" has become an axiomatic ground zero for these economic and discursive flights, what then is the symbolic economy that emerges from the widening sphere of philanthrocapitalism and its touchpoint "Africa"?

For scholars and policymakers alike, discussions on market instability, fiscal planning or even notions of "modernity" concerning Continental Africa invariably come to land on the question of aid. In these moments, aid can emerge as a panacea, as catalytic or as an obstacle; the positions are as variable as they are oppositional. Economist Jeffrey Sachs holds a prominent edge in those quarters that tend toward the urgency of aid, adding, as he does, a further layer of aid as a global moral imperative. Waxing poetic aid becomes twice blessed, blessing she who gives and she who receives, or as Sachs would suggest, for us "to turn away from the world's poorest people and leave them to die, [becomes] devastating for our souls" (cited in Leonzon, 2010). In the face of dire poverty, anemic social indicators and markets, "Africa" emerges as having the "greatest need for more and better aid" (Sachs, 2005). Aid not only ensures improved health indicators but extends its triumphs to poverty reduction, particularly when interventions are targeted to Africa's agricultural sector (McArthur and Sachs, 2018). In Sachs's embrace of aid, market and governance inefficiencies, such as state-sanctioned embezzlement of the very aid itself, are systemic market and distributive failings, for after all, "Africa's governance is poor because Africa is poor" (Sachs, 2006, p. 308). While Sachs might see aid as a panacea, others see it as ineffective to sustainable growth and/or as little more than a stage prop in a world theater of profit-inequity. Voices opposing aid highlight its capacity to exacerbate competitive tendencies within the socio-economic fabric of the receiving territory. A vocal critic, Dambisa Moyo (2009), positions aid to Africa as an instrument that de-incentivizes the pursuit of growth strategies, weakens the "accountability mechanisms, [encourages] rent-seeking behaviour" and tears at the already weak social fabric of trust (p. 58). In a similar vein, Léonce Ndikumana and James K. Boyce (2011) trouble the popular narrative of Africa as a drain on the world's resources. Their incisive analysis of loan-related capital flight brings into sharp focus the ways that external financing programs, such as international financial institution (IFI) loans, bring African nation-states into a structural and cyclical debt trap. Financing is a profitable business, and African nation-states are particularly vulnerable to internal and external predatory behaviors in which they repeatedly pay "more in debt service than [they] receive[s] in new money" (Ndikumana and Boyce, 2011, p. 36).

Given the centrality of interest on all forms of financing, Ndikumana and Boyce are clear that negative net transfers are not a possibility but a "mathematical certainty" (2011, p. 36). And so, for them, external financing has significantly undermined the very goal for which they are presumed to exist—the recipient country's development. Contrary to the perception of Africa as a drain on the world's resources, the terms of debt servicing push us to consider the profitability of inequity or, as the authors suggest, that Africa, and in particular, sub-Saharan Africa stands as a "net creditor to the rest of the world" (Ndikumana and Boyce, 2011, p. 53). If loan servicing proves detrimental to a country's long-term economic stability, then Ndikumana and Boyce's work begs the question: what of aid? Does aid present nation-states with a similar conundrum of capital flight, unencumbered as it is by debt servicing and interest? On this, Ndikumana and Boyce offer little to no sanguinity; aid is, after all, a "lootable resource" (2011, p. 67) and, so, not exempt from the machinations of flight. In this sense, we might hear echoes of Sachs's constitutive framing of poor governance as both the cause and consequence of economic poverty; structural inequity will make everything fair game for gain. But, capital flight in relation to aid is obscure. It is difficult to ascertain what structural benefits exist for donor countries and agencies that continue to grant aid, even with the recognition of the potential inefficiencies, misdirections and flight. The lure of national/regional financing is less obscure if we agree with Ndikumana and Boyce that there is money to be made from poverty and that the "winners" and "losers" are trackable phenomena. Their work, however, is not clear on whether there are structural benefits to be derived for donor countries and donor agencies; who gains in the granting of aid, and what does a "gain" look like in this exchange? While Ndikumana and Boyce position Africa as a *net creditor* to the world, I want to suggest that in the context of the "aid," Africa becomes the *moral mirror* of the world, a conduit for self-adulation and absolution.

We live in what Moyo (2009) has pointedly referred to as a "culture of aid" (p. xvii), which for Moyo, capaciously encompasses "concessional loan[s] and grant[s]" (p. 9). My use of "aid" is decidedly narrower; I am interested in the subjectification processes and discursive gains that accompany financial exchanges that are not shaped by the terms and expectations of loan servicing. Why do we give when there are no immediate *material rewards*, and what is the symbolic economy associated with such giving? As such, I distinguish loans from debt-free grants and market-driven micro-consumption. If we consider how narratives of aid are interwoven into the fabric of culture, we then have to consider a range of related and commensurate questions. A culture of aid implicates itself in the moral codes that infuse the language used for aid; it reorders the hierarchies, places and values that are assigned to those who are aid-givers and aid-receivers; and it structures *how* we give aid—through cause or through the more explosive moment of aid as consumption. In this swirling constellation, philanthrocapitalism enters the scene as the putative bridge between markets and morality.

This chapter holds a deep curiosity about the possibilities of philanthrocapitalism but is decidedly less optimistic about its capacity to "benefit everyone." Alongside the question of markets and morality, philanthrocapitalism is both premised on and *produces* specific kinds of humans. Philanthrocapitalism depends on and activates a form of modern humanism that positions human suffering as "unnecessary and unjust" (Wilkinson, 2016, p. 67). The human that turns away from such suffering, from the spectacle therefore becomes complicit with "a moral obscenity" (Wilkinson, 2016, p. 67). One might say that philanthrocapitalism allows us to look away but for the price of a coffee, but let us parse the structures that are imbricated in the production of human suffering, the definition of human suffering and the presumption that the frames that produce these spectacles of suffering can somehow save the ailing body.

I argue that for these market/aid practices to work, they must deploy an age-old erasure of an African body politic in ways that I find woefully instructive if we were to look at Voltaire's *Candide, ou l'Optimisme* (1759/2000).[21] In *Candide*, Voltaire crafts a journey set in the 18th century, in which the main protagonist, Candide, the "illegitimate" son of a German aristocrat who is schooled in his father's house, undertakes a series of misadventures in Europe and beyond. Candide is subject(ed) to a series of catastrophic events and fast-paced, fantastic scenarios (e.g., torture, war, natural catastrophes, wealth acquisition and dire poverty). The allegorical novel was an assault on German philosopher Leibniz's belief that "we live in the best of all possible worlds." This creed of Western optimism and celebration, inculcated under the tutelage of Candide's teacher, Pangloss, initially guides Candide. In his odyssey, however, with each harrowing episode, Candide increasingly questions his teacher's wisdom, resulting in the novel's resolution that in life, humanity is best served when we "tend to our own garden" ("il faut cultiver notre jardin").

Candide's odyssey challenges him to reconcile a number of irreconcilable moments and events (e.g., mass death, his sweetheart's rape). However, even at my high school encounter with this novel, the scene that has always captured my postcolonial imagination was that, on his entrance to Suriname, Candide encounters an enslaved man who has horrifically lost his leg and arm to the terrors of slavery.[22] The enslaved man attributes his dismemberment to the gruesome cost of the pleasures of European sugar consumption ("C'est à ce prix que vous mangez du sucre en Europe"). With this articulation, the enslaved body becomes the site from which political economy extracts both its pains and pleasures. The body of *Le nègre de Suriname* marks the hidden contradictions of consumption; indeed, the very pleasure of consumption is premised on not seeing these forms of extraction and dismemberment ("C'est l'usage").[23] As such, we learn of *Le nègre's* existence only because he has become the object of Candide's gaze, a gaze that is made possible after Candide has been violently thrown out of the comforts of "Westphalia" in Europe and finds himself in South America. For those who do not make such a journey, the enslaved body remains disconnected from the site of consumption as well as the gaze of the consumer. Yet, even at the point at which the consumer encounters the laboring body, it is still an instrumentalized encounter in that the slave's dismembered, laboring body is positioned in the text primarily to advance Candide's knowledge and critical awareness of himself.

What, then, does Voltaire's *Candide* have to do with a piece that aims to interrogate the upsurge of philanthrocapitalism as evidenced in celebrity-driven "development" campaigns such as the (RED) Campaign? To make these connections, we must first acknowledge that capitalism has not only embedded itself into our quotidian but it has, in essence, become a "foundational principle of social life" (Mohanty, 2003, p. 183). The discursive tropes that guide these foundational principles are infused with presumptions and structural inequities that shape how colonized, racialized and gendered laboring bodies are deployed in the processes of profit-making. Despite the argued merits of philanthrocapitalism, it, too, is not immune. Indeed, it is premised on the very logic of neoliberalism, a logic that is analogous to what I have described in Voltaire's treatment of *Le nègre de Suriname*. In similar ways, contemporary moves toward "philanthropy as development" render the unknown laboring/ailing body as familiar, but this is a tropological familiarity. It is a familiarity that is confined by signs and symbols that draw on a set of legitimated colonial narratives that hide much more than they reveal about the bodies that labor and pain. These signs and symbols, similarly, do not centralize or visualize the laboring/ailing body; once again, in the foreground, we find a campaign that focuses on the realization of a new "first world consumer" in need of greater awareness of herself and the politics of her purchasing power.

The seamless fusion of philanthropy and capitalism (philanthrocapitalism) and its compatibility with modern humanism ensures that those of us who would usually grapple with the politics of giving and ethics of care can find very little wrong with global good emerging out of our quotidian practices—what we wear, how we listen to music, what we eat. Each of these economic decisions can make us feel good about ourselves and our part in building a global civil society; further, this is a civil society that tells us to trust our celebrities and not worry about corruption and capital flight; that coffee you had today saved a child (Mitchell, 2016, p. 289). Social groups rather than territories and nation-states become the primary actors, and as with any populist formation, which clique you belong to determines place and value (Robinson, 2002, p. 1048). This peculiar deterritorialization feeds a narrative of aid, development and even the relationship harnessed between aid-giver and aid-receiver "as a distanceless and borderless" phenomenon (Scholte, 2005, p. 72). The very production of this presumption of affective proximity is aided and abetted by these campaigns' deft use of digital platforms, used to sell goods, set trends, build brand-based communities, but most of all, to depoliticize the politics of capitalist production (Burns, 2019, p. 1102). Yet, the constellation of effects and inflections enables a global civil society in which the embrace of "profit philanthropy as development" simultaneously produces, if not requires, disturbing erasures of the very bodies that should be the beneficiaries of this philanthropy.

I have argued here that there are economic, textual and rhetorical practices in philanthropic models, such as the (RED) campaign, that are inimical to the long-term well-being of peoples on the African continent. Primary among these is the disarticulation of operational and analytical spheres. This disarticulation masks the asymmetrical relations that exist between and among economic regions and the ways in which individual lives are affected by these inequities. This is a disarticulation that also hides the ways in which consumption in the North facilitates the underdevelopment of the Global South. Rather than address these inequities frontally, these campaigns' dependence upon consumption and profit generation reflects a model that becomes complicit in "*explaining away the international equality problem*" (Myrdal, 1970, p. 277, emphasis in the original).

The indicators on the economic, political and health status of the peoples of Africa are undeniably worrying. In 2007, at the inception of (RED)'s work, the Joint United Nations Program on HIV/AIDS (UNAIDS) estimated that 22.5 million people were living with HIV/AIDS in sub-Saharan Africa; this accounted for 68 percent of adults and 90 percent of children living with HIV/AIDS worldwide (2007, pp. 7–8). In the intervening period to the present, there has been a notable decline, but the number of people living with HIV/AIDS in sub-Saharan Africa recently stood at 20.6 million.[24] Despite falling poverty rates between 1999 and 2004, by 2007, persistent population growth in sub-Saharan

Africa had resulted in 300 million people living below the poverty line, and, in the midst of debt-forgiveness programs, external debt responsibilities remained high (International Monetary Fund, 2007, p. 5). Despite the multitude of aid-related interventions, the structures of poverty continue to constrain the region's possibilities, a matter of unimaginable urgency given that future projections suggest that by 2100, three out of every four people added to the world population will live in sub-Saharan Africa.[25]

The lack of fiscal expenditure on health-related services is a critical factor when confronting the HIV/AIDS crisis. The disparity between disease burden and care infrastructure continues to be in chronic disarray. In 2006, the African region accounted for 24 percent of the global disease burden but only 3 percent of the world's health workers, commanding less than 1 percent of world health expenditure—even with loans and grants from abroad (WHO, 2006, p. 8). This translated into a deficit of approximately 2.4 million healthcare providers in 57 countries; 36 of the countries affected by this deficit are in sub-Saharan Africa (WHO, 2006, p. 12). In 2015, the total spent on HIV/AIDS in sub-Saharan Africa was US$18.0 billion (averaging between $16.3 billion and $20.5 billion), of which only 31.0 percent (averaging between 24.6 percent and 39 percent) came from governments.[26] In sub-Saharan Africa in 2017, 75 percent of deaths resulted from HIV/AIDS, and the region maintained a new infection rate of 65 percent (Dwyer-Lindgren et al., 2019). At the same time, healthcare systems in sub-Saharan Africa struggle to redress fiscal vulnerabilities: the region's healthcare sector had a financing gap of US$66 billion (UN Economic Commission for Africa, 2019).

Sub-Saharan Africa's health infrastructure instability cannot, and ought not, be isolated from the economic instability arising, in part, from structural adjustment programs (SAPs) imposed on the region. Reduced public expenditure and privatization of state services are now a well-known and standard feature of SAPs. While IFIs offered a moratorium on debt payments during 2020 and 2021 to free national budgets to address COVID-19-related strains to existing health infrastructures, the pandemic has shown itself to not be a zero-sum game—with health infrastructure, service providers and the most vulnerable on the losing end.[27] In lieu of comprehensive and permanent debt forgiveness, a post-pandemic, post-moratorium world is invariably leading to even further mired conditions for some of the world's most vulnerable economies. The COVID-19 global pandemic made the exponential effect of these structural vulnerabilities keenly felt, with UNAIDS estimating an additional 500,000 HIV/AIDS-related deaths should there be a six-month complete disruption of access to HIV treatment in sub-Saharan Africa (2020–2021) and the World Health Organization noting that malaria deaths are still targeted to far exceed COVID-19 mortalities.[27, 28]

Philanthropic models such as (RED) are so deeply imbricated in neoliberal assumptions that consumption and poor health are rendered as discrete properties rather than as phenomena that hold an obverse and occasionally parasitic relationship with each other. It is here that I (re)turn to Abderrahmane Sissako's

Bamako (2006) for the ways in which the film resists the compartmentalization of the impact of global political economy on individual lives and in its defiance of the laryngectomy that results when the North tells "Africa's" story—a vehicle that takes on even greater significance in the context of the global pandemic and the expected disastrous humanitarian crisis that has resulted from and is left in the pandemic's wake.

Bamako is set in a residential compound surrounded by a rural village atmosphere in the capital of Mali. An outdoor court of law has been convened, with judges and prosecuting and defense attorneys to consider an indictment of IFIs and globalization more generally for socioeconomic injustices based on villagers' testimonies. *Bamako* tells no single story but rather interweaves a panoply of lives, with people telling parts of their stories as formal testimonies or through cutaways to their daily lives and conversations outside the courtroom, in and beyond the village setting. The closest that *Bamako* comes to a coherent storyline is through a secondary narrative of a young couple: Melé, who sings in an upscale, urban bar at night, and her unemployed husband, Chaka, are caught in a marriage on the verge of demise. Their communication with each other is perfunctory, and the only signs we have that there must have once been love between them are the still photograph of the young couple on the wall and their love and affection for their young daughter. While this story unfolds, we are also the audience for the seemingly bizarre trial of IFIs and globalization that occurs daily in the compound in which Melé and Chaka live.

In *Bamako*, testimony and witnessing work along a continuum of words, silence and unintelligibility to convey the grief and mourning resulting from living under the exigencies of globalization. As the trial continues, a reporter covering it re-engages one of his interviewees, Chaka, by prompting, "You were saying that the worst part of structural adjustment policies is the destruction of the social fabric—that entire part got erased—say it again." To which Chaka responds, "No one will listen … don't waste your time." Yet, Sissako places the film's moral burden on the importance of testimony and witnessing. Through the trial testimonies, Sissako humanizes the social and economic variables of macroeconomics; these variables are made flesh in the forms of whistle-blowers formerly employed by exploitative corporations; migrant workers with harrowing tales of near-death experiences on their forced journeys across African deserts to seek work in Algeria; laid-off teachers in the wake of education cuts; infirm but stoic elderly, who have seen so much loss; and "the folk," particularly the female folk, who go about the daily-ness of some vestige/semblance of social reproduction as the trial goes on, preparing food, cleaning shelters and clothes and dying textiles. The multiplicity of narratives is a reminder, in the words of one witness, that "[the] goat has its ideas but so does the hen." Villager after villager steps forward to tell her/his story, some through sophisticated analyses and others through personal tales, with the prosecuting attorney providing mountains of additional statistical evidence of human costs for which there is little defense. In these ways, we learn of the complex and far-reaching effects of globalization.

Through the use of testimony and voice, Sissako engages in a poignant re-narration of Africa, which challenges the language and form of, and legitimated stories told by, traditional jurisprudence and economic policy. However, the emotional and psychological losses attendant to the economic crisis are most poetically rendered by Sissako through silence and unintelligibility. As witnesses come forward when called, so, too, does a former school teacher made redundant by reduced state expenditure on education. Asked to state his testimony, he becomes overwhelmed by his story, rendering him silent; he is able merely to record his existence, rendering his humanity through no more than the utterance of his name and date of birth before departing in response to a final nothing to say ("Rien à déclarer?").

The narrative culmination of the film comes through the voice of an elder, a *griot*, who, at the beginning of the film, disrupts the conventional legal narrative and walks to the podium to speak before he is called. As he is sent back, he responds, "Words are something, they can seize your heart if you keep them inside." This elder again defies convention by poignantly breaking into a song that is never translated, at which point all non-Bambara-speaking viewers and the French-speaking magistrates are left unable to decipher what is being conveyed. If words are inadequate to tell these woes, at this moment, Sissako appeals to the human spirit, not so that we, the viewers, can understand, but so that we can feel. The song's profound emotive effect rests in its very unintelligibility that we do not know, understand and are not enabled to understand (through subtitles) requires us to deploy a different register. Here, Sissako seems to suggest a connectedness through the power of the human spirit and the possibility, through alternative engagements, for a new socioeconomic arrangement that can be reached when other, typically rationalist, discourses are suspended. To treat any emotional register as though it were transcendent may not always be effective; however, in this scene, we are faced with the very important reminder that there are parts of these narratives that will always be impossible for us, the Western viewer, to fully comprehend.

The camera shuttles into Melé and Chaka's room and out into the courtyard, following the trial in the compound and following Melé and Chaka when they leave the compound. Sissako skillfully ensures that these are parallel and occasionally intertwined narratives. They never seamlessly mesh into each other but maintain the tension of an imbricated messiness. The confined location and the occasional character movement from one narrative to the other reminds us that these stories matter to each other; however, the most intimate connection is at the epistemological level. That these private and public knowledge worlds confront each other is a deliberate attempt to merge the personal connections and costs between the worlds of production and consumption. The personal is made prominent and the political accountable. As such, these narrative structures and spatial contrivances are not allowed the deception of separation.

Sissako skillfully presses the unseen hand of the market against the slow and quotidian aspects of economic tyranny and, in so doing, makes the market hypervisible. Sissako weaves these worlds into each other so that, as lawyers debate the impact of SAPs on the healthcare system, we see the immediacy of the ailing body when the compound dwellers keep vigil for a sick and dying neighbor. Heated exchanges between legal teams on China's economic prowess are punctuated by a toddler's squeaking synthetic shoes as she learns to walk. A cameraman, there to film the historic trial, announces that he now does most of his business filming funerals, suggesting a lucrative, homonymic play on "death" and "debt." Throughout the entire film, the local economy is represented by Malian women who dye fabric; their steady and adaptable centrality is reflected by an equally steady, yet flexible, flow of dyed water that winds its way on the ground in almost every scene of the film.

As the proceedings unfold, we find twin brothers among the community members: they wear the same style of shirt in different colors, they are always visible during the proceedings and they never speak audibly. In my reading of the film, *Bamako* is edited as if to suggest that they are simultaneously inside and outside of the proceedings so that they remain in the camera's eye, even when partially hidden. It is difficult not to interpret these twins as both observers and observed, as the metaphoric, mystical omnipresence of the twin Bretton Woods institutions, the World Bank and the International Monetary Fund (IMF), always in the backdrop.

Sissako employs the absurd in his critique of the IFIs' impact on the economic and moral worlds of the continent. He offers a particularly strong indictment of the promise of technology and prescriptive infrastructural development, for which World Bank funds are released through a set of ironies. For example, the film opens with a mass of scaffolding constructed upward into nothingness with no connected building or other construction. Meanwhile, Melé's husband has begun to learn Hebrew and is presently wrestling with sentences to explain that he has lost his wallet. His intended goal for such a task? To work as a security guard for an Israeli embassy that will one day open in Mali. Each symbolic offering moves us closer to nothing.

I am not suggesting that Sissako offers a "truer" narrative about the effects of structural adjustment, but his filmic account is undoubtedly one that resists disembodiment and one that contextualizes inequity. The use of testimony and witnessing resists the erasure of the laboring/ailing body without sacrificing the poetic. *Bamako* resists the conventional heroic narrative through the use of decentralized narratives: this is a film that neither needs nor desires a "star" (or savior) from/in the North, but one that demands equity in trade and economic practices, which makes it possible for nations to heal themselves. *Bamako* is a testimony and an epistemological challenge that echoes the words of one viewer to the filmmaker: "At least they'll know that we know." And it is here that a hero of sorts emerges—civil society. The heroes of *Bamako* are the teachers/professors, whistle-blowers, writers and migrant workers, who, despite the Sisyphean dimensions of their task, continue to tell their stories so that at least the world will know that they know.

These narratives challenge the disembodied, silencing erasures of projects such as (RED). I have argued that the neoliberal logic that now drives globalization and development projects forces a purposeful distancing of markets from their effects. Throughout this chapter, I have wrestled with one dominant question: why is it that centralizing the consumer and centralizing laboring/ailing bodies are presented as mutually exclusive, noncompatible sites of critique? My examination of celebrity-driven philanthropy for-profit models shows that not only are states displaced within conversations on the global political economy, but so, too, are citizens. In this model, it is the brand identity that takes preeminence and becomes the medium of transnational dialogue between consumers in the North and perceived need in the South. These are not inconsequential activities; by 2021, the (RED) website noted that more than 3 million people have been impacted by "HIV/AIDS programs supported by ... (RED) purchases."

However, through a reading of Sissako's work, I have called for a lived literacy of oppression which, for many marginalized bodies, is critical to survival. The pleasures of contemporary consumerism come with embodied costs, as was the case with Candide's *Le nègre du Suriname*. Unless we connect the worlds of production and consumption, it becomes too easy to individualize and commercialize responses to global inequity. Such policy solutions focus on the importance of individual "behavioral adjustments," whether on the part of the consumer to buy more "responsibly" or on the part of laboring bodies to work harder. This individualist logic masks the ways in which underdevelopment is historically and structurally determined, and it further masks the ways in which individual consumers in the North are implicated in the construction of the very inequity that their consumption is supposedly designed to change.

Notes

1 See Hozic, Maiic and Ibrahim's "'It is not about me ... but it kind of is': Celebrity humanitarianism is late modernity" for a further discussion of what they refer to as a "politically disengaged but emotionally supercharged" audience for whom "enthusiasm" trumps political engagement (2018, p. 180).

2 Since this chapter's first publication in 2011, a number of scholars have taken up the politics, affective circuits and economic presumptions of the (RED) campaign. See, for example, Farrell (2012), Richey and Ponte (2009 and 2011), and Hozic et al. (2018). Taken together, the body of work on this topic helps us to map the overall trajectory of a campaign that is inherently mercurial because of its changing product inventory, ephemeral digital life and populist bent. While I have revised the conceptual frame and where appropriate updated the campaign's accomplishments, I have deliberately kept some of the content of the earlier publication as a means of archiving the early formation of the (RED) campaign. Additionally, the earlier title of the piece, "Where the Streets Have No Name," referenced one of U2's more iconic songs to capture the way that African geographies and bodies are remade as invisible and nameless within development discourses. This revised chapter again draws from U2's extensive cache to center this piece as both a conversation with the earlier rendering as well as my ongoing inability to see hope in these models of philanthropic development.

3 At the risk of being deterministic, neoliberalism's ability to produce the conditions for its own survivability now relies heavily on an intermingling of politics and profit, or more precisely rendering profit as politics. Using narratives such as "ethical

consumption" or "progressive politics," neoliberalism makes allies of some of its fiercest critics, see, for example, Jemma Repo's (2020) discussion of "commodity feminism."

4 See Ananya Roy's video "Can we shop to end poverty?" for a discussion of the contradictions that remain embedded within global circuits of consumption, ethics of care and laboring bodies within the Global South. Available at https://www.youtube.com/watch?v=mpuf-N66CGI&ab_channel=GlobalPOV (accessed 17 December 2021). Lisa Ann Richey and Dan Brockington's "Celebrity humanitarianism: Using tropes of engagement to understand North/South relations" (2019) also highlights the relational circuits and flows that inform contemporary practices of celebrity humanitarianism.

5 Accompanied by Annie Leibovitz's iconic portraiture, Lisa Robinson gives us an in-depth look at the extensive celebrity network that Bono has harnessed to drive (RED).

6 Bono appeared with Bill and Melinda Gates on the cover of *Time* magazine as "Persons of the Year" in 2005. "The good Samaritans: Bill Gates, Bono, Melinda Gates," *Time*, December 26, 2005/January 2, 2006. Online. Available at http://content.time.com/time/specials/packages/article/0,28804,1946375_1947772_1947758,00.html (updated June 14, 2020). Bono was also featured in the "2006 TIME 100." See Helms (2006).

7 Both ONE and (RED) are the brainchild of Bono and fundraiser Bobby Shriver. See http://www.one.org.

8 See Jon Blistein's "Bono's One Campaign launches 'Pandemica' series to raise awareness of Covid-19 vaccine access crisis," *Rolling Stone,* March 25, 2021. Available at https://www.rollingstone.com/music/music-news/bono-one-campaign-pandemica-covid-19-vaccine-shortage-1146233/.

9 (RED)'s Annual Report (2019) identified an expanded portfolio that now includes TikTok, Primark, Dannon and Johnson & Johnson's BAND-AID, and attempted to make inroads in France by partnering with Agnès B., Balmain, Louis Vuitton, Stella Luna and Atelier Paulin (ONE.org, 2019, p. 11).

10 See https://www.nytimes.com/2008/02/06/business/06red.html.

11 GAP Inc., as part of its (RED) campaign. has worked with comedian Chris Rock; actors Don Cheadle, Penelope Cruz and Jennifer Garner; singers Mary J. Blige, Wyclef Jean and John Legend; and director Steven Spielberg.

12 This, of course, parodies the Brundtland Report's (1987, p. 43) definition of sustainability as "development which meets the needs of the present without compromising the ability of future generations to meet their own needs" . For example, the (RED) Manifesto advertisements initially aired on MTV, whose monopoly captured a demographic that includes preadolescents to young 30-year-olds, thereby ensuring a generational reach for (RED)'s "sustainable flow of private sector money." (RED) "FAQs." Available at https://www.red.org/faq-contact.

13 I refer to the use of fashion as a "glocalized" expression of political economy to point to the ways in which the production process requires global labor. However, I also recognize that there is a collective recognition of the (RED) brand among the cosmopolitan elite. In a more direct way, Bono has also partnered with designer Rogan Gregory in 2005 to create a line of "socially responsible" fashion, EDUN.

14 "The (RED)^{TM} Manifesto." Available at http://www.joinred.com.

15 At www.joinred.com, there is the occasional exchange between the iconic (PRODUCT) RED motif and (YOU) RED. Similarly, at www.one.org, we find "POWERED BY: YOU." Both instances generate a very powerful appeal to an individual sense of global responsibility while engaging in the process of commodifying both consumer and recipient.

16 See the advertisement featuring supermodel Gisele Bundchen and Maasai warrior Keseme Ole Parsapaet used for the launch of American Express (RED). https://www.seattletimes.com/nation-world/kenyan-supermodel-glad-to-be-back-herding-cattle/ (updated January 24, 2021).

17 This absence is nowhere more readily apparent than on the 20 covers released in July 2007 by *Vanity Fair*. For this issue, guest-edited by Bono, photographer Annie Leibovitz paired 21 individuals, all identified for their connection with or concern for "Africa." The list is remarkable for the sheer political heft of the individuals who participated in this project. Among the individuals who sat for these covers were then-President George Bush, then-Secretary of State Condoleezza Rice, pop star Madonna (noted for her adoption of an African child), peace activist Bishop Desmond Tutu, Oprah, then-US Senator Barack Obama, former prize boxer Muhammad Ali and philanthropists William Warren Buffet and Bill and Melinda Gates. Of the 21 individuals selected, two presently reside on the continent (Bishop Tutu and Queen Rania Al-Abdulla of Egypt). In my introductory analysis of Candide's encounter with the nameless *Le nègre du Suriname*, I pointed to the fact that even when we encounter the laboring/ailing body, it is a moment in the text that serves to advance Candide's knowledge and critical awareness of himself. Similarly, the blurbs that accompany the individual photographs tell us something more about the individual as they gaze on "Africa" and, in so doing, learn something more about themselves.

18 CSR places emphasis on the pursuit of ethical business practices, as well as a holistic corporate model that makes connections between economic development, communities and the quality of life of the workforce (Watts and Holme, 1999, p. 6).

19 See "International Information Programs of the U.S. State Department." Available at http://usinfo.state.gov/xarchives/display.html7p=washfile-english&x=20071031123014mlenuhret0.538357.

20 The global COVID-19 pandemic brought several global health inequities into even starker relief. Despite a lower prevalence and spread rate, the Global South and African countries in particular will no doubt experience more long-term and more dire effects (e.g., hunger, agricultural threats, co-impacting morbidities) because of these very preexisting weak health inequities and infrastructure. See https://www.unocha.org/story/ocha-calls-support-against-%E2%80%98triple-threat%E2%80%99-covid-19-flooding-and-desert-locusts-horn-africa.

21 See also Bellhouse's discussion of the dismembered enslaved body within French imperial imaginaries (2006).

22 The encounter is rendered in *Candide* in the following manner: "En approchant de la ville, ils rencontrèrent un nègre étendu par terre, n'ayant plus que la moitié de son habit. c'est-à-dire d'un caleçon de toile bleue; il manquait à ce pauvre homme la jambe gauche et la main droite. 'Eh, mon Dieu! lui dit Candide en hollandais, que fais-tu là, mon ami, dans l'état horrible où je te vois? – J'attends mon maître, M. Vanderdendur, le fameux négociant,' répondit le nègre. – 'Est-ce M. Vanderdendur,' dit Candide, 'qui t'a traité ainsi?' – 'Oui, monsieur,' dit le nègre, c'est l'usage. On nous donne un caleçon de toile pour tout vêtement deux fois l'année. Quand nous travaillons aux sucreries, et que la meule nous attrape le doigt, on nous coupe la main: quand nous voulons nous enfuir, on nous coupe la jambe: je me suis trouvé dans les deux cas. C'est à ce prix que vous mangez du sucre en Europe" (Voltaire, 1759/2000, p. 96).

23 "It is the custom," however, in French we are compelled to reckon with the juxtaposition of the "custom" and "use value."

24 See https://www.avert.org/professionals/hiv-around-world/sub-saharan-africa/overview.

25 See https://www.newsecuritybeat.org/2011/06/one-in-three-people-will-live-in-sub-saharan-africa-in-2100-says-un/.

26 See https://gh.bmj.com/content/4/1/e001159.

27 See https://www.worldbank.org/en/news/factsheet/2020/05/11/debt-relief-and-covid-19-coronavirus.

28 See https://www.unaids.org/en/resources/presscentre/pressreleaseandstatementarchive/2020/july/20200706_global-aids-report.

29 See https://www.who.int/teams/global-malaria-programme/reports/world-malaria-report-2020.

References

Asongu, J.J. (2007) "Generating sustainable funds through branding: RED campaign introduces new business model for CSR," *Journal of Business and Public Policy*, 1(1), pp. 1–15.

Bellhouse, M.L. (2006) "Candide shoots the monkey-lovers: Representing Black men in eighteenth-century French visual culture," *Political Theory*, 34(6), pp. 741–784.

Bishop, M. and Green, M. (2008) *Philanthrocapitalism: How the Rich Can Save the World*. New York: Bloomsbury Press.

Browne, H. (2013) *The Front Man: Bono (In the Name of Power)*. London: Verso.

Brundtland, G. (1987) *Report of the World Commission on Environment and Development (WECD): Our Common Future*. United Nations General Assembly document A/42/427.

Burns, R. (2019) "New frontiers of philanthrocapitalism: Digital technologies and humanitarianism," *Antipode*, 51(4), pp. 1101–1122.

Cooper, A.F. (2008) *Celebrity Diplomacy*. Boulder, CO: Paradigm Publishers.

DeCurtis, A. (2007) "Interview with Bono for 40th RS anniversary issue," *Rolling Stone*, 1039, pp. 60–62.

Dwyer-Lindgren, L., Cork, M.A., Sligar, A. *et al.* (2019) "Mapping HIV prevalence in sub-Saharan Africa between 2000 and 2017," *Nature*, 570, pp. 189–193.

Escobar, A. (1995) *Encountering Development: The Making and Unmaking of the Third World*. Princeton, N.J.: Princeton University Press.

Farrell, N. (2012) "Celebrity politics: Bono, Product (RED) and the legitimising of philanthrocapitalism," *The British Journal of Politics and International Relations*, 14(3), pp. 392–406.

Gap Inc. (2005–2006) "What is a company's role in society?" *Social Responsibility Report Fact Sheet*, https://shorturl.at/cjmnN (accessed September 4, 2023).

Gruenwald, G. (1997) *How to Create Profitable New Products*. New York: McGraw-Hill.

Hamelman, P.W. and Maze, E. (1972) "Improving product abandonment decisions," *Journal of Marketing*, 36, pp. 20–26.

Helms, J. (2006) "Bono: The 2006 Time 100," *Time*, May. Available at https://content.time.com/time/specials/packages/article/0,28804,1975813_1975847_1976565,00.html.

Hozic, A.A., Majic, S. and Ibrahim, I.Y. (2018) "It is not about me … but it kind of is': celebrity humanitarianism is late modernity," in Persaud, R.B. and Sajed, A. (eds.) *Race, Gender, and Culture in International Relations: Postcolonial Perspectives*. New York: Routledge, pp. 80–199.

International Monetary Fund. (2007) *Regional Economic Outlook: Sub-Saharan Africa*. Washington DC: IMF.

Klein, N. (2000) *No Logo: Taking Aim at the Brand Bullies*. New York: Picador.

Leonzon, R.M. (2010) "Jeffery Sachs: Why development aid is a win-win solution." Available at https://www.devex.com/news/jeffrey-sachs-why-development-aid-is-a-win-win-solution-70225 (accessed June 9, 2020).

McArthur, J.W. and Sachs, J.D. (2018) *Agriculture, Aid and Economic Growth in Africa*, Policy Research Working Paper 8447. World Bank Group, Development Economics Vice Presidency Strategy, and Operations Team.

McGoey, L. (2015) *No Such Thing as a Free Gift: The Gates Foundation and the Price of Philanthropy*. London: Verso.

Mitchell, K. (2016) "Celebrity humanitarianism, transnational emotion and the rise of neoliberal citizenship," *Global Networks*, 16, pp. 288–306.

Mohanty, C. (2003) *Feminism without Borders: Decolonizing Theory, Practicing Solidarity*. Durham: Duke University Press.

Moyo, D. (2009). *Dead Aid: Why Aid Is Not Working and How There Is A Better Way for Africa*. New York: Farrar, Straus and Giroux.

Mugubane, Z. (2008) "The (Product) Red man's burden: Charity, celebrity, and the contradictions of coevalness," *The Journal of Pan African Studies*, 2(6), pp. 102–125.

Myrdal, G. (1970) *The Challenge of World Poverty*. New York: Pantheon Books.

Ndikumana, L. and Boyce, J.K. (2011) *Africa's Odious Debts: How Foreign Loans and Capital Flight Bled a Continent*. London: Zed Books.

One.org. (2019) *2019 Annual Review*. Available athttps://cdn.one.org/pdfs/ONE-Annual-Review-2019.pdf.

Peterson, V. Spike. (2003) *A Critical Rewriting of Global Political Economy: Integrating Reproductive, Productive and Virtual Economies*. London: Routledge.

Ponte, S., Richey L.S. and Baab, M. (2009) "Bono's product (RED) initiative: Corporate social responsibility that solves the problems of 'distant others," *Third World Quarterly*, 30 (2), pp. 301–317.

Repo, J. (2020) "Feminist commodity activism: The new political economy of feminist protest," *International Political Sociology*, 14, pp. 215–232.

Richey, L. and Brockington, D. (2019) "Celebrity humanitarianism: Using tropes of engagement to understand North/South relations," *Perspectives on Politics*, 18(1), pp. 1–17.

Richey, L. and Ponte, S. (2011) *Brand Aid: Shopping Well to Save the World*. London: University of Minnesota Press.

Robinson, L. (2007) "It's Bono on line one." Available at https://archive.vanityfair.com/article/2007/7/its-bono-on-line-one (accessed January 27, 2021)

Robinson, W. (2002) "Remapping development in light of globalization: From a territorial to a social cartography," *Third World Quarterly*, 23(6), pp. 1047–1071.

Sachs, J. (2005) "Why aid does work." Available at https://www.earth.columbia.edu/site files/file/about/director/documents/BBCOnlineSept2005-WhyAidDoesWork.pdf (accessed June 9, 2020).

Sachs, J. (2006) *The End of Poverty: Economics Possibilities for our Time*. New York: Penguin Books.

Scholte, J.A. (2005) *Globalization: A Critical Introduction*. New York: Palgrave Macmillan.

Sissako, A. (dir.) (2006) *Bamako* [film]. France: Icarus Films.

UNAIDS. (2007) *AIDS Epidemic Update*. Geneva: UNAIDS and WHO. Available at https://data.unaids.org/pub/epislides/2007/2007_epiupdate_en.pdf (updated September 4, 2023).

UN Economic Commission for Africa (UNECA). (2019) *Economic Report on Africa 2019: Fiscal Policy for Financing Sustainable Development in Africa*.

Voltaire (1759/2000) *Candide, ou, l'optimisme: conte philosophique*. Darcos, X. (ed.). Paris: Hachette Groupe Livre.

Watts, P. and Holme, R. (1999) *Corporate Social Responsibility Meeting Changing Expectations*. Geneva: World Business Council for Sustainable Development.

Wilkinson, Iain M. (2016) "The problem of understanding modern humanitarianism and its sociological value," *International Social Science Journal*, 65(215–221), pp. 65–78.

World Health Organization (WHO). (2006) *Working Together for Health: The World Health Report. 2006*. Geneva: WHO.

World Economic Forum (2006) "Bono and Bobby Shriver launch Product Red to harness power of the world's iconic brands to fight AIDS in Africa." Available at https://allafrica.com/stories/200601260272.html (updated June 14, 2020).

5 The gendered imperatives of the financialization of remittances in Mexico

Listening to the subjects-to-be-financialized

Rahel Kunz and Brenda Ramírez

Introduction

Since the late 1990s, remittances—the money that migrant workers send to their families or communities of origin—have become heralded by the international development community as a key tool to promote development and reduce poverty.[1] Officially recorded remittance flows[2] to lower- and middle-income countries reached US$529 billion in 2019 and constitute more than 30 percent of GDP in countries such as Haiti or Tonga (World Bank and KNOMAD, 2019). In the wake of the global financial crisis and in a context of enduring stagnating levels of official development aid, the international community has started to promote the linking of remittances to the global financial inclusion (FI) agenda. This financialization of remittances (FOR) represents a shift from earlier paradigms referred to as the "remittance-based development model" (Delgado Wise and Marquez, 2007) or the "global remittance trend" (Kunz, 2011), whereby remittances no longer necessarily contribute to development per se but need to be financialized to do so (Kunz, Maisenbacher and Paudel, 2020). As part of the FOR, various international, governmental, nongovernmental and private actors promote the formalization, digitalization and securitization of remittances (Guermond, 2014; Hudson, 2008; Kunz, 2012). Remittance senders and receivers are targeted with financial education programs and financial services to encourage them to spend more time managing personal finance, risk management and planning for the future. The overall objective of the FOR is to promote the "productive" investment of remittances in financial products to promote FI and development.

One key feature of the FOR is its explicit emphasis on empowering women and reducing gender inequality through linking remittances to FI (Kunz and Maisenbacher, 2021). While earlier forms of the remittances-based development agenda mostly ignored gender equality but implicitly drew on and reproduced gender dynamics (Kunz, 2011), the FOR portrays and targets women who send and receive remittances as financial customers, untapped resources and entrepreneurs. These FOR gender tropes are embedded in two broader global agendas: the "gender as smart economics" and the FI agenda (Kunz and Maisenbacher, 2021). Yet, in the emerging literature analyzing the manifestations and implications of the

DOI: 10.4324/9781003036425-6

FOR, gender dimensions of the FOR have not yet received much attention (for exceptions, see Kunz, 2018; Mullings, 2014).

In this chapter, we contribute to addressing this gap through an analysis of the FOR in the context of Mexico. In the first part, we present the FOR in Mexico, based on an analysis of major documents, websites, advertising and information material, and newspaper articles related to key governmental, nongovernmental and financial institutions (published after 2008, around which the FOR emerged). We identify three main gendered FOR imperatives: the formalization imperative, the financial products imperative and the entrepreneurial imperative. In the second part, we focus on how women remittance senders and receivers interpret experience, manage and resist these FOR imperatives in various creative ways.

We draw on research that includes observation and interviews with women receiving and sending remittances from a community in the state of Puebla. During 2019–2020, we conducted in-depth interviews with 21 women in the age range from 30 to 60 years: 4 return migrants, 13 remittance recipients and 4 women with both sending and receiving experience.[3] We selected our respondents randomly during our visits to the community and through snowballing. We focus on women in Puebla as they have been targeted in particular ways through FOR policies (Kunz and Ramírez, 2021). Puebla is among the top six emigration and receiver states in Mexico: in 2017, it was the destination of US $1558 million in remittances (BBVA and CONAPO, 2018, p. 128). It has developed various policies targeting Mexicans living in the US and return migrants, which makes it a particularly interesting site to study the FOR and its gender dimensions (Marchand et al., 2017; Marchand and Ramírez, 2019; Buznego, Lee and Pérez, 2020).

The selected community is one of the 17 *juntas auxiliares*[4] of the municipality of Puebla and has a high level of marginalization and a not-too-distant agricultural past. Since the 1980s, in just three decades, the percentage of the population from this community employed in the primary sector has dropped from 88.8 percent to 25.3 percent. Meanwhile, employment in the secondary sector has increased from 2.0 percent in the 1980s to 50.8 percent in 2000. Of the total population, around 7 percent are in formal employment (as compared to 54.98 percent for the city of Puebla). Most people work in the informal sector, mostly in the retail trade sector, but also in the service and manufacturing sectors. Based on our observations, most of the women in the community are working as domestic workers in nearby communities, and the men as construction workers in nearby construction sites. The community has a long tradition of emigration, embedded in broader migration patterns from central Mexico, and in particular the state of Puebla, toward destinations such as Chicago, New York, Atlanta and more recently toward the East Coast (D'Aubeterre Buznego and Rivermar, 2015). Recent urbanization trends have accelerated the emigration from the community, both to urban centers and toward the US.

For our analysis, we combine insights from three strands of literature. First, critical finance scholars highlight the contradictions and limits of financialization and FI agendas (Bernards, 2016; Loomis, 2018; Mader, 2018; Wichterich, 2017; Zanotelli, 2013). They emphasize that the FI agenda is a "contested enterprise" and challenge key assumptions underlying this agenda, such as "poor people gain poverty alleviation through financial inclusion" and "financial inclusion is good business" (Mader, 2018, p. 461). In the case of Mexico, anthropologist Bazán (2018, p. 163) argues that financial inclusion does not necessarily imply social inclusion, challenging public policies and private initiatives to encourage financial inclusion without really understanding the needs, habits and strategies of low-income populations. A few studies also focus on resistance to financialization and FI, documenting the activities of "unwilling subjects of financialization" (Fields, 2017; Forsberg and Stockenstrand, 2014; Kutz, 2018; Montgomerie and Tepe-Belfrage, 2019). The second source of inspiration is the literature on the migration-development nexus and the financialization of remittances (Kunz, Maisenbacher and Paudel, 2020; Rodriguez and Schwenken, 2013; Zapata, 2013; Guermond, 2020). This literature analyzes the ways in which migrants and their families experience, negotiate and resist the various imperatives established for them, such as the "good migrant" (Findlay et al., 2013; Rodriguez and Schwenken, 2013) or the "transnational financial subject" (Zapata, 2013). Third, we draw on the feminist literature analyzing the gendered dimensions of FI and financial subjectivity creation (Joseph, 2013; Maclean, 2013; Roy, 2012). This literature shows, for example, that financial education programs destined to overcome women's reluctance to become financially included promote "gendered notions of morality and respectability" on how to become "good financial citizens" (Loomis, 2018, p. 2).

So far, few studies center the narratives and experiences of embodied, gendered subjects to examine the ways in which they negotiate and resist these imperatives of the FOR. One exception is Guermond's (2020) analysis of the contestation of the FOR in the context of Ghana and Senegal, which shows how transnational families engage in various individual and collective "acts of refusal" to resist financialization through a rich "repertoire of reluctance, refusal, and dissent." Such empirical research is crucial if we are to listen to and learn from the experiences of what we term "subjects-to-be-financialized" and to understand the lived realities of financialization. These insights also contribute to a better understanding of the limits and fragile nature of financialization processes. Our analysis shows how women subjects-to-be-financialized resist FI and prefer to follow their own complex financial strategies. Their experiences and insights challenge basic assumptions of the FOR, revealing its temporary and nonlinear character, challenging its dichotomous approach to FI, and destabilizing the idea that FI is necessary for empowerment or necessarily empowering.

The gendered FOR imperatives in Mexico

Mexico ranks third among remittance-receiving countries (US$35.7 billion in 2018) (World Bank and KNOMAD, 2019), and remittances are one of the country's largest sources of foreign exchange and help cover the living expenses of millions of Mexicans (Labastida Tovar et al., 2014). In the Mexican context, only about 14.5 percent of remittances are sent through banks, the majority are transferred through nonbanking institutions and collected at a store, or money transfer operator, and 94.1 percent of remittances are handled in cash (BBVA and CONAPO, 2018, pp. 134–135). Mexico also ranks quite low on FI: the 2017 Global Financial Inclusion Index of the World Bank indicates that only 23 percent (17 percent in rural areas) of the Mexican population reports using mobile money, a debit or credit card, or a cell phone to make payments from an account or internet banking, and only 5.55 percent of the Mexican population had a mobile money account (3.95 percent in rural areas). Around 21 percent reported not having a financial institution account because financial institutions are too far away (cited in Cruz-García, Macedo and Tortosa-Ausina, 2020). This has prompted the Mexican government and financial institutions to emphasize the need to provide financial education and financial services, in particular to migrants and their families, in order to use remittances more efficiently and to include them in the formal financial system (Comité de Educacion Financiera, 2017).[5, 6]

The FOR in the context of Mexico manifests in a number of gendered ways. It resonates with the gender tropes in the international context that portray women who send and receive remittances as ideal financial customers, untapped resources and entrepreneurs (Kunz and Maisenbacher, 2021). This FI, through remittances, aims to empower women and to improve the economic situation of women and their families and communities. This agenda presupposes that including women in the formal financial system will push them to abandon informal financial practices and institutions that are widely used in many contexts. Thus, the FOR in Mexico invokes women sending and receiving remittances as subjects-to-be-financialized through remittances. This manifests in three FOR imperatives, understood as guidance to shape the being and behaving of women who send and receive remittances.

First, people sending and receiving remittances are encouraged to use formal transfer mechanisms. This formalization imperative is embedded in the broader FI agenda that aims to extend financial services to those traditionally excluded from the mainstream financial system to bank the unbanked (Weber, 2004; Rankin, 2013). In the context of the FOR, this is combined with the targeting of women as a particularly financially excluded group, drawing on preexisting targeting strategies within microcredit schemes. Thereby, the expansion and deepening of finance is understood as a way to lead the global economy out of recession while simultaneously addressing the problem of gender inequality. FI is linked to broader global tendencies of the financialization of everyday life, for example, the increasing importance of finance in people's lives and the growing role of debt in financing social reproduction (Rankin, 2013, p. 549). Remittance policies play a crucial role in FI and financialization processes: gendered narratives and policies target women who send and receive remittances to include them into the global financial architecture through remittances, for example, through microcredit initiatives or subprime mortgage lending (Kunz, 2018). Similarly, in the context of Mexico, remittances are seen as "an opportunity for financial inclusion" (BBVA, 2018). The National Financial Inclusion Policy promotes the use of formal financial services to underserved populations, such as women and Mexicans living abroad (CONAIF, 2016, pp. 29–30). It emphasizes the need for financially including remittance senders and receivers, as the majority of remittances are sent informally or through electronic transfers and the rate of integration of migrants and their families into the formal banking system remains low. An estimated 68 percent of Mexicans living in the US and 34 percent of remittance-receiving households have bank accounts, but only 28 percent of these coincide in both ends having a bank account (CONAIF, 2018, p. 135).

One key strategy of FI is financial education programs. The National Strategy for Financial Education mentions the need to provide financial education to migrants and their families to use remittances more efficiently (Comité de Educacion Financiera, 2017). The government institution Instituto de los Mexicanos en el Exterior (IME)[7] and its state- and municipal-level equivalents work both in the US (through Mexican consulates) and in Mexico to provide financial education and services to transnational families. On the government internet portal for financial education (EDUFIN),[8] migrants are targeted as one particular group in need of financial education. Other policies promoting the formalization imperative include the *Directo a México* program that was launched in 2005 by the Federal Reserve Bank and the Banco de México to incorporate Mexican migrants in the US and their families in Mexico into the formal financial system (Bakker, 2015, p.163).[9] This agenda was also reinforced by the linking of remittances, sending and receiving to the bank accounts opened through the social welfare program PROSPERA.[10] This conditional cash transfer scheme provided money to "poor" households—mostly women who made up 96 percent of beneficiaries—in exchange for regular school attendance of children and periodic health check-ups of household members (Luccisano, 2006, p.67). While initially support was paid in cash, the program later delivered the money to savings accounts. These electronic payments were understood to be "the first entry point for the poor into the financial system" and to provide them with options for "risk management and investment portfolios" (Masino and Niño-Zarazúa, 2018, p. 5). The FOR linked into this strategy by encouraging migrants to remit through transfer to the bank accounts of PROSPERA beneficiaries, which creates an imperative for women to receive remittances through formal financial channels, to acquire financial products and to get financially included through remittances.

Second, the FOR creates an imperative for women receiving remittances to open a bank account, save part of the money they receive and acquire other formal financial products, such as credits or insurances. In the context of Mexico, various governments and financial institutions contribute to this imperative. As mentioned, the government encouraged PROSPERA beneficiaries to use their accounts for remittance reception and to acquire remittance-linked financial products. In another attempt, AMUCSS (Asociación Mexicana de Uniones de Crédito del Sector Social), an NGO with longstanding experience in the field of rural microfinance, aimed to provide financial services in marginalized rural and indigenous communities to increase the saving and investing of remittances (Ambrosius, Fritz and Stiegler, 2014, p. 743). In 2008, it established Envíos Confianza to facilitate remittance transfers to such communities and promote financial education.[11] In partnership with the Inter-American Dialogue and supported by the Western Union Foundation, it carried out a financial literacy project in 2013 "to attract the informal savings of remittance recipients into the formal sector by intercepting remittance recipients as they left AMUCSS with their money" (Inter-American Dialogue, 2014).[12]

This strategy of exerting pressure at the collection point to encourage women to save or acquire financial products is widely practiced in the context of the community where we conducted our research and was experienced by all our respondents. For example, one financial cooperative offers remittance-receiving services without commission only up to a certain amount, past which people need to become a member and open a savings account. During our observation at the cooperative branch in August 2019, we saw customers face an intense campaign to promote a saving culture: big posters advocate saving, for example, by encouraging people to reduce their consumption of sweets, sodas and alcohol. The local branch director reported: "Many women come here to collect their remittances, even cooperative members, and they don't save, so we invite them to save, we tell them: think of the future!" The staff of the cooperative exerts intense pressure on receivers, presenting the withdrawal of the full amount of remittances as normatively unacceptable and irresponsible.

Remittance receivers using banks face similar pressures, as our observation in a Banco Azteca branch in August 2019 shows. Banco Azteca was established in 2002 by Grupo Elektra, one of Mexico's largest retailers of electronics and household goods, and launched 815 branches in preexisting stores, targeting low- and middle-income customers, which comprise an estimated 70 percent of Mexican households (Bruhn and Love, 2014). This bank has low documentation requirements and is very popular among remittance receivers who combine picking up remittances with opening a savings account, contracting a credit or buying consumer products (mostly on credit)[13] from Elektra stores. Prices for products on credit are indicated in big letters across the store. Interest on Banco Azteca credits is relatively high (around 40 percent) but lower than other financial nonbank institutions. Once they have provided their contact details, our respondents report receiving frequent credit offers by SMS. When we entered the Banco Azteca branch to request information about the different possibilities for receiving remittances, we were immediately directed to an executive who asked us to provide our personal details and present documents to open an account. The option of receiving remittances without opening an account was not even mentioned. This illustrates the FOR imperative that aims to shape women's financial behavior to open a bank account to receive and save remittances.

Relatedly, the third FOR imperative encourages women to acquire credits linked to remittances and to become entrepreneurs and open (small) businesses. Thereby, in resonance with the global agenda promoting women's entrepreneurship, women remittance receivers are targeted as ideal clients and micro-entrepreneurs. Thus, various financial institutions involved in remittance transfer operations also offer business credits. Financial institutions and NGOs offer financial education and business training courses that aim to shape people's financial behavior toward responsible risk-taking and entrepreneurship. In the context of the FOR, such initiatives target migrants and remittance receivers. In the community where we conducted research, there are various such initiatives underway that aim to financially educate women receiving remittances and offer business training courses to receivers and return migrants (Interview with financial education and business training facilitator, October 2019). The idea is that financially educated people will become financially included through bank accounts and other financial services and that business training will foment an entrepreneurial spirit, push people to obtain credits for a small business, and thereby promote jobs, economic well-being and growth in the community. Mexican government institutions also contribute to this FOR imperative. For example, the Puebla state government institution Instituto Poblano de Atención a Migrantes (IPAM) offers business education and skills training for women with migrant spouses to develop their own microbusiness.

However, in the context of the FOR in Mexico, government and financial institutions portray women's microbusinesses often in instrumental ways as contributing to the well-being of the family and the children. Women receivers are understood as "marginal entrepreneurs" with small businesses that improve well-being, whereas men migrants are associated with successful businesses that provide income (Kunz and Ramírez, 2021). Broader microfinance policies in Mexico also reflect this: women are more often targeted with group rather than individual credit. They represent 99 percent of group credit clients, as compared to 52 percent of individual credit of *ProDesarrollo* (CONAIF, 2018, p. 186). Group credits have been critiqued for their tendency to restrain women to marginal economic activities with low-profit rates and based on the household (Cruz, 2016).[14]

These three FOR imperatives push women to increasingly use formal financial instruments to send, receive, save and invest remittances, with the overall aim of contributing to the well-being of the children, the family and the community. Informal financial products and practices are discredited as risky, ineffective and illegitimate. This establishes a dichotomy between informal and formal finance. In order to move toward more FI, financial education programs are promoted. They are widely based on the assumption that "poor" people are financially illiterate and that more financial education for target groups, such as women and migrants, will bring them into formal finance. Thereby, the ideal process of FI is understood as a linear and durable shift from informal to formal finance. More broadly, FI is promoted as an instrument to empower women, to end discriminatory practices toward "unbanked" (and mostly female) populations by providing access to formal finance and specific remittance-linked financial products and to increase economic well-being and business success. We now move to explore how women experience and manage these imperatives of the FOR.

Negotiating and resisting the gendered FOR imperatives

The women we spoke with experience and deal with FOR imperatives in complex ways. Unsurprisingly, in our research, we did not meet any woman who followed the FOR imperatives to the letter. Instead, most respondents partially adopt, negotiate and resist these imperatives to become financially included through remittances in creative ways and develop their own financial strategies. In the process, they also challenge the assumptions and dichotomies established by the FOR.

The community where we carried out research is characterized by various financial institutions, both informal and formal. There is one formal financial institution that has a mixed reputation among the community members (see later). This institution allows people to withdraw remittances (up to a certain amount) and offers various financial services. Alongside, various informal financial credit providers, often called *prestamistas*, offer loans at relatively high rates but with low access requirements. Several women in the community have been hired by these informal institutions as local credit promoters (Interview with microcredit promoter, May 2019). There are also a number of loan sharks (*agiotistas*) who offer loans at extremely high rates (we heard up to 110 percent) (Interview with financial institution, April 2019). All these financial institutions target remittance receivers and senders in various ways to nudge them to formalize their financial practices and acquire financial products. Finally, there are numerous and very popular *tandas*, a form of rotating credit and savings associations (ROSCAs) (Bazán 2018; Campos, 1998). ROSCAs exist globally and are "association(s) formed upon a core of participants who agree to make regular contributions to a fund which is given, in whole or in part, to each contributor in rotation" (Ardener, 1964, p. 201). In the case of Mexico, *tandas* are frequently used by low-income households (Bazán, 2018). In the community where we carried out research, *tandas* consist of a group of community members who organize to regularly contribute a certain amount of money at an agreed date. At the beginning, they generate a raffle to determine the turn in which each member will receive the total sum of the money collected until that date. From the beginning, each participant knows the date on which they will receive the sum of payments so they can plan how to spend the money (which sometimes contributes to essential expenses of the family). As Bazán (2018) explains, *tandas* can be used as a loan for those who receive the sums of money at the beginning of the rotation cycle or as a form of savings for those situated toward the end of the rotation cycle. Based on our observations in the community, *tandas* were mostly used by women, but there were also some mixed groups. All our respondents have participated in *tandas* several times.

Formalization imperative

As studies for the context of Mexico show, the percentage of remittances sent through banks is very low (only about 14.5 percent), and 94.1 percent of remittances are handled in cash (BBVA and CONAPO, 2018, pp. 134–135). This was also the case in the community where we conducted our research in 2019: most of our respondents do not use bank accounts to send and receive remittances. They either send money in cash through a relative or through the post (*paqueterías*), or they use money transfer services that do not require opening an account and allow receivers to withdraw the full amount in cash (Interview with Ruben, *paqueteria* worker, April 2019). Some women open an account with a formal financial institution to receive remittances but use it mostly to withdraw in cash or close it after some time.

Our respondents mentioned several reasons for refusing to use formal financial services or only using them temporarily. Given that economic life in the community is based on cash, many of our respondents do not see the need to have an account. Several other women temporarily opened a bank account during the period of receiving or sending remittances, only to close it after the end of the migration experience. For example, when asked about why she opened a bank account, Magali explains:

> Well, because it was a lot of money and we could not keep it in the house, it was not a huge amount, but it was some money, that's why my husband decided to keep it (in the bank), and when he returned he withdrew it all, and bought his things … land.

Similarly, after the return of her husband from the US, Rosa decided she no longer needed an account, given that most of her daily financial practice happens in cash:

> No, not anymore, I had an account when my husband was in the US, but since he no longer sends me money and as I told you I don't save … well not now. In any case, the expenses that I have or the payments that the people make for the dresses and everything is all in cash. Right now, I almost don't use banks.

Still another motive is the lack of trust in, or bad experiences with, formal financial institutions. This is not surprising, as Mexican financial institutions have a long history of discrimination against poorer populations, also linked to the banking and peso crisis of the 1990s (Zanotelli, 2013). This was reflected in our research: generally speaking, there is a lot of disappointment and frustration with formal financial institutions in this community. Many respondents complained about discriminatory treatment, lack of information or sometimes deliberate misinformation on behalf of financial representatives. For example, Rosa told us that when she opened a bank account, they did not explain to her how it works and she did not like the way she was treated, so she decided to close her account. Others had bad experiences with particular banks, whereby staff failed to give clear information regarding complex regulations or pushed clients to contract insurance policies, as Rosa explains:

> That was what I didn't like because, you know which was the only bank that didn't ask me for anything? At Bank X they just opened my account with 1000 pesos and my husband could deposit money for me normally but at Bank Y, I had to open my account with more than 2000, and 1000 were going to go to insurance, home insurance, car insurance, life insurance. Everything, we practically had to pay for everything.

Moreover, in the community where we carried out our research, there have been some problems with the local financial institutions where people lost their savings (Interview with Elena, May 2019). As a result, the institution has a relatively bad reputation among a part of the population, as various respondents told us. For example, Renata explains that she does not trust much in financial institutions: "Sometimes they disappear, or the accounts or the money."

Most of our respondents resist the FOR formalization imperative. Our interviews show that they refuse to have bank accounts or use them only temporarily. Refusing or moving away from formal financial institutions is a conscious choice of our respondents, who either do not trust or do not perceive a need for bank accounts (any longer). It is not, as is often suggested in the FOR discourse, that women refuse to become financially included because of financial illiteracy or based on irrational behavior. Instead, our interviews show that these are conscious, well-reflected, situated and experience-based choices. Most of our respondents perceive the informal financial sector as being closer to the community and more visible and "material" than formal financial institutions (see later). As a result, they trust informal institutions more. Some women consciously self-exclude from formal financial institutions and either move to cash, use informal financial institutions, such as *tandas*, or decide to buy land or livestock to save and invest their money. Others are themselves involved in informal finance as local promoters of informal credit institutions. Some also combine formal bank accounts and informal financial services, as we shall see later.

Financial products imperative

The FOR imperative to acquire financial products from formal financial institutions and save remittances is felt very strongly by most of our respondents. The strategy of exerting pressure at the remittance collection point to encourage women to save or acquire financial products is widely practiced in the context of the community and was experienced by all our respondents. This strategy to attract new customers and savings and create new markets is used by most formal financial institutions, for example, banks and financial cooperatives. As our respondents report:

> I really didn't like this ... the last time I went, they told me that I had to open an account otherwise, they could no longer send us money ... it's like they threatened us. Grandparents like my mother-in-law are going to collect their money there and they tell her that it is the last time they will give her money if she doesn't open an account, they will not be able to give her money.
>
> (Interview with Rosa, August 2019)

> For example, once when he sent me money, the bank wanted to take it from me for savings, credit, insurance ... and they wanted to leave me with nothing ... but as I told you when I saw that, I wanted to change bank because this didn't suit me.
>
> (Interview with Adriana, October 2019)

> In Bank A, oh forget it, they offered me insurance for the car, for the dog, for the house ... (laughs). Uff, imagine if I don't have (money) for myself, how would I have it for my dog (laughs)?
>
> (Interview with Socorro, October 2019)

In another example, Esperanza told us that after she had saved more than 50,000 pesos with the local financial institution, they started pressuring her to buy an insurance to guarantee the protection of her money. As a result, she decided to withdraw her money and invest it in a business. Many of our respondents have similar experiences and reactions. They do not see the need for financial products, do not trust the institutions or simply do not have the necessary money to deposit or pay interest. All of our respondents refused to contract insurance policies for these same reasons, as Rosa told us: "Insurance? Well, no, I don't trust insurance. I doubt that they are really going to give me money or that if I die, they will give it to my family." This echoes a study of the negative perception and widespread failure of microinsurance products in the context of rural Mexico that reports that most people are not interested in contracting microinsurance products (Sulmont, 2014).

For some women, saving is not an option due to a lack of income, as they use all their remittances for living expenses. For others, saving and opening a bank account is for "wealthy people," as Gabriela explained when we asked her whether she has a bank account: "No, no, because I have no money to put in, and no, I'm living by the day." Similarly, Magali told us: "Well, for those who have a lot of money, the bank is a good option ... and if they trust them, yes. But not for someone like me who is living by the day."

Some respondents give in to the pressure and open bank accounts and use formal financial instruments. But most do not really trust formal financial institutions and tread with utmost care when using financial services. Thus, for example, Adriana had a bad experience with a formal financial institution where she had an account. The procedures were not explained well to her, and when she started receiving remittances, they were deducted to pay the interest on her credit with the institution without her knowledge. After a while, she decided to close the account and only receive remittances. But given that there is a maximum sum of remittances that she could withdraw without having an account, she reopened an account in order to be able to receive remittances without having to travel. Adriana now leaves the minimum amount of savings necessary to keep her account open but withdraws all the rest of the remittance. She closely monitors the institution and refuses to contract other services, such as insurance or credit, even though she has received various offers. Thus, she chooses her financial products very strategically, based on her experience and knowledge.

An underlying assumption of the FOR saving imperative is that saving should happen in formal financial institutions. However, not having an account does not necessarily mean women do not save:

> I like to save my money, although I don't keep it in the bank, I like to keep my money, so it's there in case of an illness, or for a small pleasure, for anything you need to have some money saved, for an emergency.
>
> (Interview with Adriana, July 2019)

> No, well … I like to breed animals, for example, two cows or three, and when I see that they are ready, we sell them, and we can earn 20,000 or 15,000 depending on how the animal is.
>
> (Interview with Magali, October 2019)

> I think that *tandas* are better than loans. Because there (at financial institutions) they charge us interests and everything.
>
> (Interview with Rosa, August 2019)

As these quotes illustrate, many of our respondents save money through informal financial practices such as *tandas* or by investing in land or livestock. Thus, saving is not necessarily linked to inclusion in the formal financial system. Some women also combine various informal and formal financial practices either simultaneously or over time, depending on their economic situation, needs and time availability. Esperanza explained her saving strategy as follows: "Well, when I don't have any loan from bank Z, I participate in *tandas*. I invest like 200 pesos from me and 200 from my husband."

For many respondents, the key criteria for placing their money are "visibility" and "accessibility": they want to have easy access to their money and see it invested in something tangible and visible, which is not a bank account number (Interview with Asunción, May 2019). This is the reason why most of our respondents are engaged in *tandas* and sometimes in various *tandas* simultaneously. Contrary to the FOR imperative that discredits *tandas* as risky, illegitimate and inefficient, our respondents see various advantages in *tandas*' accessibility, relative flexibility (when compared to fixed commitments in the formal financial sector) and the possibility to save small amounts. They also mentioned that *tandas* are a collective endeavor, where people who decide to participate in a *tanda* commit to pay their share based on a sense of responsibility toward neighbors and the community. This resonates with Zanotelli's (2013) study of women's participation in *tandas* in rural Western Mexico. He finds that women use their participation in *tandas* as a form of "strategically diversified indebtedness" that allows them to create "new conditions for power negotiation" in the household and the community (Zanotelli, 2013, pp. 193–194). Thereby, *tandas* are understood as a form of freeing oneself from social dependence through collectivity and "the multiplication and differentiation of relations of dependency," rather than through the "individually conceived autonomy of a liberal model of citizenship" (Zanotelli, 2013, p. 193).

Our respondents also deplored that saving through bank accounts yields very little interest. Moreover, banks' saving conditions are sometimes not totally clear to them. As a result, they prefer *tandas* because they know that at the end of a certain period, they will receive a specific amount of money that is visible and that they can invest in a particular project. None of our respondents had bad experiences; they select their *tandas* very carefully. Yet, they are aware of the potential risks of *tandas* and reported hearing about fraudulent *tandas*. [15] Our respondents did not report feeling guilty or shameful for using *tandas*. On the contrary, they told us that they are aware of the risks associated with *tandas*, but in their opinion, it is the government that does not understand their situation and financial needs and strategies (Interview with Karla, October 2019). Our interviews show that the women did not let themselves be conditioned by the discrediting of *tandas* that the FOR imperative attempts to install.

Overall, while some of our respondents follow the FOR imperative to open bank accounts to save money and to consume other financial products linked to remittances, most either refuse to do so or do so only periodically. Some women also use bank accounts very strategically to allow them to continue most of their financial practices in cash, always with the underlying aim of taking the money out. This partial and temporary FI of some of our respondents does not mean that they abandon informal financial practices; on the contrary, most of them combine informal and formal financial practices. And again, they do so in strategic ways based on their experience and their plans. Based on our interviews, women save mostly informally. Several women also told us stories of how they used *tandas* to realize their projects, for example, to open a small business.

Entrepreneurial imperative

The entrepreneurial imperative of the FOR encourages women to contract credits and other financial products linked to remittances and to open (small) businesses. Various informal and formal financial institutions offer business credits to migrants and remittance receivers. Many of our respondents constantly receive and refuse formal credit or insurance offers:

> Bank M is always sending messages ... as I've emigrated they offer me a credit for up to 40,000 pesos because I used to be a client there ... But I don't respond. Sometimes they are bothering me two or three times per week, but I don't give in.
>
> (Interview with Josselin, July 2019)

Financial literacy and business training also form part of the FOR entrepreneurial imperative. Most of our respondents refuse to participate in such training. Some of the women we interviewed had their own small businesses but did not wish to participate in training. They told us that with their workload in the household and the business, they do not have time to attend training (Interview with Renata, August 2019). Other women do not trust the institutions offering the training; they prefer to trust their own business experience and knowledge (Interview with Magali, October 2019). Still, other respondents had bad experiences with women's group-credit businesses and decided to part ways with formal financial institutions and continue their entrepreneurial activities through informal financial institutions, such as *tandas* (Interview with Claudia, August 2019).

Some of our respondents reported having participated in such training. Yet none of them accepted a start-up credit offered by the training institution to start a business. They considered it either too risky or too low of an amount to start a real business. Or they simply preferred to invest their savings instead of financing their business through credit. They wanted to make sure to have enough money to start their businesses rather than assuming huge debts that might turn out to be unmanageable (Interviews with Rosa, August 2019; Adriana, July 2019; and Esperanza, October 2019). Yet, many financial institutions push women to take credits rather than use savings for investing in their businesses. For example, Esperanza told us that when she wanted to withdraw her savings from the local financial institutions, the bank representative tried to convince her to take a credit instead of using her savings. This illustrates the attempts by financial institutions to link people to banks and foment a culture of credit and indebtedness, with the aim of financially including them. Adriana went through business training but refused to take a credit and open a bank account, successfully resisting this pressure. She is the owner of a successful business and not just a microbusiness: she has a liquor store and a clothes shop and is also renting out three commercial properties.[16] She participates in *tandas* and even acts as a *tanda* organizer. When asked whether she accepted to contract a credit following her participation in the business training, she responded:

> No, no, I just took the training. We opened this business four years ago but then we took a break because we had rented a place. Later, when he started sending money, we built this store that I now have, that was two years ago.
>
> (Interview with Adriana, July 2019)

Rosa, a return migrant, is also a successful entrepreneur with three small businesses in the community (two in the food sector and a tailor shop). She used the money she earned in the US and the remittances she received from her husband as well as *tanda* money to finance her business. Based on her bad experiences with banks and informal credit institutions, she decided to completely withdraw from all formal financial institutions. She now holds neither bank accounts nor credit; she has decided to remain financially excluded yet is a very successful entrepreneur doing all her transactions in cash. She has an explicit strategy for managing her finances, for example, by saving money in particular categories (some for herself, some for her children and so on). And she continues to invest in *tandas*. When asked about whether she trusts *tandas*, she replied:

> Yes, well it depends on who gets into the *tandas*. [...] The first time, I bought a machine because they gave me about 7,000 pesos. The second time, I don't remember what I invested in, but as we were building at the time, I think I invested in buying one of these displays. But *tandas* do work because they don't charge us interest and it's a way of saving.
>
> (Interview with Rosa, August 2019)

Thus, our interviews show that women's entrepreneurship can be funded through both formal and informal sources. Some women did participate in business training but refused to become financially included through a formal credit offered after the training. This challenges the underlying assumption of the FOR that entrepreneurship and small businesses necessarily need to be funded through formal credit. It also challenges the assumption that successful entrepreneurship rhymes with FI. As some of our respondents demonstrate, women establish successful businesses without being financially included. Moreover, there seems to be an implicit assumption within the FOR that to open a business, you need remittances. Yet, the experiences of some of our respondents show that they did not necessarily use remittances to establish their businesses. Instead, they used other funding sources, such as money saved through *tandas*.

Finally, our research shows that financially including people through credits does not necessarily contribute to increasing their well-being but ends up throwing people into over-indebtedness. Even though none of our respondents directly experienced this, during our research, they told us about several relatives and friends who received remittances or returned from migration and found themselves in situations of high indebtedness and economic hardship. Thus, they would be financially included through credits, but this did not mean increased economic well-being.

Conclusion

Women who send or receive remittances face various FOR imperatives that aim to turn them into subjects-to-be-financialized. These imperatives manifest in policies and practices that push women to use formal financial institutions for sending and receiving remittances, to follow financial literacy training and acquire formal financial products linked to remittances and to take business training to invest remittances in small businesses. Yet, most of our respondents refuse to use bank accounts and other financial services or use them in their own ways and resist credit and insurance offers. Their testimonies emphasize that the financial services proposed by formal financial institutions in this context do not meet their needs. Our respondents manage and resist FOR imperatives in various ways and prefer to follow their own financial strategies, experience and knowledge, defying the figure of the illiterate subject in need of financial education. Their choices are conscious and well-reflected.

First, our interviews challenge the assumption that linking FI to remittances is a linear and permanent process. Instead, we find that FI is a complex, messy, unstable and inherently temporary process. People who use bank accounts to send and receive remittances will not automatically remain financially included. Instead, the women we interviewed move in and out of financial inclusion or are simultaneously included and excluded in complex ways. Women might be included in formal finance through a bank account but experience exclusion through discrimination by formal financial institutions or through over-indebtedness. They experience attempts to financially include them as a form of constraint or violence and, as a result, decide to self-exclude from formal finance. Instead, they move to informal institutions or to a cash-only strategy based on previous experience and conscious decisions. Thus, financialization and de-financialization processes happen in close connection, and financial inclusion/exclusion takes various forms. This pushes us to move beyond dichotomous and fixed understandings of financial inclusion/exclusion toward a more cyclical understanding that focuses more on the quality of FI and financialization processes.

Second, the dichotomy between formal and informal financial practices central to the FOR and the FI agenda does not resonate with the experiences and accounts of the women we interviewed. Indeed, their experiences challenge conventional distinctions between formal and informal finance. For most respondents, these are intimately linked, and they combine various forms of financial practices in their lives, either simultaneously or over time. As we have seen, *tandas* are being used to pay interest rates on formal credits, or formal credit is invested in *tandas*. This happens either out of necessity and increasing indebtedness or out of conscious and well-informed choice. Our respondents are themselves involved as promoters of informal financial practices, such as informal credit providers or *tandas*.

Third, the FOR imperative promises economic well-being and empowerment for women, their families and communities through FI, based on the assumptions that FI is necessarily empowering and is necessary for empowerment. Yet, our interviews challenge these assumptions in various ways. On the one hand, FI does not always rhyme with economic well-being or successful business. Sometimes, women experienced FI as leading to high indebtedness, which prevented them from continuing their economic activities, pushed them to abandon formal finance, or threw them into hardship. Thus, they experience FI not necessarily as empowering, and many find participating in *tandas* more empowering than getting included in the formal financial system through a bank account or a credit. On the other hand, some of our respondents have opened and maintained successful businesses while remaining totally outside formal finance: instead of using bank accounts or credits, they finance their entrepreneurial activities through *tandas* and conduct all their business transactions in cash. Many women find there is a price to pay for being financially included, such as high indebtedness, and choose to opt out. They perceive being outside the formal financial system as a form of freedom: they do not have to feel guilty or worry about getting trapped in debt cycles or being taken advantage of. Listening to these insights and experiences exposes the limits, fragility and contradictions of the FOR and the broader FI agenda.

Notes

1 Special thanks go to the editors Marianne Marchand and Anne Sisson Runyan. We would also like to thank Julia Maisenbacher and Lekh Nath Paudel for very stimulating discussions in the context of our collaborative research project "The Financialisation of Remittances," https://www.unil.ch/crhim/en/home/menuinst/recherche/projets-en-cours/the-financialisation-of-remittances.html. Funding by the Swiss National Science Foundation (10001A_172945) is gratefully acknowledged.
2 Official numbers do not include "informal" remittances, thought to be substantial. Yet, the increase in official remittances figures is also influenced by the increased capacity to register such flows.
3 We would like to thank our interview partners. All interviews have been anonymized for confidentiality.
4 These are small towns, ranches or ejidos, and even municipalities that were absorbed by the city and now form part of the metropolitan urban area. See http://www.pueblacapital.gob.mx/guia-general/185-gobierno/2018-juntas-auxiliares-del-municipio-de-puebla.
5 We refer to formal financial institutions as those under the regulation of the National Banking and Securities Commission. According to the 2018 Mexican *National Survey of Financial Inclusion,* informal financial practices refer to "money stored in the house, with a relative or through mechanisms such as bundles, piggy banks or unauthorized institutions." See http://en.www.inegi.org.mx/app/glosario/default.html?p=enif2018.
6 Financial inclusion presents large profit opportunities for the financial sector. The Center for Financial Inclusion estimates that "full [financial] inclusion could contribute a potential of 6 to 8.5 million US dollars in the [Mexican] financial sector" (quoted in Bazán, 2018, p. 146).
7 See https://www.gob.mx/ime.
8 See https://www.edufinmexico.gob.mx/indexgobmx.php.
9 See http://www.directoamexico.com/.
10 Progresa was launched in August 1997 and renamed Oportunidades in 2001 then PROSPERA in 2010. By the end of 2015, the program supported 6.1 million households living in poverty, 25 percent of Mexico's population (Masino and Niño-Zarazúa, 2018, pp. 1–2). The program was suspended in 2019.
11 See https://www.amucss.org/index.php/acercade.
12 This project provided financial counseling to over 9,000 people, of which 25 percent acquired a financial product (e.g., insurance or credit) and approximately 40 percent planned on using new savings methods. See https://www.ilo.org/dyn/migpractice/migmain.showPractice?p_lang=en&p_practice_id=115.
13 Some 70 percent of Elektra's merchandise is sold on credit (Smith, 2003).
14 For an extended critique of microcredit in Mexico, see Bazán (2018).

15 Esperanza shared with us the experience of her brother and his partner who experienced *tanda*-related fraud. The organizers of this *tanda* came from outside the community and disappeared after a few payments. Her brother had taken a loan from a financial institution to pay for the *tanda* and ended up with a growing debt and had to ask for money from their relatives and sell his land (Interview with Esperanza, October 2019).

16 It is important to note that women's entrepreneurship does not necessarily rhyme with women's empowerment. Yet, it goes beyond the scope of this chapter to engage with this debate.

References

Ambrosius, C., Fritz, B. and Stiegler, U. (2014) "Remittances for financial access: Lessons from Latin American microfinance," *Development Policy Review*, 32(6), pp. 733–753. doi:10.1111/dpr.12087.

Ardener, S. (1964) "The comparative study of rotating credit associations," *The Journal of the Royal Anthropological Institute of Great Britain and Ireland*, 94(2), p. 201. doi:10.2307/2844382.

Bakker, M. (2015) *Migrating Into Financial Markets: How Remittances Became a Development Tool*. Oakland: University of California Press.

Bazán, L. (2018) "Microfinanzas ¿ para abatir la pobreza? Desencuentros entre instituciones microfinancieras y practicas fiancieras populares," in de la Rocha, Mercedes González, and Saraví, Gonzalo Andrés (eds.), *Pobreza y vulnerabilidad: debates y estudios contemporáneos en México*. Mexico City: CIESAS.

BBVA. (2018) *Remesas: una oportunidad de inclusión financiera en México*. Available at https://www.bbva.com/es/remesas-oportunidad-inclusion-financiera-mexico/ (accessed June 24, 2019).

BBVA and CONAPO. (2018) *Anuario de Migración y Remesas México 2018*. p. 184. Available at https://www.bbvaresearch.com/wp-content/uploads/2018/09/1809_AnuarioMigracionRemesas_2018.pdf (accessed June 24, 2019).

Bernards, N. (2016) "The International Labour Organization and the ambivalent politics of financial inclusion in West Africa," *New Political Economy*, 21(6), pp. 606–620. doi:10.1080/13563467.2016.1183115.

Bruhn, M. and Love, I. (2014) "The real impact of improved access to finance: Evidence from Mexico: Impact of access to finance on poverty," *The Journal of Finance*, 69(3), pp. 1347–1376. doi:10.1111/jofi.12091.

Buznego, M.E.D., Lee, A.E. and Rivermar, M.L. (2020) *Class, Gender and Migration: Return Flows between Mexico and the United States in Times of Crisis*. London: Routledge.

Campos, P. (1998) "Las tandas en México: un enfoque de acción colectiva," *Sociológica*, 13(37), Universidad Autónoma Metropolitana Unidad Azcapotzalco, pp.189–212.

Comité de Educacion Financiera. (2017) *Estrategia Nacional de Educación Financiera*. Available at https://www.gob.mx/cms/uploads/attachment/file/254597/Estrategia_Nacional_de_Educacio_n_Financiera 002.pdf (accessed July 18, 2019).

CONAIF. (2016) *Reporte Nacional de Inclusion Financiera*. Available at https://www.gob.mx/cms/uploads/attachment/file/190321/PNIF.pdf (accessed July 26, 2019).

CONAIF. (2018) *Reporte Nacional de Inclusion Financiera*. Available at https://www.cnbv.gob.mx/Inclusi%C3%B3n/Documents/Reportes%20de%20IF/Reporte%20de%20Inclusion%20Financiera%209.pdf (accessed July 18, 2019).

Cruz, I. (2016) *Los diarios financieros, la inclusión financiera y las remesas de México.* Available at https://www.elfinanciero.com.mx/opinion/isabel-cruz/los-diarios-financieros-la-inclusion-financiera-y-las-remesas-de-mexico (accessed August 6, 2019).

Cruz-García, P., Macedo, M. del C.D.P. and Tortosa-Ausina, E. (2020) *What drives financial exclusion in Mexican municipalities?* Working Paper 19, Universitat Jaume I. Available at: http://www.doctreballeco.uji.es/wpficheros/Cruz_et_al_19_2020.pdf (accessed August 6, 2019).

D'Aubeterre Buznego, M.E. and Rivermar, M.L. (2015) "Flujos migratorios tardíos y retornos en el estado de Puebla," in D'Aubeterre Buznego, M.E. and Rivermar, M.L. (eds.). *Lo que dejamos atrás ... Lo que vinimos a encontrar. Trabajo precario, nuevos patrones de asentamiento en Estados Unidos y retorno a México.* Mexico: BUAP.

Delgado Wise, R. and Marquez, H. (2007) "Migration and development in Mexico: Toward a new analytical approach," *Journal of Latino/Latin American Studies*, 2(3), pp.101–119.

Fields, D. (2017) "Unwilling subjects of financialization," *International Journal of Urban and Regional Research*, 41(4), pp. 588–603. doi:10.1111/1468-2427.12519.

Findlay, A., McCollum, D., Shubin, S., Apsite, E. and Krisjane, Z. (2013) "The role of recruitment agencies in imagining and producing the 'good' migrant," *Social & Cultural Geography*, 14(2), pp. 145–167. doi:10.1080/14649365.2012.737008.

Forsberg, P. and Stockenstrand, A.-K. (2014) "Resistance to financialization: Insights about collective resistance through distancing and persistence from two ethnographic studies," *Journal of Organizational Ethnography*, 3(2), pp.169–187. doi:10.1108/JOE-05-2013-0009.

Guermond, V. (2014) *Financialising Remittances: Exploring the Causes and Consequences (I).* Available at http://www.columnf.com/financialising-remittances-exploring-the-causes-and-consequences-i/ (accessed January 15, 2016).

Guermond, V. (2020) "Contesting the financialisation of remittances: Repertoires of reluctance, refusal and dissent in Ghana and Senegal," *Environment and Planning A: Economy and Space*, 54(4). doi:10.1177/0308518X20976141.

Hudson, D. (2008) "Developing geographies of financialisation: Banking the poor and remittance securitisation," *Contemporary Politics*, 14(3), pp. 315–333. doi:10.1080/13569770802396360.

Inter-American Dialogue. (2014) *Financial Literacy in Mexico.* Available at https://www.ilo.org/dyn/migpractice/docs/185/Handout.pdf (accessed July 18, 2019).

Joseph, M. (2013) "Gender, entrepreneurial subjectivity, and pathologies of personal finance. social politics: International studies in gender," *State & Society*, 20(2), pp. 242–273. doi:10.1093/sp/jxt009.

Kunz, R. (2011) *The Political Economy of Global Remittances: Gender, Governmentality and Neoliberalism.* London: Routledge.

Kunz, R. (2012) "Remittances," *Academic Foresights*, 6. Available at http://www.academic-foresights.com/Remittances.pdf (accessed September 12, 2016).

Kunz, R. (2018) "Remittances in Global Political Economy," in Elias, J. and Roberts, A. (eds.), *Handbook on the International Political Economy of Gender.* Handbooks of Research on International Political Economy. Cheltenham, UK: Edward Elgar, pp. 265–280. Available at https://www.elgaronline.com/view/edcoll/9781783478835/9781783478835.00027.xml.

Kunz, R. and Maisenbacher, J. (2021) "Gender and Remittances," in Mora, C. and Piper, N. (eds.), *The Palgrave Handbook of Gender and Migration.* Cham: Palgrave Macmillan. doi:10.1007/978-3-030-63347-9.

Kunz, R., Maisenbacher, J. and Paudel, L.N. (2020) "The financialization of remittances: governing through emotions," *Review of International Political Economy*, pp. 1–25. doi:10.1080/09692290.2020.1785923.

Kunz, R. and Ramírez, B. (2021) "'Cambiando el chip': The gendered constellation of subjectivities of the financialisation of remittances in Mexico," *Environment and Planning A: Economy and Space*, 54(24), pp. 779–799. doi:10.1177/0308518X211006110.

Kutz, W. (2018) "Financialization interrupted: Unwilling subjects of housing reform in Morocco," *City*, 22(4), pp. 568–583. doi:10.1080/13604813.2018.1507109.

Labastida Tovar, M.E., Ortiz de Zarate, A., Pavon, L.I. and Tacujan, P. (2014) "Financial inclusion, mobile banking, and remittances in Mexico and the Philippines," *Journal of Political Risk*, 2(1). http://www.jpolrisk.com/financial-inclusion-mobile-banking-and-remittances-in-mexico-and-the-philippines/.

Loomis, J.M. (2018) "Rescaling and reframing poverty: Financial coaching and the pedagogical spaces of financial inclusion in Boston, Massachusetts," *Geoforum*, 95, pp. 143–152. doi:10.1016/j.geoforum.2018.06.014.

Luccisano, L. (2006) "The Mexican *Oportunidades* program: Questioning the linking of security to conditional social investments for mothers and children," *Canadian Journal of Latin American and Caribbean Studies*, 31(62), pp. 53–85. doi:10.1080/08263663.2006.10816902.

Maclean, K. (2013) "Gender, risk and micro-financial subjectivities," *Antipode*, 45(2), pp. 455–473. doi:10.1111/j.1467-8330.2012.01005.x.

Mader, P. (2018) "Contesting financial inclusion," *Development and Change*, 49(2), pp. 461–483. doi:10.1111/dech.12368.

Marchand, M.H., Lee, A.E., Osorno Velázquez, R. del C. and Ramírez Contreras, B. (2017) *Agenda de Atención Inmediata para la atención de la población migrante del estado de Puebla: Mujeres migrantes de retorno en Puebla*. Cholula, Mexico: Instituto Nacional de las Mujeres, p. 91.

Marchand, M.H. and Ramírez, A.S.O. (2019) "Globalising cities at the crossroads of migration: Puebla, Tijuana and Monterrey," *Third World Quarterly*, 40(3), pp. 612–632. doi:10.1080/01436597.2018.1540274.

Masino, S. and Niño-Zarazúa, M. (2018) "Improving financial inclusion through the delivery of cash transfer programmes: The Case of Mexico's Progresa-Oportunidades-Prospera Programme," *The Journal of Development Studies*, pp. 1–18. doi:10.1080/00220388.2018.1546845.

Montgomerie, J. and Tepe-Belfrage, D. (2019) "Spaces of debt resistance and the contemporary politics of financialised capitalism," *Geoforum*, 98, pp. 309–317. doi:10.1016/j.geoforum.2018.05.012.

Mullings, B. (2014) "Neoliberalization gender and the rise of the diaspora option in Jamaica," in Oberhauser, A. and Johnston-Anumonwo, I. (eds.), *Global Perspectives on Gender and Space*. London and New York: Routledge, pp. 53–70. Available at https://scholar.google.com/scholar?hl=fr&as_sdt=0%2C5&q=neoliberalization+gender+and+the+rise+of+the+diapsora+optoion&btnG=.

Rankin, K.N. (2013) "A critical geography of poverty finance," *Third World Quarterly*, 34(4), pp. 547–568. doi:10.1080/01436597.2013.786282.

Rodriguez, R.M. and Schwenken, H. (2013) "Becoming a migrant at home: Subjectivation processes in migrant-sending countries prior to departure," *Population, Space and Place*, 19(4), pp. 375–388. doi:10.1002/psp.1779.

Roy, A. (2012) "Subjects of risk: Technologies of gender in the making of millennial modernity," *Public Culture*, 24(1), pp. 131–155. doi:10.1215/08992363-1498001.

Smith, G. (2003) *Buy a Toaster, Open a Bank Account: Banco Azteca caters to the little guy–in appliance stores*. Available at https://www.bloomberg.com/news/articles/2003-01-12/buy-a-toaster-open-a-bank-account (accessed July 28, 2019).

Sulmont, A. (2014) "La microassurance des familles transnationales: une fausse bonne idée," *Autrepart*, 67–68, pp. 247–263. http://www.cairn.info/resume.php?ID_ARTICLE=AUTR_067_0247.

Weber, H. (2004) "The 'new economy' and social risk: banking on the poor?" *Review of International Political Economy*, 11(2), pp. 356–386. doi:10.1080/09692290420001672859.

Wichterich, C. (2017) "Microcredits, Returns and Gender: Of Reliable Poor Women and Financial Inclusion in South Asia," in Xaxa, V., Saha, D. and Singha, R. (eds.), *Work, Institutions and Sustainable Livelihood*. Singapore: Springer Singapore, pp. 275–301. doi:10.1007/978-981-10-5756-4_11.

World Bank and KNOMAD. (2019) *Migration and Development Brief* 31. Washington, D.C: World Bank. Available at https://www.knomad.org/sites/default/files/2019-04/Migrationanddevelopmentbrief31.pdf (accessed January 14, 2020).

Zanotelli, F. (2013) "Multiplying debt and dependence: Gender strategies and the social risks of financial inclusion in Western Mexico," in Guérin, I., Morvant-Roux, S. and Villareal, M. (eds.), *Microfinance, Debt and Over-Indebtedness*. Abingdon, Oxon: Routledge, pp. 212–230.

Zapata, G.P. (2013) "The migration–development nexus: Rendering migrants as transnational financial subjects through housing," *Geoforum*, 47, pp. 93–102. doi:10.1016/j.geoforum.2013.03.010.

6 Restructuring, revolution and women's elusive economic empowerment

The case of Tunisia

Valentine M. Moghadam

Introduction

The Arab Spring, which began with protests in Tunisia in December 2010, initially raised expectations of democratic transitions, along with new social and gender contracts (Karshenas, Moghadam and Alami, 2014). Many studies attributed the structural causes of the protests to the fallout from two decades of neoliberalization, including rising prices, high unemployment and deteriorating public services (Achcar, 2013; Hanieh, 2013). Scholarship also noted the unprecedented presence of women protesters and the vocal and visible feminist demands in Tunisia (Charrad and Zarrugh, 2014; Khalil, 2014; Moghadam, 2013, 2020; Stephan and Charrad, 2020). Indeed, as the first country to experience the protests and the only one to embark on a celebrated but turbulent democratic transition (2011–2021), Tunisia is an instructive case study of the effects of economic restructuring and political revolution on women's empowerment.

Tunisia's legacy of "state feminism" and a dynamic civil society—including labor, human rights, student and feminist organizations—had long placed Tunisian women in advance of their Arab sisters, with women present across an array of professions and occupations. Despite frequent repression, political society included secular and left-wing parties. In the aftermath of the 2011 political revolution, Tunisian feminists worked with secular allies to prevent the legislative backsliding that newly empowered Islamists were planning. Women's parliamentary representation increased, and new laws and policies—including several constitutional articles—were adopted to strengthen and extend women's rights. Yet structural and institutional challenges prevented the full realization of women's welfare and rights.

One challenge was the dangerous neighborhood and especially the chaotic situation in post-"liberation" Libya following the 2011 NATO assault that ended the rule of Muammar Ghaddafi; this increased cross-border flows of arms and terrorists and compelled the Tunisian government to increase military spending (World Bank, 2017; Mako and Moghadam 2021, pp. 199–200).

A critical second challenge was the difficult economic environment, coupled with weak institutional support for working women, which continued to depress women's labor incorporation, prevent the availability of good jobs and

DOI: 10.4324/9781003036425-7

keep unemployment rates high. Tunisia may have been widely hailed as the one democratic success story of the Arab Spring, but the state struggled to respond to the people's socioeconomic grievances and demands. In particular, the various governments were unable to address the specific problems of the country's less privileged areas and social groups. Having occurred during the post-2008 Great Recession, Tunisia also experienced declining foreign investments, problems that were then compounded by the COVID-19 surges.

This points to the third challenge: the growing pains of the democratic transition. One feature of the country's political opening was the rise of Islamization, leaving Tunisian feminists and secularists struggling to maintain a political and social presence. Political polarization, along with the aforementioned economic difficulties and the absence of sufficient international economic support, engendered tensions and resignations within government and across political parties, which in turn heightened citizens' dissatisfaction and disillusionment. In such a context, and in response to protests and parliamentary paralysis, President Kais Saied, in July 2021, assumed vastly enhanced executive powers, fired the prime minister and suspended parliament.

Informed by feminist political economy, this chapter surveys the gendered nature of Tunisia's economic restructuring, with a focus on the liberalization policies adopted in the decades prior to the 2011 revolution, the impact of the Great Recession and the loss of investments and jobs in the aftermath of the revolution and the terrorism threat. I show how these developments affected the lives and livelihoods of Tunisian women in general and those in the peripheral regions in particular. Economic restructuring was expected to produce dynamic economic growth and inclusion in Tunisia but eventually generated the inequality, unemployment and cronyism that fueled the 2010–2011 mass protests. The 2020 COVID-19 pandemic only added to the country's economic, social and political travails. The chapter draws on my observational, interview and documentary data over years of research on and in Tunisia, along with the relevant academic sources, documents produced by government agencies, Tunisian economists, women's rights organizations and international surveys.

The chapter is organized as follows. I begin with an overview of Tunisia's post-colonial developments, highlighting the shift to privatization and liberalization that began in the 1980s and was deepened in the 1990s, and responses from the country's formidable trade union as well as feminist organizations. The subsequent section unpacks the difficulties of implementing the progressive social and economic reforms demanded by protesters in 2011 and since. Weak state capacity undermined citizen expectations of expanded social rights and rendered women and their families, especially in the peripheral regions, economically deprived. As such, and despite the fairly impressive democratization that the country experienced in its first decade, economic empowerment has remained elusive for most Tunisian women. Among other conclusions, years of economic difficulty in the aftermath of a political revolution underscores the limits of democratization in a global neoliberal capitalist environment faced with one crisis after another.

From socialism to privatization: Economic policy shifts

Following independence from France, Tunisia's first leader, the French-educated lawyer Habib Bourguiba, began his presidency (1957–1987) on a wave of popularity and optimism. As in other newly independent or modernizing Third World states, Bourguiba and his team implemented a plan for the country's economic development and sociocultural modernization. Rather audaciously, Bourguiba challenged his countrymen to put the country's productivity and growth before religious observance, urging them to work during the fasting month of Ramadan. He also called the veil "an odious rag" and encouraged women to discard it (Charrad, 1997, p. 284). A significant measure was the adoption of a liberal family law, the 1956 Code du Statut Personnel, which banned polygamy and gave women the right to divorce. The National Union of Tunisian Women (Union nationale de la femme tunisienne, UNFT) was formed in 1958 and, with its close links to the ruling party, Bourguiba's Socialist Destourian Party was able to establish training centers for rural women and girls (CREDIF, 1996). The 1959 Constitution established Tunisia as a republic, eschewed reference to Islamic law and stipulated the equality of all citizens, women and men alike. Public schools and universities, along with the possibility of further education in France, produced at least two generations of educated, employed and politically aware Tunisian women. Except for a brief conservative period in the 1970s, when Bourguiba turned on the country's growing left movement and parties and reaffirmed Islamic values, his presidency was known for a version of "state feminism" that continued into the rule of his successor, Zine el Abedin Ben Ali (1989–2011).[1]

Before examining Tunisia's economic policy models and experience with economic restructuring, a word on civil society organizations is needed to anticipate their periodic political intervention and later role in the democratic transition. The Union générale tunisienne du travail (UGTT) was established by Farhat Hached in 1946, while Tunisia was still a French protectorate. Its origins lie in the short-lived Conféderation géneral des travailleurs tunisiens (1924–1925), co-founded by Taher Haddad, the famous intellectual and champion of workers' rights and women's rights. The UGTT became the most powerful civil society organization, alternating between cooperating with the state and challenging it. The Ordre National des Avocats de Tunisie, the Arab region's first bar association, was founded in 1887, and the human rights organization League Tunisien des Droits de l'homme was established in 1977, before many others in the Arab region (Bellin, 1995). The Club Taher Haddad was formed by left-wing women's rights advocates in the 1970s who later established two influential feminist organizations, the Association tunisienne des femmes démocrates (ATFD) and the Association des femmes tunisiennes pour la recherche sur le développement (AFTURD). The 1980s saw the rise of an Islamist movement, the Mouvement de tendance Islamique, which was banned after confronting the state in the late 1980s; renamed Ennahda, it became a key political party in 2011.

Economic development

Import substitution industrialization (ISI) was a common economic development strategy across the Third World, and in Tunisia, resource extraction (of phosphates and oil), agricultural production, and ISI became the main pillars of economic development. Initially, the state pursued a socialist planned economy, largely the brainchild of the planning minister and former UGTT secretary-general, Ahmed Ben Salah, who favored ISI and agricultural cooperatives. State-owned enterprises' share of the economy rose from a mere 1.8 percent in 1961 to 33.7 percent in 1970 (Murphy, 1999, p. 82). The socialist period came to an abrupt end with Ben Salah's dismissal in 1969. Bourguiba's resentment of Ben Salah's popularity and the weak growth of the agricultural sector replaced the socialist plan with a more open economic policy toward export manufacturing and encouragement of European foreign direct investment (FDI). This move pleased the World Bank, which praised the Tunisian government for "reducing Government's direct intervention in the economy, relaxing administrative controls, and strengthening indirect support to productive activities in the private sector" (cited in Aliriza, 2020, p. 27). Government subsidies continued, however, as did government promotion of education and employment. Women with high school and university degrees began careers in education, healthcare and public administration, while those with basic schooling or from working-class or low-income households in urban and rural settings found jobs in the growing manufacturing sector—especially textiles and garments—or in the agricultural cooperatives. By the 1980s, not only was a large proportion of Tunisia's total female labor force involved in manufacturing, but the majority of workers in textiles and garments came to be women (Moghadam, 1998, Table 3.4, p. 66).

Tunisia's introduction in the mid-1980s to International Monetary Fund (IMF) lending and World Bank structural adjustment precipitated its evolution toward privatization of state-owned enterprises and liberalization of trade and labor markets.[2] The World Bank's 1982 review of Tunisia's Sixth Development Plan raised the question of bread subsidies, and the next year, the government more than doubled the price of bread for the first time in 15 years (Aliriza, 2020, p. 28). What followed were "bread riots" that were violently repressed (Seddon, 1984). Tunisia's government nonetheless gave in to promises of aid, loans, foreign investments in key sectors and market access for Tunisian exports. The first loan and structural adjustment package covered the period 1986–1992. (Those years coincided with the end of Bourguiba's rule, the crackdown on the growing Islamist movement and the beginning of Ben Ali's presidency.) The emphasis at the time was on privatizing Tunisia's textiles and agriculture sectors, which happened to be where many women were employed formally as well as informally.

In return for the World Bank and IMF loans, the Tunisian government sold off its holdings in banking, tourism and textiles manufacturing, and was praised for its ability to reduce the budget deficit and inflation rate. However, income inequality rose, the reduction in poverty may have been a statistical artifice (the poverty line was set too low) and unemployment was rising (Harik, 1992; Moghadam, 1998, pp. 57, 62; Aliriza, 2020). The results for women's economic participation and empowerment were mixed at best. Tunisia's state spending on education doubled between 1960 and 1990, from 3.3 percent to 6.1 percent of the GDP (United Nations Development Programme, 1995, pp. 174–175). Public expenditure on education helped create a middle class and a stratum of women professionals that became especially visible in the 1990s and increasingly vocal in the new century. For working-class households, the new economic strategy helped urban women earn an income and contribute to the household budget. However, a study by the Tunisian women's policy agency study CREDIF found that little had changed in the country's interior and peripheral regions. Patriarchal attitudes and practices had not lessened significantly; work had not afforded women a way out of poverty, and there were no mechanisms in place to alleviate the double burden of productive work and domestic responsibilities (CREDIF, 1996).

If the 1980s was a period of structural change, the shift was consolidated in the 1990s, following the collapse of world communism and the embrace of capitalist democracy in Eastern Europe and the former Soviet Union. In Tunisia, the UGTT could not halt the advance of privatization and liberalization. It did, however, organize wide-scale protests in 1984 and provide refuge for dissidents and the country's weakened left activists (Netterstrom, 2016; Omri, 2015; Zemni, 2013). Meanwhile, left-wing women were active in building women's organizations in the 1980s. They encouraged the UGTT to form a Women's Committee, which represented women workers in the formal sector of textiles and garments production as well as in health and education. They formed the Club Taher Haddad and the "Democratic Women" (Femmes Démocrates), supporting the Palestinian struggle and other international causes, Tunisia's striking workers and women's advancement (Debuysere, 2018; Tchaicha and Arfaoui, 2017). In 1989 the Ben Ali government formally recognized the ATFD and the AFTURD.

1990–2010: Privatization and its discontents

Tunisia progressively took steps to integrate into international markets, joining the World Trade Organization in 1995 and signing a free trade agreement with the European Union (EU) in 1995. The Foreign Investment Promotion Agency offered tax incentives for FDI. Investments were concentrated in the energy sector, although that sector generated less employment overall than the manufacturing and service sectors. Exports included textiles, electrical and automotive components, agricultural goods and phosphates—mainly to Europe and especially to France and Italy. Most of Tunisia's large employers came to be concentrated in those sectors, and especially in textiles and phosphates. Integrating Tunisia into European markets had its advantages, but ultimately, it deepened Tunisia's dependence on those markets and made it vulnerable to swings in European investors' fiscal decisions. The extraction of natural resources in the Gafsa basin contributed enormously to the state budget but did little to lift local communities out of poverty and unemployment or develop the region's infrastructure, while also creating environmental and health problems.[3]

The 1990s cemented Tunisia's standing in the world polity, as the Ben Ali government presented itself as a champion of women's rights, lifted previous restrictions on civil society organizing and introduced new social protection policies. In 1990, the government established the Centre de Recherches, d'etudes, de Documentation, et de l'information sur la femme (CREDIF), a women's policy agency charged with carrying out studies on urban and rural women's status. The government also formalized meetings that had existed since the 1970s with the UGTT and the employers' group Union Tunisienne de l'industrie du Commerce et de l'artisanat (UTICA). In regular triennial meetings, the three groups negotiated wage increases and other economic policies. The UGTT was also included in different government bodies, such as the Economic and Social Council (Netterstrom, 2016, p. 387–388). Post-colonial Tunisia had developed a social policy regime that was generous and well-managed, but after the late 1980s, households began bearing more healthcare costs (Ben Romdhane, 2006), and just 20 percent of public investment was devoted to the interior and southern region (Boukhars, 2017, p. 12). To deal with poverty and social exclusion, the National Solidarity Bank was created in 1997, but Ben Romdhane (2006) highlights "clientelistic" practices. Entrepreneurship was promoted as another way of addressing poverty. ENDA Inter-Arabe Tunisia, co-founded by Esma Ben Hamida in 1990, was the first microcredit organization, with the goal of poverty alleviation through loans to "the most rejected customers of the traditional financial system" and to focus "more on productive projects than on consumer loans."[4]

The privatization and liberalization program continued. In the early years of the new century, the Ben Ali government tried to break up the national airline, Tunis Air, into smaller companies, privatize them and sell them one at a time. Netterstrom (2016) explains how the UGTT's airport workers' union opposed the gradual privatization, leading the national body to call a strike. The government tried to buy off union leaders with generous retirement packages, but the issue continued until the 2011 revolution, after which Tunis Air was renationalized.

In the 1980s and 1990s, manufacturing was by far the most female-intensive sector of the economy and the labor force (Moghadam, 1998, p. 68; PNUD and UNIFEM, 2003). Production of garments in Tunisia had close links with enterprises abroad through FDI, foreign contracting and localization in export-processing zones. However, the success of the Tunisian garment industry was contingent on special trade policies giving it preferential access to the EU market. Once other countries, mostly in Eastern Europe, received similar treatment and Tunisia lost this privileged position, the performance of the garment industry worsened (Aita et al., 2008, p. 164). Later, the Great Recession took a toll. The major trading partners and foreign investors in Tunisia's manufacturing sector were from France, Spain, Italy and, to a lesser degree, Germany, and overconcentration of exports in EU markets, especially southern ones, exposed Tunisia to recessions in those markets from 2009 onward (Jaud and Freund, 2015, p. 11–12), resulting in job losses and even higher unemployment. This outcome is consistent with studies highlighting gender bias in hiring and firing decisions and the vulnerability of women workers who cluster in low-skill manufacturing sectors that are subject to global economic trends (Elson, 1999; Kucera and Tejani, 2014).

Middle-class women's access to professional jobs continued. Whereas in 1980, Tunisian women accounted for just 15 percent of the paid labor force, the proportion rose to 28.6 percent in 2014 (République Tunisienne, 2014, p. 14). On the eve of the revolution, women made up 39 percent of the staff in the civil service (Ben Salem, 2010, p. 501). In the health field, 42 percent of doctors, 72 percent of pharmacists, 57 percent of dental surgeons and 42 percent of university teaching staff were women. Most university students were female. And yet, for those in the private sector, and for some in the public sector, work contracts no longer guaranteed long-term, stable employment (CREDIF, 2015, p. 47). Private universities increasingly relied on temporary rather than permanent teaching staff (Boughzala, Ghazouani and Ben Hafaiedh, 2016, p. 17).

Growing unemployment

Until the 1980s and early 1990s, the public sector and government agencies and enterprises absorbed those Tunisians with high school and especially university degrees who sought jobs. In the aftermath of the structural adjustment policies, and especially after the government embraced neoliberalism, the number of public sector jobs shrank. At the same time, access to university increased, in part through the removal of vocational tracks in secondary schools.

By 2000, when a law enabled the formation of private universities, the government had decreased funding to state-run universities. The number of university graduates almost tripled between 1997 and 2007, but the coveted jobs in the public sector—stable and prestigious, with good benefits—became scarce. The official total unemployment rate remained between 13 and 14 percent during the 2000s, but unemployment rates of educated youth steadily increased, reaching almost 23 percent in 2010. Tertiary school enrollment rates increased from about 8 percent in 1990 to 35 percent in 2010, enabling more Tunisian women to acquire university degrees. Their labor-force participation rates were high, but so too were their unemployment rates.[5] One reason was that the preferred stable public-sector jobs had become increasingly unavailable, while those that were available came with "flexible" employment contracts. The elusive nature of good jobs led to the 2005 formation of a union for unemployed graduates (Union des Diplômés Chômeurs, UDC), which remains in place today.

Working-class women were also affected by the changing political economy, albeit differently than middle-class university graduates. The first set of job losses occurred with denationalization and the shift to privatization in the mid to late 1980s. Later in the 1990s, more women's jobs in the textiles and manufacturing sector began to vanish as European investors turned their attention to the newly opened markets of the former socialist countries that had joined the European Union. As total unemployment increased, worker protest action flared, some organized by the UGTT and others spontaneous. In 2004, women employees of a Dutch-owned textile factory in Moknine went on strike and occupied the factory after the owner decided to close the factory, leaving 275 women without work and income (Debuysere, 2018). When protests broke out in the phosphate mining basin in Gafsa in January 2008 over poverty, unemployment and perceived cronyism in hiring, women joined the call for jobs, fair pay and a decent infrastructure. They marched on the city hall and held a sit-in calling for their arrested sons, brothers and fathers to be released, and at one point, a group began walking toward the border with Algeria, threatening to seek asylum (Gantin and Seddik, 2008). Soon afterward, some 800 workers in Ben Arous—a governorate south of Tunis, home to the biggest port and a large UGTT regional chapter—protested their factory closure (Debuysere, 2018). These were important signals of the widespread opposition to come.

Throughout this period, to remain competitive and continue to attract foreign investment, "flexible" employment contracts expanded in Tunisia's private sector, which meant lower wages, more temporary work and less job security for workers. Flexible forms of employment included job rotation, short-term contracts, part-time work, flexible work hours, weekend work, night work and overtime work. A study found that workers involved in flexible work practices faced a higher risk of work injuries and more mental strain than workers in a more traditional work organization (Haouas and Yagoubi, 2008). The situation was especially dire in the country's interior regions.

Mining and agriculture were the primary sources of employment in Tunisia's interior, but social development lagged behind that of the more affluent and privileged coastal areas. Roughly 90 percent of new jobs and enterprises prior to 2011 were created in the coastal governorates of Tunis, Bizerte, Monastir, Nabeul, Sfax and Sousse (Boughzala, 2013). In contrast, the country's interior—especially its western and southern regions—suffered disadvantage and deprivation, with poor indicators in poverty, housing, school enrollment, illiteracy, fertility, infant mortality and access to healthcare. Life expectancy in Kasserine and Tatouine was just 70 years, compared with 77 years in Tunis and Sfax. In 2010 the poverty rate was 32 percent in the center and west compared to 8–9 percent in the Center-East and in Greater Tunis (Sadiki, 2019). The shift to neoliberalism had created more problems than it had solved.

Left-wing women and those who formed ATFD and AFTURD were allied with the UGTT in its periodic confrontations with the government, and their many publications reveal critiques of the social effects of restructuring and privatization. A large proportion of the UGTT rank-and-file was female, from sectors such as textiles and garments, tourism, education and healthcare. Feminist trade unionists supported the 2008 Gafsa mine protests, and they joined the local and national protests after word spread in December 2010 of the self-immolation of Mohamed Bouazizi, the young man whose frustration at his inability to make a living came to represent the nation's loss of dignity. According to one observer, the participation in the 2011 revolution of "women and lawyers, an important and historically active body of resistance in Tunisia, led the way in parts of the country, and articulated – and even raised – the demands of the people to a more political level" (Omri, 2015, p. 17). The mass protests led to the resignation and exile of President Ben Ali, the dissolution of his government, the appearance of multiple political parties, democratic elections, new institutions, an invigorated civil society and a Constituent Assembly (2011–2014) to finalize a new constitution.

Whither social and economic reforms?

Tunisia's democratic transition was hailed internationally for its peaceful and procedural nature despite growing political polarization. But the revolution's socioeconomic demands—including full employment and quality public services—remained unmet. Growth and FDI plummeted. Much-needed reforms and enforcement stalled under repeated cabinet reshuffles. Between October 2011 and January 2014 (when the constitution was adopted), the Constituent Assembly, dominated by the Islamist Ennahda party, spent much time debating cultural and religious matters (for example, whether the constitution should include a reference to the Sharia, whether women and men were "complementary" or "equal") rather than focusing on pressing socioeconomic policy issues. Ennahda came to be known as a moderate Islamist party, but it also was a socially conservative party comfortable with market capitalism.[6]

The 2013 political crisis caused by the assassinations of two left-wing politicians was alleviated and resolved through the mediation of the UGTT and three civil society partners—UTICA, the lawyers' association and the human rights league. For their efforts, the "National Dialogue Quartet" received the 2015 Nobel Peace Prize. However, two terrorist attacks on foreign tourists in 2015 nearly toppled Tunisia's lucrative tourism industry.[7] The problem of female unemployment worsened when FDI sharply declined in most sectors following the revolutionary upheaval and the terrorist attacks. FDI flows decreased by 29 percent in 2011, and 182 foreign firms—Italian, French and German—closed, with the loss of 10,930 jobs (Ayadi and Mattoussi, 2014, p. 6). The decline of FDI in the tourism sector was severe. All told, FDI fell from a peak of over $3 billion in 2006 to just under $989 million in 2018.[8] Tensions within government and across the political parties, including resignations, cabinet reshuffles and accusations of corruption, continued to prevent concerted efforts to alleviate poverty, reduce income inequality and improve women's economic conditions. The nation's once-sizable share of phosphate production dropped steeply, remaining depressed due to protests by the unemployed in the poor southeast region; consequently, commodity exports overall declined, constraining government revenue.

Meanwhile, liberalization of trade and labor markets remained intact. In 2012, workers benefiting from indeterminate-length contracts constituted 43 percent of the working population, but 44.6 percent had no contract at all, while 12.3 percent were on fixed contracts (CREDIF, 2015, p. 47). Young women did better than young men in the type of work contract, but their unemployment rates were much higher. After a high of 18.3 percent in 2011–2012, the unemployment rate hovered at around 15 percent between 2014 and 2020.[9] Youth unemployment rates were much higher, at around 30 percent, and those of young women even higher. In 2012, the unemployment rate reached 25.6 percent for women, compared with 14.6 percent for men. The surge in unemployment from 2011 to 2014 was almost entirely absorbed by women: nearly 54 percent of the 137,000 jobs lost (CREDIF, 2015, p. 70; Mouelhi and Goaied, 2017, p. 4; République Tunisienne, 2014, p. 14). Studies found that the highest female unemployment rates were in the country's less-developed interior, reaching 40–46 percent in Kebili, Gafsa and Tataouine—rates that were two to three times higher than men's (République Tunisienne, 2014, p. 16; see also République Tunisienne, 2012). Years of neglect had rendered Tunisia's interior lacking in the infrastructure, transformational knowledge and information networks enjoyed by the northeast and the coastal areas. In low-income Jendouba, Le Kef, Kasserine and Gafsa, some 60 percent of women suffered from health problems, and just 10 percent had access to healthcare (Elrahi, 2015). One study estimated a 46 percent participation rate in the informal sector in the third quarter of 2020, generated by the long-standing contraction of formal sector employment as well as the effects of the pandemic.[10]

Many Tunisian feminist legal scholars and advocates have cited the lack of decent work and support for working mothers, weak enforcement of positive laws, unequal inheritance and domestic violence as problems that keep women from advancing further (AFTURD, 2006, 2010; Arfaoui and Moghadam, 2016; CREDIF, 2014, 2017; Moghadam, 2019; Tchaicha and Arfaoui, 2017). Others emphasize conservative social norms. Women's unpaid care burdens are considerable throughout the Arab region (UN Women, 2020, p. 49). In Tunisia, the labor law differentiated between the public and private sectors, disadvantaging many low-income and working-class women. In the public sector, social insurance was provided, and women were entitled to two months of paid maternity leave and on-site childcare facilities at workplaces with more than 50 workers (Ben Salem, 2010, p. 502). For the private sector, the law stipulated a leave of 30 days and a year-long right for new mothers to leave work daily to breastfeed, but the law was not enforced, and small enterprises were exempt. There was no gender distinction in social security provisions, but the mandatory requirements applied to civil servants only (Bernard-Maugiron, 2015, p. 8). Unsurprisingly, many employed women found it difficult to balance work and family life (Ben Salem, 2010, p. 501; Moghadam, 2019). Large numbers of young women from working-class households who wished to enter the labor market out of economic need, or those from middle-class households who aspired to a professional career, found that both the lack of demand and the unappealing working conditions in the private sector blocked their entry into the workforce—hence the high unemployment rates and overall low economic activity rate.

In the private sector, women were concentrated in low-skill employment, with little capacity for promotion (Ayadi and Mattoussi, 2014, p. 5). In a 2017 interview, Samia Bouslama Letaief, head of the UGTT health sector and a long-standing AFTURD member, explained:

> By law, women workers should have good work conditions, but the reality is otherwise, especially in the private sector and in agriculture. In effect, no social insurance, 10–12 hour days, bad transport conditions, no paid maternity leave, no job security, a work stoppage at any time, and continued exploitation. … Textiles and electronics workers generally work within legally stipulated conditions. They are unionized and better organized.[11]

In a show of solidarity, the World Social Forum (WSF)—established in 2001 as the progressive alternative to the World Economic Forum—convened in Tunis in March 2013 and again in March 2015. At the Women's Assembly of the 2013 WSF, Ahlem Belhaj, then president of ATFD, cited the feminization of poverty, violence against women and "an economic system that exploits women and men" as the main challenges facing the world's women and Tunisia.[12] In a 2014 interview, Nadia Chaabane, a member of the Constituent Assembly from the left-wing coalition group El Massar, expressed her preference for a socio-economic program that combined the welfare state of the Nordic countries and the *modèle participatif* of the left-wing Latin American countries of the time. As she explained: "We tested liberalism, and see where it brought us. We want an interventionist state that is not anti-business but is people-oriented."[13] A long-time left-wing activist and university professor who briefly joined the government in 2014 spoke of his frustration with those in the coalition government and in parliament who were reluctant to tackle neoliberal policies head-on. A health expert and left-wing professor committed to women's equality emphasized the importance of providing for poor and marginalized women in the country's interior regions. Letaief, the feminist trade unionist, told me: "We work for equality of public and private labor law, social insurance for all workers, maternity leave and crèches, healthy workplaces and against sexual harassment. We want the government to ratify ILO Convention 183 [on maternity protection]."[14]

To address high unemployment and the development needs of the country's interior, Tunisia's government in 2013 turned to the IMF for a $2.8 billion loan, and the final $247 million tranche was disbursed in June 2016. This was in part to help fund its 2016–2020 Development Plan (République Tunisienne, 2016; see also International Monetary Fund, 2016). The plan set several goals for the productive capacity of the economy, including the promotion of modern agriculture, food processing and food security; protection of natural resources; and promotion of the knowledge economy, which would entail transforming half the universities into STEM (science, technology, engineering and math) institutions. For manufacturing, the government's note to the IMF stated that the former development model that "is based on pervasive state intervention that led to an economy dependent on low-value-added exports, excessive regulation, and limited competition—will be changed swiftly" (République Tunisienne,

2016, p. 24). The plan was to provide incentives and allow competition for "backbone services" such as telecoms, transport and professional services (République Tunisienne, 2016, p. 21), for which Tunisia was seen as having significant export potential. Especially relevant to women's employment were the goals to significantly increase women's share of the labor force to 35 percent, expand the size of the social care sector by raising kindergarten enrollments from 35 percent in 2015 to 53 percent in 2020 and invest in child protection, sports and home-care support. Such goals, if realized, could have generated jobs for women in the social or care sector, releasing mothers for employment and improving the quality of citizens' social rights.

The plan's goals, however, came to be at odds with what were seen as austerity measures, including government spending cuts and the dinar's devaluation, which were detailed in the government's 2018 Finance Bill. Tunisians reportedly lost 40 percent of their purchasing power, while foreign investment fell by a further 7.6 percent in 2019 (Volkmann, 2020). A 2017 report stated that across certain regions, female unemployment rates ranged from 22 percent to 50 percent, compared to 15 percent for men; some 40 percent of young university-educated women were unemployed.[15] Frustration with persistent unemployment and the high cost of living triggered a new wave of protests across Tunisia in early January 2018. Opinion polls showed a steep decline in public faith in government and democracy. Out-migration to Italy and other European countries continued, this time on the part of educated and middle-class Tunisians.[16]

After the 2011 revolution, voices within Tunisia's civil society and internationally called for debt cancellation, as debt-servicing repayments were high at a time of decreasing government revenue. Tunisia's public debt-to-GDP ratio increased from about 40 percent in 2010–2011 to 77 percent at the end of 2018 (Aliriza, 2020, pp. 35–36).[17] The IMF continued to monitor Tunisia for currency devaluation, containment of the public sector wage bill (through retirement packages and wage and hiring freezes), "flexibility" with the minimum wage, recapitalizing the banks and strengthening the Central Bank's "independence" (Aliriza, 2020, pp. 37–38). The UGTT did compel the government to approve salary increases in 2018, but these were offset by inflation. Protests and strikes in the country's interior, where residents demanded more employment and investment, paralyzed gas, petroleum and phosphate production. Most of Tunisia's debt was external debt, and in July 2020, with a shrinking economy but increased spending to offset the effects of the pandemic, the government sought to delay debt repayment to Saudi Arabia, Qatar, France and Italy.[18] Meanwhile, strikes and protests continued across Tunisia in 2020 and into the new year, demanding the same socioeconomic welfare policies that had been central to the uprising in 2011.

Despite political polarization and economic difficulties, Tunisia's feminists helped effect the passage of several women-friendly legal and policy reforms in the years following the 2011 revolution. These included parity in political representation, the removal of a 1973 decree banning a Muslim Tunisian woman from marrying a non-Muslim man and the strongest legislation to date on violence against women (see Moghadam, 2016; Tripp, 2019, p. 113). However, attitudes and values remained more favorable to male employment than to female employment, albeit with differences between women and men. The large agreement among women that preschool children suffer if the mother works reflected the reality of inadequate policies and facilities for working mothers of small children (see Table 6.1). In 2020, confinement due to the COVID-19 virus raised the specter of increased domestic violence, and the Ministry of Women created a toll-free number operated by 11 pro bono psychologists to help victims. Tunisia had the lowest self-reported cases of domestic violence, according to the Arab Barometer.[19] Even so, the ATFD president said in an interview that she worried about a return to patriarchy in the home, public spaces and the public sphere (Boukhayatia, 2020). What occurred was a halt to the democratic transition, when the confluence of economic difficulties and political dysfunction enabled the newly elected president to enhance his executive powers in July 2021.

Discussion and conclusions

Economic restructuring in Tunisia followed the playbook of global restructuring, and its gendered effects were similar to those in many other countries in the capitalist world-economy's periphery and semi-periphery. In the years after the introduction of privatization and liberalization, especially in the early years of the new century, Tunisia seemed to be benefiting from neoliberal capitalist globalization: tourism was booming, foreign direct investment grew and exports of natural resources and manufactured goods generated considerable revenue. Economic history reveals, however, that the capitalist world economy is beset by periodic crises and often fails vulnerable and dependent economies. As a peripheral country dependent on exports, tourism and foreign investment, Tunisia has been vulnerable to the vagaries of the world economy, the volatility of commodities prices, the changing fortunes of European partners and the demands of international financial institutions.

This chapter has shown the effects of the debt crisis of the 1970s–1980s, growing unemployment in the 1990s, the Great Recession and the post-revolutionary turmoil compounded by the 2020 COVID-19 pandemic. Over the years, a combination of internal and external factors and forces has prevented the economic empowerment of Tunisian women: most Tunisian women remain economically inactive, unemployment plagues many educated young women and private-sector working conditions are often undesirable. The three challenges identified at the start of this chapter—the dangerous neighborhood, the severity of Tunisia's economic conditions and the travails of democratization—continue to prevent women's economic empowerment.

Tunisia's democratic transition was impressive in many ways, with a constitution that called on the state to protect women from violence and achieve political parity, and a constitutional article on environmental protection. The *Global Gender Gap Report*, issued by the World Economic Forum, routinely ranked Tunisia high on women's political empowerment, and in the 2020 report, Tunisia's ranking on that indicator was higher (at 67) than that of the

US (at 86). In 2017, President Beji Caid Essebsi created a high-level commission on liberties and rights (known by its French acronym COLIBE), which was led by a well-known feminist legal scholar. Its report included a recommendation for equal inheritance within the family, along with decriminalization of homosexuality and other recommendations aimed at aligning Tunisia's legal frameworks with international conventions. In 2019, the Council of Ministers adopted a bill on the extension of paid maternity leave to three months.[20] Following President Essebsi's death, the new president, Kais Saied, appointed a government that included a female prime minister (Najla Bouden Romdhane), the first in the Arab world, and the largest number of women ministers. However, the bill on equal inheritance was put on hold because of opposition from Ennahda and its supporters and because President Saied did not support it (Moghadam, 2022). And Najla Bouden was dismissed in August 2023.

Tunisia's untoward macroeconomic environment created a gap between women's considerable legal rights and political representation on the one hand and their limited economic empowerment on the other. The gap has been especially wide for women from lower-income or working-class households and those in the country's interior. The same *Global Gender Gap Report 2020* ranked Tunisia 142 on economic participation and opportunity. As the dire economic conditions persist, feminist goals such as equal inheritance rights are put to the side—even though women's more equal access to family wealth could provide part of the start-up capital needed for women-owned small businesses and thus the alleviation of poverty. Given the economic situation, it is difficult to envision how Tunisia could achieve the Sustainable Development Goals.

There is also the issue of attitudes and norms, some liberal and others quite conservative. As is seen in Table 6.1, the World Value Survey for Tunisia

Table 6.1 Selected attitudes on women, work and family in Tunisia, World Values Survey, Waves 6 and 7 (combined, 2013, 2019)

Wave 6/Wave 7	*Total*	*Women*
V45/Q33: When jobs are scarce, men should be preferred (% agree/strongly agree)	68	57*
V47/Q35: There is a problem if woman earns more than her husband (% agree/strongly agree)	43	38.5**
V48: A job is the best way for a woman to be independent (% agree/strongly agree)	52.2	62.7
V50/Q28: Pre-school children suffer if the mother works (% agree strongly/agree)	73.8	69
V139/Q249: Essential to democracy is that women have the same rights as men (scale from 1 not essential to 10 essential)	T Mean 7.29 (36.4% essential) T Mean 6.30 (23.1% essential)	F Mean 8.11 (47% essential) F Mean 6.40 (24.7% essential)

*About 20% reply: Neither agree nor disagree.
** About 35% reply: Neither agree nor disagree.

showed that attitudes were not strongly gender-egalitarian on questions of women, work and family or on the relationship of women's rights to democracy. The Arab Barometer (AB) surveys show a lack of confidence in institutions and limited support for equal inheritance. The AB's fifth wave, conducted in Tunisia between October and December 2018, revealed frustration with economic conditions. Just 7 percent of respondents rated the economy as good or very good, which was 20 points lower than in the months after the revolution and 7 points lower than in 2016 (Arab Barometer, 2019). Only a third expected the economy to improve in the coming years. Nearly half of all respondents (48 percent) stated that the most important challenge facing Tunisia was economic; terrorism came in next at 14 percent and corruption at 13 percent. Trust in government fell from 60 percent in 2011 to a mere 20 percent in 2018 (Robbins and Thomas, 2019, p. 6). Most respondents were highly satisfied with the government's provision of security but far less so with public services such as education and housing. The World Value Survey seventh wave, conducted in Tunisia in 2019, found similar results in attitudes toward the country's economic travails, along with expectations of proactive government policies. The majority of Tunisians agreed that the government should tax the rich and subsidize the poor and that a democratic government should provide state aid for unemployment (WVS 7, Q241, Q244). Given the high rates of youth unemployment, it is not surprising that a majority of young Tunisians, especially those with university degrees, stated that they wished to emigrate (Robbins and Thomas, 2019, p. 11); as noted earlier, they have been doing so. The AB found that most Tunisians considered democracy as not functioning well, though there was little support for an alternative system of governance.

Global restructuring had not been serving the world's population well even before the onset of the COVID-19 pandemic. Income inequalities had been widening, the quality and accessibility of public services deteriorating and the cost of living increasing. One reaction to democracy deficits and discontentment with globalization was the spread of right-wing populist-nationalist movements (Moghadam and Kaftan, 2019) and democratic backsliding (V-Dem, 2020). Tunisia's version occurred in July 2021. Not only have arrests increased of political opponents across the spectrum, from Islamists to trade unionists and journalists, but the July 2022 Saied-constructed constitution that was instituted after very low voter turnout replaced the parliament with a loyal assembly and concentrated power in the presidency. At the same time, import costs rose after the onset of the Russia–Ukraine–NATO war, and unemployment continued to grow, particularly among youth, further increasing out-migration. President Saied has led a campaign against migrants coming to Tunisia, and in 2023, he reached a lucrative agreement with the EU to keep migrants from reaching European shores. Such developments have put into question Tunisia's democracy and future political stability (Saleh, 2023). As this case study elucidates, both democracy and women's economic empowerment depend very much on favorable global, regional and national environments—which neoliberal capitalism has failed to provide in Tunisia and elsewhere.

Notes

1. For details on Bourguiba's conservative turn, as well as on the Tunisian state's policy shifts on women between the 1950s and 1990s, see Charrad (1997). She also compares the Bourguiba era's top-down "state feminism" with the post-Bourguiba era that enabled women's agency and institution-building. See also ATFD (2008) for a discussion of the state and women's rights from the perspective of an activist feminist organization.
2. Third World governments had found themselves in debt in the aftermath of either oil price increases in the early 1970s or interest rate hikes on bank loans in the early 1980s, or both. The World Bank and the International Monetary Fund (IMF), urged on by the US Treasury, stepped in to provide loans in return for extensive policy shifts—from state-owned enterprises to the promotion of the private sector, from government subsidies of staples and public services to price increases and "cost recovery" through "user fees." Key sources on Tunisia's structural adjustment experience and shift to privatization are Harik (1992), Murphy (1999) and Seddon (1984). See also Moghadam (1998, ch. 3).
3. See https://ejatlas.org/conflict/phosphate-mining-in-gafsa.
4. On ENDA's work, see https://media.iese.edu/research/pdfs/OP-08-11-E.pdf. More Tunisian microcredit organizations were formed after 2011: Tayssir in March 2014, Microcred in October 2014, Advans in January 2015, Center Financier aux Entrepreneurs (CFE) in April 2015 and Zitouna Tamkeen in May 2016. All are under the supervision of the Microcredit Control Authority. See http://nawaat.org/portail/2016/07/13/lutte-contre-la-pauvrete-les-risques-du-microcredit/.
5. CREDIF (2013a); and author interview with Dalenda Largueche, director-general of CREDIF, Tunis, June 22, 2017.
6. In this respect, Ennahda diverged more from the hard-left Front Populaire than with its erstwhile governing partner, Nidaa Tounes. For details, see Rousselin (2016).
7. Because of the NATO assault on Libya, the porous border with Tunisia enabled infiltration by ISIS, as seen by the March 2016 terror assault on security forces in the border town of Ben Guerdane. See https://www.cnn.com/2016/03/07/africa/tunisia-militants-killed-ben-guerdane/index.html (accessed September 2024).
8. The World Bank, foreign direct investment, Tunisia, available at https://data.worldbank.org/indicator/BX.KLT.DINV.CD.WD?locations=TN (accessed September 2024).
9. See https://www.statista.com/statistics/524516/unemployment-rate-in-tunisia/ (accessed September 2024.
10. See https://www.statista.com/statistics/1191154/informal-employment-rate-in-tunisia/.
11. Samia Letaief, response to a question via email, June 4, 2017; my translation from French.
12. Author notes, World Social Forum, Tunis, March 26, 2013.
13. Nadia Chaabane, interview, Tunis, March 6, 2014. The interview took place at the Bardo parliament building, of which Mme. Chaabane proudly gave me a tour.
14. Personal communications, M.B. and H.B., Tunis, March 2015; Samia Letaief, personal interview, Tunis, March 4, 2014, at AFTURD offices.
15. See Maghreb Emergent (March 1, 2017), https://maghrebemergent.net/tunisie-40-des-femmes-diplomees-du-superieur-sont-au-chomage/. See also Boughzala (2019) and Moghadam (2019).
16. See https://protectproject.w.uib.no/migration-flows-to-europe-a-new-tunisian-exodus/.
17. There is consensus among economists that a debt-to-GDP ratio of beyond 60 percent becomes worrisome. The ratio may be higher in rich countries such as Japan and the US, but these are core countries with strong economies and international standings; a peripheral economy such as Tunisia cannot afford its own debt level. In 2022, Tunisia's debt-to-GDP ratio was estimated to be about 85 percent.

18 See Reuters (July 13, 2020), "Tunisia seeks late debt payments as crisis hits economy, state budget," available at https://www.reuters.com/article/business/finance/tunisia-seeks-late-debt-payments-as-crisis-hits-economy-state-budget-idUSKCN24E18V/ (accessed September 2024).

19 See https://www.arabbarometer.org/2020/06/domestic-violence-and-arab-womens-false-choice-during-covid-19-pandemic/. See also Arfaoui and Moghadam (2016) for details on Tunisian feminist initiatives against domestic violence, including hotlines and shelters.

20 See https://www.nawaat.org/portail/2020/03/10/reforme-du-conge-de-maternite-urgence-sociale-atermoiement-politique/ (accessed September 2024).

References

Achcar, G. (2013) *The People Want: A Radical Exploration of the Arab Uprising*. Berkeley: University of California Press.

AFTURD. (2006) *Egalité dans l'héritage: pour une citoyenneté pleine et entière*. Vol. 1: *Histoire, droits et sociétés*; vol. 2: plaidoyer pour l'egalité dans l'héritage. Tunis: AFTURD. [Equality in inheritance; for full citizenship (for women). Vol. 1: History, Laws, and Societies; Vol 2: An appeal for equality of inheritance]

AFTURD. (2010) *Les aides ménagères à temps complet: Violences et non droits. Présentation des résultats de l'étude dans le cadre du project 'Répercussions économiques des violences sur les jeunes filles dans le grand Tunis, 2008–2010'*. Samira Ayed and Abdessatar Sahbani (eds.). Tunis: AFTURD Espace Tanassof. [Full-time household help: Violence and lack of rights. Presentation of results of a study on economic repercussions of violence against young women in greater Tunis.]

Aita, S. (2008) *Employment and Labor Law in the Arab Mediterranean Countries and the Euromediterranean Partnership: Comparative Study*. Madrid: Fundación Paz y Solidaridad Serafin Aliaga de Comisiones Obrereas.

Aliriza, F. (2020) "Perpetual periphery: IFIs and the reproduction of Tunisia's economic dependence," in Radwan, Tarek (ed.), *The Impact and Influence of International Financial Institutions on the Economies of the Middle East and North Africa*. Tunis: Friedrich Ebert Stiftung Regional Project, pp. 26–41.

Arab Barometer. (2019) *Arab Barometer V Tunisia country report 2019*. https://www.arabbarometer.org/wp-content/uploads/ABV_Tunisia_Report_Public-Opinion_2018-2019.pdf. (accessed May 2020).

Arfaoui, K. and Moghadam, V. (2016) "Violence against women and Tunisian feminism: Advocacy, policy, and politics in an Arab Context." *Current Sociology* 64, pp. 637–653.

ATFD. (2008) *Femmes et république: un combat pour l'égalité et la démocratie*. Tunis.

ATFD. (2010) *Declaration: Women's Rights in Tunisia*. Summary of Key Concerns Submitted by the Association Tunisienne Des Femmes Democrats (ATFD) to the United Nations Committee on the Elimination of Discrimination against Women, 4th Session.

Ayadi, M. and Mattoussi, M. (2014) *Scoping of the Tunisian Economy*. Working Paper 2014/074. Helsinki: WIDER.

Bellin, E. (1995) "Civil society in formation: Tunisia," in Norton, Augustus R. (ed.), *Civil Society in the Middle East*, Vol. 1. Leiden: E.J. Brill, pp. 120–147.

Ben Romdhane, M. (2006) "Social policy and development in Tunisia since independence: A political perspective," in Karshenas, Massoud and Moghadam, Valentine M. (eds.), *Social Policy in the Middle East: Economic, Political, and Gender Dynamics*. London: Palgrave Macmillan and UNRISD, pp. 31–77.

Ben Salem, L. (2010) "Tunisia," in Kelly, Sanja and Breslin, Julie (eds.), *Women's Rights in the Middle East and North Africa: Progress amid Resistance*. Lanham: Rowman & Littlefield and Freedom House, pp. 487–516.

Ben Salem, M. and Soumaya B. C. (2013) *Politique et jeunes femmes vulnérables en Tunisie: Étude qualitative Gafsa – Kasserine – Tozeur*. Tunis: CAWTAR, UNESCO, Royaume des Pays-Bas.

Bernard-Maugiron, N. (2015) *Supporting Women as Economic Actors in the Middle East and North Africa Region*. Draft report of Experts Meeting. Paris: Programme MENA-OCDE Pour l'Investissement.

Boukhars, A. (2017) "The fragility of elite settlements in Tunisia." *African Security Review*, 26(3), pp. 257–270, doi:10.1080/10246029.2017.1294093.

Boukhayatia, R. (2020) "Covid-19: Women, violence and confinement. An interview with Yosra Frawes." *Nawaat* (April 15). Available at http://nawaat.org/portail/2020/04/15/covid-19-women-violence-and-confinement-an-interview-with-yosra-frawes/.

Boughzala, M. (2013) *Youth Unemployment and Economic Transition in Tunisia*. Global Economy and Development Working Paper no. 57. Washington, DC: Brookings Institution.

Boughzala, M. (2018) "Employment and the functioning of the labor market," in Assaad, Ragui and Boughzala, Mongi (eds.), *The Tunisian Labor Market in an Era of Transition*. Oxford: Oxford University Press.

Boughzala, M. (2019) "Unemployment in Tunisia: Why it's so high among women and youth." ERF Policy Forum (May 21). https://theforum.erf.org.eg/2019/05/07/unemployment-tunisia-high-among-women-youth/.

Boughzala, M., Ghazouani S. and Hafaiedh, B.A. (2016) *Aligning Incentives for Reforming Higher Education in Tunisia*. Working Paper No. 1031. Cairo: Economic Research Forum.

CAWTAR. (2006) *Gender Impact of Trade Liberalization in the MENA Region*. Tunis.

CAWTAR. (2007) *Women entrepreneurs in the Middle East: characteristics, contributions and challenges*. Tunis and Washington, DC: CAWTAR and International Finance Corporation.

CAWTAR and Oxfam. (2016) *Women in political and civil life: obstacles and challenges to overcome them in Morocco, Tunisia, Occupied Palestinian Territories, Yemen*. Tunis: CAWTAR.

Charrad, M. (1997) "Policy shifts: State, Islam, and gender in Tunisia." *Social Politics*, pp. 284–319.

Charrad, M. and Zarrugh, A. (2014) "Equal or complementary? Women in the new Tunisian constitution after the Arab Spring." *Journal of North African Studies* 19(2), pp. 230–243.

CREDIF. (1996) *Femmes rurales de Tunisie*. Tunis.

CREDIF. (2002) *Les femmes en Tunisie 2000*. Tunis.

CREDIF. (2013a) "L'autonomisation économique des femmes: un pari à gagner." *Revue du CREDIF*, no. 46.

CREDIF. (2013b) "Tunisienne et action politique." *Revue du CREDIF*, no. 45.

CREDIF. (2014) *Autonomisation économique des femmes: emploi et entrepreneuriat*. Tunis: Ministère de la jeunesse, des sports, de la femme et de la famille; Secrétariat d'état de la femme et de la famille; Centre de recherches, d'études, de documentation et d'information sur la femme.

CREDIF. (2015) "Chômage des femmes diplômées du supérieur." *Revue du CREDIF*, no. 49.

CREDIF. (2017) "En attendant la loi intégrale: la violence à l'econtre des femmes, une réalité alarmante." *Revue du CREDIF*, no. 50.
Debuysere, L. (2018) "Between feminism and unionism: The struggle for socio-economic dignity of working-class women in pre- and post-uprising Tunisia." *Review of African Political Economy* 45, pp. 25–43. https://doi.org/10.1080/03056244.2017.1391770.
Elrahi, N. (2015) "Rural women in Tunisia: 'We have been silent for too long'." *The Guardian*. Available at https://www.theguardian.com/global-development/2015/mar/30/rural-women-rights-tunisia-world-social-forum.
Elson, D. (1999) "Labor markets as gendered institutions: Equality, efficiency, and empowerment Issues." *World Development* 27(3), pp. 611–627.
Gantin, K. and Seddik, O. (2008) "Révolte du « peuple des mines » en Tunisie." Available at https://www.monde-diplomatique.fr/2008/07/GANTIN/16061.
Hanieh, A. (2013) *Lineages of Revolt*. Chicago: Haymarket Books.
Haouas, I. and Yagoubi, M. (2008) *The Flexible Forms of Employment and Working Conditions: Empirical Investigation from Tunisia*. Working Paper 407. Cairo: Economic Research Forum.
Harik, I. (1992) "Privatization and development in Tunisia," in Harik, Ilya and Sullivan, Denis (eds.), *Privatization and Liberalization in the Middle East*. Bloomington: Indiana University Press, pp. 210–232.
International Labor Organization (ILO). (2012) *Global Employment Trends for Women 2012*. Geneva: International Labour Organization.
International Monetary Fund (IMF). (2016) *Tunisia: Request for an Extended Arrangement under the Extended Fund Facility—Press Release; Staff Report; and Statement by the Executive Director for Tunisia*. Country Report No. 16/138. Washington, DC: IMF.
Jaud, M. and Freund, C. (2015) *Champions Wanted: Promoting Exports in the Middle East and North Africa*. Directions in Development. Washington, DC: World Bank Group.
Karshenas, M., Moghadam, V.M. and Alami, R. (2014) "States and social rights: Social policy after the Arab Spring." *World Development* 64, pp. 726–739.
Khalil, A. (2014). "Tunisia's women: partners in revolution" *Journal of North African Studies* 19, pp.186–199.
Kucera, D. and Tejani, S. (2014) "Feminization, defeminization, and structural change in manufacturing." *World Development* 64, pp. 569–582.
Mako, S. and Moghadam, V.M. (2021) *After the Arab Uprisings: Progress and Stagnation in the Middle East and North Africa*. Cambridge and New York: Cambridge University Press.
Moghadam, V.M. (1998) *Women, Work, and Economic Reform in the Middle East and North Africa*. Boulder, CO: Lynne Rienner.
Moghadam, V.M. (2013) "What is democracy? Promises and perils of the Arab Spring." *Current Sociology* 61, pp. 393–408.
Moghadam, V.M. (2016) "Feminist movements in the Maghreb," in Basu, Amrita (ed.), *Women's Movements in a Global Era*. Boulder, CO: Westview Press, pp. 333–360.
Moghadam, V.M. (2019) "Women's employment in Tunisia: Structures, institutions, advocacy." *Sociology of Development* 5(4), pp. 337–359. Available at https://online.ucpress.edu/socdev/article/5/4/337/109350/Women-and-Employment-in-TunisiaStructures.
Moghadam, V.M. (2020) "Gender regimes in the Middle East and North Africa: The power of feminist movements." *Social Politics: International Studies in Gender, State & Society* 27, pp. 467–485, https://doi.org/10.1093/sp/jxaa019.
Moghadam, V.M. (2022) "Institutions, feminist mobilizations, and political economy: Debating equal inheritance in Tunisia." *British Journal of Middle East Studies*, pp. 1–18. doi:10.1080/13530194.2022.2117133.

Moghadam, V.M. and Kaftan, G. (2019) "Right-wing populisms north and south: Varieties and gender dynamics." *Women's Studies International Forum* 75, pp. 1–9. Available at https://www.sciencedirect.com/science/article/abs/pii/S027753951830390X.

Mouelhi, R.B.A. and Goaied, M. (2017) *Women in the Tunisian Labor Market*. Working Paper 1160. Cairo: Economic Research Forum.

Murphy, E. (1999) *Economic and Political Change in Tunisia from Bourguiba to Ben Ali*. New York: St. Martin's Press.

Netterstrom, K.L. (2016) "The Tunisian General Labor Union and the advent of democracy." *Middle East Journal* 70, pp. 383–398.

Omri, M. (2015) "No ordinary union: UGTT and the Tunisian path to revolution and transition." *Workers of the World* 1, pp. 14–29. Available at https://www.academia.edu/19291239/No_Ordinary_Union_The_role_of_UGTT_in_the_Tunisian_path_to_revolution_and_transition.

PNUD and UNIFEM. (2003) *La Dimension genre dans la liberalization economique de la Tunisie*. Tunis: Programme de Nations Unies pour le Développement et Fonds de Développement des Nations Unies pour la Femme.

République Tunisienne. (2012) *Enquête nationale sur la population et l'emploi 2012*. Tunis: Statistiques Tunisie.

République Tunisienne. (2014) *Recensement en chiffres/statistique Tunisienne*. Available at http://census.ins.tn/fr/recensement.

République Tunisienne. (2016) *Synthèse du plan du développement 2016–2020*.

Robbins, M. and Thomas, K. (2019) *Tunisia at a Crossroads: Findings from the Fifth Wave of the Arab Barometer*. Available at https://www.arabbarometer.org/publication/tunisia-at-a-crossroads/.

Rousselin, M. (2016) "In the name of Allah and of the market: The capitalist leanings of Tunisian Islamists." *Science and Society* 80 (2), pp. 196–220.

Sadiki, L. (2019) *Regional Development in Tunisia: The Consequences of Multiple Marginalization*. Brookings Doha Center Publications. Available at https://www.brookings.edu/research/regional-development-in-tunisia-the-consequences-of-multiple-marginalization/.

Saleh, H. (2023) "The 'Slow Coup' Taking Tunisia Back to Autocracy." *Financial Times*. https://www.ft.com/content/993bf045-a2f0-45fc-855b-4588dc300a5c.

Seddon, D. (1984) *Winter of discontent: Economic crisis in Tunisia and Morocco*. MERIP Reports, no. 127.

Stephan, R. and Charrad, M.M. (eds.) (2020) *Women Rising: In and Beyond the Arab Spring*. New York: New York University Press.

Tchaicha, J. and Arfaoui, K. (2017) *The Tunisian Women's Rights Movement: From Nascent Activism to Influential Power-Broking*. London: Routledge.

Tripp, A.M. (2019) *Seeking Legitimacy: Why Arab Autocracies Adopt Women's Rights*. Cambridge and New York: Cambridge University Press.

United Nations Development Programme (UNDP). (1995) *Human Development Report 1995: Gender and Human Development*. New York: Oxford University Press.

UN Women. (2020) *The Role of the Care Economy in Promoting Gender Equality: Progress of Women in the Arab States 2020*. New York: UN.

V-Dem. (2020) *Autocratization Surges – Resistance Grows: Democracy Report 2020. Gothenburg: Varieties of Democracy Institute*. Available at https://v-dem.net/documents/14/dr_2020_dqumD5e.pdf.

Volkmann, E. (2020) "For Tunisia, recovery means modernizing economy." Available at https://www.al-monitor.com/pulse/originals/2020/03/tunisia-government-plan-economic-crisis-gateway-africa.html#ixzz6GyBSbQLz.

World Bank. (2017) *Republic of Tunisia Impact of the Libya Crisis on the Tunisian Economy*. Report No: ACS16340. Washington, DC: The World Bank.

World Economic Forum. (2020) *Global Gender Gap Report*. Geneva.

Zemni, S. (2013) "From socio-economic protest to national revolt: The labor origins of the Tunisian revolution," in Ghana, N. (ed.), *The Making of the Tunisian Revolution: Contexts, Architects, Prospects*. Edinburgh: University of Edinburgh Press, pp. 127–146.

7 "Empowerment" training for women workers in Bangladesh's garment factories

Corporate social (ir)responsibility (SIR)

Laura Dudley Jenkins

Introduction

This chapter's focus is on three initiatives, each led by a partnership between transnational corporations (TNCs) and nongovernmental organizations (NGOs) and targeting women in ready-made garment (RMG) factories. The first is women's empowerment training lessons sponsored by Walmart and CARE. The second consists of menstrual health awareness posters sponsored by Bayer and an NGO called Business for Social Responsibility (BSR). The third is financial literacy instructional videos for women, sponsored by Mastercard and BSR. Rather than empowering women in meaningful ways, they instead fortify status quo power relations between women and men, and between workers, managers and TNCs. The TNCs involved benefit from the clothing produced, painkillers sold to keep women working during their periods and electronic financial transaction fees. NGOs with missions to advance women have supported programs that fail to disrupt the root causes of patriarchy or poverty.

In the sections that follow, I first introduce critiques of the watered-down version of "women's empowerment" prevalent in contemporary international development initiatives. Discussing this reduced form of empowerment in the context of another concept, corporate social responsibility (CSR), I delineate how this chapter contributes to critical scholarship on both empowerment and CSR. I outline my research method and then analyze the context of RMG factories in Bangladesh, the production and distribution of these instructional texts, and the texts themselves (lesson plans, posters and videos). As a counterpoint, I offer examples of what more meaningful empowerment could entail, describing programs that prioritize the demands of RMG workers, enhance solidarity, reduce stigma and enable RMG workers to earn college degrees. To conclude, I reflect on empowerment, irresponsibility and the stakes for women in global supply chains.

Women's empowerment and corporate social responsibility

Women in the Global South, including women working in the RMG industry, have demanded women's empowerment, meaning political mobilization to transform gender subordination and the oppressive structures supporting it. But

DOI: 10.4324/9781003036425-8

development programs for "women's empowerment" have diluted the concept, reducing it to "providing women with economic livelihoods" or "technical programming required to improve education and health" (Cronin-Furman, Gowrinathan and Zakaria, 2017, pp. 1–2). The training programs examined in this chapter align with this tendency to depoliticize Global South women's empowerment and to tinker with—rather than transform—power relations. Often, they focus on changing workers' behavior rather than the actions of powerful governments, TNCs or factory owners.

Several trends produced this meager version of "empowerment." Neoliberalism, discussed throughout this book, includes both policies (privatization, deregulation and "free" trade) and ideologies (self-help, competition and efficiency as primary values) (Ganti, 2014, p. 91). Neoliberal trade policies in Bangladesh encouraged the growth of RMG manufacturing for export, including the establishment of export processing zones in the 1980s to attract investors with low wages and few taxes or regulations (BEPZA, 2021). Another aspect of neoliberalism is reducing the social welfare role of the government. Without adequate government support for social and economic safety nets, the growing need to raise private funds from individuals and corporations for women's initiatives in the Global South has contributed to dramatic portrayals of women as "abject victims stripped of all agency." Meanwhile, the "growing mania for measurement in the aid industry" has incentivized temporary and/or technical fixes over transformative structural changes led by the women themselves (Cronin-Furman, Gowrinathan and Zakaria, 2017, pp. 6, 2; Suchomel, 2018; Merry, 2016).

This "anti-politics" version of development (Ferguson, 1994) is evident in TNC–NGO-sponsored initiatives purporting to help women in the RMG industry. Rather than solidarity, rights or justice, the "neoliberally imagined empowerment logic seeks to enable grassroots actors, and especially women, to fulfill their own needs through market mechanisms instead of relying on state largesse" (Sharma, 2008, pp. xvi–xx). The intersection of sexism and racism is clear from interventions to "develop" or "empower" women in the Global South, including RMG workers. The widespread assumption that women workers are simply victims, and that their main threat is local patriarchy (eliding the role of corporate malfeasance), results in "responses that prioritize interveners' judgment about what these women need," resulting in some "laughably off-base interventions" (Cronin-Furman, Gowrinathan and Zakaria, 2017, p. 6). Development NGOs often take an expert-driven "charity" approach, in contrast to a "mutual aid" approach. Mutual aid is voluntary, flattens hierarchies, promotes solidarity and mobilizes broader political participation (Spade, 2020, pp. 61–64). Because mutual aid can be disruptive, TNCs and mainstream NGO donors often prefer "aid work disconnected from other tactics, depoliticized, and distanced from disruptive or root causes-oriented tactics" (Spade, 2020, p. 63).

Truncated "empowerment" tries to fix women rather than the world (Chant and Sweetman, 2012) and reinforces the profitable status quo for TNCs.

Businesses are increasingly partnering in global development initiatives to advance women as part of their CSR commitments. The United Nations Global Compact calls on corporations to commit to taking actions that support human rights, labor and the environment, and fight corruption. The United Nations' Women's Empowerment Principles (WEPs) encourage corporate participation, including "supply chain and marketing practices that empower women," but critics note these efforts also "naturalize the broader fusing of gender equality to participation in the capitalist market economy" (Roberts, 2015, p. 214). In the current context of obscene and growing wealth disparities, we must take a closer look at corporate virtue signaling (Giridharadas, 2018; Wu, 2018, 2019). As corporations become increasingly irresponsible for the workers making their products through convoluted subcontracts and supply chains around the world, it is time to rethink what "just responsibility" (Ackerly, 2018) would entail, not only for corporations but for us all.

This project connects critiques of NGOs that turn women's demands for power into limited forms of "empowerment" and growing concerns about corporate greed despite the rise of CSR. I examine the products of three partnerships between TNCs and NGOs, a common neoliberal collaboration because it sidesteps government involvement. I argue that the three training programs for RMG workers I examine are not just too little too late but actually help TNCs evade transformative change. With the assistance of NGOs, they provide a thin veneer of pro-women CSR messaging to shield longstanding business practices that endanger and underpay women. The extent of corporate social irresponsibility in Bangladesh will become evident in the discussion of context.

Methods

I use a form of critical discourse analysis inspired by Brosnan's (2016) examination of textbooks. She analyzes three dimensions, including (1) the context, (2) text production and distribution and (3) the text. I start with the context of the challenges RMG workers face. Second, I introduce the corporations and NGOs producing the training materials and the three modes of their distribution (in-person, posters and streaming videos). Third, I analyze the content of the texts, including words and images.

The analysis throughout is feminist in that it is guided by "a normative commitment to transforming the social order to promote gender justice" (Ackerly and True, 2020, p. 2). My gendered critique of texts and images illustrates how they perpetuate sexist and heteronormative hierarchies. The intersectionality of race, gender and class plays out at a global scale, with large international corporations and NGOs curating "empowerment" for women of color working in capitalist supply chains in a postcolonial context (Hawkesworth, 2016, pp. 6–17). Attuned to Arruzza, Bhattacharya and Fraser's manifesto on "feminism for the 99%," this chapter exposes the problems of a "corporate feminism" that "asks ordinary people, in the name of feminism, to be grateful that it is a woman, not a man, who busts their union" (2019, p. 2).

The empowerment lesson plans (for instructors) are in English. The health awareness posters are available in Bangla and English, so I quote the English versions. The financial literacy videos are in Bangla but have English subtitles, which I use for quotations. Future research should engage additional dimensions of discourse and visual analysis, such as how workers interpret and respond to these materials, but that is outside the scope of this chapter.

The context

The context of RMG work exposes the disconnect between what kinds of empowerment workers are demanding and what kinds of empowerment TNC–NGO training programs are providing. There is a tendency of white feminists—and the programs examined in this chapter—"towards rescuing non-Western women from their own societies, cultures and contexts" (Cronin-Furman, Gowrinathan and Zakaria, 2017, p. 2). Instead, the context I scrutinize is the international political economy of RMG factories and how this global industry impacts women's lives in factories.

Ready-made garment workers in Bangladesh, a majority female workforce, experience below-poverty wages, long hours, sexual harassment, other forms of harassment and intimidation, a risk of being fired for pregnancy, retaliatory mass dismissals after protests, industry-wide blacklisting of protesters, fabricated criminal charges, violent police raids of workers' homes, locked exits in workplaces, factory fires and building collapses, punctuated by arrests and killings of labor leaders (Clean Clothes Campaign, 2020a; Human Rights Watch, 2017b, 2019; Kashyap, 2018; Manik and Bajaj, 2012; Paul, 2016). In order to compete for contracts with TNCs, RMG factory owners in Bangladesh operate on very thin margins, meaning they must offer the garments at very low prices and are constantly struggling to remain profitable. Wages are so low that a 2018 *raise* in the monthly minimum wage for garment workers (from 5,300 Tk or 63 USD to 8,000 Tk or 96 USD per month) sparked protests because it was so inadequate. Worker's organizations, unions and protesters demanded at least double that, or 16,000 Tk, to get closer to a living wage that covers a minimal cost of living for one in Dhaka (Business and Human Rights Resource Centre, 2018; Clean Clothes Campaign, 2020a).

The government of Bangladesh relies on the ready-made garment sector, which employs 4.5 million people and exports apparel worth $34 billion per year, as a key component of the national economy and has done very little to advance or enforce worker protections, basic needs, safety, pay or rights (Paton, 2020). The government of Bangladesh prioritizes maintaining this sector's extremely cheap production and inhibiting unionization in order to keep TNCs from shifting production to factories in other countries. Aminul Islam, a union organizer with the Bangladesh Center for Worker Solidarity (BCWS), was tortured and murdered with impunity in 2012, with no meaningful response by the Bangladeshi government (Manik and Bajaj, 2012; Human Rights Watch, 2017a).

After a series of deadly RMG factory collapses and fires, the Rana Plaza building, which housed several RMG factories in Dhaka, collapsed, killing over a thousand workers in 2013 (Paul, 2016). The government of Bangladesh and transnational corporations sourcing clothing from Bangladesh faced an international outcry from victims' families, workers, journalists and human, labor and women's rights organizations (International Labour Organization, 2018). Some TNCs developed voluntary worker safety agreements and initiatives. For instance, some North American apparel companies, including Walmart, formed the Alliance for Bangladesh Worker Safety, which ran from 2013 to 2018. Another factory safety consortium of primarily European TNCs (the Bangladesh Accord on Fire and Building Safety) included union involvement, a binding arbitration clause and data transparency, but the Alliance for Bangladesh did not.

Both the Alliance for Bangladesh and the Bangladesh Accord were advantageous for TNCs, or "brand" owners because they allowed "buyers new methods for controlling liability over their global supply chains" while claiming to be taking meaningful actions in the name of corporate social responsibility (Salminen, 2018, pp. 412, 414). In other words, while taking incremental and temporary steps, these corporate social responsibility initiatives also made it easier to *avoid* responsibility for workers harmed in factories supplying their products. The government of Bangladesh claims to be continuing aspects of the Bangladesh Accord through a new Ready Made Garment Sustainability Council. People monitoring labor conditions in this sector predict that the council will be weaker than the Bangladesh Accord and will do more to protect the sustainability of the factories and their owners than the sustainability and safety of the workers (Clean Clothes Campaign, 2020b; Paton, 2020). In addition to these corporate and government agreements and initiatives after the Rana Plaza tragedy, some training programs specifically for women emerged.

Text production and distribution

CSR often involves partnerships. The Alliance for Bangladesh Worker Safety and the Bangladesh Accord on Fire and Building Safety discussed earlier were "private–private" partnerships between multiple for-profit companies for "social impact" (Moser and Lowes, 2017, pp. 2–4). Also discussed earlier, the new Ready Made Garment Sustainability Council is a public–private initiative between government and industry partners. A third form, TNC–NGO partnerships, were responsible for producing and distributing these training materials to "empower" women in RMG factories:

- Walmart/CARE: "Women in Factories" program, part of Walmart's "Global Women's Economic Empowerment Initiative"
- Bayer/BSR: HERproject menstrual hygiene posters
- Mastercard/BSR: HERfinance financial literacy videos

The TNCs involved include Walmart, the world's largest retailer; Bayer, a chemical and agribusiness giant; and Mastercard, a financial technology company. Walmart sources clothing from factories in Bangladesh. Bangladeshis are a source of profits for Bayer through agribusiness and pharmaceutical sales. Mastercard profits from digital financial transactions in Bangladesh.

Although many participants were mentioned in the acknowledgments sections, each project had one major NGO partner. Walmart's "Women in Factories" empowerment program teamed with CARE, an international NGO with a mission to "save lives, defeat poverty, and achieve social justice" (CARE, 2021). Bayer's menstrual hygiene posters and Mastercard's financial literacy videos were produced in collaboration with BSR, which has a mission to "work with business to create a just and sustainable world" (BSR, 2021).

The modes of distribution range from more active to passive. "Women in Factories" is designed for in-person instruction at factories, with lessons that include role-playing, discussions, games and other active learning techniques. In the case of menstrual hygiene posters, not only is the learning more passive, but the distribution is passive as well: digital (pdf) files to be printed at the factories at the local owners' expense. The financial literacy videos are streaming but require access to the internet and a device with a screen to view them; again, the onus is on the factory owners or workers themselves to actually access them. Digital distribution helps the TNC–NGO partners save money and remain disconnected from the conditions at factories. Often the content reflects that disconnect.

The texts

The curricula reinforce gendered hierarchies in the workplace, patronize and stigmatize women and perpetuate stereotypes. In all three sets of lessons, women are the problem that needs to be fixed in order to become empowered. Improving brand image or glossing over their own culpability for women's labor exploitation is not enough for the TNCs involved. In all three cases, corporate sponsors stand to benefit from aspects of their so-called women's empowerment initiatives. They benefit not only from the idea that they are helping women, marketed to Western consumers and shareholders, but also from the content taught to the workers themselves: Walmart and factory owners "own" women's empowerment and reinforce the status quo of male managers; Bayer's materials suggest bringing painkillers to work; and Mastercard stands to profit from digital financial transactions and consumer data.

Various parts of the "Empowering Women in Factories" program actually reinforce worker-management power disparities and gender hierarchies. These intersectional inequalities are evident in the PowerPoint presentation to introduce facilitators to the curriculum. Factory management objectives include: "inclusively identify and develop talent within the factory," "retain a strong workforce, reaping the benefits of investment in talent development," "enhance factory efficiency" and, in a telling turn of phrase, "take ownership of women's empowerment"

(CARE and Walmart, n.d., p. 31). Who is reaping the benefits and taking ownership? In the images on the management objectives slide, factory management is represented by a man seated at a desk, with women sewing in the background or standing to address him or to sign a paper on his desk. The last image is all women. One woman, possibly in a leadership role, addresses the others, but they are all standing around a sewing machine. No woman in the images on this slide gets to sit at the desk. These images normalize gendered work hierarchies and divisions of labor.

Objectives for workers include: "obtain skills necessary for career advancement and increase earning potential" and "gain practical knowledge" to "enhance quality of life for workers and their families," which are, throughout the curriculum, heteronormative families (CARE and Walmart, n.d., p. 30). Images on the workers' objectives slide largely reinforce traditional and binary gender roles, such as women in family caregiving roles. One, for instance, is a woman cleaning her toddler's butt.

The "Sanitation" lesson contains two more images of other women cleaning their toddler's butts, one of the most frequently pictured activities in these women's empowerment learning plans (CARE and Walmart, n.d., pp. 30, 65, 66). For instance, pictures to facilitate a role-play exercise feature a woman preparing food while minding her child, cleaning the child's butt with a cloth and putting a sick child to bed (CARE and Walmart, n.d., p. 65). The following three pictures feature a woman preparing food with a child in a much neater room, washing her child's butt with water somewhere else and holding a happy child (Care and Walmart, n.d., p. 66). While imparting sanitation lessons, the images and role-play exercise also reinforce gendered expectations about the work women should do at home, in addition to their long factory shifts.

Another form of sexism is explaining basic information that women already know, infantilizing women, even while expecting them to single-handedly improve their own health without access to basic resources. The true-or-false menstruation awareness poster begins, "Menstruation happens for most women about once a month." The same poster instructs: "pain relievers, a hot bath, or a warm compress can help ease pain from cramps" (US AID, Bayer and Evidence Project, 2017). So, women should buy some Bayer aspirin and take baths.

Many people in Bangladesh take bucket baths, and garment workers' living conditions often do not include private bathrooms. A bathtub with enough clean hot water to fill a tub to soak in is not a realistic scenario for women working in RMG factories. Even a hot bucket bath might be difficult due to limited water and sanitation facilities. For instance, some garment workers in southeast Dhaka had access to "two toilets for an entire block of at least 40 people" (Gavin, 2019). In the Mirpur slum of Dhaka,

> an area in which a majority of the community members work in one of the many garment factories ... There are no female toilets in the community,

> which makes it uncomfortable for girls and women, especially during their menstruation. Often, they await darkness to go to the toilet in the open and risk being assaulted.
>
> (Sustainable Sanitation Alliance, n.d.)

Suggesting a hot bath illustrates the disconnect between the training materials and the women's lives. This poster also shows how empowerment initiatives focus on changing individual women rather than broader structural changes, like better wages, adequate water and sanitation at work and home, bathroom breaks for workers or affordable housing with plumbing.

Another poster, titled "Stay healthy during your period," has this suggestion:

> **Wear darker colored clothing.**
> During menstruation, you may bleed through your clothes. Consider wearing dark clothes on days when you're expecting your period or when your flow is at its heaviest in order to prepare and avoid embarrassment.
> (US AID, Bayer and Evidence Project, 2017, emphasis in original)

While this is good advice to keep workers working, it has little relevance to health unless it is emotional health; in that case, the poster does more harm than good by describing visible bleeding as an "embarrassment." Stigma about menstruation, reinforced by this poster, is a powerful form of sexism that is unaddressed by the "growing trend within international development, often called 'Menstruation Hygiene Management' (MHM), to help menstruators in the global south," which has made sanitary pads the "'It Girl' of Global Development" (Zhu, 2019). The poster series is called menstrual "hygiene" rather than health, which reinforces the idea that menstruation is dirty.

Additional advice on this poster has more to do with embarrassment and work interruptions than women's health: "**Be prepared.** Your period may start at work. If you carry sanitary pads and a pain reliever, then regular work activities can continue" (US AID, Bayer and Evidence Project, 2017, emphasis in original). In addition to pads, this poster also promotes sales of pain relievers—Asia is an important and growing market for Bayer (Bayer, 2020). To be sure, open communication on public posters about menstruation is progress in a sense. But of all the messages that could be put on menstrual health posters, those chosen reinforce a notion of women as ignorant about their own cycles, prone to humiliating bleeding that interrupts work and an emerging market for pharmaceutical and menstrual products.

Sexism in HERfinance videos includes the stereotype that women are frivolous spenders who would benefit from the discipline of digital banking. Interestingly, TNCs with programs to empower women in the Global South often tell the opposite tale about the economic behavior of women to their shareholders and consumers: "there is a growing tendency to view women as more risk averse than men and to have longer-term goals," another essentialized generalization about women (Roberts, 2015, p. 214). That story reassures shareholders that helping women is also good for the bottom line and blames short-sighted, risk-taking men of the Global South for impoverishing their families. But in HERfinance live-action short films, in which actors portray everyday situations in Bangladesh to impart financial lessons, one storyline centers on women's need to curb their spending—with the help of cash-free digital banking. The film "Intro to digital financial services" takes place near a small, outdoor vendor, where three women with factory IDs on lanyards are walking home. Shabana holds up her earrings but says her purse contains only her mobile phone and a few taka (the currency of Bangladesh) because the rest of the money is in her account. Her older sister or colleague, Rinaa, observes, "That is a very good thing. Maybe now you will stop buying unnecessary things like earrings, ribbons, etc." (HERfinance, 2020c).

Rinaa's husband, Sohan, then enters the scene, telling Rinaa they should go home because their daughter must be hungry. Another man drives by on a red motorcycle. Sohan: "Oh, that's what I want. What a beautiful motorcycle. It's worth saving money for" (HERfinance, 2020c). This storyline reinforces the idea of women as central to the problem of deficient savings (due to their ribbons and earrings purchases) as well as key to its solution: They should save to help men buy important things (a husband's new motorcycle, or, in another video, a brother's mobile phone minutes). An older woman, Ratna, pipes in with her own dream of saving to move back to her village, where she can spend time playing with her future grandchildren instead of working. In this case, she would be saving for her own needs (retirement) in her accepted role as mother and grandmother, providing some of the free care work that allows factory owners to hire couples like Rinaa and Sohan (Patel and Moore, 2017, ch. 4). The heteronormative family and traditional, binary gender roles are reinforced throughout the video.

To be sure, the storylines and images are not entirely sexist. The film "Savings" features young Shabana walking into the spacious courtyard of Sohan and Rinaa's home (where Sohan is seen helping to remove dry laundry from a line) for savings advice because she wants to open a shop. Rinaa tells her that she discusses the monthly budget together with her husband, Sohan, and that both need to save—she did not buy a shawl, and he spends less time at the tea stall with friends. They are saving for the future education of their young daughter, who is shown drawing a helicopter. This drama thus hits all the right notes for a corporate-friendly vision of women's empowerment (women's entrepreneurship, girls' STEM education, men helping out with light housework) in addition to the takeaway, an endorsement of digital banking: "What really helps me save is to keep money on my digital account" (HERfinance, 2020d). The idyllic home and spacious courtyard (unrealistic with the incomes of most workers in the RMG industry) convey the message that it is not low wages but low savings that are the major problem facing workers, and digital savings are the solution.

Despite the "aura of emancipation" (Arruzza, Bhattacharya and Fraser, 2019, p. 12) in this story, the main point is that technology helps curb women's natural impulses to overspend (a sexist stereotype) and turns them into responsible consumers and entrepreneurs. The drama artfully combines sexism and the neoliberal impulse to upgrade women rather than their socioeconomic conditions. Together, these videos exhort women earning sub-poverty wages to save money and thus gain access to a phone (to receive their pay), transportation, retirement, business opportunities and education for their children.

In addition to the narrative of spendthrift women frittering away time and money buying earrings and ribbons, another sexist element, most evident in the "Savings" video, is the recurring narrative of women and girls in danger, which functions to try to scare women into mobile banking. Rinaa says, "It makes me feel safer to not have cash at home. I've heard about these break-ins to people's houses. And my daughter is still very young. It scares me even to think about it." Ratna laments that she is tired of "not feeling safe carrying it [cash] around" (HERfinance, 2020d). Yet an impact report on RMG workers' shift to digital wages, despite rosy conclusions about their overall benefits, includes more complicated findings about safety:

> Many women in Bangladesh are expected to hand over part, if not all, of their earnings to a male family member. When paid in cash, some women circumvent control over their salaries by hiding some of their earnings for their own use or to send to relatives ... the transparency of the digital wages system can put women at risk of conflict or even domestic violence if they are caught hiding a portion of their wages.
>
> (Bill & Melinda Gates Foundation, 2020, p. 20)

Here the report problematically emphasizes local rather than global patriarchy, sidestepping the exploitation of women in supply chains, but this finding about women potentially losing some financial freedom with the move to digital wages also reveals that we cannot hack our way out of patriarchy. We need to consider the unintended consequences of digital innovations rather than assume they empower women (see Kunz and Ramírez, this volume).

Moreover, to achieve the feeling of safety that is (perhaps) provided by mobile banking, women need to purchase or share a phone or, at least, a SIM card to use on a shared phone (with unproven implications for their financial or personal security) and pay fees for their digital financial transactions. HERfinance videos encourage women to purchase mobile phones, both directly by advising women to buy a phone for financial security (HERfinance, 2020a) and indirectly by instructing women how to do financial planning to save and buy something expensive, featuring, as the primary example, a mobile phone (HERfinance, 2020b). In addition to providing fees to Mastercard and other financial technology companies, digital banking encourages women to buy phones and spend money via their phones, which become conduits for consumer data and marketing (Zuboff, 2019).

Like the "Women in Factories" lessons and the menstrual hygiene posters, the financial literacy videos instruct workers to be better neoliberal "subjects" and "human capital" (Brown, 2015). RMG workers are supposed to empower themselves by adjustments to their own behavior and by saving to pay for things (such as dark clothing, phones and retirement). In contrast to individual economic and behavioral adjustments, transformative empowerment would entail both solidarity and political power.

Counterpoints and alternatives

Women workers in Bangladesh apprehend the limitations of programming spearheaded by corporations. Indeed, thousands of garment workers have marched to demand a living wage, at least double the current minimum wage for garment workers (Agence-France Presse, 2019; Business and Human Rights Centre, 2018). Some workers have organized and offered their own workshops to achieve substantive and material changes. For instance, despite the murder of one of their organizers, the BCWS offers leadership training that—in contrast to Walmart's—emphasizes "women's rights, workplace safety and security, gender-based violence at the workplace and community and how to take action against different types of violence and exploitation." BCWS computer training enables workers to "communicate with BCWS, brands, and oversight institutions, prepare written complaints and present evidence" (BCWS, 2020b). Due to the globalization of anti-union law firms and consultants hired to hold sessions in factories to prevent unionization (Logan, 2020; Bognar and Reichert, 2019), the BCWS "know your rights" programs on why and how to form a union are increasingly vital to achieving workers' rights (BCWS, 2020a).

Such BCWS training programs and garment workers' ongoing demands for better wages and safe working conditions provide a mutual aid (Spade, 2020) counterpoint to the meager forms of empowerment discussed earlier. They do so by incorporating (1) labor solidarity instead of neoliberal individual improvement; (2) intersectional approaches that challenge poverty, gender inequalities and gender-based violence instead of repeating sexist narratives; and (3) political actions such as joint complaints that document and fight widespread labor exploitation.

Solidarity and political actions are also central to another initiative. After working on the "Women in Factories" program, CARE subsequently developed another program (with noncorporate funding from the EU and the Austrian government) for workers in Bangladesh. The program was called OIKKO (or "unity" in Bangla) and ran from 2015 to 2018. In contrast to CARE's earlier collaboration with Walmart, a key part of the OIKKO program was forming "EKATA groups" of women—*ekata* means "one" in Bangla—to identify issues and form collective action plans in safe spaces. CARE found that

> the EKATA approach, combined with support to trade unions, is far more effective than training for supporting worker empowerment. Our experience shows individual training approaches on rights and life skills can

> support individuals to make better-informed decisions and raise some demands on their own behalf, but this is unlikely to facilitate the collective action on a broader scope of rights-based issues seen as a result of EKATA.
> (CARE, 2019, p. 1)

CARE's shift from a self-help approach to a program based on solidarity and rights puts into relief the limitations of the "Women in Factories" type of empowerment funded by Walmart, which is "one of the most aggressive anti-union companies" (Greenhouse, 2015).

On the specific issues of empowerment related to menstruation, Bobel provides several practices for "putting menstrual literacy at the center" by providing menstrual literacy for everyone, not just women and girls, by teaching the whole menstrual cycle, not just the period, by recognizing menstruation's value as another "vital sign" of health and by prioritizing trained and trusted teachers (2019, pp. 282–321). An example of a "rights-based" and "women-centered" program that utilizes such principles in Bangladesh is Ritu, funded by The Netherlands (Simavi, 2021).

In regard to women's financial literacy, the push for "cashlessness for development" needs much more research to determine the impacts of the shift to digital transactions on informal economies, privacy, poverty and women. Masiero and Das's (2019) research in South Asia begins to problematize the "orthodoxy of 'inclusive cashlessness'" and examine the implications of digital wages and transactions in the Global South. Couldry and Mejias (2019) argue that digital data collection about spending followed by targeted marketing, all facilitated by cashless economic transactions, are a new form of colonization, which they call "data colonialism." Programs to empower women financially will need to take these significant critiques into account.

A final counterpoint to the factory-based initiatives discussed in this chapter is the Pathways for Promise program at the Asian University for Women in Chattogram, Bangladesh. Chattogram is the location of Bangladesh's first export processing zone and many RMG factories. Through this program, women in the RMG industry can pursue college degrees (Asian University for Women, 2021). College degrees can do more than temporary training initiatives to benefit women and help them take on leadership roles. Providing funding and time for educational opportunities for women—and enabling them to achieve college degrees while continuing to work if they need or want to—is an important way to advance gender equity (Dye and Jenkins, 2021).

Conclusion: A gendered critique of social (ir)responsibility (SIR)

Robust power and mutual aid are necessary to transform women's lives in meaningful ways, as opposed to watered-down, neoliberal "empowerment" schemes that protect powerful people and corporations. At best, the three TNC–NGO training initiatives for RMG workers examined in this chapter tinker around the edges of neoliberal capitalism; at worst, they shore it up.

Such programs link a set of feminist-sounding ideas to the interests of global capitalism (Roberts, 2015, p. 211). At first glance, the programs make TNCs look good and bolster their CSR commitments, but they reinforce gendered hierarchies and gloss over corporate social irresponsibility (SIR).

Walmart, which sources garments from Bangladesh, is a member of the UN Global Compact of businesses committing to advance human rights—but only in Chile and Mexico, not Bangladesh (UN Global Compact, 2021). By partially participating in the UN Global Compact in certain places and offering women's "economic empowerment" training in others, corporations like Walmart can say they are fulfilling some social responsibility obligations while selectively ignoring several of the UNGC's ten principles, which include "the right to collective bargaining" (Moon, 2014, p. 93; Greenhouse, 2015).

The menstruation posters provide tips that put the onus on women to maintain factory production by purchasing pads and painkillers rather than guaranteeing the material resources and labor rights (for instance, more bathroom facilities and breaks) needed to actually maintain menstrual health. These awareness posters prioritize managing menstruation in ways that do not disrupt production over advancing women's health or destigmatizing menstruation.

The financial literacy videos suggest that inadequate savings, rather than inadequate pay, is the main problem—and that women need digital discipline to save their wages to buy motorcycles for their husbands. They also promote digital financial transactions and technologies that benefit Mastercard and other financial technology companies through fees, consumer data and targeted marketing opportunities. The financial literacy curriculum prioritizes corporate profits over women's power.

One ideology associated with corporate initiatives to empower women and girls in their supply chains in the Global South is the maxim that what is good for women is also good for business (Roberts, 2015, p. 210). This chapter refutes that win-win story. These empowerment programs for women in RMG factories may look good on corporate and NGO websites, advertisements and annual reports, but they are a losing prospect for women workers. Not only do they help corporations avoid doing what actually needs to be done to advance women, but they also harm women by perpetuating sexist stereotypes and profiting off of them. Stereotypical roles and images in these training programs include women as frivolous spenders, as the primary caregivers for children in heteronormative families, and as workers hovering around but not sitting at the boss's desk. They aim for limited empowerment for workers in the Global South rather than power for all women. These programs facilitate gendered SIR. At the same time, other noncorporate and more mutual aid- and labor rights-oriented initiatives suggest on-the-ground resistance to neoliberal SIR, lending additional evidence to Bergeron's (Chapter 11, this volume) claim that there are always cracks in neoliberal and neoliberal feminist-inflected projects.

References

Ackerly, B. (2018) *Just Responsibility: A Human Rights Theory of Global Justice*. New York: Oxford University Press.

Ackerly, B. and True, J. (2020) *Doing Feminist Research in Political and Social Science*. London: Macmillan.

Agence-France Presse. (2019) "Bangladesh strikes: thousands of garment workers clash with police over poor pay." *The Guardian*. Available at https://www.theguardian.com/world/2019/jan/14/bangladesh-strikes-thousands-of-garment-workers-clash-with-police-over-poor-pay (accessed December 2, 2020).

Arruzza, C., Bhattacharya, T. and Fraser, N. (2019) *Feminism for the 99%: A Manifesto*. London: Verso.

Asian University for Women. (2021) "Impact: pathways for promise." Available at https://asian-university.org/impact/our-partners-2/ (accessed March 29, 2021).

Bayer. (2020) "Important market: the Asia/Pacific region." Available at https://www.bayer.com/en/worldwide/asia-pacific (accessed January 12, 2021).

BCWS. (2020a) "Know your rights program." Available at https://www.bcwsbd.org/page/know-your-rights-program/ (accessed December 3, 2020).

BCWS. (2020b) "Skills development." Available at https://www.bcwsbd.org/page/leadership-skills-development/ (accessed December 3, 2020).

BEPZA. (2021) "About BEPZA." Available at https://www.bepza.gov.bd/content/about-bepza (accessed March 18, 2021).

Bill and Melinda Gates Foundation. (2020) *Digital Wages: Positive Impact for Women and Business*. Available at https://herproject.org/files/reports/HERproject-digital-wages-positive-impact-for-women-business.pdf (accessed December 4, 2020).

Bobel, C. (2019) *The Managed Body: Developing Girls and Menstrual Health in the Global South*. London: Palgrave Macmillan.

Bognar, S. and Reichert, J. (dirs.) (2019) *American Factory* [film]. USA: Higher Ground Productions.

Brosnan, A. (2016) "Representations of race and racism in the textbooks used in southern black schools during the American Civil War and Reconstruction Era, 1861–1876," *Paedagogica Historica*, 52 (6), pp. 718–733.

Brown, W. (2015) *Undoing the Demos: Neoliberalism's Stealth Revolution*. New York: Zone Books.

BSR. (2021) "Overview." Available at https://www.bsr.org/en/about (accessed March 19, 2021).

Business and Human Rights Resource Centre. (2018) "Bangladesh: Widespread garment worker protests over minimum wage increase; leads to mass dismissals." Available at https://www.business-humanrights.org/en/latest-news/bangladesh-widespread-garment-worker-protests-over-minimum-wage-increase-leads-to-mass-dismissals/ (accessed December 2, 2020).

CARE. (2019) *OIKKO: Unity, Women Working Together for Change*. Available at https://care.org/wp-content/uploads/2020/08/oikko_learning_brief_sept2019.pdf (accessed December 3, 2020).

CARE. (2021) "Mission and vision." Available at https://www.care.org/about-us/mission-vision/ (accessed March 19, 2021).

CARE and Walmart. (n.d. [circa 2011–2012]) *Women in Factories Training Program: Foundational Training—Trainer's Guide and Module Learning Plans*. Available at https://corporate.walmart.com/media-library/document/foundational-training-trainers-guide-and-mod ule-learning-plans/_proxyDocument?id=0000016b-8b69-d026-a17f-8f792cbd0000 (accessed January 12, 2021).

Chant, S. and Sweetman, C. (2012) "Fixing women or fixing the world? 'Smart economics,' efficiency approaches, and gender equality in development." *Gender and Development*, 20 (3), pp. 517–529.

Clean Clothes Campaign. (2020a) "A year after crackdown on wage protests in Bangladesh, hundreds of workers still face retaliatory charges." Available at https://cleanclothes.org/news/2020/a-year-after-crackdown-on-wage-protests-in-bangladesh-hundreds-of-workers-still-face-retaliatory-charges (accessed December 2, 2020).

Clean Clothes Campaign. (2020b) "Amidst Covid-19 crisis, untested industry group assumes safety responsibilities for Bangladesh garment factories despite concerns." Available at https://cleanclothes.org/file-repository/accord_witness_signatory_assessment.pdf/view (accessed March 19, 2021).

Couldry, N. and Mejias, U. (2019) *The Costs of Connection: How Data Is Colonizing Human Life and Appropriating It for Capitalism.* Palo Alto: Stanford University Press.

Cronin-Furman, K., Gowrinathan, N. and Zakaria, R. (2017) "*Emissaries of empowerment.*" Colin Powell School for Civic and Global Leadership, The City College of New York. Available at https://www.ccny.cuny.edu/colinpowellschool/emissaries-empowerment (accessed March 30, 2021).

Dye, J. and Jenkins, L. (2021) "Women's equality and development through political representation, food sovereignty, and education," in Snarr, M. and Snarr, D. (eds.) *Introducing Global Issues*, 7th ed. Boulder: Lynne Rienner Publishers.

Ferguson, J. (1994) *The Anti-politics Machine: "Development," Depoliticization, and Bureaucratic Power in Lesotho.* Minneapolis: University of Minnesota Press.

Ganti, T. (2014) "Neoliberalism," *Annual Review of Anthropology*, 43, pp. 89–104.

Gavin, I. (2019) "Fairer fashion begins with better access to water & toilets for workers in clothing supply chains." *IPS Inter Press Service News Agency.* Available at http://www.ipsnews.net/2019/09/fairer-fashion-begins-better-access-water-toilets-workers-clothing-supply-chains/ (accessed November 17, 2020).

Giridharadas, A. (2018) *Winners Take All: The Elite Charade of Changing the World.* New York: Alfred A. Knopf.

Greenhouse, S. (2015) "How Walmart persuades its workers not to unionize." *The Atlantic.* Available at https://www.theatlantic.com/business/archive/2015/06/how-walmart-convinces-its-employees-not-to-unionize/395051/ (accessed December 3, 2020).

Hawkesworth, M. (2016) *Embodied Power: Demystifying Disembodied Politics.* New York: Routledge.

HERfinance. (2020a) "HERfinance digital wages Bangladesh animation 1 of 10: Intro to digital financial services." *YouTube.* Available at https://www.youtube.com/watch?v=WXcKbbSY_k8 (accessed January 7, 2021).

HERfinance. (2020b) "HERfinance digital wages Bangladesh animation 5 of 10: Intro to financial planning and managing." *YouTube.* Available at https://www.youtube.com/watch?v=R2jE8Hm0CU4 (accessed January 7, 2021).

HERfinance. (2020c) "HERfinance digital wages Bangladesh film 1 of 7: Intro to digital financial services." *YouTube.* Available at https://www.youtube.com/watch?v=3A-PAzKltlc (accessed January 14, 2021).

HERfinance. (2020d) "HERfinance digital wages Bangladesh film 5 of 7 savings." *YouTube.* Available at https://www.youtube.com/watch?v=v9-rlDx-6Bc (accessed January 14, 2021).

Human Rights Watch. (2017a) "Bangladesh: 5 years on, no justice for Aminul Islam, government promises to expedite high-level investigations yield nothing." Available at

https://www.hrw.org/news/2017/04/04/bangladesh-5-years-no-justice-aminul-islam (accessed December 2, 2020).
Human Rights Watch. (2017b) "Bangladesh: stop persecuting unions, garment workers." Available at https://www.hrw.org/news/2017/02/15/bangladesh-stop-persecuting-unions-garment-workers (accessed December 2, 2020).
Human Rights Watch (2019) "Bangladesh: investigate dismissals of protesting workers: unions claim at least 7,500 dismissed arbitrarily from work, others targeted in violent policy raid." Available at https://www.hrw.org/news/2019/03/05/bangladesh-investigate-dismissals-protesting-workers# (accessed December 2, 2020).
International Labor Organization. (2018) "The Rana Plaza accident and its aftermath." Available at https://www.ilo.org/global/topics/geip/WCMS_614394/lang--en/index.htm (accessed December 2, 2020).
Kashyap, A. (2018) "When clothing labels are a matter of life or death." *Human Rights Watch*. Available at https://www.hrw.org/news/2018/05/02/when-clothing-labels-are-matter-life-or-death (accessed December 2, 2020).
Logan, J. (2020) "The U.S. union avoidance industry goes global," *New Labor Forum*, 29(1), pp. 76–81.
Manik, J. and Bajaj, V. (2012) "Killing of Bangladeshi labor organizer signals and escalation in violence." *New York Times*. Available at https://www.nytimes.com/2012/04/10/world/asia/bangladeshi-labor-organizer-is-found-killed.html?module=inline (accessed December 2, 2020).
Masiero, S. and Das, S. (2019) "Cashlessness for development: a dangerous orthodoxy." DATACTIVE: The Politics of Data According to Civil Society. Available at https://data-activism.net/2019/09/cashlessness-for-development-a-dangerous-orthodoxy/ (accessed January 28, 2021).
Merry, S. (2016) *The Seductions of Quantification: Measuring Human Rights, Gender Violence, and Sex Trafficking*. Chicago: University of Chicago Press.
Moon, J. (2014) *Corporate Social Responsibility: A Very Short Introduction*. Oxford: Oxford University Press.
Moser, H. and Lowes, S. (2017) "Catalyzing private-private partnerships for social impact." *Center for Strategic and International Studies*. Available at https://www.csis.org/analysis/catalyzing-private-private-partnerships-social-impact (accessed January 7, 2021).
Patel, R. and Moore, J. (2017) *The History of the World in Seven Cheap Things*. Oakland: University of California Press.
Paton, E. (2020) "After factory disaster, Bangladesh made big safety strides. Are the bad days coming back?" *The New York Times*. Available at https://www.nytimes.com/2020/03/01/world/asia/rana-plaza-bangladesh-garment-industry.html (accessed December 2, 2020).
Paul, R. (2016) "Factbox: major industrial accidents in Bangladesh in recent years." *Reuters*. Available at https://www.reuters.com/article/us-bangladesh-fire-factbox/factbox-major-industrial-accidents-in-bangladesh-in-recent-years-idUSKCN12C2PR (accessed April 2, 2019).
Roberts, A. (2015) "The political economy of 'transnational business feminism': Problematizing the corporate-led gender equality agenda." *International Feminist Journal of Politics*, 17(2), pp. 209–231.
Salminen, J. (2018) "The accord on fire and building safety in Bangladesh: A new paradigm for limiting buyer's liability in global supply chains?" *The American Journal of Comparative Law*, 66(2), pp. 411–451.

Sharma, A. (2008) *Logics of Empowerment: Development, Gender, and Governance in Neoliberal India*. Minneapolis: University of Minnesota Press.

Simavi. (2021) "Ritu." Available at https://simavi.org/what-we-do/programmes/ritu/ (accessed March 23, 2021).

Spade, D. (2020) *Mutual Aid: Building Solidarity During This Crisis (and the Next!)*. London: Verso.

Suchomel, K. (2018) "Gender in humanitarian imagery: The case of CARE international." Centre for Feminist Foreign Policy. Available at https://centreforfeministforeignpolicy.org/journal/2018/9/4/gender-in-humanitarian-imagery-the-case-of-care-international (accessed April 5, 2021).

Sustainable Sanitation Alliance. (n.d.) "Addressing WASH crisis in Mirpur for garments workers Bangladesh: 2018–2021." Available at https://www.susana.org/en/knowledge-hub/projects/database/details/595 (accessed January 5, 2021).

UN Global Compact. (2021) "Our Participants." Available at https://www.unglobalcompact.org/what-is-gc/participants/search?utf8=✓&search%5Bkeywords%5D=Walmart&button=&search%5Bper_page%5D=10&search%5Bsort_field%5D=&search%5Bsort_direction%5D=asc (accessed March 24, 2021).

US AID, Bayer and Evidence Project. (2017) "Do you know the Facts about menstrual hygiene and management? Check your knowledge: T or F," and "Stay healthy during your period." Poster. Available at http://evidenceproject.popcouncil.org/resource/health-education-materials-for-the-workplace/ (accessed November 17, 2020).

Wu, T. (2018). *The Curse of Bigness: Antitrust in the New Gilded Age*. New York: Columbia University Press.

Wu, T. (2019) "The virtuous corporation is not an oxymoron." *New York Times*. Available at https://www.nytimes.com/2019/09/23/opinion/stakeholder-capitalism.html (accessed September 23, 2019).

Zhu, A. (2019) "Sanitary pads, the 'it girl' of global development." *BRIGHT Magazine*. Available at https://brightthemag.com/sanitary-pads-the-it-girl-of-global-development-a38c7b3fda3 (accessed March 23, 2021).

Zuboff, S. (2019) *The Age of Surveillance Capitalism: The Fight for a Human Future at the New Frontier of Power*. New York: PublicAffairs.

8 Inclusive innovation

Feminist perspectives

Gillian Youngs

Introduction

Innovation is one of the most overused and underexplained terms in contemporary times. Its significance and application have grown in step with the continually expanding and deepening definition of human development as primarily technologically driven. In this context, our minds are directed immediately to the West-centered and increasingly globalized agrarian, industrial and high-tech revolutions and economic growth models of the past several hundred years. We can go even deeper into the fundamental facts that human invention of tools, organizations and all forms of social, economic and cultural processes have involved different kinds of innovation throughout history.

Cities have stood out as hubs of cutting-edge knowledge and economic power, spearheading innovation, and more recently, attention has been directed to the network of global cities steering globalization—London, New York, Beijing and Tokyo, to name a few. This signals how innovation is dependent on links across government, research, finance, investment and business, as well as transport and trading networks. Innovation is embedded in the economic growth paradigm. In the recent era of small and medium-sized enterprises (SMEs) as key powerhouses of the economy, it has been closely associated with entrepreneurship. As increasing numbers of people have been involved in founding and growing SMEs, there has been, not surprisingly, expanding awareness of issues of inclusion related to innovation and entrepreneurship. Less evident has been fundamental questioning of how innovation is understood and ways in which these impact who is most likely to become an innovator, and, equally importantly, how and what kind of innovation is supported by institutions and different kinds of public and private funding and investment. This chapter focuses on how related areas have been addressed by feminist theory and analysis, as well as women's activism and practice.

The predominance of technological framings of innovation is driven by the masculinist history of science and technology in theory and practice, as well as the state and market entities that define, shape and support the economic growth paradigm. Defense research and development (R&D) and spending dominate this picture as an expression of masculinist power and framings of

DOI: 10.4324/9781003036425-9

innovation across state and market. In wider societal regards, the effects of structural factors, constraining innovation within primarily scientific and technological parameters, reflect masculinist limitations on agenda and horizon setting. This critical point was boosted in significance by the global COVID-19 pandemic starting in 2020 and only subsiding by 2023. The dramatically disruptive nature of this crisis in relation to long-established and relatively stable patterns of state and market activity, employment and mobility, consumption and leisure and social and family life led to talk about the *new normal*. The highly contagious nature of the virus resulted in patterns of what had been regarded as normal life and social engagement being substituted by various forms of nationwide and small-scale lockdowns and restrictions of movement. A position of intense mobility established through processes of modernity and globalization was replaced by a range of conditions of immobility and isolation, both physical and social. Digital connectivity and dependence expanded dramatically as working, learning, socializing, shopping and entertainment became substantially virtual by default. Digital divides were among the array of inequalities related to race, age and a range of socioeconomic factors, resulting in the crisis impacting most of the least advantaged communities through deaths, illness and loss of educational opportunities, livelihoods and homes.

This chapter reflects in part on the disruptions of the pandemic and their destabilization of assumptions related to the economic growth paradigm, particularly the extent to which it is underpinned by increasingly complex and interconnected sets of inequalities and extreme and widening gaps between those with most and least. The discussion begins by setting out the vital and long-standing contributions of feminism's critique of the reductionism of masculinist approaches to innovation, and feminist calls for more effective and integrated perspectives. This feminist work mirrors substantially some new mainstream realizations and pressures resulting from the pandemic, steering innovation toward more comprehensive and historically-informed perspectives and pressing for greater policy attention to embedded socioeconomic inequalities.

Such priorities directly challenge the restricted definitions of innovation in STEM (science, technology, engineering and math), which have driven the growth model of contemporary capitalism and maintained its masculinist orientations. The chapter begins by considering the past, present and future of innovation, reflecting on the many resources feminist work and women's activism have made available to address contemporary challenges. This reaches well beyond the dominant technologically-driven approaches to innovation and is distinguished by its interdisciplinarity and recognition of the distribution of power, defining winners and losers in terms of resources and influence. The discussion examines how well-established feminist critiques are a basis for developing new forms of innovation, adequate to long-standing social inequities as well as fit for a post-pandemic world, where the most tragic results of those inequities have been dramatically demonstrated through millions of deaths and cases of long-term illness.

The points covered make it clear that we need to look outside the traditional boundaries and trajectories of STEM for fresh and more equitable answers while also recognizing that, with the intensification of technological developments, the power of STEM is likely to continue to assert itself in major, if possibly some changed ways. The chapter goes on to consider gender issues in STEM in this recognition that its dominant position in mainstream power structures of knowledge and production is unlikely to be significantly dislodged in the immediate future. The discussion stresses the importance of both improving gender balance and women's advancement and leadership in STEM, and gender critiques' disruption of the masculinist assumptions around definitions of research excellence within it. The chapter moves on to examine the radical transformation in innovation promoted by the feminist new green deal, integrating interdisciplinary approaches into human-centered and environmentally-grounded ways forward. This section touches on the values-driven nature of such approaches, and the extent to which they destabilize established masculinist assumptions, and makes connections with the growing mainstream attention to design thinking as a methodology for innovation, bringing value and process together. The discussion considers how the principles of design thinking mirror some feminist priorities and offer the potential to contribute to the development of new inclusive trajectories for innovation.

Innovation past, present and future: Transformative feminist paths

Innovation has to be considered in the wider context of science and technology with which it has traditionally been most closely associated. The status of science as the dominant form of knowledge in modernity is a key part of this picture, especially for understanding the hurdles to be overcome in mounting critiques of it in theory and practice. The power of science and its embedding in state and market structures and institutions are foundational elements of West-centered male domination and masculinist cultures and values (Harding, 1998, 2008). Feminist theorists and activists have, throughout a long history, interrogated and challenged embedded assumptions and distortions maintaining this gendered hegemony of thought and practice. Key trajectories in this vast and diverse body of work revolve around revealing and exploring how these assumptions and distortions generate and perpetuate binary framings. These have featured gendered separations of productivity (in market and public terms) in a hierarchical fashion *over* human and social reproduction (in domestic and private terms), the former predominantly aligned with masculine identities and positionings, and the latter with feminine ones (Wollstonecraft, 1792/1985; Pettman, 1996; Peterson, 2003). This structure extends to traditional roles and identities, with subject status granted to men and the masculine realm, and object status to women and the feminine realm (Pateman, 1988; Thompson et al., 2018). Such framing of productivity drives the mainstream economic growth model and places human and social reproduction in service to it. Masculinity is largely aligned with the public construction of productivity, and femininity with the private reproductive sphere, and as male power is dominant, it extends across public and private, whereas female power struggles to establish itself in either (Walby, 1990, 1997; Gill and Bakker, 2003). The complexities of gendered inequalities have continued to expand, with growing numbers of women doing different forms of work outside the home and processes of globalization increasing exploitation, forced labor and enslavement of women as transnational phenomena, including in the care, domestic and sex trafficking areas (Youngs, 1999; Marchand and Runyan, 2011; United Nations Office on Drugs and Crime, 2018). Feminist scholars such as Sylvia Walby, quoted next, highlight the importance of understanding contrasting forms of dynamics across public and private.

> Some ways of thinking about varieties of gender regime have a simple division between production and reproduction: women may be women predominantly working in the home or predominantly in the workplace. That is too simple. I differentiate between different forms of women's engagement in the public and divide the public gender regime into social democratic and neoliberal varieties. In both forms, women are in the public, for example, in employment and education. They differ in the levels of democracy and organisation of care work. In the social democratic variety of public gender regime, democratic pressures lead the state to provide care work; in the neoliberal variety of public gender regime, where democracy is less deep, care-work is organised through the market.
>
> (Kocabicak, 2017)

There is an integrated emphasis in feminist analysis, contesting fundamentally the masculinist binary structuring of public and private and asserting instead the primacy of embodied reality, incorporating all dimensions of lived experience across them (Youngs, 2000). This overturns the oppositional framings of the binary power configurations of male (subject) over female (object) and the characteristics associated with them, such as rationality, objectivity, courage and independence in the case of the former, and emotion, vulnerability, caring and dependence in the case of the latter. The categories of rationality and objectivity stand out as key drivers of masculinist power expressed through STEM and its constrained definitions of innovation through a combination of knowledge processes and their transformation into application and practice. The masculinist abstractions resulting from the workings of the binary structure through institutional and other social processes can also be considered disembodied in the ways they deny the entirety of lived experience. Feminists have also charted extensive territory beyond the binary in the complexities of that lived experience, including in terms of the "intersectional," varied and often overlapping forms of racial, socioeconomic and cultural inequality impacting groups and individuals and the wide range of embodied gendered and sexual identities (UN Women, 2020; Butler, 1990, 1993; Grosz, 1994; hooks, 2015).

The unequal impacts of the COVID-19 crisis in deaths, illness and damage to or loss of livelihoods, as it intensified through 2020 and 2021, was a dramatic and enduring feature of public focus and debate. While the big STEM news was concentrated on the development of the life-saving vaccines, there were growing revelations about diverse ways in which the pandemic hit hardest those with intersecting inequalities related to race, gender, income, job type and location. The scale and speed of the human loss could not have highlighted more forcefully and tragically that STEM's perspectives on innovation, while vital in their contributions, were sorely inadequate to overturn the historically entrenched divides, placing some at much greater risk than others of death, severe illness, damage to or loss of livelihood and homelessness. This was clear evidence, if it was needed, that the integrated perspectives of feminist analysis were essential to an interdisciplinary understanding of innovation, focused on social reproduction as much as production, and taking account of the range of overlapping inequalities that shape lived realities and relative vulnerabilities. This was even more notable in terms of growing awareness that socioeconomic and other negative effects of the pandemic were likely to be long-lived and deep.

> In general, the already disadvantaged, such as women, children, persons with disabilities and indigenous people, stand to see their conditions worsen disproportionately through increasing poverty, reduced access to services and heightened vulnerability within the household. Women, for instance, are mostly employed in the informal sector—70 percent globally and over 90 percent in developing countries, while single mothers and older women are already more likely to be poor than men in similar circumstances. Prolonged stays at home can increase the burden of care work, as well as make it harder to escape domestic violence.
>
> (United Nations Department of Economic and Social Affairs, 2020, p. 2)

The pandemic impacts signaled the increase of multiple burdens and inequalities affecting women and other disadvantaged groups. The concentration of women working in the health and care sectors, as well as other low-paid, part-time and insecure key worker roles, increased their exposure to the virus as well as the subsequent risks of passing it on to their families, including highly vulnerable elders (Blundell et al., 2020). One striking aspect in relation to women and children was the exposure of the home as an unsafe environment and the negative outcomes of more enforced time there due to repeated lockdowns to curb the spread of the virus and ease the pressure on already underresourced healthcare facilities. UN Women identified the increase in violence against women and girls, particularly domestic violence, as a "shadow pandemic," and emphasized the importance of data collection on the problem, a long-standing area in need of greater policy focus (UN Women, 2020; United Nations, 2020a; UN Women and World Health Organization, 2020). UN statistics showed the depth of global gender inequalities, including women doing three times as much unpaid care work as men, limiting their access to paid work and experiencing a gender pay gap of 16 percent, rising to 35 percent in some countries (United Nations, 2020a, pp. 6–7). Women aged 24–35 globally were 25 percent more likely to live in extreme poverty than men. The effects of the pandemic threatened not only to inhibit the efforts to improve this situation but, even worse, to push it back significantly.

A by-product of the pandemic and the lockdowns and restrictions on physical movement was a boost to digital transformation, and dependence on online access and communication across all areas of activity—family and social life, education, work, shopping and entertainment. This boosted the profits of digital giants such as Amazon, Apple and Facebook; intensified the uses of social media in daily lives; raised concerns about market dominance, risks to privacy and fake news; and expanded public debate about the need for regulatory controls (Foer, 2020; Paul and Rushe, 2020). The online boom pushed the issues of global and national digital divides concerning access to the internet, digital tools, and equipment and skills into the spotlight.

Gendered socioeconomic and rural/urban digital divides have long been the subject of much research, policy work and activism (OECD, 2018; Youngs, 2006, 2007, 2013, 2014). The case of children and young people was seen as particularly urgent, with homeschooling and online learning across the world as a result of pandemic lockdowns (UNICEF, 2020). Digital inclusion was already understood as a dimension of human rights and empowerment, and integral to access to knowledge, networks and professional and other opportunities in contemporary life. An issue for children and young people was the long-term impact of digital inequalities during the pandemic on their opportunities in life.

> The digitalization of society has made ICT skills and access to technology important, but the COVID-19 pandemic has turned these things into essential human rights in terms of the educational, social and professional needs of children and young people. The lack of connectivity among the most marginalized populations—children and young people from poor households and rural areas—places them at an extreme disadvantage, and all but eliminates any chance they might have of participating in the modern economy. ... Today, 2.2 billion children and young people are still unconnected, deprived of the digital technologies and services that have proved so essential during the pandemic. Closing the digital divide will require significant resources, cooperation and dedication. But we must act—the ability of many children and young people to achieve their full potential depends on it.
>
> (UNICEF, 2020, p. 1)

When we consider gender and digital inequalities, the family context is central. As mothers and carers, women's digital empowerment has direct links to children and others in the family, especially in the context of homeschooling. Intersectional inequalities, such as time poverty due to the nature of women's paid work, can add to limitations in these areas. The importance of digital inclusion for opening opportunities to access information, networks, skills and professional opportunities in the contemporary economy continues to be a gender issue.

> The road ahead is uphill: today, worldwide, some 327 million fewer women than men have a smartphone and can access the mobile Internet. Women are under-represented in ICT [information, communication, and technology] jobs, top management, and academe and … men are four times more likely than women to be ICT specialists. At 15 years of age, on average, only 0.5% of girls wish to become ICT professionals, compared to 5% of boys. Women-owned start-ups receive 23% less funding and are 30% less likely to have a positive exit compared to male-owned businesses.
> (OECD, 2018, p. 5)

Gendered inequalities in STEM, linked to education and career opportunities, are part of the explanation for digital divides impacting women and girls, and the pandemic-related growth in shifts to online only served to heighten the importance of addressing them.

Gender and STEM: Feminist issues inside the mainstream innovation structure

In light of the global picture of gendered inequalities being worsened by the pandemic in the short and possibly the medium and long term, it continues to be vital to interrogate the state of play within STEM. It would not be an overstatement to say that STEM represents one of the most influential and secure masculinist bastions of power in concrete as well as symbolic terms. It represents a major foundation stone of masculinist domination and binds together forms of knowledge and its transformation into application and practice. The STEM sphere incorporates knowing and doing, and its emphasis on technology shapes substantially the modernist paradigm of economic growth and progress. It is worth stressing that this is as much the case for states (through policy and public funding) as it is for markets (through profit and investment-driven activities), with the defense sector featuring strongly in the interests and strategies of actors in both. There is little evidence that the paramount position of STEM will be significantly disrupted in the near future, so feminist work to challenge its limitations needs to be equally matched by efforts to dramatically increase women's presence and influence within it. This is not least the case because of the lion's share of resources, policy priorities and investment committed to STEM across state and market processes and institutions. Despite major efforts at national and international levels, through policy and practice, progress has been highly uneven and, in many cases, relatively slow in changing the gender balance in science. At the most basic level, there is not even consistent statistical data collection on the number of women in science across the world, which in itself reflects the low profile of the issue on many national agendas. This suggests that available calculations are best regarded as no more than approximate and indicative. In their limited reliability, they signal the need for higher-level global attention to mapping, in granular terms, not only the numbers but their specificities in sectors, leadership and other roles. Recent research emphasizes the need for capacity building in data collection on gender in STEM as well as better measurement and evaluation of women's and girls' situation in science (UNESCO, 2017, p. 12; UNESCO, 2016)

At the global level, available data for 2016 put the number of women in scientific R&D at less than 30 percent, with regional ranges between, at best, just over 48 percent for Central Asia, and, at worst, just over 18 percent for South and West Asia, with the figure for North America and Western Europe nearly 33 percent (UNESCO, 2019, p. 2). What is often referred to as "the leaky pipeline" also reflects a concentration of women at the lower levels of scientific education and training and a concentration of men at the upper levels—in 2013, 53 percent of bachelor's and master's numbers were women, and 43 percent were at the PhD level with a dramatic drop to 28 percent in the researcher category (Huyer, 2015, p. 86). Experts point out that the glass ceiling is very much intact in science and technology (European Parliament, 2015). "Each step up the ladder of the scientific research system sees a drop in female participation until, at the highest echelons of scientific research and decision-making, very few women are left" (Huyer, 2015, p. 86). This highlights the importance of integrated feminist perspectives, incorporating production and social reproduction, for working toward improvements. Work–life balance and career progression present specific challenges for women, with regard, for example, to career breaks related to maternity and childcare, as well as other caring activities. There is unevenness in gender parity across economies, emphasizing the importance of policies and action for change in national as well as global contexts. For example, while Malaysia, the Philippines and Thailand are reported to have achieved gender parity, high-income countries such as France, Germany and The Netherlands have one in four women in the research category (Huyer, 2015, p. 86). The countries with the highest proportion of female researchers are Bolivia (63 percent) and Venezuela (56 percent) (Huyer, 2015, p. 86).

The gender imbalances within and across different sectors are equally if not more important than the global figures. In tertiary education, women are reported to dominate the broad fields of health and welfare in most countries and regions, but no other areas of science. They are the least in evidence in engineering (Huyer, 2015, p. 91). These imbalances contribute directly to gendering innovation along predominantly masculinist lines, and counter possibilities for more inclusive forms of innovation, drawing on the insights, expertise and imagination of women as well as men. A 2017 report on researchers by Elsevier referred to the bleak picture of patents as well as imbalances across the sciences.

> In the Physical Sciences, women are still generally and markedly underrepresented, with women comprising less than 25% of researchers in these fields in the majority of comparators. The global share of women among inventors listed in patent applications increases between 1996–2000 (10%) and 2011–2015 (14%), yet women remain strongly underrepresented across all comparators.
>
> (Elsevier, 2017, p. 6)

The gendered picture in STEM indicates a number of factors that need to be taken into consideration if real change is to be achieved. These relate but are not restricted to scales of reward, both direct and indirect; levels of influence and decision-making; opportunities to impact how hierarchies are shaped and operate; day-to-day conditions of work such as environment, hours and use of less or more advanced equipment and resources; access to training and retraining; and flexibilities of time and work management. Research on gender and women in STEM is vital for understanding how such areas can be actively addressed in practical ways. At the heart of this is recognition, based on feminist analysis, of the need to give equal weight to social reproduction and production. Recent global policy work emphasizes the comprehensive focus that is required to effect real change. This work prioritizes promoting gender in research content, practice and agendas. This includes specific gender-oriented R&D and research on gender in STEM; gender factors in the evaluation of research projects; gender sensitivity in shaping hypotheses; and gender awareness in research dissemination strategies (UNESCO, 2016, p. 9). The research area is among seven priorities identified, the remaining being in changing social norms and stereotypes around women in STEM; engaging girls and young women in STEM in primary and secondary education and training; attracting and retaining women at all levels of STEM higher education; ensuring gender equality in promotion in science and engineering; promoting gender equality in STEM-related policymaking; and promoting gender equality in science and technology-based innovation and entrepreneurship (UNESCO, 2016, pp. 6–7).

A 2014 survey of more than 5,000 women in the UK aged 20–60 with STEM-related qualifications identified a range of practical barriers perpetuating gender imbalances (Women's Engineering Society, 2014). These barriers were largely linked to the inflexible nature of jobs and career paths, the former predominantly in the full-time mode and the latter failing to cater adequately for maternity and career breaks. These are all areas that can be addressed through changes in management and work culture, restructuring of work patterns and training and retraining opportunities, as well as career formats taking overt account of maternity leave and caring responsibilities. The findings were notable, however, for the extent to which they reported the need for change in these areas, alongside the extreme gender imbalance in leadership and influence, giving women few possibilities to effect that change. For example, the survey found that only 12 percent of respondents identified as a senior leader, director or CEO, and on completion of their qualifications, only 0.1 percent had set up their own business. Very few were benefiting from flexible working, with 73 percent working full-time, 19 percent part-time, 6 percent on flexi-time and 1 percent on condensed hours. The problem of barriers to returning to work after maternity or career breaks was reported by what was described as an "alarming" 60 percent of respondents to the survey. Barriers fell into a number of different categories: financial, including childcare costs (52 percent); insufficient flexible and part-time working, job sharing and condensed hours (27 percent); insufficient help and support on training and guidance (25 percent); and inability to move to find work (16 percent). This range of gender issues presses home the urgent need to increase and diversify leadership roles for women in STEM to speed up change, including through disruption of embedded and institutionalized implicit or unconscious bias influences blocking such change. The scale of incidences of violence against and oppression of women is evidence of some of the worst impacts of the gender imbalance in STEM. A recent report by the National Academies of Sciences, Engineering, and Medicine identified significant levels of sexual harassment and ways it can be addressed.

> Through our work it became clear that sexual harassment is a serious issue for women at all levels in academic science, engineering, and medicine, and that these fields share characteristics that create conditions that make harassment more likely to occur. Such environments can silence and limit the career opportunities in the short and long terms for both the targets of the sexual harassment and the bystanders—with at least some leaving their field. The consequence of this is a significant and costly loss of talent in science, engineering, and medicine.
>
> However, we are encouraged by the research that suggests that the most potent predictor of sexual harassment is organizational climate—the degree to which those in the organization perceive that sexual harassment is or is not tolerated. This means that institutions can take concrete steps to reduce sexual harassment by making systemwide changes that demonstrate how seriously they take this issue and that reflect that they are listening to those who courageously speak up to report their sexual harassment experiences. (National Academies of Sciences, Engineering, and Medicine, 2018, Preface)

Sexual harassment demonstrates extreme objectification of women and is witness to masculinist cultures of power, which disempower women in damaging and life-restricting ways. Representation and stereotyping in popular culture are part of the wider symbolic environment reflecting and normalizing gender imbalances, and it is clear that in an age of media, including digital saturation, change is well overdue. A study by the Geena Davis Institute on popular films across 11 countries in 2014 reported that men were depicted nearly five times more than women in computer science and technology roles, and 10 times more than women in engineer roles (Smith, Choueiti and Pieper, 2014, p. 22). Representation and stereotyping impact identity and empowerment in relation to professional aspirations, levels of engagement and endurance (Macdonald, 2014). There has been increasing attention to persistent problems of implicit or unconscious bias, as well as stereotype threat, whereby fear of reinforcing a negative stereotype, such as assumptions that an engineer is male rather than female, can have disempowering effects. In this context, research points to the importance of role models and the presence of women at all levels of organizations (Corbett and Hill, 2015, p. 3; UNESCO, 2017).

Issues of representation and stereotyping also highlight the importance of education at all levels to effect change. This includes primary and secondary school levels as well as vocational and higher education. Research points to the need for changes in curricula, including more learning through hands-on experience and experiments, as well as enhancing knowledge about science and engineering career issues (UNESCO, 2016, p. 6). Mainstreaming of gender in teacher training, materials and methods, and promoting gender balance among STEM teachers are among other aspects identified. Visibility of women in science and engineering, and their achievements, is an area where professional organizations have been particularly active. The Women's Engineering Society (2020), for example, launched "The Top 50 Women in Engineering Awards" in 2016. The aim of the awards, focusing on a different theme each year, such as sustainability in 2020, is to "raise awareness of the skills shortage facing the industry and the huge discrepancy between the number of men vs. women currently in engineering professions, to change perceptions and encourage young women to consider engineering as a viable and rewarding career."

The steep hill yet to climb in achieving greater and more consistent gender equality in STEM, reflected in the research and statistics, has to be considered against the scale of intensification of societies' focus on it, as well as public and private investment in it. Looking toward 2030, UNESCO (2015, p. xx) identified at the macro level three major trends in 2015: the growth of expenditure, particularly in applied sciences by the private sector; the narrowing of North–South divides; and growth in North–South and South–South collaborations, notably in areas of common concern such as climate change, a topic on which there was an increase of more than 20 percent in researchers' attention and publications worldwide between 2007 and 2014. The global political economy and its key drivers, in policy as much as market terms, are increasingly oriented toward STEM, pointing to inclusion and diversity within it as growing priorities. In other words, as STEM increasingly defines what happens with public and private resources, and the shape of core areas of society—environment, health and infrastructures of all kinds, physical and virtual—the consequences of its limited diversity continue to deepen. Feminist analysis has explored how information society and digital developments have, in the main, developed further the masculinist orientations of the industrial economy (Peterson, 2003; Youngs, 2007). Cyberfeminism and digital activism and empowerment work have been substantial movements, and have increased opportunities for women and girls in the digital sphere (Spender, 1995; Plant, 1997; Harcourt, 1999; Klein and Hawthorne, 2003; Youngs, 2006). Nevertheless, it has to be admitted that the masculinist grip on innovation, reflected through established STEM-based structures and priorities, is best understood as having, if anything, expanded in the digital age, leaving the opportunity for alternative perspectives, visions and priorities significantly constrained.

This situation sits within the larger context in society and business, where there is growing awareness of, and emphasis on, the value and benefits of diversity. A 2020 report stressed the importance of deepening inclusion and diversity for business success, including in relation to the COVID-19 crisis:

> A third of the firms we have tracked over the past five years have significantly improved both gender and ethnic diversity on their executive teams, while the majority have stalled or gone backwards.
>
> We also find that the dynamics around inclusion are a critical differentiator for companies. Our evidence is that an emphasis on representation is not enough; employees need to feel and perceive equality and fairness of opportunity in their workplace. Companies that lead on diversity have taken bold steps to strengthen inclusion.
>
> Early signs suggest that the COVID-19 crisis could deepen these trends. Companies that already see I&D [inclusion and diversity] as a strength are likely to leverage it to bounce back quicker—and they will use this time to seek new opportunities to boost representation and inclusion to strengthen performance and organizational health.
>
> (McKinsey & Company, 2020, p. 2)

In research, there have been developments in mainstream STEM in recent years, highlighting and examining the relevance of gender to the quality of processes and results. The fundamental nature of these steps can be regarded as a notable force for change to the extent that they represent some challenge to long-established masculinist limitations of scientific ontology. Part of their value is in doing so within traditional scientific parameters, stressing gender considerations as intrinsic to objective research, as well as the production of accurate and meaningful results. Gendered Innovations has been a leading project in addressing these issues. It was launched at Stanford University in the USA in 2009 and linked to related expert group work under the European Union Horizon 2020 program at the European Commission (2013). The comprehensiveness of this gender analysis addresses serious gaps in scientific research and technological application.

> It is crucially important to identify gender bias. But analysis cannot stop there: Gendered Innovations offer state-of-the-art methods of sex and gender analysis. Integrating these methods into basic and applied research produces excellence in science, health & medicine, and engineering research, policy, and practice. The methods of sex and gender analysis are one set of methods among many that a researcher will bring to a project.
>
> (Gendered Innovations, 2020a)

The project emphasizes the added value gendered innovations bring: "by ensuring excellence and quality in outcomes and enhancing sustainability" in research and engineering; by making research "more responsive to social needs"; and "by developing new ideas, patents, and technology" (Gendered Innovations, 2020a). It is clear that this kind of work addresses the research process as a whole, including how research questions are generated and what they cover; the extent of the reach of their relevance to members of society;

research methodologies and testing frameworks; who is part of the dissemination and knowledge-sharing networks; and what kinds of innovation are generated. As a member of an interdisciplinary Horizon 2020 Advisory Group on Gender in 2015–2016, I noted, in particular, the complexities involved in addressing gender bias at all stages of the research process: from the outset through the various review stages of projects and makeup of teams to deciding which get funded and which do not as well as assessing in detail the excellence of proposals and outcomes. The expert group's discussions concentrated on the persistent nature of unconscious bias and the need for it to be repeatedly addressed at all stages, including as an element of preparing for assessment processes. This emphasizes the embedded nature of bias and the amount of work that has to be undertaken to address it. Success depends on operational cultures and processes and their capacities to intensify critical reflection on bias as standard practice.

Case studies undertaken as part of the Gendered Innovations project across different areas of science, engineering and health provided examples of how sex and gender analysis enhanced what research could discover and illustrated how methodologies could be improved (Gendered Innovations, 2020a; European Commission, 2013). The work also included a focus on the communication of science and stressed the importance of reviewing language, visual representations and content in textbooks to incorporate sex and gender analysis.

> Word choice, charts, graphs, and images have the power to shape scientific practice and reinforce beliefs about gender roles. Words and images selected to illustrate scientific principles in textbooks may influence: who participates in science, how research priorities are set, and how scientific findings are interpreted. Fundamental concepts in any field should not be taken for granted; they should be critically analyzed for gender and other assumptions. Challenging unconscious gender bias helps to ensure rigor in generating hypotheses, testing them, and conveying knowledge to students.
> (Gendered Innovations, 2020b)

Tracking through to leadership in knowledge generation and attribution, the slow rate of change is in large part due to male domination in fields such as engineering. The Elsevier (2017, p. 48) research project showed that between 2011 and 2015, men were substantially ahead of women in terms of lead scholarly output in collaborative engineering papers involving both men and women—for example, 69 percent of men versus 35 percent of women in Japan, 63 percent versus 43 percent in the USA, 55 percent versus 39 percent in France and 63 percent versus 48 percent in Brazil. In an associated finding, while generally, international collaborations in scholarly outputs have grown since 1996, they continue to be gendered along predominantly male lines. The figures show differences across countries:

> Japan has relatively low shares of papers reflecting international collaboration for both men and women (18% for women; 22% for men); in

> contrast, the United Kingdom (43% for women; 49% for men), Denmark (48% for women; 55% for men), and Chile (46% for women; 56% for men) have relatively high rates of international collaboration.
>
> (Elsevier, 2017, pp. 51)

Findings on the comparative mobility of researchers parallel those on international collaboration, with women generally being less mobile than men.

> We can hypothesize that the findings around international collaboration and mobility are linked: if women are less internationally mobile, it may also restrict their network and international collaboration opportunities. If international collaboration occurs less frequently for women than men, their networks may remain small and this may negatively affect opportunities for career progression and mobility.
>
> (Elsevier, 2017, p. 58)

These critiques and research on gender distortions in STEM show the depth of the need for fundamental disruption and redressing of entrenched masculinist underpinnings of scientific knowledge and practice. The extent of the task also indicates that a substantial amount of persistent effort and continuing critical reflection will be required to achieve meaningful change, even in mainstream contexts. Such change in areas like research funding is intrinsic to moving toward a new interdisciplinary culture of excellence, as inclusive of women and gender as it is of men and masculinist priorities, as well as comprehensively addressing spheres of social reproduction and production, and overlapping inequalities across them.

Radical transformation of innovation: The feminist green new deal and values

Interdisciplinarity and intersectionality in relation to the planetary threats of climate change point toward the need for radical transformation of innovation, taking full account of long-standing environmental impacts of all human activity, and the need to counter deeply damaging trajectories. In response to the UN Climate Summit, a broad coalition of feminist climate and rights activists launched the feminist green new deal in 2019, advancing further efforts to overturn the full array of historically entrenched inequalities.

> The 'Feminist Green New Deal Principles' … call for Green New Deal policies and actions to '*advance a transformative feminist agenda that centers the leadership of women, and acknowledges and addresses the generational impacts of colonization and anti-Black racism. It must end oppression against and be led and articulated by frontline, impacted communities—especially women of color, Black women, Indigenous women, people with disabilities, LGBTQIAP+ people, people from the Global South, migrant and refugee communities, and youth.*' The 10 key principles

> call for advancing reproductive justice, the creation of regenerative economies centered on feminist analysis and understanding of the care economy, a shift from exploitative and unsustainable production patterns and a rejection of false solutions to the climate crisis.
>
> (Women's Environment and Development Organization, 2019, emphasis in original)

This campaign represents a feminist drive of dramatic proportions away from masculinist abstractions, including in relation to the links between the dynamics of human processes and nature. Alternative perspectives and fundamental forms of epistemological and structural change linked to them are central to feminist analysis and revisioning. Feminist critiques of science and technology have explored their colonial and gendered patterns of male domination, masculinist knowledge processes and constrained definitions of scientific rationality (Keller, 1985, 2010; Harding, 1986, 1993, 1998, 2008, 2015; Wajcman, 1991, 2004; Rose, 1994). The aligning, in power terms, of women with nature in the object position versus men and capitalist production in the subject position has underpinned masculinist modes of control and the economic growth model of modernity. In this context, feminist work has examined the limited parameters within which STEM operates, and the extent to which its knowledge and practice reflect them, including through innovation. Feminist critiques of STEM can help disrupt mainstream approaches to innovation, and enable and support inclusive innovation and a genuine blank-page approach toward such possibilities. This would work to identify values reflecting the diversity of societies and their full breadth of needs and desires, as well as processes toward goals engaging diverse participants and reflecting shared horizons. This involves new forms of complexity in thought and action. It is inevitable that inclusive innovation will require the upending of many assumptions and exclusions, which have been in place and unquestioned for far too long.

The slow pace of transformation of masculinist STEM and related innovation points to the need for new approaches. What is clear in feminist analysis and activism, including in work around the feminist new green deal, is that many fundamental and long-established assumptions have to be dislodged and interrogated for their abstractions and the values implicit within them. These values have to be open to question in a profound and inclusive manner—what do they prioritize, whose interests do they represent most, who do they advantage and disadvantage, what kinds of damage do they do socioeconomically, culturally and environmentally? Complexities include recognition of the unequal outcomes of historical and contemporary processes, and how they have shaped and embedded dominant values, often in extreme *taken-for-granted* ways (Horton and Patapan, 2004; Harding, 2008; Kofman and Youngs, 2008). Intersectional issues are part of this complexity (Crenshaw, 1989; African American Policy Forum, 2020; Gender in Design Stanford, 2020). These focus on aspects of inequality and exclusion, such as race, ethnicity, gender, age, socioeconomic status, education, location and sexual orientation, which come together and overlap in individuals and groups in diverse combinations. Focus on intersectionality grew in intensity as a result of the COVID-19 crisis, including in the case of the short- and longer-term impacts of the pandemic, as well as in relation to the communities and individuals hit by the most deaths, illnesses and threats to livelihoods. The scale of the crisis and range of impacts highlighted the past gross deficits in addressing inequalities and significantly expanded focus, in policy and public debate, on imperatives to do much better in the future (United Nations Department of Economic and Social Affairs, 2020; Blundell et al., 2020). This increased general awareness of winners and losers in contemporary societies, and the varied and intersecting bases for inequalities, potentially improving the possibilities for a shift to more human-centered values and priorities in future trajectories.

In the USA and beyond, alongside the COVID-19 crisis and its unequal impacts, the Black Lives Matter protests in 2020 placed a sharp focus on entrenched and institutionalized inequalities and their historical roots, as well as contemporary manifestations (Black Lives Matter, 2020). The facts of compounded inequalities were sharply highlighted by the unequal impacts of COVID-19, adding to existing factors of inequity, meaning that those already struggling most were hit hardest. The UN's hope was that this would not ultimately take the world backward to worsening structural inequalities but act as a catalyst for new positive paths.

> Much like with earlier crises, COVID-19 is a fork in the road. An insufficient response to the crisis and its economic and social impacts will likely deepen inequality, intensifying public discontent and weakening trust in institutions. However, this tragedy ushers in new awareness of the social and economic risks of deficient social protection systems and inadequate public services. It also underscores the importance of collective action and global collaboration. The crisis can therefore lead to the transformational changes needed to build more equitable societies and better align policy frameworks with the aspirations of the 2030 Agenda for Sustainable Development.
>
> (United Nations Department of Economic and Social Affairs, 2020, p. 2; United Nations, 2020b)

António Guterres, secretary-general of the United Nations, underlined the nature of this COVID-19 challenge on the wider development front and for marginalized groups in the foreword to the United Nations Sustainable Development Report 2020:

> Although the novel coronavirus affects every person and community, it does not do so equally. Instead, it has exposed and exacerbated existing inequalities and injustices. In advanced economies, fatality rates have been highest among marginalized groups. In developing countries, the most vulnerable—including those employed in the informal economy, older people, children, persons with disabilities, indigenous people, migrants and refugees—risk being hit even harder.

> Across the globe, young people are being disproportionately affected, particularly in the world of work. Women and girls are facing new barriers and new threats, ranging from a shadow pandemic of violence to additional burdens of unpaid care work.
>
> (United Nations, 2020b, p. 2)

In a mainstream context, mirroring some feminist concerns, design thinking was gaining growing attention as an approach to innovation with cross-sector familiarity and interdisciplinary relevance. Design's wide applicability as a tool in STEM areas, as well as creative industries such as architecture and fashion, was matched by its use to develop systems and processes in businesses and organizations. The wider utility of design thinking had generally been less familiar but has received increased attention in recent years, especially in policy settings (Kimbell, 2013; Mintrom and Luetjens, 2016; Nesta, 2016). At its core, design thinking has a human-centered focus and explores values and processes. The Design Council draws on the familiar trio of head, heart and hand to point toward the comprehensive nature of the dynamics involved in design processes: the head in "problem solving" and "the ability to visualise and conceptualise the intangible"; the heart in maintaining a "humanity centred" approach connecting "passion and curiosity to design solutions that are right for people and planet"; the hand in "practical" ways, using "technical skills to enable the end goal to be reached" (Design Council, 2020, p. 6; see also Rose, 1983) Design thinking lends itself to co-creative and collaborative approaches engaging diverse voices and perspectives. It offers one useful route to developing new interdisciplinary approaches to innovation, which are more inclusive of diverse and interconnected human, socioeconomic and environmental values, as well as processes reflecting them.

Feminist futures: Potential for radical new trajectories in innovation

The global human and socioeconomic impacts of the COVID-19 pandemic produced an unprecedented platform for challenging reductionist masculinist framings of innovation. The multiple imperatives of this platform, as we entered the third decade of the 21st century, signaled the potential for change as well as the urgency for it. These included laying bare a gathering momentum of diverse and increased inequalities before the pandemic, exacerbated by it, and likely to extend into at least the medium-term, if not long-term, future. These inequalities were clearly based on historically-entrenched forces of oppression associated with gender, race, socioeconomic and cultural structures. They affected patterns of education, housing, job opportunity, quality of life and longevity, and reflected masculinist hierarchies of production over social reproduction and the associated generation of a care economy driven by capitalism over human values. These inequalities operated at every level, within and across countries, and were increasingly affected and restructured by complex processes of globalization. The pandemic dramatically highlighted the extent to which these processes were virtual as much as material, with physical mobility replaced by the exponential growth of virtual mobility in conditions of lockdown and restrictions of movement. The major beneficiaries were the digital giants, whose market dominance and distance from regulatory reach had long been a major concern. Their businesses boomed while digital divides added to prominent debates about inequalities, especially with lengthy closures of schools and reliance on homeschooling and online learning, and universities moving to largely remote connections with students. The socioeconomics of home as a locus of nurturing, a *safe* or *unsafe* space, were increasingly recognized, as the vulnerabilities related to poverty and all forms of domestic violence and neglect expanded.

STEM's established primacy was reaffirmed through necessary investments in the life-saving global work to produce effective vaccines and treatments at greater speeds than ever before, with the political economy of global inequalities raising deep concerns about how quickly poorer as well as richer countries would have access to these. The crisis expanded public focus on the pre-eminence of science and technology but also signaled that, in social as well as human terms, they could not be the limit of innovation. The full power of interdisciplinary and human-centered perspectives was needed to ensure innovation addressed integrated models of social reproduction as well as production, and the complexities of intersectional inequalities and environmental issues. The Black Lives Matter movement brought critical perspectives on history center stage, and climate change activism did the same with regard to the planetary damage of the economic growth model. There was a boost in attention to green technology, with some new awareness of the environmentally-disconnected nature of masculinist abstractions of technological *progress* of the past. The feminist new green deal represents a call for a radical transformation of innovation to incorporate interconnections across human and planetary concerns as well as all aspects of inequality. If ever there was a time when radical approaches could make headway, the COVID-19 era could be it. Even with this possible prospect, the workings of STEM would be likely to continue to be pivotal, so feminist perspectives and gendered improvements continued to be high priorities in that context.

Influential NGOs such as Oxfam were at the forefront of calls for the crisis of the pandemic to be a time of radical change rather than a return to the *old normal*.

> The coronavirus pandemic has the potential to lead to an increase in inequality in almost every country at once, the first time this has happened since records began. The virus has exposed, fed off, and increased existing inequalities of wealth, and race. Over two million people have died, and hundreds of millions of people are being forced into poverty while many of the richest—individuals and corporations—are thriving. Billionaire fortunes returned to their pre-pandemic highs in just nine months, while recovery for the world's poorest people could take over a decade. The crisis has exposed our collective frailty and the inability of our deeply unequal

economy to work for all. Yet it has also shown us the vital importance of government action to protect our health and livelihoods. Transformative policies that seemed unthinkable before the crisis have suddenly been shown to be possible. There can be no return to where we were before. Instead, citizens and governments must act on the urgency to create a more equal and sustainable world.

(Oxfam, 2021, p. 2)

References

African American Policy Forum. (2020) Available at https://aapf.org/ (accessed July 1, 2020).

Black Lives Matter. (2020) *News – Black Lives Matter*. Available at https://blacklivesmatter.com/ (accessed July 1, 2020).

Blundell, R., Costa Dias, M., Joyce, R. and Xu, X. (2020) "COVID-19 and inequalities." *Fiscal Studies*. Available at https://ifs.org.uk/journals/covid-19-and-inequalities (accessed September 12, 2023).

Butler, J. (1990) *Gender Trouble: Feminism and the Subversion of Identity*. London: Routledge.

Butler, J. (1993) *Bodies That Matter: On the Discursive Limits of Sex*. London: Routledge.

Corbett, C. and Hill, C. (2015) *Solving the equation: The variables for women's success in engineering and computing*. Washington: American Association of University Women (AAUW). Available at https://www.aauw.org/app/uploads/2020/03/Solving-the-Equation-report-nsa.pdf (accessed July 1, 2020).

Crenshaw, K. (1989) "Demarginalizing the intersection of race and sex: A black feminist critique of antidiscrimination doctrine, feminist theory and antiracist politics." *University of Chicago Legal Forum*, 1989 (1), Article 8. Available at http://chicagounbound.uchicago.edu/uclf/vol1989/iss1/8 (accessed July 1, 2020).

Design Council. (2020) *Using design as a force for change: Strategy 2020–24*. London: Design Council. Available at https://www.designcouncil.org.uk/fileadmin/uploads/dc/Documents/Design%2520Council%25202020-24%2520Strategy.pdf (accessed September 12, 2023).

Elsevier. (2017) *Gender in the global research landscape: Analysis of research performance through a gender lens across 20 years, 12 geographies and 27 subject areas*. Available at https://www.elsevier.com/__data/assets/pdf_file/0008/265661/ElsevierGenderReport_final_for-web.pdf (accessed July 1, 2020).

European Commission. (2013) *Gendered innovations: How gender analysis contributes to research*. Report of the Expert Group 'Innovation Through Gender'. Available at: https://op.europa.eu/en/publication-detail/-/publication/d15a85d6-cd2d-4fbc-b998-42e53a73a449 (accessed September 12, 2023).

European Parliament. (2015) *Women's careers in science and universities and glass ceilings encountered*. Report 2014/2251(INI) 09/09/2015. Available at: https://oeil.secure.europarl.europa.eu/oeil/popups/printficheglobal.pdf?id=653436&l=en (accessed July 1, 2020).

Foer, F. (2020) "What Big Tech wants out of the pandemic." *The Atlantic*. Available at: https://www.theatlantic.com/magazine/archive/2020/07/big-tech-pandemic-power-grab/612238 (accessed January 21, 2021).

Gender in Design Stanford. (2020) Available at https://genderedinnovations.stanford.edu/ (accessed September 12, 2023).

Gendered Innovations. (2020a) "What is gendered innovations?" Available at http://gendered innovations.stanford.edu/what-is-gendered-innovations.html (accessed July 1, 2020).

Gendered Innovations. (2020b) "Textbooks: Rethinking language and visual representations." Available at: http://genderedinnovations.stanford.edu/case-studies/textbooks.html#tabs-2 (accessed July 1, 2020).

Gill, S. and Bakker, I. (eds.) (2003) *Power, Production and Social Reproduction: Human In/Security in the Global Political Economy*. London: Palgrave Macmillan.

Grosz, E. (1994) *Volatile Bodies: Toward a Corporeal Feminism*. Bloomington, IN: Indiana University Press.

Harcourt, W. (ed.) (1999) *Women@Internet*. London: Zed.

Harding, S. (1986) *The Science Question in Feminism*. Ithaca, NY: Cornell University Press.

Harding, S. (1991) *Whose Science? Whose Knowledge?*Ithaca, NY: Cornell University Press.

Harding, S. (ed.) (1993) *The Racial Economy of Science: Toward a Democratic Future*. Bloomington, IN: Indiana University Press.

Harding, S. (1998) *Is Science Multicultural? Postcolonialisms, Feminisms and Epistemologies*. Bloomington, IN: Indiana University Press.

Harding, S. (2008) *Sciences from Below: Feminisms, Postcolonialisms and Modernities*. Durham, NC: Duke University Press.

Harding, S. (2015) *Objectivity and Diversity: Another Logic of Scientific Research*. Chicago: Chicago University Press.

hooks, b. (2015) *Feminist Theory: From Margin to Center*, 3rd ed. New York: Routledge.

Horton, K. and Patapan, H. (eds.) (2004) *Globalisation and Equality*. London: Routledge.

Horizon (2020) "Advisory Group on Gender." Available at https://ec.europa.eu/transparency/expert-groups-register/screen/expert-groups/consult?lang=en&do=groupDetail.groupDetail&groupID=3034 (accessed September 12, 2023).

Huyer, S. (2015). "Is the gender gap narrowing in science?" in *UNESCO Science Report: Towards 2030*. Available at http://uis.unesco.org/sites/default/files/documents/unesco-science-report-towards-2030-part1.pdf (accessed July 1, 2020).

Keller, E.F. (1985) *Reflections on Gender and Science*. New Haven, CT: Yale University Press.

Keller, E.F. (2010) *The Mirage of a Space Between Nature and Nurture*. Durham, NC: Duke University Press.

Kimbell, L. (2013) *Applying Design Approaches to Policy Making: Discovering Policy Lab*. Brighton: University of Brighton. Available at https://researchingdesignforpolicy.files.wordpress.com/2015/10/imbell_policylab_report.pdf (accessed July 1, 2020).

Klein, R. and Hawthorne, S. (eds.) (2003) *Cyberfeminism: Connectivity, Critique and Creativity*. Melbourne: Spinifex.

Kocabicak, E. (2017). "A conversation with Sylvia Walby about crisis, Brexit and changes in gender regimes" [blog interview]. *The Sociological Review*. Available at https://thesociologicalreview.org/collections/sociology-of-brexit/a-conversation-with-sylvia-walby-about-crisis-brexit-and-changes-in-gender-regimes/ (accessed September 12, 2023).

Kofman, E. and Youngs, G. (eds.) (2008) *Globalization: Theory and Practice*, 3rd ed. London: Continuum.

Macdonald, A. (2014) *"Not for people like me": Under-represented groups in science, technology and engineering*. Bradford: WISE. Available at https://www.sciencecentres.org.uk/documents/50/not_for_people_like_me.pdf (accessed September 12, 2023).

Marchand, M.H. and Runyan, A.S. (eds.) (2011) *Gender and Global Restructuring: Sightings, Sites and Resistances,* 2nd ed. London: Routledge.

McKinsey & Company. (2020) *Diversity wins: How inclusion matters.* Available at https://www.mckinsey.com/featured-insights/diversity-and-inclusion/diversity-wins-how-inclusion-matters (accessed July 1, 2020).

Mintrom, M. and Luetjens, J. (2016) "Design thinking in policymaking processes: Opportunities and challenges." *Australian Journal of Public Administration* 75(3). Available at https://www.researchgate.net/publication/305622603_Design_Thinking_in_Policymaking_Processes_Opportunities_and_Challenges_Mintrom_and_Luetjens.

National Academies of Sciences, Engineering, and Medicine. (2018) *Sexual harassment of women: Climate, culture and consequences in academic sciences, engineering and medicine.* Washington, DC: The National Academies Press. Available at https://www.nationalacademies.org/our-work/sexual-harassment-in-academia (accessed January 21, 2021).

Nesta. (2016) *Designing for public services: A practical guide.* Available at https://media.nesta.org.uk/documents/nesta_ideo_guide_jan2017.pdf (accessed July 1, 2020).

OECD. (2018) *Bridging the digital gender divide: Include, upskill, innovate.* Available at http://www.oecd.org/digital/bridging-the-digital-gender-divide.pdf (accessed January 25, 2021).

Oxfam. (2021) *The inequality virus: Bringing together a world torn apart by coronavirus through a fair, just and sustainable economy.* Available at https://oxfamilibrary.openrepository.com/bitstream/handle/10546/621149/bp-the-inequality-virus-250121-en.pdf (accessed January 25, 2021).

Pateman, C. (1988) *The Sexual Contract.* Cambridge: Polity.

Paul, K. and Rushe, D. (2020) "Tech giants shares soar as companies benefit from COVID-19 crisis." *The Guardian.* Available at https://www.theguardian.com/business/2020/jul/30/amazon-apple-facebook-google-profits-earnings (accessed January 21, 2021).

Pettman, J.J. (1996) *Worlding Women: A Feminist International Politics.* London: Routledge.

Peterson, V.S. (2003) *A Critical Rewriting of Global Political Economy: Integrating Productive, Reproductive and Virtual Economies.* London: Routledge.

Plant, S. (1997) *Zeros + Ones: Digital Women + The New Technoculture.* London: Fourth Estate.

Rose, H. (1983) "Hand, brain and heart: A feminist epistemology for the natural sciences." *Signs: Journal of Women in Culture and Society* 9(1), pp. 73–90.

Rose, H. (1994) *Love, Power and Knowledge: Towards a Feminist Transformation of the Sciences.* Cambridge: Polity Press.

Smith, Stacey L., Choueiti, M. and Pieper, K. (2014) *Gender bias without borders: An investigation of female characters in popular films across 11 countries.* Los Angeles: University of Southern California, Geena Davis Institute on Gender and Media. Available at https://seejane.org/wp-content/uploads/gender-bias-without-borders-full-report.pdf (accessed July 1, 2020).

Spender, D. (1995) *Nattering on the Net: Women, Power and Cyberspace.* Melbourne: Spinifex.

Thompson, S., Hayes, L., Newman, D. and Pateman, C. (2018) "The sexual contract thirty years on: A conversation with Carole Pateman." *Feminist Legal Studies* 26, pp. 93–104.

UNESCO. (2015). *UNESCO science report: Towards 2030.* Available at http://uis.unesco.org/sites/default/files/documents/unesco-science-report-towards-2030-part1.pdf (accessed July 1, 2020).

UNESCO. (2016) *Measuring gender inequality in science and engineering: The SAGA Science, Technology and Innovation Gender Objectives List (STI GOL) working paper* 1. Paris: UNESCO. Available at http://uis.unesco.org/sites/default/files/documents/saga-sti-objectives-list-wp1-2016-en.pdf (accessed July 1, 2020).

UNESCO. (2017) *Measuring gender in science and engineering: The SAGA toolkit working paper* 2. Paris: UNESCO. Available at http://uis.unesco.org/sites/default/files/documents/saga-toolkit-wp2-2017-en.pdf (accessed July 1, 2020).

UNESCO. (2019) *Women in Science Fact Sheet* No. 55. FS/2019/SCI/55. Available at http://uis.unesco.org/sites/default/files/documents/fs55-women-in-science-2019-en.pdf (accessed July 1, 2020).

UNICEF. (2020) *How many children and young people have internet access at home? Estimating digital connectivity during the COVID-19 pandemic.* Available at https://data.unicef.org/resources/children-and-young-people-internet-access-at-home-during-covid19 (accessed January 21, 2021).

United Nations. (2020a) *Policy Brief: The impact of COVID-19 on women.* Available at https://unsdg.un.org/resources/policy-brief-impact-covid-19-women (accessed September 12, 2023).

United Nations. (2020b) *The Sustainable Development Goals report 2020.* New York: United Nations. Available at https://unstats.un.org/sdgs/report/2020/The-Sustainable-Development-Goals-Report-2020.pdf (accessedJuly 1, 2020).

United Nations Department of Economic and Social Affairs. (2020) *Responses to the COVID-19 catastrophe could turn the tide on inequality.* COVID-19 Response Policy Brief No. 65. Available at https://www.un.org/development/desa/dpad/wp-content/uploads/sites/45/publication/PB-65.pdf (accessed July 1, 2020).

United Nations Office on Drugs and Crime. (2018) *Global report on trafficking in persons 2018.* New York: United Nations. Available at https://www.unodc.org/documents/data-and-analysis/glotip/2018/GLOTiP_2018_BOOK_web_small.pdf (accessed January 18, 2021).

UN Women. (2020) "Violence against women and girls: the shadow pandemic." Available at https://www.unwomen.org/en/news/stories/2020/4/statement-ed-phumzile-violence-against-women-during-pandemic (accessed January 20, 2021).

UN Women and World Health Organization. (2020) *Violence against women and girls: Data collection during COVID-19.* Available at https://www.unwomen.org/en/digital-library/publications/2020/04/issue-brief-violence-against-women-and-girls-data-collection-during-covid-19 (accessed September 12, 2023).

Wajcman, J. (1991) *Feminism Confronts Technology.* Cambridge: Polity.

Wajcman, J. (2004) *Technofeminism.* Cambridge: Polity.

Walby, S. (1990) *Theorizing Patriarchy.* Oxford: Blackwell.

Walby, S. (1997) *Gender Transformations.* London: Routledge.

Wollstonecraft, M. (1985) *Vindication of the Rights of Woman.* Harmondsworth: Penguin Books. (Original work published 1792)

Women's Engineering Society. (2014) *Women in STEM: Are you in or out? Survey overview.* Available at https://www.wes.org.uk/content/women-stem-are-you-or-out-survey-results (accessed July 1, 2020).

Women's Engineering Society. (2020) "*The top 50 women in engineering awards.*" Available at https://www.wes.org.uk/activities/events-and-awards/wes-we50awards/ (accessed September 12, 2023).

Women's Environment and Development Organization. (2019) "*Women's rights and climate activists launch a feminist agenda for a new green deal.*" Available at https://wedo.org/feminist-green-new-deal-press-release (accessed January 20, 2021).

Youngs, G. (1999) *International Relations in a Global Age: A Conceptual Challenge*. Cambridge: Polity.

Youngs, G. (ed.) (2000) *Political Economy, Power and the Body*. Basingstoke: Macmillan.

Youngs, G. (2006) "Gender and technology: The internet in context," in Sarikakis, K. and Thussu, D. (eds.) *Ideologies of the Internet*. Cresskill, NJ: Hampton Press, pp. 47–62.

Youngs, G. (2007) *Global Political Economy in the Information Age: Power and Inequality*. London: Routledge.

Youngs, G. (ed.) (2013) *Digital World: Connectivity, Creativity and Rights*. London: Routledge.

Youngs, G. (2014) "Digital transformations of transnational feminism in theory and practice," in Baksh, R. and Harcourt, W. (eds.) *The Oxford Handbook of Transnational Feminist Movements*. Oxford: Oxford University Press, pp. 857–870.

9 Engagements with multipolarity

Sites and struggles of African–Chinese cooperation

Rirhandu Mageza-Barthel

Introduction

One of the most prominent shifts that has marked political and economic relations in the Global South in the past 20 years has been the renewed interest of the People's Republic of China to act as a leader of the Third World, a role it especially played as a leader of the Non-Aligned Movement also associated with "Third Worldism" in the 1950s. Africa has been at the forefront of China's diplomatic relations, its companies' investments and its development enterprises in the new millennium. Initially hailed as the beacon of a new Southern-centered global order, these revived ties have also shown themselves to be controversial. Despite governmental proclamations that this wave of Chinese–African relations should be mutually beneficial, they cannot be regarded as a phenomenon removed from the wider processes of global restructuring or from the political changes that have taken place on both continents. Poignantly, the ties are critiqued for the neoliberal orientations and hegemonic relations they replicate, yet, at the same time, they also (re)present new possibilities for development, and political and trade relations. This becomes important in a world still shaken by the COVID pandemic, as the pandemic appears to have heightened unequal relations and sociopolitical conflicts. The dynamics of the pandemic have exposed the rifts in the current global order but also shown the points of tension that exist within the Global South, including in the case of South Africa and China, at a time when their political and international agendas are aligning. Both countries, in lockstep with each other, have spearheaded transregional politics and have been active internationally, contributing toward the ongoing engagement with one another. In this chapter, I discuss how African–Chinese relations and the politics of both South Africa and China have been playing out at international forums and how gender activists have played crucial roles in forging African–Chinese relations in such forums. My chapter shows that conferences and delegation exchanges have always been important sites in state-led African–Chinese relations, as well as in the development of relations between African and Chinese gender activists who, in many ways, laid the foundations for the intensification of Chinese–African relations. These conferences, from the UN Women's World Conferences (one held in Africa and one in China) to the more recent Forum on Chinese–African Cooperation

DOI: 10.4324/9781003036425-10

(FOCAC) conferences held in Africa, create, at times tentative, ties between Africa generally (and South Africa specifically) and China and bring to light their commitments to multipolarity and South–South solidarity in international politics, as emergent features, I argue, of contemporary global restructuring. Owing to the prominence of a Southern feminist agenda forged through the Women's World Conferences, African and Chinese feminists have insisted that a gender focus must be formally included in the FOCAC. As I discuss, South African feminist energies, forged in the anti-apartheid struggle, have provided particular impetus for this effort toward a Southern-centered, nonandrocentric multipolarity. I conclude with the continued barriers to realizing women's full participation in African–Chinese relations within and outside the FOCAC, which also stand in the way of a Southern-centered multipolarity that promotes just relations, just development and gender and social justice.

Multipolarity as a site of global restructuring

One of the current debates that seems to be of particular relevance to those countries previously dubbed as "developing" and that suggests a shift in current discussions on development, poverty, and global inequality pertains to how different parts of the globe, which have been regarded as belonging to the Third World, are now being widely embraced as "emerging powers" and "emerging economies" (Mawdsley, 2012; Gray and Gills, 2016). Discussions on "The Rise of the Global South" and captured by such catchphrases as "Africa Rising" that have been promoted by such development agencies as the World Bank, gained press attention by 2013, coinciding with the hope of recovery from the financial crisis in 2008–2009 that had major repercussions across the world. Although the global crisis impacted the Global South and North similarly, a declining status of "the West" and a changing world order has served as a background against which these debates are being led (Woodley, 2015). Nevertheless, analyses that have raised the African continent's enduring political and economic dependence question these overly hopeful tones, suggesting that economic growth alone would not solve Africa's development woes (Taylor, 2016). If structural problems, among them governance, production and sustainability, are not addressed, such critics warn that "Africa Rising" remains a narrative that not only detracts from pressing issues facing people on the continent but also bolsters an ongoing neoliberal agenda that sidelines far-reaching structural changes.

Alongside concerns about entrenched economic differences across the globe that put into question the rise of the South has been attention to what implications a rising South has for the balance of power in the international system. The term *multipolarity* is increasingly used to denote a diffusion of power among different actors who can now influence the global order. In its earliest form, multipolarity referred to a concentration of geopolitical power in terms of "poles" of influence, primarily raised in relation to the state-based security-related affairs of bipolar alliance politics and used to discuss the United States or the Soviet Union as superpowers (see Beres, 1972). It has more recently taken on a new meaning that is cognizant of changed global relations, which, on the one hand, describes declining US power and, on the other hand, accentuates the increased influence of such countries as China, Brazil, and/or such regional blocks as the European Union (EU) (Murray, 2012a, p. 4). Now, multipolarity also implies economic power and international cooperation as sources of global influence rather than a focus on state-driven security and mutually assured destruction. With the simultaneous decline of the West and the rise of China, multipolarity refers to increased cooperation within the Global South that is different from North–South relations. Africa is actively negotiating such an emerging South–South multipolarity and presents an opportunity for balancing an otherwise fraught international order (Shaw et al., 2009; Dietz et al., 2011; Engel and Ramos, 2013). These political changes become increasingly significant as part of a global restructuring that shapes people's lives and livelihoods. As was argued in a previous edition of this volume, such political restructuring can "create new, but not necessarily uncompromised, openings for women's resistance to ongoing and new oppressions" (Marchand and Runyan, 2011, pp. 183–184). Thus, engagements with South-centered multipolarity shift our perspective on international political dynamics, cultural interactions and transnational politics with gender implications. Chinese–African relations are a part of these processes—and integral to any analysis of changing global relations—as they represent increasingly intense transregional ties and thereby symbolize aspirations toward a multipolar order, which, on the face of it, may create openings for a changing gender order.

Most of these discussions—whether of multipolarity or of global restructuring—cannot take place without taking into account China's role in the world or, more specifically, Chinese–African relations. Even though the Chinese leadership has been wary of being considered a new superpower, it has managed to make the Chinese economy one of the leading economies in the world, having in recent decades had the most foreign reserves, been the largest holder of US bonds, and been considered the world's largest trading partner (Murray, 2012b, p. 53). It still leads the world on these indicators despite some slowing of its economy over the last few years. For countries in the Global South, China's global prominence is noteworthy on several counts: under a so-called Chinese development model, the Chinese government has celebrated unprecedented development successes and its own substantial experience in curbing poverty has been built on a state that remains a key economic actor, specializing in infrastructure investment and the export of manufactured goods. As a foundation of a "Beijing Consensus," this model has superseded the more commonly known "Washington Consensus" built on neoliberal principles and pushed by Western donors as well as international financial institutions (see Brautigam, 2009; Dent, 2011; Mawdsley, 2012). These major accomplishments on a national and global scale have undoubtedly raised debates among critics, such as whether China, like South Korea, still belongs to the Global South or whether China's development priorities may supplant democratic principles. What cannot be disregarded is that the Chinese state takes pride in its image as a Third World leader and continues to build transregional relations.

For many states in the Global South, and in Africa specifically, a part of the attraction to enter into agreements with China lies in the principles China claims distinguish it from the traditional donors or powers in the Global North. These principles are based on equal treatment, claim to be mutually beneficial by bringing about win-win arrangements, reference ideals of South–South cooperation, aim at common development, and adhere to the One-China policy. They also include respect for sovereignty and noninterference in domestic affairs, as well as the goals of reciprocity and common prosperity. Rather than one-way arrangements, economic and technical cooperation are framed as attempts at mutual learning (Dent, 2011; Mawdsley, 2012; Tan-Mullins and Mohan, 2016).

Chinese investment in Africa has rapidly grown since China's Africa Policy was unveiled in 2006 and displays the extent of its foreign policy. Compared to Western-dominated institutions such as the Organization for Economic Cooperation and Development (OECD) and the World Bank, China's range and level of economic activity is astounding. In 2006, China surpassed the World Bank as a source of loans to Africa—and provided a mix of debt cancellation, trade, low-interest loans and aid packages to support its promise of friendship extended to African states (see Murray, 2012b, pp. 54–55). These financial investments and development tools toward Africa set the stage for the era after the financial crisis that also affected the continent. In 2015, the commitments made by the Chinese government toward its African counterparts reached US$35 billion in loans, US$5 billion in grants and US$15 billion in trade and investment funds for the period up to 2018 (Eom et al., 2018). By 2019, trade levels between China and Africa reached US$208.7 billion, having "only" recorded US$10 billion in 2000, according to media reports (Wang and Xie, 2020). Beyond economic development, however, we also find a change in China's political relations with Africa as a part of its South–South relations. These include prestigious gifts and a different quality of relations than Western states have practiced.

On the regional front, China has also been a driving force behind transregional institutions, such as the block of BRICS states originally consisting of Brazil, Russia, India, China and South Africa before the BRICS expansion in 2024 to include Saudi Arabia, Iran, Ethiopia, Egypt, Argentina, and the United Arab Emirates. The most wide-ranging instrument that Chinese and African governments have used to engage each other has been the FOCAC, which was initiated by China just over two decades ago. Within this forum, as I will further address, a gender equality agenda has not been as prominent as in other international regimes, yet advocacy toward including this has been ongoing (Mageza-Barthel, 2017). The aforementioned financial commitments made to African states in 2015 were made at the FOCAC VII, the summit held in South Africa. Since the first FOCAC meeting, which took place in 2000, Chinese government representatives have regularly met with their African partners. The locations have alternated every three years between an African capital and a Chinese city. Each meeting has brought with it a thematic focus, with the 2018 meeting, for instance, emphasizing local capacity-building in various initiatives, whereas, in 2021, it drew attention to security and sustainability issues during the COVID pandemic (Tiezzi, 2018; Large, 2022). Next to Ministerial Conferences, other meetings for businesses, think tanks, and civil society have also taken place. Almost all African states, except eSwatini and the African Union's Commission, have taken up relations with China and partake in the FOCAC mechanism as a foreign policy instrument dedicated to the African continent. FOCAC has also led to the creation of similar multilateral regimes between Asian and African states, such as the India–Africa Forum Summit, South Korea's Africa–Korea Forum and Japan's Tokyo International Conference on African Development (TICAD). FOCAC underscores the Chinese government's agenda by pursuing central political goals, among them limiting Taiwanese influence, producing a counterbalance to a Western liberal world order and containing globalization. These objectives supplement the ongoing economic relations and have opened the door for the burgeoning trade between Africa and China. As a cornerstone of implementing China's African policy, China applies its national interests and positions itself within a tradition of South–South cooperation and China's relations with Africa that was cemented during the Mao era (Taylor, 2011, pp. 24–29). Because of its now capitalist orientation that dramatically pushes for increased trade and investment, China effectively implements China's "going out" strategy. According to Ian Taylor (2011), this implicates China in the wider discussion of globalization as opposed to seeing it as conducting neo-colonial relations; however, he warns that a globalizing China in Africa has also had drawbacks. Concerning the effects that Chinese foreign and development policies have had across the continent, he argues:

> What can be stated is that Sino–African relations are processes not of colonization but of globalization and the reintegration of China into the global economy—a project that has enjoyed the hitherto enthusiastic support of Western capitalism. … At present the picture appears mixed—there are instances where the Chinese role in Africa is clearly positive and appreciated. Equally, there are issues where Beijing is, at present at least, playing an equivocal role. Beijing's current role in Africa is, like all other external actors, diverse, and its effect in the continent varies widely depending on local economic and political circumstances.
>
> (Taylor, 2011, pp. 33–34)

While this insight is useful to understand that there are pros and cons in Chinese–African relations, it downplays the foundation on which the relations become possible and on which they build, to which I now turn.

The legacy of Third Worldism reveals that the current mode of South–South cooperation is more than a nostalgic exercise. More than being an economic and political phenomenon, Third Worldism affects how the Global South constitutes itself geographically and epistemologically (Carmody, 2013; Kristensen, 2015). It further bears upon how the Global South imagines itself in relation to the Global North (Bachmann, 2019). In this context, South–South cooperation has become the preferred mode of engagement between China and its African counterparts. It is based on the principles established at the Bandung Conference in Indonesia in 1955. It extends the spirit of Third Worldism that was propagated at the conference into the current era (Taylor, 2006, pp. 16–34). At the very least, it has continued as a rhetorical frame under which countries in the Global South interact with each other. Bandung has influenced Chinese ideals of international politics, its perception of its position within the Global South and its African policy too (Fennell, 2013). However, in China's current engagement with Africa, the tension between its Third World, anti-capitalist roots and its current global economic program is evident (Dent, 2011).

Nevertheless, given South–South cooperation contours the foreign and development policies of states in the Global South (Mawdsley, 2012), it has afforded much to African societies. It produces the opportunity to be subjects of international awareness (see Modi, 2011). Specifically, as Quỳnh N. Phạm and Robbie Shilliam (2016, p. 3) point out, Bandung's significance lies in the ways the conference sought to expressly mediate between the two poles of the United States and the Soviet Union that were emerging at the outset of the global Cold War. Set up to bring together various states (and social movements), mainly from Africa and Asia, to forge a possible future of decolonization politics, Bandung was firmly set against Cold War politics. The aspirations and principles that came out of the conference aimed to fundamentally change international politics and the existing world order. As Phạm and Shilliam put it: "Crucially, attendees at Bandung introduced anti-colonialism and anti-racism as constitutive principles of a new world order rather than as background aspirations in a bipolar rivalry of great powers" (2016, p. 11). Bandung's implications on a theoretical level marked a point of rupture—constituting the Global South outside or beyond the definitional power that the Global North had hitherto claimed for itself (Pasha, 2013). Bandung, therefore, was a site at which its participants steered the agenda of formulating "visions of political order and just relations" (Phạm and Shilliam, 2016, pp. 17–18). These are issues I further discuss in terms of feminist involvement in these legacies.

Engendering multipolarity: Southern legacies and current politics

While it is more common to regard South–South cooperation as a state-driven project, such multipolarity has also deeply impacted transnational movement politics and shaped South–South civil society solidarities. However, despite the rise of South-centered multipolarity constituting one of the most significant developments affecting African politics and societies, feminist attention to African–Chinese relations is scarce. Related to the preference for the concept of global restructuring(s) that informs this and past volumes to redirect attention from the supposedly sweeping macro-processes of globalization to the more variegated changes being experienced at the level of lived realities that make visible and center gender relations (Marchand, 2003, pp. 148–149), a feminist perspective on multipolarity necessitates a discussion of African–Chinese politics beyond the state. China's use of soft power in Africa claims to regenerate Asian and African agency as a form of positive global restructuring brings with it negotiations on the ground by civil society actors, including women. Women, as traders, migrants or cultural intermediaries, for instance, contend with these new dynamics. They also seek to affect the structures governing them; it is this latter point that I focus on here, which corresponds to a more feminist understanding of global restructuring as an "open-ended, historically-produced social, cultural, and political construction with uneven and contradictory dimensions and effects that are subject to change" (Marchand and Runyan, 2011, p. 99).

As has long been stressed in feminist analyses, the study of international relations (IR) requires an intersectional analysis that goes beyond a critical perspective on North–South relations and takes postcolonial positions seriously (Chowdhry and Nair, 2004). It acknowledges localized feminist struggles as belonging to a wider phenomenon of global relations and appreciates Southern women's movements as part and parcel of a transnational political dynamic (Mohanty et al., 1991; Basu, 2010).

Inasmuch as Southern-centered multipolarity has been closely entwined with postcolonial visions in international relations, it has also always been a feminist subject. Despite the varying emphasis assigned to social categories such as race, class, gender, sexuality and nation, the study and practice of critical, including feminist, international politics is understood as taking place on the so-called margins of the field, in global peripheries, and through subaltern agents. While Mustapha Kamal Pasha (2013) emphasizes the racialized division of international politics and the possibility of alternative imaginaries when coining the phrase of a "Bandung Impulse," L.H.M. Ling (2004) reveals how gender underlies the binary categories of the "West" and the "Rest," and how these gendered dichotomies were redeployed during the Asian financial crisis in the late 1990s. In a bid to reassert Western power and discipline over struggling Asian economies, she explains, the dichotomies of feminized "developing" nations and masculinized "developed" nations were replicated. Rather than engaging in such discursive critiques of imprisoning Northern gendered hegemonies, my attention is given to social movements—be they liberation movements or feminist movements—that have been active in engaging Southern-centered multipolarity and shaping its outcomes. Rereading the Bandung Conference as involving women as agents in progressive Third World politics allows us to see how gender politics stood in opposition to a bipolar world. Bandung provides an entry point for a postcolonial IR (Acharya, 2016, p. 344). By bringing together African and Asian states and peoples, Bandung provided an ideological common ground that still generally influences the principles governing political relations within the Global South and Chinese–African ties more specifically.

Just as gender issues and women's politics at the Bandung Conference have been a relatively neglected avenue of inquiry, little attention has been paid to gender politics in the FOCAC, which is explored in more detail later and taking place under fundamentally changed international conditions. This is so even though societal actors have come to the fore in the FOCAC, either in the guise of state feminisms or through social movements, who have brought gender politics onto the FOCAC agenda. Although not all gender activists in this context necessarily organize within or only within women's movements and bring other agendas with them, gender activists are making feminist claims in the FOCAC, seeking to inscribe themselves into a newly developing South-centered multipolar order and promulgate alternative visions of such multipolar politics. Revisiting Bandung and its legacy serves to reevaluate women's agency during Cold War politics and in the Non-Aligned Movement (NAM) by not only identifying women as actors at the time and since in these international relations but also by underlining how South–South conferences and forums then and now are sites of gender politics.

One problematic reality and legacy of the Bandung Conference, as the foundational event of South–South cooperation and Third Worldism, is that women were excluded from it, and masculinist images and narratives dominated it. But as exclusionary as Bandung was with respect to women, Laura Bier (2010), who recognizes that it was a space at which socialist and nonaligned "brotherliness" was celebrated, finds that it still left deep inspirational imprints on Egyptian feminists who had just experienced a revolution in their own country and were aspiring to become involved in international feminism(s). Additionally, although Aida Hozić (2016) finds that Jovanka Broz, the wife of Josip Broz Tito, the leader of the then nonaligned Yugoslavia and a major actor in the NAM after Bandung, had not been at Bandung, despite her claims that she had, the role she claimed to have in giving rise to the NAM did have an impact on Southern women's sense of international agency. Because the NAM served to mediate the animosity between the two poles during the Cold War, and due to the claim that Broz made about being influential in its creation, Hozić argues, Southern women were part of the internationalist dream that was being created at Bandung. In turn, according to Hozić, Southern imaginaries were a key element of their political subjectivity. Thus, Southern women have been a part of the "lineages of struggle within which Bandung can be situated as a crucial intervention into global order, lineages yet to be grasped in IR" (Phạm and Shilliam, 2016, p. 5).

In another rereading of Bandung through a gender lens, Anna Agathangelou (2016) reiterates its centrality to seeking alternative global constellations. However, she focuses on social movements that have taken up the gauntlet of solidarity that was fashioned then and applied it to today's situation. Specifically, she refers to new social movements, both local and cross-border, that continue to challenge the global order through their social justice claims.

> Indigenous movements, black lives movements, and occupy movements are calling for political, economic, and ecological decentralization of the world's resources, better and fair distribution of these resources. These movements demand self-determination and participation in the invention of worlds and lives that are not terror ridden and exclusive.
>
> (Agathangelou, 2016, p. 111)

Faced with social, political, economic, and ecological crises of a seeming insurmountable magnitude, they stand in opposition to states and/or transnational corporations to transform the existing system. Her assessment of new transregional politics is as mixed as Taylor's assessment of the FOCAC, which, as addressed earlier, found tensions between Chinese and African positionings and aspirations. For Agathangelou, the rise of the BRICS signifies a shift in the global order while representing an obstacle to a more egalitarian society (see also Domínguez, Chapter 10, this volume). The BRICS—and consequently the FOCAC—are more than a regional block or institution. Despite the promise of multipolarity, they may represent, the BRICS (and FOCAC) can also be seen as an alliance of hegemonic states promoting neoliberal market policies across the Global South (Agathangelou, 2016, p. 111). Thus, multipolarity simultaneously holds the promise of critically questioning the world we live in yet falls short of questioning the epistemic and power shifts needed to make a sufficiently meaningful change to international politics. Given this significant shortfall, Agathangelou suggests that rather than advocate for a multipolar world, it is better to "seek governance institutions that allow for cooperation and partnerships benefitting larger numbers" (2016, p. 111). In short, multipolarity marks both Southern solidarities and the tensions and problematics that arise within these, including how it is gendered (and racialized). But I still see value in it as it ties together Southern agency from the 1950s through to today and can, if exclusivities, hegemonies, neoliberal proclivities and masculinism can be effectively challenged, point toward a utopian future.

Juxtaposed to the picture of women and gender activists sidelined from transregional Southern politics at and since Bandung, even as it proved inspirational to such activists, women's conferences and forums on a broader scale reflect the centrality of Southern politics to transnational and transregional women's movements. Among the key events that have mobilized women's movements through South–South cooperation are the UN World Women's Conferences (1976, 1980, 1985 and 1995) and, as I also argue, within the FOCAC regime. These examples demonstrate the dynamic nature of these Southern relations—and the extent of gender politics within them. The Fourth World Women's Conference, held in Beijing in 1995, would be the most familiar to feminist scholars as a site for feminist encounters. The culmination of the World Women's Conference series not only represents the peak of transnational feminism but also further brought North–South differences among women to the fore. The conference stands out because African gender equality proponents from across the continent still associate Beijing with a politics of transnational solidarity. It reinforced their efforts to engage in multilevel politics and to straddle state-driven and civil society-led politics. In Rwanda, this mattered particularly for a women's movement borne out of genocide; in Ethiopia, the conference outcomes are seen as a guiding principle for gender policies, governmental activities and women's activism (Mageza-Barthel, 2015, 2017). At the same time, Third World women exposed the transnational women's movement for implying sameness among women. Critically, Chinese feminism experienced a turning point in its transnational relations.

On the one hand, the heightened North–South tensions following the Tiananmen demonstrations propelled the Chinese state to host the 1995 Beijing Conference with the consequence of bringing international influences closer to home (Howell, 1997). On the other hand, similar to a widespread critique of Western feminism in the Global South, the translatability of Western feminist concepts and approaches remained controversial among Chinese feminists (Min, 2017; Spakowski, 2011). As the first review of the UN Women's Decade, Beijing corroborated the progress made in gender politics through the 1985 World Women's Conference in Nairobi, where Southern feminist voices were particularly strong. There, women's movements were, for the first time, collectively confronted with forces of neoliberal globalization—especially the effects of structural adjustment programs in the Global South—and their weaknesses to adequately address these new dynamics were also exposed, despite the advances in mainstreaming gender politics.

Nairobi was as vital as Beijing to reinforce transnational feminist successes. Nairobi was indeed forward-looking regarding shifting the global gender agenda by recasting approaches to development and such concepts as empowerment through Third World perspectives. At Nairobi, Chinese women were initially represented in the conference series and translated their experiences into the Chinese context (Zhang and Hsiung, 2010). And it was after Nairobi that exchanges between Chinese and African women began to pick up steam. After the Nairobi Conference and before hosting Beijing, the Chinese Women's Federation returned to Kenya and visited with the principal Kenyan women's organization that was closely aligned with the Kenyan government. Having attended the Beijing conference, Ethiopia has repeatedly sent women's delegations to China and/or received Chinese women's delegations in Ethiopia (Mageza-Barthel, 2017). Such relationships have been carried over into the current era. These carry weight due to the pervasive transformation processes that have taken place over the past three decades in the Global South, where boundaries between the state and civil society are much more fluid than in the Global North. Suffice it to say that the World Women's Conferences and gender politics delegation exchanges they enabled have been a stepping stone and a cornerstone of African–Chinese relations.

While transregional relations between politically organized women from Africa and the All-China Women's Federation (ACWF) took place *before* the current era of Chinese–African relations, gender issues have either been notably absent from or very narrowly defined within the policies that set the terms for transregional relations. This stands in sharp contrast to how gender issues have been more central to other Afro-Asian relations; they have benefited from the presence of activists in those relations whose politics and projects have been openly and simultaneously feminist, radical and queer (see Reddy and Sudhakar, 2018).

FOCAC, as a current instrument to promote Chinese–African relations and representative of a new era of these relations, has consolidated various initiatives under its capitalism-friendly umbrella, including women's exchanges and interventions based on those forged post-Nairobi and post-Beijing. However, whereas agents from other sectors of Chinese–African politics have met frequently and been included in the triannual official meetings, there has only been one FOCAC Women's Forum in the past two decades. It was held in Cairo in 2009 with 110 delegates from 29 countries and aimed to bring state-led women's organizations and gender machineries into contact with one another. The final declaration adopted after the forum was then submitted to the ensuing Ministerial Conference, out of which the first mention of gender issues in such a FOCAC document emanated. The women's demands showed their concerns were linked to the financial crisis at the time. The Chinese news agency Xinhua, cited them as follows:

> In response to the financial crisis, the declaration states that governments should give full consideration to the interests of both men and women with regard to developing economic recovery plans and avoid the risk of aggravating the gender gap and gender inequality by applying a gender perspective.
>
> (People's Daily Online, 2009)

What potential for change this forum holds remains unclear. For example, Egyptian feminists have been vocalizing more far-reaching feminist demands since the early 20th century. Yet, the FOCAC forum was hosted by the dictatorial Mubarak regime before the Arab Spring. It was short-lived, leaving Egyptian and several other North African feminists to continue their struggles under subsequent dictators. Moreover, gender seems to be still quite marginal in the FOCAC given that, to date, no other women's forum has been held even though there have already been five China-Africa People's Forums to promote people-to-people exchanges, with two being held in Africa, as well as nine FOCAC Think Tank Forums, with the last being in 2020 to address development issues during the COVID crisis and to celebrate the 20th anniversary of FOCAC. The last BRICS summit attended by South Africa and China was held in 2023 in South Africa but was dominated by the expansion of the BRICS, and it is likely, with the expansion, that gender will remain a marginal concern, at best subsumed under people-to-people exchanges.

The current state of affairs within FOCAC disregards the decades-long history of mobilization between the ACWF and its African counterparts. Exchanges between Chinese and African women began in the 1950s, not long after the People's Republic was founded, and the ACWF had found its place in its institutional landscape. This is a history that the ACWF claims for itself and asserts within the FOCAC era. It is woven into the international(ist) role that China has assigned itself, and it seems inconceivable how China's reentry into the international community and project of "going out" would have succeeded without the legitimacy garnered through hosting the Beijing conference. Against this backdrop, we find some commitment to gender equality in the FOCAC framework, even though such issues are tucked into the more prominent mantles of people-to-people or cultural exchanges. Chinese–African feminist relations are building on what I see as the African strength of pushing for sociopolitical change, and African calls for increased measures to support women's political participation to secure gender equality within FOCAC. For example, a commitment was made to promote exchanges between women at the 2015 Johannesburg Summit. This commitment is representative of the, in fact, long feminist engagements with South-centered multipolarity and long South–South transnational feminist mobilizations and resolve, despite women being excluded at Bandung and being rendered more invisible within the FOCAC, one of the most significant forms of global restructuring in the Global South. In this sense, the legacy of Third Worldism is ever-present. It not only exists in the governmental rhetoric supporting the proclaimed friendship between China and African nations but permeates many of the transnational relations that have developed since Bandung, most notably transregional feminist interactions.

South African struggles and Chinese–African engagement

South African struggles for democracy and social justice provide a *longue durée* view of Chinese–African engagement. South Africa has traditionally had a strong feminist movement embedded in international discourses and alliances. Economically, it is one of the few African countries that can almost balance the power asymmetries in its relations with China. It has attracted much political attention—whether as a leader or a pariah on the continent—and exemplifies African–Chinese relations from the Bandung to the FOCAC eras. South Africa's current relations with China are broadly based on the promise of friendship that China has extended to the continent, primarily through increased cooperation and trade alongside the principles emanating out of the Bandung Conference. This friendship looms large over all relations that have come into being since then.

Under the stewardship of the African National Congress (ANC), the continent's oldest liberation movement, there were few major changes in economic policy over the first decade it came to power in 1994, but the government's international politics has shifted with the ruling party's changes in leadership. FOCAC-centered South African–Chinese relations were most prominent during the Zuma era (2009–2018), in which the transregional agenda also included South Africa's admission into the BRICS and also saw a flurry of local Chinese organizations engaged in delegation exchanges with South African organizations.[1] The nascent Ramaphosa era (from 2018) has resumed the (sub-)continental leadership role embraced by Thabo Mbeki (1999–2008) and is still dealing with the repercussions of the COVID pandemic and subsequently his party's losses in the 2024 election. The sharp economic downturn and increased levels of international debt that have plagued the country in recent years amplify many of the struggles for equality and social justice that were already a part of the national fabric since the country's post-apartheid dispensation began.

Whereas development has been a mutual goal of the administrations in Pretoria and Beijing, there are asymmetries between China and South Africa in terms of their economic positionings in the global economy, and South Africa has faced greater difficulties in redressing the socioeconomic needs of its people post-apartheid in the face of global economic imperatives. Just as China was once largely cordoned off as it pursued its own political and development paths before it entered world markets (and became a dominant player in them), South Africa experienced an era of almost absolute economic and political isolation before its democratic transformation after 1994, which can be seen as a feature of processes of global restructuring. However, South Africa's comparatively late-stage entry into the global economy as it democratized meant that it was only privy to the repercussions of international trade and investment. Any possibilities for South Africa to facilitate social mobility or undo the political injustices of the past rested on economic redistribution. However, this was rendered impossible in a climate where fiscal constraints and international investment were built into the government's policies. Such conditions also affected the diverse South African–Chinese immigrant community, who, despite their contested social status in South Africa, maintains social and cultural ties with China, Taiwan and South Africa (see Yap and Man, 1996).

Official South African–Chinese relations only began once the Chinese boycott of the South African government ended and the ANC-led administration switched its allegiance from Taipei to Beijing. How close these social, political and cultural ties would become were not yet imagined when these "new" friendly relations translated into an early quintessential Chinese–African development project known as Tembisa's Friendship Town (Ying Chen and Alden, 2011). Beyond such economic relations, ideological support has been pivotal in producing the current wide range of South African–Chinese relations, which can be traced to Third Worldism initially fostered at Bandung.

South Africa did not officially attend the Bandung Conference, nor was the apartheid government represented in Nairobi. Ostracized by the international community and defined as the last bastion of colonialism within Africa, the government was fairly isolated and did not find many allies in the world. Other African states, particularly those with relations with China and other members of the international community targeted South Africa with sanctions intended to curtail its political and economic domination of the continent (see Monson and Haifang, 2011).

However, the apartheid government's isolation in the international community did not preclude South African liberation movements from sending representatives, or even high-ranking delegations, to either of the pivotal Bandung and Nairobi conferences. Moses Kotane and Ismail "Maulvi" Cachalia skipped the country to attend Bandung as observers on behalf of the ANC and South African Indian Congress, respectively (Acharya, 2016, p. 343; Taylor, 2006, p. 20). Kotane, who had led the delegation and returned on his own, was received as a hero on his return to Johannesburg. The liberation movements would also receive military training during their armed struggle against apartheid and directly visit China on various occasions. Their mobilization continued beyond Bandung and carried the Bandung Conference premises of Third Worldism and South–South solidarity forward in their international engagements.

At Nairobi, the South African social movement representatives rallied against a possible inclusion of the apartheid government. With the ANC sending political stalwarts from its Women's Section, including Ruth Mompati, Ray Simons, Frene Ginwala and Gertrude Shope, activist positions dominated proceedings, including the struggle against apartheid in the conference deliberations. At a press conference recorded by the ANC's propaganda channel "Radio Freedom," ANC President Oliver Tambo, as a Nairobi attendee, provocatively took up the gauntlet proclaimed by the conference themes of equality, peace, and development to lobby others:

> Women – how do the women of the world come to Africa – as my colleague has been saying – and we are a stone's throw away from that [apartheid South Africa and South West Africa] situation and not delve into it?! What equality are we talking about when there is such evidence of inequality for women? What development have we come to discuss, if we cannot discuss the fate of women in South Africa and Namibia in relation to development? Which arises from the fact of that [apartheid] oppression and domination. What peace? When there is no peace for them?
>
> (Tambo and Nujoma, 1985)

The ANC called out the American administration's collaboration with the apartheid regime and mobilized further to connect gender politics with national liberation struggles. The conference came on the heels of a NAM meeting that further bolstered the delegation's approach (Hassim, 2004, p. 448). Nairobi would become a pivotal moment at which South African resistance to apartheid, to gender politics untethered to other liberation struggles and to unequal development was articulated. Before Nairobi, though, and immediately before the July 1980 World Women's Conference in Copenhagen, the ANC Women's Section had made a similarly strategic appearance at a 1980 seminar in Prague. They used this particular platform to garner transnational support for the Women's Section's cause of struggling against apartheid but also simultaneously rebuffed China's hegemonic involvement in Asia (Participants of the International Seminar of African and Asian Women, 1980). However, later, South African gender activists, through their interactions with the ACFW, would pioneer relations with China and stabilize them.

The World Women's Conferences were critical nodes for such feminist encounters that led to other ones. The ANC and the Pan Africanist Congress of Azania (PAC), another major South African liberation movement, sent women's delegations to China on separate occasions. A delegation from the ANC Women's Section visited the ACWF in 1985 (Pekane, 2004 [1985]) after geopolitical differences behind the Iron Curtain had caused a rift between the ANC and the Chinese Communist Party. The PAC, on the other hand, used its visit to China after the Nairobi Conference to revive its relations with the ACWF and fundraise to begin systematically building a women's wing distinct from its parent body in conjunction with the "Gender and Development" discourses that were circulating globally (Pan Africanist Congress of Azania, 1985–1986). Since then, China has always been the PAC's strategic ally, which shows the significance of its women's wing turning to the ACWF for assistance.

More generally, such delegation exchanges were a trademark of African–Chinese friendship politics. Jamie Monson (2020) finds that during the visit of Tanzanian freedom fighter, gender activist and later politician Bibi Titi Mohamed to China in 1963, development became an approach through which the Chinese leadership aimed to build closer ties with Africans. She, in turn, secured material support from her Chinese counterparts by receiving medical treatment during her visits to China. Medical exchanges, as in this example, are tied to Chinese–African gender politics and have continued to be so in the FOCAC era. For example, the African Union Commission received donations of medical delivery kits in 2011 from the ACWF on the occasion of International Women's Day, and during the COVID pandemic, the Chinese government gifted the African Union personal protective equipment (PPE) and other medical equipment (African Union Commission, 2011, 2020).

As sites of African–Chinese engagement, FOCAC meetings have provided opportunity structures to build bridges between Chinese and African women, who have worked together through South African-based networks at the FOCAC Women's Forum in 2009 and at the 2015 FOCAC conference held in Johannesburg. That conference coincided with widespread protests in South Africa that sought to reclaim the ideals of the liberation struggle. Interestingly, Egypt, which hosted the 2009 Women's Forum, was about to embark on its, albeit short-lived, Arab Spring in 2011, in which feminists played a central role. Both locations marked the possibilities for setting an African–Chinese gender agenda. The Johannesburg Action Plan that came out of the 2015 conference included repeated references to promoting women's development and participation chances. It recommitted to the concessions made after Cairo, including acknowledging Chinese and African women's centrality to Africa's "self-development," sponsoring programs focused on reducing poverty for women and children and supporting gender equality through dialogues and cultural exchanges. In this sense, the Johannesburg Action Plan marks a turning point for gender politics in the current FOCAC era. In it, FOCAC leaders are held accountable for the commitments they had previously made in 2009, which were made possible by earlier transregional gender activist encounters since Bandung and particularly deepened during the World Women's Conferences. These declarations in the Johannesburg Action Plan, while consequential in and of themselves, need to be seen as outcomes achieved through the contribution of feminist activists and gender machineries in FOCAC. They build on the accomplishments of African women freedom fighters at Nairobi, informed by the spirit of Bandung—and on South African women's achievements in toppling the apartheid government.

What has not been discussed here are those activists and organizations who distance themselves from or remain skeptical of how Southern-centered multipolarity, particularly through African–Chinese relations, is playing out in South Africa. Even today, similar to the position taken by the Women's Section of the ANC at the Prague seminar in 1980, there are those who critique China for its hegemonic designs and Chinese involvement in Africa and its rising influence in the current world order. These historic and current tensions stand in the way of more sustainable feminist South African–Chinese relations. Beyond these political obstacles, there are numerous challenges in bringing about South African–Chinese feminist exchanges outside of the state-led and top-down FOCAC. These include political differences, language and cultural gaps, the requirement of travel and/or access to delegation exchanges, as well as widening social inequalities that persist on both sides. A mutual recognition as belonging to a Southern sisterhood contributing to an inclusive and more just vision of South–South cooperation seems more of a pronounced necessity than ever if these governmental interactions and people-to-people relations are to push against current persistent and overlapping crises associated with global restructuring and produce gender- (and race-)sensitive South-centered multipolar alternatives to restructure the current world order.

Conclusion: Africa and China in a new era

Beginning in the mid-1950s, when Afro-Asian solidarity was fostered, continuing into the early 1960s, when outreach between China and African peoples and countries began in earnest, and later further developing amid the South African struggles against apartheid, Chinese–African relations have significantly intensified in the past 20 years as a result and a feature of global restructuring. As I have shown, the World Women's Conferences and other exchanges between Chinese and African women's organizations played a crucial role in this intensification and a rising role in the context of the FOCAC. South African–Chinese and Chinese–African gender activists have struggled against apartheid, endorsed nonalignment and multipolarity and challenged an androcentric multipolar world. The question we have to ask ourselves, following Agathangelou (2016), is whether the FOCAC can fulfill the potential of increased cooperation and partnerships that supersede the state level and facilitate more equity on the ground. It seems that these are issues that FOCAC leaders are increasingly aware of. Increased economic strain, social conflicts and pandemic-related racial tensions have obviated such changes. Especially in light of the COVID crisis, FOCAC leaders have pledged to prioritize vaccine cooperation, economic recovery and transformative development. The next meeting, set for late 2024, will, according to the Chinese Foreign Ministry, also seek to revitalize solidarity and cooperation and to benefit more people expressly. This would require a departure from the predominantly state-led and largely capitalist development mode of Chinese–African friendship that has contributed to the relative marginalization of gender and has characterized the FOCAC era to date. Reflecting on Bandung and Nairobi has allowed me to highlight the spirits and commitments that initially informed African–Chinese relations and which can better inform them going forward—commitments to South–South cooperation and solidarity, multipolarity and gender and social justice. Women's activism, past and present, in these relations challenges us, reminiscent of Tambo's provocation, to once more ask how substantive equality and social justice might be attained and which direction development should take to foster these in a multipolar world.

Note

1 Under the presidency of Nelson R. Mandela (1994–1999), a new foreign policy based on human rights prerogatives was established, and the Mbeki era saw the promotion of an African Renaissance agenda and regional integration.

References

Acharya, A. (2016) "Studying the Bandung conference from a global IR perspective," *Australian Journal of International Affairs*, 70 (4), pp. 342–357.

African Union Commission. (2011) "Chairperson receives donation of medical equipment from All-China Women's Federation." Available at https://au.int/en/pressreleases/20110308.

African Union Commission. (2020) "China donates medical supplies to African Union Commission." Available at https://au.int/en/pressreleases/20201023/china-donates-medical-supplies-african-union-commission.

Agathangelou, A.M. (2016) "Casting off the 'heavenly rule book': Bandung's poetic revolutionary solidarities," in Phạm, Q.N. and Shilliam, R. (eds.) *Meanings of Bandung: Postcolonial Orders and Decolonial Visions*. London: Rowman and Littlefield, pp. 101–112.

Bachmann, V. (2019) "(Trans)regionalism and South–South cooperation: Afrasia instead of Eurafrique?," *Third World Quarterly* 40(4), pp. 688–709. doi:10.1080/01436597.2019.1573634.

Basu, A. (2010) *Women's Movements in the Global Era: The Power of Local Feminisms*. Boulder, CO: Westview Press.

Beres, L.R. (1972) "Bipolarity, multipolarity, and the reliability of alliance commitments," *Political Research Quarterly* 25(4), pp. 702–710. doi:10.1177/106591297202500409.

Bier, L. (2010) "Feminism, solidarity, and identity in the age of Bandung: Third World women in the Egyptian women's press," in Lee, C.J. (ed.) *Making a World after Empire: The Bandung Moment and Its Political Afterlives*. Athens, OH: Ohio University Press, pp.143–171.

Brautigam, D.A. (2009) *The Dragon's Gift: The Real Story of China in Africa*. Oxford: Oxford University Press.

Carmody, P. (2013) *The Rise of the BRICS in Africa: The Geopolitics of South-South Relations*. London: Zed Books.

Chowdhry, G. and Nair, S. (eds.) (2004) *Power, Postcolonialism and International Relations: Reading Race, Gender and Class*. New York: Routledge.

Dent, C.M. (2011) "Africa and China: A new kind of development partnership," in Dent, C.M. (ed.) *China and Africa Development Relations*. New York: Routledge, pp. 3–20.

Dietz, T., Havnevik, K., Kaag, M. and Oestigaard, T. (eds.) (2011) *African Engagements: Africa Negotiating an Emerging Multipolar World*. Leiden: Brill.

Engel, U. and Ramos, M.J. (2013) *African Dynamics in a Multipolar World*. Leiden: Brill.

Eom, J., Brautigam, D. and Benabdallah, L. (2018) *The path ahead: The 7th forum on China-Africa cooperation*, SAIS-CARI Briefing Paper 1. Available at http://www.sais-cari.org/s/Briefing-Paper-1-August-2018-Final.pdf.

Fennell, V.L. (2013) "Race: China's question and problem," *The Review of Black Political Economy* 40(3), pp. 245–275. doi:10.1007/s12114-013-9160-z.

Gray, K. and Gills, B.K. (2016) "South–South cooperation and the rise of the Global South," *Third World Quarterly* 37(4), pp. 557–574. doi:10.1080/01436597.2015.1128817.

Hassim, S. (2004) "Nationalism, feminism and autonomy: The ANC in exile and the question of women," *Journal of Southern African Studies* 30(3), pp. 433–455.

Howell, J. (1997) "Post-Beijing reflections: Creating ripples, but not waves in China," *Women's Studies International Forum* 20(2), pp. 235–252. doi:10.1016/S0277-5395(97)00009-5.

Hozić, A.A. (2016) "False memories, real political imaginaries: Jovanka Broz in Bandung," in Phạm, Q.N. and Shilliam, R. (eds.) *Meanings of Bandung: Postcolonial Orders and Decolonial Visions*. London: Rowman and Littlefield, pp. 95–100.

Kristensen, P.M. (2015) "How can emerging powers speak? On theorists, native informants and quasi-officials in international relations discourse," *Third World Quarterly* 36(4), pp. 637–653. doi:10.1080/01436597.2015.1023288.

Lan, S. (2019) "Reconstructing blackness in grassroots interactions between Chinese and Africans in Guangzhou," *Anthropological Quarterly* 92(2), pp. 481–508. doi:10.1353/anq.2019.0023.

Large, D. (2022) "China, Africa and the 2021 Dakar FOCAC," *African Affairs* 121(483), pp. 299–319. doi:10.1093/afraf/adac014.

Ling, L. .M. (2004) "Cultural chauvinism and the liberal international order: 'West versus Rest' in Asia's financial crisis," in Chowdhry, G. and Nair, S. (eds.) *Power, Postcolonialism and International Relations: Reading Race, Gender and Class*. New York: Routledge, pp. 115–141.

Liu, R. and Shange, S. (2018) "Toward thick solidarity," *Radical History Review* 2018 (131), pp. 189–198. doi:10.1215/01636545-4355341.

Mageza-Barthel, R. (2015) *Mobilizing Transnational Gender Politics in Post-Genocide Rwanda*. New York: Routledge.

Mageza-Barthel, R. (2017) "Beyond the state in Sino-African Relations?," in Graf, A. and Hashim, A. (eds.) *African-Asian Encounters: Creating Cooperations and Dependencies*. Amsterdam: Amsterdam University Press, pp. 103–132.

Marchand, M.H. (2003) "Challenging globalisation: Toward a feminist understanding of resistance," *Review of International Studies* 29(1), pp. 145–160. doi:10.1017/S0260210503005965.

Marchand, M.H. and Runyan, A.S. (eds.) (2011) *Gender and Global Restructuring: Sightings, Sites, and Resistances*, 2nd ed. London: Routledge.

Mawdsley, E. (2012) *From Recipients to Donors: Emerging Powers and the Changing Development Landscape*. London: Zed Books.

Min, D. (2017) *Translation and Travelling Theory: Feminist Theory and Praxis in China*. New York: Routledge.

Modi, R. (ed.) (2011) *South-South Cooperation: Africa on the Centre Stage*. Basingstoke: Palgrave Macmillan.

Mohanty, C.T., Russo, A. and Torres, L. (eds.) (1991) *Third World Women and the Politics of Feminism*. Bloomington: Indiana University Press.

Monson, J. (2020) "Futures in the past of Africa-China engagement," in Achenbach, R., Beek, J., Karugia, J.N., Mageza-Barthel, R. and Schulze-Engler, F. (eds.) *Afrasian Transformations: Transregional Perspectives on Development Cooperation, Social Mobility and Cultural Change*. Leiden: Brill, pp. 21–43.

Monson, J. and Haifang, L. (2011) "Railway time: Technology transfer and the role of Chinese experts in the history of Tazara," in Dietz, T., Havnevik, K., Kaag, M. and Oestigaard, T. (eds.) *African Engagements: Africa Negotiating an Emerging Multipolar World*. Leiden: Brill, pp. 226–251.

Murray, D. (2012a) "Introduction," in Murray, D. and Brown, D. (eds.) *Multipolarity in the 21st Century: A New World Order*. London: Routledge, pp. 1–16.

Murray, D. (2012b) "The Chinese dragon," in Murray, D. and Brown, D. (eds.) *Multipolarity in the 21st Century: A New World Order*. London: Routledge, pp. 48–79.

Pan Africanist Congress of Azania. (1985–1986) *PAC Women's Wing Assistance Project* (Correspondence, 1985–1986), Dar es Salaam, PAC Tanzania Papers, Box 20. Alice: NAHECS Archive.

Park, Y. J. (2012) "Chinese South Africans now black!: Race and belonging in the 'new' South Africa," in Fois, M. and Pes, A. (eds.) *Politics and Minorities in Africa*. Rome: Aracne, pp. 101–125.

Participants of the International Seminar of African and Asian Women. (1980) *Communique of the International Seminar of African and Asian Women Held in Czechoslovakia from June 27 to July 10, 1980*, Prague, African National Congress Papers, ANC Women's Section, Box 6. Alice: NAHECS Archive.

Pasha, M.K. (2013) "The 'Bandung Impulse' and international relations," in Seth, S. (ed.) *Postcolonial Theory and International Relations: A Critical Introduction*. London: Routledge, pp. 144–165.

Pekane, M. (2004 [1985]) *ANC Women's Delegation visit to the People's Republic of China African National Congress Papers*, ANC Women's Section, Box 013, Folder 0184. Alice: NAHECS Archive.

People's Daily Online. (2009) "Forum on China-Africa Cooperation Women's Forum 2009 ends in Cairo." Available at http://en.people.cn/90001/90776/90883/6783667.html (accessed March 14, 2021).

Phạm, Q.N. and Shilliam, R. (2016) "Reviving Bandung," in Phạm, Q.N. and Shilliam, R. (eds.) *Meanings of Bandung: Postcolonial Orders and Decolonial Visions*. London: Rowman and Littlefield, pp. 3–19.

Reddy, V. and Sudhakar, A. (eds.) (2018) *Feminist and Queer Afro-Asian Formations*. Available at http://sfonline.barnard.edu/feminist-and-queer-afro-asian-formations (accessed September 11, 2020).

Shaw, T.M., Cooper, A.F. and Chin, G.T. (2009) "Emerging powers and Africa: Implications for/from global governance?," *Politikon* 36(1), pp. 27–44. doi:10.1080/02589340903155385.

Spakowski, N. (2011) "'Gender' trouble: Feminism in China under the impact of western theory and the spatialization of identity," *Positions: Asia Critique* 19(1), pp. 31–54. Available at https://muse.jhu.edu/article/444419.

Tambo, O.R. and Nujoma, S. (1985) *Press Conference at the Third World Conference for Women* (Radio Freedom Audio Recording), Nairobi, Kenya, RF 152. Cape Town: Mayibuye Archives.

Tan-Mullins, M. and Mohan, G. (2016) "China's relations with Africa," in Kavalski, E. (ed.) *The Ashgate Research Companion to Chinese Foreign Policy*. London: Routledge, pp. 275–285.

Taylor, I. (2006) *China and Africa: Engagement and Compromise*. London: Routledge.

Taylor, I. (2011) *The Forum on China-Africa Cooperation (FOCAC)*. New York: Routledge.

Taylor, I. (2016) "Dependency redux: Why Africa is not rising," *Review of African Political Economy* 43(147), pp. 8–25. doi:10.1080/03056244.2015.1084911.

Tiezzi, S. (2018) "FOCAC 2018: Rebranding China in Africa," *The Diplomat*. Available at https://thediplomat.com/2018/09/focac-2018-rebranding-china-in-africa/.

Wang, W. and Xie, W. (2020) "Ninth China-Africa Think Tanks Forum to boost development amid pandemic," *Global Times*. Available at https://www.globaltimes.cn/content/1205891.shtml (accessed March 10, 2021).

Woodley, D. (2015) *Globalization and Capitalist Geopolitics: Sovereignty and State Power in a Multipolar World*. New York: Routledge. doi:10.4324/9781315798165.

Yap, M. and Man, D.L. (1996) *Colour, Confusion and Concessions: The History of the Chinese in South Africa*. Hong Kong: Hong Kong University Press.

Ying Chen, A. and Alden, C. (2011) "Chinese development co-operation and Africa: The case of Tembisa's friendship town," in Dent, C.M. (ed.) *China and Africa Development Relations*. New York: Routledge, pp. 103–117.

Zhang, N. and Hsiung, P.-C. (2010) "The Chinese women's movement in the context of globalization," in Basu, A. (ed.) *Women's Movements in the Global Era: The Power of Local Feminisms*. Boulder, CO: Westview Press, pp. 157–192.

10 Transnational feminist networks resisting economic restructuring

The cases of WIDE/WIDE+ and BRICS Feminist Watch

Edmé Domínguez Reyes

Introduction

This chapter considers different levels and strategies of transnational feminist resistance to contemporary global restructuring through the presentation of two cases: the nongovernmental organization (NGO) Women in Development Europe that became the WIDE+ network and the more recent BRICS Feminist Watch.[1] These networks consisting largely of feminist economists are focusing on feminist political economy concerns and adopting different strategies. These include studies and projects that look into gendered European free trade, structural adjustment policies and other political economy issues; critique gendered financialization; and serve as interventions that expose non-gender-inclusive banking practices among the BRICS countries (Brazil, Russia, India, China and South Africa).[2] The chapter examines their strategies and goals, seeking to find commonalities to map trends in global resistance to varying processes shaped by capitalist development in order to confront the multiple crises that are threatening women's survival in various parts of the world.

Transnational feminist resistance has been the subject of much feminist scholarship, including my own (see, for example, Antrobus, 2004; Moghadam, 2000; Eschle and Maiguashca, 2007; Domínguez, 2014; Marchand and Domínguez, 2019), especially since neoliberal policies were found to be negatively affecting women of all social groups, particularly in the Global South. Such resistance has been growing, taking on different aspects, strategies and forms since the beginning of the 1970s United Nations (UN) Decade for Women through the UN Conference for Women in Beijing in 1995.

We are now witnessing large-scale transnational feminist networks (TFNs) that include or are led and solely composed by many Global South organizations with agendas of their own but always linked to issues engaging both North and South activists. The forging of shared agendas provides clear evidence that there are fundamental gender issues that are binding women activists across levels of development, class locations and ethnic divides. Behind the latest great movements for abortion rights and against gender-based violence in various parts of the world, including in most countries in Latin America, are groups of activists who play a crucial role in the shaping of strategies sustaining such mobilizations.

DOI: 10.4324/9781003036425-11

These TFNs are being mobilized to defend against all kinds of backlashes directed at globally acknowledged rights for women, such as reproductive ones, since Beijing 1995, but that are now being put at risk at national and global levels. TFNs have long mobilized around the gendered impacts of globalization or global economic restructuring, but are responding more recently to the rise of right-wing populism seen by some as a backlash to globalization as well as a backlash to women's rights. These networks include many academic activists for whom feminist perspectives on economic issues have become their main topic of research or teaching and whose theoretical expertise, in combination with the experience and practical skills of activists, shape a distinct, scholarly- and activist-informed network capable of confronting not only international institutions and governments in order to reverse the negative gender effects of global capitalism, but also extreme right-wing populism.

After presenting some historical background on transnational feminist networking in relation to economic globalization, this chapter presents two examples of networks that are shaping transnational feminist resistance. This comes out of my previous study of the Mesoamerican Women in Resistance (Mujeres Mesoamericanas en Resistencia or MMR) (see Domínguez, 2014) to which I briefly speak before introducing the main cases. The first one is a well-known European-based network in the form of an NGO—WIDE, and its successor, WIDE+—which has had considerable influence on European development and gender policies but also on discussions about global neoliberal restructuring and economic capacity-building of grassroots women in both the Global South and Global North. The second one, the BRICS Feminist Watch, is a new network based mostly in the emerging countries of the Global South and created to monitor, from a feminist economic perspective, investment processes conducted by the BRICS group. These two networks exemplify in a concrete way the latest kind of feminist resistance to global economic restructuring, a resistance highly informed by and productive of feminist scholarly critiques of globalization and related neoliberal restructuring policies but one also sufficiently linked to the daily realities of women affected by these phenomena in several different geographical and cultural contexts.

The material for this chapter consists of documents provided by and interviews of participants in these two transnational networks of feminist economist scholar-activists. The interviews with selected members of each network were done virtually in the fall of 2020. These interviews were conducted in English, and I quote from some at length to allow the interviewees' words to come through. Additional material comes from the websites of the networks themselves or from the online archives of WIDE. It is also important to note that I am a member of WIDE+, so I provide an insider perspective in one case as well as a scholarly one on both cases through interviews conducted and materials analyzed.

Some theoretical and contextual reflections

The subject of transnational resistance from a feminist perspective has received a great deal of attention over the last 30 years (see Alvarez, 1999; Domínguez, 2014; Eschle and Maiguashca, 2007; Marchand and Runyan, 2011; Marchand and Domínguez, 2019; Moghadam, 2000; Moghadam, 2020). Resistance can take many shapes, but here it is conceptualized as "actions against a certain order that can be perceived as permanent or transitional and harmful to the interests of a certain group" (Domínguez, 2014, p. 195). The networks presented here are good examples of strong platforms in which academics and activists from different perspectives and geographical locations combine to produce new assertive programs of action in the struggle against an order unfair to most women, particularly in the Global South.

These are alliances of heterogeneous forces that go beyond divisive identity politics of gender, class, race/ethnicity or nation alone, and are shaping a new commonality around marginality in order to attain new forms of political agency (Eschle and Maiguashca, 2007, p. 292). While social movements in civil society have been depicted as "counterhegemonic," reflecting the collective will to change radically class (or other) forms of oppression (Eschle and Maiguashca, 2007, p. 292), the groups under study here are not just domestic social movements but rather transnational networks, which are more representative of "activist campaigns" constituting actions of resistance to an order that has become unbearable across borders. Such resistance can also be seen as an "ongoing social process in which solidarity is continually subject to dissent and renegotiation" (Eschle and Maiguashca, 2007, p. 293). Also, in such resistance, "the pursuit of identity is not an end in itself, but rather a means to a wider end, involving the articulation of a political critique of the status quo and of an alternative vision of the future" (Maiguashca, 2005, pp. 135–136). However, there is a shared identity in the feeling of collective outrage and injustice and the need to redress such injustice. There is also transnational solidarity that can be nevertheless interpreted in diverse ways (Eschle and Maiguashca, 2007, p. 293). It is also important to recognize the importance of organizational forms of resistance, including whether and how networks of organizations are flexible in their commitment to sharing diverse experiences, exhibit empathy and agree to the need to strategize together. In the case of transnational networks resisting globalization, additional understandings and practices are needed.

> Whether framed in terms of 'global crises' brought on by neoliberal restructuring, 'uneven development' or 'structural contradictions' that create disjuncture between material life, realities and cognitive beliefs, the root causes of discontent and, thereby, resistance is situated within an expanding and transformative capitalist system … tracing the origins of resistance compels us to go beyond mapping power relations to the ways in which activists conceptualize oppression.
>
> (Eschle and Maiguashca, 2007, p. 294)

The networks under study here resist neoliberal restructuring in the form of economic globalization and changing relations of production but recognize these are experienced differently in different parts of the world and by women in varying social locations. Thus, transnational network critiques depend on the regional context in which they operate. Context also determines the kinds of collective resistance to gendered experiences of globalization. Those gendered experiences have many dimensions. As Eschle and Maiguashca (2007, p. 294) observe, the impact of globally produced socioeconomic relations on cultural/ideational dimensions has "confirmed that power relations are multiple, and that gender intersects with other hierarchies of power in context-specific ways."

Moreover, also following observations by Eschle and Maiguashca (2007, p. 296), the networks under study here show a "principled pragmatism"; they adapt easily to different circumstances principled in the sense of a "faith and hope for an alternative future" thus embracing a "utopian vision of social transformation." They have also managed to craft a sense of collective identity, shared meanings and common goals on the part of members (Moghadam, 2000, pp. 59–60).

Historical background

Since the mid-1980s, what Moghadam (2000, 2020) refers to as TFNs[3] have grown enormously in number, size, spread and quality, and many of them have become large professional organizations with regular forums, annual meetings, webpages and officers. They interact with other NGOs involved in issues like human rights or environmental concerns, sometimes reaching consultative status with intergovernmental organizations (IGOs), including the United Nations (UN), the World Bank, the International Monetary Fund (IMF) and the World Trade Organization (WTO) as well as the European Union (EU).

While a few Global South TFNs, such as Development Alternatives with Women for a New Era (DAWN),[4] were formed in the 1980s to promote alternatives to neoliberal capitalist development models that foregrounded gender justice and environmental sustainability, what we are seeing today is a mosaic of TFNs, all united in their efforts to press for alternatives to still dominant neoliberal capitalist development models. DAWN continues to serve as a model for feminist scholar-activist transnational networks, including those I look at in this chapter. Such TFNs are heterogeneous, and their dynamism sometimes leads to tensions as we shall see later. Nevertheless, they are extremely influential organizations that most IGOs and governments are now having to take seriously if the global challenges today are really to be confronted.

A precursor study conducted by me with the MMR had already introduced the subject of TFNs as a response to gendered neoliberal economics in the wake of resistance against a host of free trade initiatives in Central America in the 1990s (see Domínguez, 2014). The interviews conducted then already showed the transformative potential of creating spaces for the production of "collective knowledge" that enabled women to try to find alternatives. The participants in this network had been a part of the Mesoamerican School of Economics and had seen it as a political-pedagogic experience that made them feel that transformation was possible. Such transformation does not only depend on political changes, but on social movement participants and everyday people's choices to transform their life patterns (consumption, nutrition, health, care of oneself and so on). This has been seen as a "radical feminist" approach with a decolonial understanding, reconstructing the relationships among diverse groups of women that had been undermined by the patriarchal order and by neoliberal capitalism. This network, which had some grassroots ties but was wary of local and national social movements that were male-dominated or more patriarchal in orientation, also formed transnational alliances with, for example, the Latin American network REMTE (Red de Mujeres transformando la economia or Women's Network to Transform the Economy), the World March of Women and the gender chapter of the hemispheric Social Alliance (Red Mesoamericana en Resistencia, 2012; Domínguez, 2014).

WIDE (Women in Development Europe) and its successor WIDE+

WIDE is an example of the combination of a powerful NGO that, after 27 years of fruitful work, was transformed into a pure network now known as WIDE+, a decentralized organization leading coordinated efforts across several areas and at different levels but with no headquarters and very little funding.

Through my analysis of the contents shared in the interviews and official documents, I identify the following regarding WIDE's achievements: (1) a commitment toward the Global South and critical thinking about neoliberalism, liberal feminist gender "mainstreaming" and the EU's development cooperation; (2) an opening toward Eastern Europe and support toward the creation of new networks there; and (3) an ambition to a provide a whole picture view, linking economics, violence, peace and security. After this NGO closed its offices at the end of 2011, its successor, WIDE+, can be characterized as (1) limiting its focus to the themes of gender and trade, migration (women migrants in Europe), feminist economics and, more recently, feminist contribution to the struggle against climate change; (2) paying more attention to Europe and the issue of feminist movement building; and (3) becoming less professionalized and more based on voluntary/activist work.

WIDE, as a network-NGO, was created in 1985 by a group of activists, members of NGOs, academics and feminists working in international institutions (Interview with W. Harcourt, September 29, 2020). It emerged in what some see as the first decade of neoliberalism, and, as WIDE's own documents reveal, the organization developed in response to the "forward-looking strategies" arising out of the third UN Women's Conference in Nairobi. It was at this conference that European NGOs, research institutions and solidarity groups working on either development or women's issues saw the need for a European network that could combine both these issues. The first meeting of the network was organized by women from the International Coalition for Development Action (ICDA) and took place in Amsterdam in late 1985. This was a time when the notion of "gender" was purely political, not bureaucratic (Interview with W. Harcourt, September 29, 2020).

WIDE's evolution

During its first five years, WIDE focused on information exchange and solidarity tasks as well as lobbying work to convince major donor agencies in Europe to integrate women's concerns into development policies. By 1990, it received funding from the European Commission and thus could open a secretariat in Dublin. By this time, according to WIDE's online "Herstory," its aims were clarified:

> to exchange information and build up more expertise on issues of importance to women's development needs in developing countries with a view to deepening and extending public awareness on these issues; to encourage and to strengthen national networks, and European development policies, priorities, and programmes directed towards Southern countries, with a view to improving support for women in the South; to promote purposeful contacts with women in partner countries so that their development priorities will become the guiding principles of WIDE's activities in support of women in development; to lobby European and international institutions.

Contrary to the liberal feminist approach associated with Women In Development (or WID) programs that tended to simply "add women and stir" to existing approaches, WIDE was very critical of liberal and neoliberal notions of development, being influenced by all kinds of radical feminist thought from the Global South and the search for alternative economic models. Thus, it rejected "gender mainstreaming" as a "light" approach that would not transform structures of oppression:

> It was never about gender mainstreaming or about applying policy but criticizing policy. Also going to all kinds of meetings and forums, especially the World Social Forum, and more critical thinking. There was a bit of a split of groups within WIDE, people working on trade and gender, and people within development, dismantling development itself.
>
> (Interview with Wendy Harcourt, September 28, 2020)

By 1993, WIDE moved its headquarters to Brussels to be closer to EU governance in the wake of the 1992 Maastricht Treaty. The organization also broadened its focus toward monitoring macroeconomic and trade institutions, such as the World Trade Organization (WTO). Lobbying tasks also broadened to include the UN, cooperating with organizations like the Caribbean Association for Feminist Research (CAFRA) and the African Women's Development and Communication Network (FEMNET) that were receiving funds, co-financed by the EU, in preparation for the UN World Conference in Beijing.

Inspired by Global South feminists

As attested to by WIDE's former president Wendy Harcourt (Interview, September 28, 2020), "the relationship with the global South developed mainly by caucusing with diverse feminist forums the World Social Forum context, and with individual women who moved in and out from their positions, coming from the Global South to Europe."[5]

Similar to and inspired by DAWN, WIDE became involved in most conferences that involved women in and from the Global South in the 1990s, culminating in the 1995 Beijing World Women's Conference. WIDE made an official statement during the governmental conference General Exchange of Views and at the Huairou parallel NGO Forum. By the mid-1990s, the work of WIDE focused on gaining EU and member-state compliance with the Beijing Platform of Action, mapping the gender consequences of trade policies and establishing four regional consultation groups from each continent on EU policies and their impact on women (Moghadam, 2000, pp. 69–70)

By then an influential NGO, WIDE was very critical of, for example, the contradictions between EU development cooperation and EU trade policies and its support for structural adjustment programs. However, as acknowledged by its president at its May 1995 general assembly, WIDE had to balance such criticism with the need for a good working relationship with key EU agencies and to continue applying for funding, although many of its resources came from alternative sources (Moghadam, 2000, p. 70). Another tension was the one between the headquarters in Brussels and the network established with Global South organizations.

In 1997, at its annual meeting in Finland, WIDE focused on how globalization and the role of international financial institutions were impacting women, particularly in the cases of Russia, the Nordic countries and India. In its conference report "Trade Traps and Gender Gaps: Women Unveiling the Market," the forces of deregulation are held responsible for social disintegration and environmental degradation. Transnational corporations are perceived to be behind this deregulation in order to have rules further favoring them (Moghadam, 2000, p. 71).

Networking within networking

Through WIDE's cooperation with Latin American organizations such as Grupo de Educación Popular con Mujeres (GEM), Centro Interdisciplinario de Estudios sobre Desarrollo (CIEDUR) and REMTE, they monitored trade negotiations between the EU and Latin American countries, specifically the one between the EU and Mexico and the negotiations regarding Mercosur (or the Common Market of the South consisting of South American countries). The aim was to analyze the effects of such trade exchanges on gender relations by developing such analytical tools as gender indicators. WIDE cooperated with European networks like the European Network on Debt and Development

(EURODAD), the European Solidarity Towards Equal Participation of People (EUROSTEP) and Catholic and Protestant agencies, as well as being a member of the Global Alliance for Alternative Development, which also included DAWN and Alt-WID (Moghadam, 2000, p. 68). During the first decade of the 21st century, WIDE engaged in many post-Beijing meetings, which involved strategizing forums that brought many new members and new themes around which new ideas and new alliances were to be forged, including a greater focus on Eastern Europe.

Expanding analysis and engaging Eastern Europe

In her reflections on WIDE's 20th annual conference in London, Harcourt remembered that the challenge was to gain more of a "whole" picture that would broaden WIDE's analysis of gendered economic forces.

> One issue that WIDE has begun to link to its theme of economics, trade and globalization is sexual health and reproductive rights (SRHR). The conference signaled the need to bring new analytical/policy/activist thinking on the subject as part of WIDE's broad feminist positioning in women's rights and development debates.
>
> (Harcourt, 2005, p. 3)

Beyond the focus on sexual health and reproductive rights in relation to economic issues, WIDE also began to interconnect feminist economic analysis with issues of peace and security "to unpack the multiple power relations that interlink economic, social, political and cultural inequalities" (Harcourt, 2006, p. 3). In 2006, WIDE allied with the Feminist Task Force of the Global Call Against Poverty (GCAP), the European Social Forum, the coordinating group of the European Feminist Forum and the International Feminist Dialogues.[6]

By WIDE's 2006 annual conference in Warsaw, Poland, the growing role of Eastern European feminists in the organization was acknowledged. This was seen as the beginning of a process to engage "in the 'new' and marginal Europe, embracing the shift in focus and scope that will inevitably follow, and hopefully attracting new WIDE members and platforms" (Harcourt, 2006, p. 6). In relation to the interlinkages among the state, markets and women's agency discussed at this conference, "women from the East, West and South" debated "the different ways in which they had experienced the dynamics among care work, productive and reproductive work, and sexualities in the context of neoliberalism, militarism and fundamentalisms" (Harcourt, 2006, p. 3).

According to Gea Meijers, a network officer for WIDE since 2006 and subsequently, the general coordinator of WIDE+, the integration of the Eastern European network known as KARAT into WIDE took place in the wake of the growth of EU funding for new women's organizations there to ally and collaborate with women's organizations in the EU. WIDE helped Eastern European organizations frame their own programs and shape new gender-sensitive development policies Eastern European countries could adopt concerning countries in the Global South (Interview with Gea Meijers, September 24, 2020).

Although mostly concerned with the economic dimensions of neoliberal capitalist development and feminist critiques of and alternatives to it, WIDE also sought to link analyses of gendered economics with analyses of reproductive rights, gender violence, and gendered peace and security.

The politics of translation toward WIDE+

All this expansion of connections across Europe and in the Global South obviated the need for better "translation" practices: "how to cope with the dominance of languages such as English but also how to translate complex concepts and new ideas into politically engaging strategy" (Harcourt, 2006, p. 4). This also extended to "the importance of keeping records of our 'herstories' on how we mobilize," leading to the WIDE Economic Literacy Mistress File (Harcourt, 2006, p. 4). WIDE also advanced a politics of solidarity based on "respecting our different 'herstories,' diverse viewpoints, ways of being and living" and "sharing political spaces, funding resources and being willing to adjust our own particular standpoint to build a collective vision" (Harcourt, 2006, p. 4). Such principles informed WIDE's capacity-building on gender, trade and other macroeconomic issues through "economic literacy" projects, which included collecting "herstories" from various parts of the world and offering training courses in Latin America through a platform in Ireland (Interview with Gea Meijers, September 24, 2020).

This capacity-building served WIDE well when it became a network in 2010. Prior to this, there were 13 national platforms in Europe: Austria, Belgium, Bulgaria, Denmark, Eastern Europe (KARAT coalition), Finland, Italy, Ireland, the Netherlands, Spain, Sweden, Switzerland and the UK. Each national platform consisted of one or more women's groups with their own activities and agendas but sharing information and events with the secretariat in Brussels, which housed WIDE platforms and a WIDE archive. This network strengthened WIDE's impact and presence in Europe and beyond, but there was tension between the secretariat and the network. There were problems deciding which strategies to prioritize and, in general, a lack of clarity as to members' rights and obligations. By the end of 2006, Gea Meijers was recruited as a network officer to take care of the reorganization of the network and simplify the formalities around membership, a process that took two years, according to Meijers (Interview, September 24, 2020).

Despite these internal efforts, staff problems, changes in executive directors and coordinators, too large staff costs, decreases in funding and the lack of vision or will to adjust strategies all contributed to the dismantling of the secretariat in early 2012 (Interview with Gea Meijers, September 24, 2020). The network itself reorganized, and after months of negotiations, it came back as WIDE+, a network of organizations and individuals without any secretariat or headquarters and mostly based on voluntary/activist work.

As a network, WIDE+ had no resources and very few members left. After a period of restructuring, it was able to focus on recovering and further recruiting European organizations not previously associated with WIDE. Some funding was obtained to refocus on certain themes, such as migration, but mostly limited to a focus on migrant women in Europe. Gender and trade also remained a focus, pursued through lobbying the European Parliament, networking worldwide and monitoring EU–Latin American free trade agreements, as well as joining the Gender Trade Coalition (GTC) that had been created in 2018. The network is trying to contribute to the building of the feminist movement in Europe through the organization of a European continental forum to take place in 2024 or 2025 (Interview with Gea Meijers, September 24, 2020; author's observations).

In sum, WIDE surged as an effort of resistance to neoliberal restructuring but was inspired and committed to the radical feminism from the Global South inspired by DAWN. Its modest goal from the beginning—the exchange of information and building of expertise—soon developed into ambitious projects that included lobbying efforts at the highest levels of international organizations (such as the UN, EU and WTO), extensive and effective capacity-building in the South (mostly Latin America) and contributing to a new feminist movement in Eastern Europe. WIDE had to manage a difficult balance of radical positioning and negotiation with EU authorities, thus following a principled pragmatism. Its successor, WIDE+, had to make choices regarding its areas of focus because of the scarcity of funds, turning mostly toward European issues, although keeping a foot in the global arena through its gender, migration and trade work. Both networks managed, nevertheless, to forge a strong collective identity and a goal for social transformation.

BRICS Feminist Watch (BFW): A new feminist voice from the South

As in the case of WIDE and WIDE+, the BFW was organized by several academic and activist feminists, but this time from countries with emerging economies in the Global South. The BFW is part of a discussion among feminist groups and networks that are concluding that activities such as monitoring, or the "naming and shaming" approach, might better be put toward pressuring global financial institutions to become more gender-inclusive, particularly in the wake of the Great Financial Crisis in 2008–2009.

From my analysis of my interviews and the materials I have collected, I was able to glean five main understandings of what informs the work of the BFW and the nature of it: (1) the reasoning behind the strategy to position BFW members as "watchdogs" for international financial institutions; (2) the aim to promote feminist economic literacy; (3) how collaboration and challenges are dealt with by the network in terms of knowledge sharing and transnational participation within BRICS countries; (4) their relationship with the New Development Bank and the challenges to create effective long-lasting change within market institutions; and (5) the challenges of limiting advocacy and action to particular contemporary issues, such as infrastructure, the green economy and the financing systems of the BRICS.

Formed in 2016, the network is self-described as a feminist alliance from BRICS countries (Brazil, Russia, India, China and South Africa at the time) that "brings the collective strength of feminist analysis and activism to promote gender-responsive inclusive economic development" (BRICS Feminist Watch, 2020). The network consists of researchers, activists and other partnering feminist organizations within the BRICS countries, but also in other parts of the world. Advocating for more women's participation and better gender-oriented policies in financial institutions attached to the development agenda, the group has been developing over the last few years a strategy of feminist resistance based on policy papers, studies, webinars and meetings calling out regional institutions, such as the New Development Bank or NDB (also known as the BRICS bank), for their lack of more inclusive gender policies and programs as well as working on a country level to observe projects financed by the bank.

Even though still considered a relatively small network (overall, the network had, at the time of the interviews, 100-plus members, though only 10–15 were considered consistently active), the BFW has a wide reach due to its partnerships and collaborations, including with WIDE+, attesting to the expansion of feminist networks oriented to resisting financialization as a predominant feature of contemporary global restructuring worldwide.

> We work very closely with many at a country level as well as globally. All our members are also very well connected with other networks and they bring a wider feminist solidarity in that sense. For example, many WIDE+ members engage with BRICS Feminist Watch; FemNet in Africa is also a member and the larger BRICS working group within a development and human rights coalition also works very closely, especially with monitoring the NDB. At a country level all our members are working closely with organizations, networks, groups. And together we build this collective pressure on civil society engagement and bring feminist analysis to the table.
>
> (Interview with Priti Darooka, October 6, 2020)

But, according to Priti Darooka, co-founder of the BFW, as much as the network has an increasingly global reach, it was created as and remains primarily a response to not only the growing economic influence of the BRICS but also its growing political influence in global forums as part of a shift to what Rirhandu Mageza-Barthel (Chapter 9, this volume) refers to as multipolarity.

> The collapse of the financial system in 2008 and the rise from the emerging economies highlighted a need for alternatives, questioning existing economic policies and the way things were working. There was also the emergence of emerging economies, particularly BRICS countries, and not just [in terms of] their role in global economies but also in global politics. We started seeing from early 2004/2005 how these countries, China, India

> and Brazil particularly, started to be inserted in many global forums, like the WTO and the G20. As feminists from the Global South, this was kind of a new identity for us. [...] We felt that there was an initial critical need for this feminist voice from the South to find a collective strength to articulate our perspectives from the ground and bring it to the highest level of policymaking.
>
> (Interview with Priti Darooka, October 6, 2020)

Reaching out to other activists and feminist organizations in the Global South, the BFW started to position itself as both a platform for feminist economic literacy with respect to development projects in the BRICS but also as a critic of gender-insensitive policies of financial institutions at state and global levels from a Global South feminist perspective.

> Right from the beginning, we were clear that the economic justice agenda from a South feminist perspective was very critical. This means looking at the economic justice agenda in broader terms, recognizing women as development and economic agents, their contributions and all the feminist analysis around women's work, paid, unpaid work; women in decision making; access to productive resources; livelihood, etc. This was at the heart of our analysis as a starting place.
>
> (Interview with Priti Darooka, October 6, 2020)

Like WIDE+, however, network participation is uneven and often ungainly. The group does not have equally involved and committed members in all BRICS countries. According to the interviewees, most action has been led by members from India and Brazil, with some participation from South Africa. However, getting people from China and Russia has been somewhat of a challenge. The interviewees argue that cultural differences, distance and political constraints by national governments, particularly in more or increasingly authoritarian contexts, impose extra difficulties for such involvement.

> Though we have members from all BRICS countries plus other Global South countries in solidarity, it is very challenging. Even given the current challenges of civil society participation, transparency and the shrinking civil society space, we still are able to do a lot more in countries like India and South Africa. Brazil has been on a decline but there still are very strong groups. China is somewhat able to do, they come in and out, but Russia continues to be a challenge. It's almost impossible to have even two or three strong organizations to be active. They say: 'if we do this, we will be in trouble'.
>
> (Interview with Priti Darooka, October 6, 2020)

This presents a problem for the network not only with respect to full participation but also in terms of an eventual lack of expertise to address gender exclusions in economic policymaking within and among the BRICS countries.

At the outset of the BFW, one of the main focal points of the network was to monitor trade and investment among the BRICS. However, a lack of people with expertise in all involved countries is an obstacle, despite enthusiastic participation in some, such as India, as relayed by Govind Kelkar, a member of BFW:

> It can be slow [getting people involved]. There have been internal problems because when we invite them, people do come, but on the long term and [to get] consistent involvement has been lacking. The idea was that we should consolidate our own position and our own strategy and line of thinking and then get into the larger group. This has been only about two years of existence in effect so that's why we have not been able to spread to other feminist organizations so far. But there is a keen interest in India. A lot of requests have come to be a part of it. But some of our colleagues in BFW have been slowing it down, saying that their politics are like this and that and we really want feminists, political people, progressive people, we don't want any political party hold so that has been our struggle: to consolidate ourselves and then spread.
>
> (Interview with Govind Kelkar, October 15, 2020)

Forms of resistance

According to the interviewees, there were some debates regarding the strategies for resistance that would be practiced by the network, arising in part from varying limitations within their own countries' political contexts and their different positionalities. Since the network was new, with limited resources, both financial and in terms of expertise, a more focused approach was chosen, with the first major project to monitor the New Development Bank.

> We are working in terms of changing the structure of that bank because the market also has to be responsible. We cannot allow the market or these so-called development institutions to introduce development and not showing development. That kind of development has to be inclusive. That is the international policy in regards to the sustainable development goals, it is the policy of the entire UN system. So, we want to really strengthen their accountability. All of them are accountable. If you are dealing with our money, if you are dealing with our system, then you are accountable to us.
>
> (Interview with Govind Kelkar, October 15, 2020)

For the BFW, the interviews with leaders showed that the decision-making process to limit itself to serving as a watchdog group for the financial sector made sense, taking into account the impact of international and state financial institutions on women's lives and also the resources of the network. Some of the interviews show there was a lively discussion as to which strategies were the best to pursue. "Some felt we should be a think tank; others felt we should be a ground movement or do mass mobilization. But as those conversations evolved, we realized that we didn't have the capacity for mass movements" (Interview with Priti Darooka, October 6, 2020). By pressing the newly created institutions, like the NDB, to do much more than the established ones, like the World Bank, they could sensitize them to the needs of marginalized groups and to gender perspectives, thus developing resistance in new forms. However, even this strategy proved to be difficult. My interviewees also voiced concern about how effective the project can be in actually changing the structure of the NDB or even the individual projects and programs it funds to be more gender-inclusive. There were also concerns as to whether local governments as recipients of such funding should also be targeted, but whether this too would be an added challenge.

In an earlier edition of this volume, Marchand and Runyan (2011, p. 183) argued that "a focus on large-scale protests tends to overemphasize organized and movement-based resistances, making other resistance strategies, including spontaneous or individual responses, less visible." However, the real challenge is to understand whether this kind of resistance is "problem-solving or problem posing," reactive or proactive (Marchand and Runyan, 2011, p. 186). BFW activist Govind Kelkar puts it this way:

> We often hear this questioning: are you changing the structure of the NDB? What are you going to gain out of that? Not only feminist groups but also civil society groups say that. Because policies are really dictated and formulated by national governments. And there are also others saying that the state doesn't do anything. There is a kind of ultra-left group that questions us why we are working with the market institutions. Our resistance strategies are really not thought of as the kind of resistance in effect. I don't consider it so.
>
> (Interview with Govind Kelkar, October 15, 2020)

At the same time, another BFW activist from the academic realm, Ritu Dewan, argues that financial institutions need to be directly confronted, not limiting critique to governmental action. And to take on financial institutions requires analysis and intervention at the level of financial decision-making. She argues that to "go beyond gender budgeting to feminist finance," the gender perspective must be applied before and throughout the designing of a project:

> My mantra is academic research, advocacy, and action. Unless the three are linked, I don't think any organization or institution can really make a difference. Otherwise, you keep writing articles, what does it matter? Not unless it links to policy design.
>
> (Interview with Ritu Dewan, October 5, 2020)

But challenging financial institutions requires significant knowledge about alternatives to their practices that can be used to counter claims made by financial managers. BFW particularly seeks to resist "greenwashing" claims (or the covering over of ecologically harmful projects through ecological-friendly discourses) made by NDB officials. This requires presenting such officials with what gender-inclusive green economy initiatives should entail to be worthy of financing.

> Some of our members have long years of experience monitoring the World Bank, but the NDB was a new challenge. When we first attended the Civil Society Forum with the bank managers, they kept saying how green the bank was, how efficient they were. And we know as feminists that we don't buy into this green economy business, but we didn't have the language nor the analysis to counter what they were telling us. We needed to do our homework so that we could come back strong and say, 'we don't buy for this and this reason'. We then decided to do a series of webinars and tap into the huge resource of feminist scholarship and activism around climate justice and green economy. By doing that, we got clarity in terms of, as BRICS Feminist Watch, what is our position. So, we did a position paper on green economy and our recommendations to the NDB, and we went with conviction and were able to give them very clear arguments.
>
> (Interview with Priti Darooka, October 6, 2020)

Kunz and Ramírez (Chapter 5, this volume) challenge basic assumptions made by the global financial inclusion agenda which embraces the "idea that financial inclusion is necessarily an empowering process and is necessary for empowerment," especially regarding gender. This relates to the strategy adopted by the BFW toward resisting gender noninclusivity in the NDB policies. While the bank was ostensibly created to meet the need for an alternative to the Western Bretton Woods institutions, which had failed to create sufficient spaces for new economic actors, such as poor and working-class women, this aim did not necessarily translate into the NDB's actual approaches to gender inclusivity. In the BFW publication "Taking It to the Bank," BFW authors argue that even though the creation of the bank was seen as "one of the vehicles to achieve long-term poverty reduction and inclusive growth," the NDB wasn't, in fact, changing the neoliberal framework but rather "meeting Western demands" (BRICS Feminist Watch, 2017).

> We gave them examples of how banks like ASEAN Development Bank and African Development Bank and the World Bank have their strategy on gender and gender unit and focal points within their systems. And the NDB wasn't doing anything on gender, there was no strategy. (...) We were surprised to see that this so-called bank representing the Southern countries and emerging economies, where women are very active, not doing anything on the gender question.
>
> (Interview with Govind Kelkar, October 15, 2020)

Such findings temper the hopes expressed in Mageza-Barthel's (Chapter 9, this volume) examination of the impact of women's organizing on the development of Chinese–African relations within the South–South engagements currently represented by the BRICS and the Forum on Chinese–African Cooperation (FOCAC). As long as gender equality and justice are not represented in the NDB and in the significant investments made by China into the BRICS and beyond, it is unlikely that alternatives to capitalist development or even gender-inclusive capitalist development will emerge.

Another interesting fact regarding BFW's approach to the NDB is the interaction between projects at the country and regional levels. While some of the members focused on finding gender gaps within the bank's main policies, others dedicated their efforts to monitoring local development projects to collect evidence of inattention to gender.

> Most of our work was around monitoring the NDB and learning from monitoring projects on the ground in different countries, having conversations with the management of the bank to bring an integrated gender approach to its operations and all its activities and how they implement projects and making gender a key category in that sense. In a way, BRICS Feminist Watch was one of the first networks to monitor NDB projects in the countries. And with that, they could not deny it, because these were hard facts from the ground with numbers, pictures, and we were presenting them the violations and showing that women were nowhere. It brought pressure.
>
> (Interview with Priti Darooka, October 6, 2020)

Conclusions: Resistance as professional activism, a balance between reforming or creating new structures?

As the cases of WIDE, WIDE+ and the BFW show, feminist resistance with respect to such issues as trade and finance has been led primarily by professional feminist economists or political economists across the North and South, although the WIDE networks, in both permutations, have engaged activists at the more grassroots level, particularly with respect to promoting women's economic literacy and collecting herstories of economic resistance to neoliberalism. A major reason for more professional feminist activism when it comes to trade and finance is the high engagement of such networks with states, national and regional banking systems, international financial institutions and other IGOs to try to make them more gender-sensitive through monitoring, interventions via policy research and reports, and lobbying. Such networks were formed by feminist economists who "did their homework" studying how regional and global economic structures were formed in order to challenge them.

For these networks, it was not about "gender mainstreaming," but about the gendered nature of development, trade and finance that exacerbate economic, social and bodily harms to women. They have not lost sight of more radical feminist critiques of such institutions and their practices that extend not just to gender exclusion in policymaking on development, trade and finance. In this sense, they are just as much a part of feminist resistance to restructuring as more grassroots-based struggles, even though they recognize the limitations of trying to dismantle the "master's house" with some of the "master's tools" (see Lorde, 1984). By making strategic transnational alliances within their networks and with other TFNs across the South, East and North, they stay more grounded in more radical feminist critique. These were not grassroots organizations involved in street protests, although they represented, especially WIDE's successor, WIDE+, such grassroots organizations.

In an era when gender was supposed to be reflected in all policies, these networks insisted that this was not the case through deep and well-informed critiques. However, these NGO networks try to maintain a difficult balance, exercising a "principled pragmatism" that navigates sustaining radical critique of economic and financial institutions and processes based on solid evidence and productive transnational mobilizations and maintaining good relations with institutional representatives for either funding or access or both to make change. In this sense, they navigate between institutional reform and transformation.

WIDE, WIDE+ and BFW, while sharing a commitment to heightening women's agency in and feminist impact on the highest levels of economic and financial policymaking, emerged at different periods of global restructuring and in different locations, accounting also for their shifting agendas. WIDE, while becoming a professionalized organization, emerged at a time of growing mass mobilizations against the initial effects of neoliberal globalization on the South and North and thus was a part of this wave of the growth of TFNs focused on gendered globalization (particularly strong in Latin America). As it garnered institutional resources from the EU, it too institutionalized in an attempt to coordinate and channel these transnational and transcontinental energies. But both internal difficulties and the rescinding of funding, related in part to the growing austerities before and after the Great Financial Crisis, led to its reincarnation as WIDE+, focusing its energies more on the effects of restructuring in Europe, albeit in relation to South-to-North migration and regional trade agreements as well as on the reconstruction of a European feminist movement. BFW is decidedly a more South–South network. It is also decidedly a post-Great Financial Crisis formation in the context of rising South–South engagements and investments (particularly by China) as represented by the BRICS, which is why it focuses almost exclusively on development finance. Its challenges are also resources, but also complicated by authoritarian, or rising authoritarianism of, BRICS countries that make overt political mobilizations very difficult. Thus, intervening with research on the effects of gender exclusion by Southern banking and finance systems (which too often mirror the priorities of Northern/Western systems) makes more sense in terms of making inroads at this stage of global restructuring in which financialization is further penetrating everyday lives. However, even more professionalized research and lobbying networks face significant pushback from national, regional and international financial institutions, whether Southern- or Northern-based, which claim to be gender-aware but are actually not. Again, this is also complicated by low or declining resources, particularly in a time of right-wing insurgencies pushing back against gender equality efforts as also a part of global restructuring. Such challenges give this kind of resistance legitimacy and potential contribution badly needed in these even more uncertain times.

Notes

1 I would like to thank the invaluable collaboration of Patricia da Matta in the elaboration of this chapter.
2 The BRICS group has enlarged since the XV BRICS summit in South Africa, August 22–24, 2023. The new members that joined the organization on January 1, 2024, were Egypt, Ethiopia, Iran and the United Arab Emirates. Saudi Arabia has still yet to join, but currently participates as an invited nation. Argentina was also invited to join, but the Milei government declined the invitation.
3 According to Moghadam (2000, p. 62), such networks were created based on the notion of a "commonality in the forms of women's disadvantage and the forms of women's organizations world wide … These organizations are increasingly networking and coordinating their activities, engaging in dialogue and forms of cooperation, solidarity and mutual support, sending representatives to meetings in other countries and regions and utilizing a similar vocabulary to describe women's disadvantage and the desired alternatives."
4 DAWN began as a network that brought together feminist researchers and activists from the Global South promoting alternatives to capitalist development models combined with a strive for gender justice (see www.dawnnet.org).
5 Among these forums we can note the Latin American Feminist Encuentros, which gather hundreds of feminist grassroots organizations and started in Bogota, Colombia, in 1983, continuing to take place every three years in different countries in Latin America. The 14th took place in Montevideo, Uruguay, in November 2017 and the 15th was celebrated in San Salvador, El Salvador, in November 2023. See EFLAC 15 El mayor Encuentro Feminista de América Latina y el Caribe at https://eflac.org/. For more information on the 14th EFLAC, see the 14th EFLAC "Diversas pero no Dispersas (Different but not dispersed), remarks and reflections, Montevideo, Uruguay 22-2 November, 2017," at https://wideplus.org/.
6 These were the World Social Forum International Feminist Dialogues, a transnational group of feminists from the Global South involved in the WSF who invited WIDE to represent Europe/North America on their steering committee (see Vargas, 2005).

References

Alvarez, S.E. (1999) "Advocating feminism: the Latin American feminist NGO 'boom'," *International Feminist Journal of Politics* 1(2), pp. 181–209.

Antrobus, P. (2004) *The Global Women's Movement: Origins, Issues and Strategies.* London: Zed Books.

BRICS Feminist Watch. (2017) *Taking It to the Bank.* Available at http://www.bricsfeministwatch.org/pdf/Taking-it-to-the-Bank.pdf (accessed September 26, 2021).

BRICS Feminist Watch. (2020) "About us." Available at http://www.bricsfeministwatch.org/about-us.html (accessed September 26, 2021).

Domínguez R, E. (2018) "The 14th EFLAC 'Diversas pero no Dispersas (Different but not dispersed)', remarks and reflections, Montevideo, Uruguay 22-2 November, 2017." Available at https://wideplus.org/ (accessed August 30, 2023).

Domínguez Reyes, E. (2014) "Women organizing against free trade in Latin America," *Latin American Policy* 5(2), pp. 193–206.

Eschle, C. and Maiguashca, B. (2007) "Rethinking globalised resistance: Feminist activism and critical theorising in international relations," *British Journal of Politics & International Relations* 9(2), pp. 284–301.

EFLAC 15. (n.d.) "El mayor Encuentro Feminista de América Latina y el Caribe." Available at https://eflac.org/ (accessed August 30, 2023).

Harcourt, W. (2005) "WIDE 20th Anniversary Conference – reflections on moving forward," WIDE's archive.

Harcourt, W. (2006) "Reflections on the WIDE Annual Conference, held 2–3 June Warsaw, Poland," WIDE's archive.

Lorde, A. (1984) *Sister Outsider: Essays and Speeches*. Berkeley, CA: Crossing Press.

Macdonald, L. and Ibrahim, N. (2019) *Canada's Feminist Trade Policy: An Alternative to Austerity Trade Politics?* Carleton University & Tax Justice Network. Available at laura-berlin-2019-to-post.pdf.

Maiguashca, B. (2005) "Globalisation and the politics of identity: IR theory through the looking glass of women's reproductive rights activism," in Eschle, C. and Maiguashca, B. (eds.) *Critical Theories, International Relations, and 'The Anti-Globalisation Movement': The Politics of Global Resistance*. New York: Routledge, pp. 117–136.

Marchand, M.H. and Domínguez, E.R. (2019) "Labour and gender in a global context: Contestations and backlashes," *Third World Thematics: A TWQ Journal* 4 (1), pp. 1–8.

Marchand, M.H. and Runyan, A.S. (2011) *Gender and Global Restructuring: Sightings, Sights and Resistances*, 2nd ed. London: Routledge.

Moghadam, V.M. (2000) "Transnational feminist networks: Collective action in an era of globalization," *International Sociology* 15 (1), pp. 57–85.

Moghadam, V.M. (2020) *Globalization and Social Movements: The Populist Challenge and Democratic Alternatives*, 3rd ed. Lanham, MD: Rowman & Littlefield Publishers.

Red Mesoamericana en Resistencia por una Vida Digna (2012) *Cuidados y Estrategias en Tiempo de Crisis*. Available at https://www.cooperaccio.org/wp-content/uploads/2012/06/RED-MESOAMERICANA-EN-RESISTENCIA.pdf (accessed September 26, 2021).

Vargas, V. (2005) "Feminisms and the world social forum: Space for dialogue and confrontation," *Development* 48, pp. 107–110. doi:10.1057/palgrave.development.1100147.

11 Moving past the co-optation narrative

Gender and development as a site of economic difference and ethical negotiation

Suzanne Bergeron

Introduction

After years of struggle to get women's issues included in institutional development frameworks, many feminist political economists who study development are very frustrated with the way that inclusion has now occurred. Significant critical literature has observed that while the gender equity initiatives by key institutional actors might vaguely resemble feminist concerns, they do so largely as feminism's "uncanny double," to use Nancy Fraser's phrase: a neoliberal project related to women's empowerment in name only (2009, p. 114). The critiques of what is now referred to widely as the neoliberalization of feminism (Calkin, 2017; Prügl, 2015) have emerged from multiple disciplinary locations and have been aimed at a varied set of practices. Some have targeted gender equity initiatives such as microcredit for critique in this regard, arguing that microcredit has done less to improve women's lives than to draw women into coercive global markets in a clear "co-optation of feminist empowerment rhetorics" (Keating et al., 2010, p. 172; see also Karim, 2011; Rankin, 2001; Roy, 2010). Others have pointed out the neoliberal logic of the now ubiquitous "smart economics" business case for investing in women on the grounds that it is key to poverty reduction and growth (e.g., Calkin, 2017; Chant, 2012). Still, others have shown neoliberalism at work in the widespread focus on market-based solutions in development, which crowds out considerations of structural analysis or the role of social transformation (Altan-Olcay, 2016; Elias, 2013). Still, others have examined the expansion of public–private partnerships, corporate funding and private sector-led gender equity programs in development, showing how these have narrowed gender concerns even further in line with corporate values—a trend that Adrienne Roberts (2015) has labeled "transnational business feminism." These worrying trends have led some to argue that feminism at this point has nothing to do with gender and development, and that references to gender serve only as a "legitimizing device for increasing corporate power in the governance of development" (Calkin, 2017, p. 2).

These varied discussions of the co-optation of feminist ideas by neoliberal agendas in development can be viewed as part of a broader preoccupation with neoliberal co-optation within feminism (Eschle and Maiguashca, 2018; Prügl,

DOI: 10.4324/9781003036425-12

2017). As feminist ideas made significant inroads into mainstream politics over the past few decades, researchers have noted the ways those ideas were distorted or appropriated to further neoliberal goals. As Eschle and Maiguascha (2018) write, this led to a growing sense of crisis regarding the possibilities for feminist resistance in the late 2000s, with many feminist scholars contending that movement politics had become nearly completely subsumed to the capitalist agenda. Thus, critical political economy scholars writing about the neoliberalization of feminist ideas in development are contributing to a sizable chorus of other feminists currently singing the "co-optation blues" (de Jong and Kimm, 2017).

However, an emerging literature engaged with gender and development is starting to sing a different tune. These scholars are challenging the co-optation narrative, arguing that the relationship between feminist struggles and neoliberal rationalities in gender and development is more complicated. Can we really reduce every gender initiative in development to another depressing instance wherein "the dream of women's emancipation is harnessed to the engine of capitalist accumulation" (Fraser, 2009, p. 111)? Are the feminists who work within development institutions so easily duped into selling out their values? Neoliberal discourses of individual freedom, self-responsibility and markets may indeed structure gender policy. But do they really control and co-opt all feminist agendas and practices in development?

This emerging challenge to the co-optation narrative in development examines a variety of sites of practice and contestation. For instance, some highlight the ambiguities at work as gender experts negotiate the every day, fragmented engagements between feminist social justice and neoliberal aims in institutional contexts (Altan-Olcay, 2020; Ferguson, 2018; Resurrección and Elmhirst, 2021). Others are examining the complexities of private sector involvement in gender equity projects, including the tensions and contradictions of feminisms inside of the corporate world (Fisher, 2012) and the ways that corporate engagements with gender and development "bring together the legacies of neoliberalism and feminism… enabling co-optations as much as new openings" (Prügl and True, 2014, p. 23). Others are highlighting the surprising power of supposedly co-opted feminist movements in challenges to global corporate power (Gregoratti, 2016).

This chapter offers another contribution to the literature on rethinking the co-optation narrative of gender and development. It provides a rereading of the "smart economics" approach to gender and development that emphasizes the spaces of economic alterity that have emerged within it. Analytically, it draws upon the feminist understandings of economic difference developed by J.K. Gibson-Graham and the Community Economies Collective (CEC) to "take back" the economy (Gibson-Graham, 2006; Gibson-Graham, Cameron and Healy, 2013). That work highlights the importance of noncapitalist economic practices and motivations such as unpaid household labor and care, many of which are devalued and marginalized in masculinist hierarchies of the economy. It does so in order to disrupt the presumptive dominance of capitalism that frames both mainstream neoliberal thought and many of its critics. A further insight of Gibson-Graham and the CEC's work is that a recognition of diverse economic practices creates the possibility of seeing the economy as a site of ethical negotiation rather than one completely determined by neoliberal logics. The hope is that in unraveling the monolithic understandings of neoliberal capitalism that haunt the co-optation literature, the chapter can help to challenge its defeatist stance and expand our thinking about possibilities for feminist social change (Eschle and Maiguashca, 2018).

The chapter begins with a brief summary of the "smart economics" approach to gender equity in development and follows that with an alternative reading of the economic diversity that is called forth, but then too often pushed to the margins, in smart economics frameworks. Then, drawing on understandings of economic difference and capitalist resistance developed by J.K. Gibson-Graham and the CEC, it discusses ways to read these frameworks for reconceptualizations of the economy that break from the singular capitalist logic imagined in mainstream smart economics approaches. Using a range of examples from gender and development practice, it then shows how such an approach might reframe gender and development initiatives as sites of ethical negotiation rather than spaces dominated completely by neoliberalism. The chapter also discusses the potential and limits for critical feminist political economists to work around the business case agenda toward more transformative outcomes.

Gender, development and "smart economics"

In the past decade or so, it seems that even the most historically resistant organizations have embraced gender equity as a goal of development. For instance, the World Bank claims that "women's empowerment and gender equality are development objectives in their own right" (World Bank, 2012, p. 2), and the director of the International Monetary Fund (IMF) declared that "women are overexploited. This needs to change ... it is a matter of justice" (Lagarde, 2014). This focus on gender justice in development, initially rooted in transnational feminist and global justice movements (Batliwala, 2007), has been adopted by a host of global development institutions. Alongside this interest in promoting gender equity is a repositioning of the activities and motivations that have long been highlighted by feminist political economists as central to human flourishing yet typically viewed as "outside" of the economy. These include care, unpaid household production, community work and cooperation. A wide range of projects rolled out over the past two decades are based on the idea that gender equity can only be achieved if attention and support are given to the previously ignored unpaid household care work that (mostly) women do in households and communities (Molyneux, 2006; Bedford, 2009). With the obvious impacts of the COVID-19 crisis on unpaid care work, there has been renewed attention to the centrality of this unpaid social reproductive labor to human well-being, and the need to value and support it through development policy today (United Nations, 2020; World Bank, 2020).

Further, in addition to recognizing nonmarket economic activities, gender equity policies have increasingly valued motivations not generally associated with self-interest and the competitive market, such as care and cooperation. For instance, much has been made of women's altruism in the gender and development literature, particularly in arguments for investing in women in order to achieve goals of growth and poverty reduction through the investments they make in their children's health and education (Kabeer, 2020). Relatedly, women's greater cooperative, caring and altruistic proclivities are now widely celebrated, but not as social relations and networks that foster solidarity. Rather, they are framed as an important form of social capital that puts women in step with market-oriented development goals (Rankin, 2001; World Bank, 2012). Because of this, women have been disproportionately drawn into microcredit lending circles that rely upon values of solidarity in order to succeed but have the ultimate aim of fostering entrepreneurial, self-managing and self-interested subjects. While the current discourse of microfinance might be framed in mostly neoliberal terms, some of the thinking behind it comes out of the alternative, participatory and human-centered development paradigm that emerged within social movements in the Global South in the 1970s. These called for the cultivation of associative and participatory forms of economy as an alternative to the top-down, capitalist and growth-centered approaches of the mainstream (Escobar, 1992).

Like attention to justice as a goal in its own right, the focus on nonmarket and noncapitalist activities and motivations marks a significant break with those earlier mainstream practices that invisibilized and/or pathologized such activities as "noneconomic," "inefficient" and/or "backward." In this sense, the valuation of nonmarket labor and care and altruistic, solidaristic behavior in the economy marks a turnaround from 50-plus years of development, which was primarily focused on changing noncapitalist mindsets toward market rationality or simply presuming that people everywhere were detached rational economic agents.

However, these glimmers of difference are made sense of in mainstream gender and development policy through a depressingly narrow approach that recenters individualism and the market, and thus constrains much of their transformative potential. That is because they are typically filtered through a "business case" for gender equity that connects women's empowerment and the existence of economic difference to the smart economics of achieving goals of growth and efficiency. For example, women's caring proclivities in households are valued only for their ability to generate human capital for enhanced productivity rather than being viewed as an alternative subjectivity that might be at odds with capitalist rationality. As the *2012 World Development Report* puts it, "(g)reater control over household resources by women leads to more investment in children's human capital, with dynamic positive effects on economic growth" (World Bank, 2012, p. 4). Further, rather than looking to cooperative microcredit lending circles to foster community and solidarity, what is highlighted in development policy is the way that cooperation functions as a risk-minimization strategy that ensures profits for investors (Roy, 2010; Karim, 2011).

This smart economics discourse has by now permeated gender equity discussions across the whole range of development institutions (Resurrección and Elmhirst, 2021; Ferguson, 2018). The smart economics framework argues for investing in women and girls because they have "untapped potential," as well as are more altruistic and caring. They are a "good investment" because they are assumed to be more likely than men to channel their incomes to their families and communities, thus increasing human capital to promote growth and poverty reduction (Chant and Sweetman, 2012). So, while significant emphasis has been placed on women's alternative economic locations (households, the informal sector) and subjectivities (care, cooperation) in the smart economics framework, progressive goals have been diverted by their placement under the umbrella of a unitary capitalist economy. In addition, these initiatives often reify rather than challenge gender norms and stereotypes in their efforts to harness women's contributions based on their presumed identities as caretakers and mothers (Bedford, 2009; Bergeron, 2011; Moeller, 2019).

It is not surprising, then, that the expanded space for addressing gender equity and economic differences in development over the past decade has not been met with much optimism by progressive feminists looking to engender alternatives to capitalist business-as-usual. In fact, a fair number of critical feminist analysts view even the recent shift in attention to nonmarket activities and motivations as a more or less complete neoliberal co-optation of feminist values and goals. As Adrienne Roberts (2008, p. 535) writes, the recognition of diverse economic practices within gender and development is a purely instrumental move, part of an effort to increase the "penetration of capital into new spaces and social relations." Other critics have noted that this new focus on gender and development calls upon values of care and altruism only to shore up its attempts to construct women as self-managing subjects who, with a little bit of investment, can make up for the withdrawal of state support for their households (Roy, 2010). Others argue that development's attention to women's labor in the reproductive sphere is because such unpaid labor mitigates the impact of neoliberal policies on household well-being (Chant, 2012). So, if attention is paid to caring labor and motivations in development policy, these critics argue, it is less about fostering economic difference, cooperation and care than it is about co-opting feminism toward neoliberal ends.

Beyond the business case

These critiques provide a much-needed reminder that feminist aims can be thwarted when they are taken up within spaces of development governance, as well as a useful counter-narrative to mainstream claims that the current approach to gender and development policy constitutes a victory for feminist alternatives when so clearly it is not. But the way that capitalism is presented in many of these critiques—as *a priori* determining all outcomes and bending all agendas to its will—makes it difficult to imagine development otherwise. The bulk of feminist criticism of current gender and development policy may, therefore, give too much power to the capitalist economy, even as these critics acknowledge the existence and value of a diversity of economic practices and motivations such as nonmarket household production, community economies and values of care and cooperation (Bergeron and Healy, 2015).

But what if instead of seeing capitalism as an impenetrable system that determines the course of everything—including the messy business of gender and development—we could imagine these glimmers of economic difference in policy as cracks or openings for thinking and doing development differently? While the "business case" approach, as presented by both its champions and its critics, views the world as a closed capitalist system in which all noncapitalist activities and motivations—including feminist motivations—function only as resources for capitalism, an alternative reading could identify the glimmers of alternative economic and social practices, rather than presenting them in terms of a closure that gives capitalism a social cohesion that is difficult to break. Of course, not all resistances will create progressive possibilities, and in fact, invocations of "community," "care," "participation," "women's empowerment" and the like may very well be integrated into projects to sustain capitalism, as the critics suggest. But when development is seen as only doing the work of global capitalism, it is itself presented as a unified force rather than a multivocal site of contestation over political projects (Ferguson, 2009). Thus, we cannot know in advance the effect of such openings, as they occupy a contradictory space between resistance and integration (Holloway, 2010; Dinerstein, 2012).

The question remains, then, as to how these glimmers and openings might allow for understandings and activities that are at odds with a completely neoliberalized "business case" being pursued by development institutions. Might we look to recent shifts in gender and development for spaces to foster projects that decenter neoliberalism in favor of noncapitalist practices and motivations of solidarity and care (Gibson-Graham, 2006, p. xxv)? By refusing to define capitalism as a determining force, could we be open to imagining ways to take these openings to recast the process of development as one not determined by capitalism but one centered on building an economy through ethical negotiation (Graham and Amariglio, 2006)?

As J.K. Gibson-Graham (2006) suggest, this orientation toward possibility is predicated upon challenging the unspoken premise of much mainstream political economy regarding the dominance of capitalism and the subordinate position of all other relationships and spaces—including development institutions, states, nonmarket production, cooperatives and households. Gibson-Graham, in contrast, imagine the economy as a diversity of economic practices that include market and nonmarket activities; individual and caring motivations; multiple class forms that include cooperative, capitalist and other modes of production; appropriation; and distribution of surplus. These insights regarding economic diversity, in tandem with the work of numerous feminist political economists who contend that globally between one-third to one-half of all economic activity, such as housework, caring labor and agricultural production, is performed outside of the market. However, instead of viewing this unpaid, nonmarket work as existing only within an overarching logic determined by the needs of capitalism, Gibson-Graham call for imagining the economy as a landscape of difference that makes heterogeneous practices visible. This, in turn, enables a different understanding of the world beyond the standard narrative, which excludes the stories, forms and practices that tend to disrupt capitalism's presumed order.

As it relates to the topic of this chapter, such an approach opens space for recognizing that capitalist logic does not necessarily co-opt all feminist ideas and practices that make their way into development policy. In the messy business of gender and development, there are multiple constituencies and forces involved, including feminist and other connected social movements, corporate interests, institutional cultures of international organizations, feminist champions working within the system, beneficiaries of development with their own ideas, the communities in which empowerment projects are rolled out and so forth. As discussed in this chapter introduction, emerging literature is focused on highlighting the openings and complex negotiations for creating transformative change in gender and development in and against institutions (Ferguson, 2018; Gregoratti, 2016; Resurrección and Elmhurst, 2021).

Further, the business case agenda can be reframed and transformed through the implementation process in the practices of local development brokers and/or the subjects who are the targets of the policy themselves. This would not be the first time such a thing happened in development. For instance, the 1970s shift to centering of "basic needs" such as nutrition in development by the World Bank was undertaken to better achieve goals of efficiency and growth, but this was "translated" by Latin American social movements into more transformative outcomes that benefited the poor, such as land reform (Porter, 1995). Similarly, the business case approach that attempts to contain equity and economic diversity concerns within a narrow efficiency framework can be potentially cracked open when it lands on the ground in certain contexts.

Negotiations and cracks in the business case: Local articulations of gender and development

Anyone familiar with the co-optation narrative in gender and development is likely well-steeped in the feminist critique of microfinance that has already been touched upon in this chapter. While touted by its proponents as an inclusive and participatory way to foster self-employment and control over income that can "emancipate the poorest women on earth" (Morduch, 1999, p. 570) while simultaneously fostering economic growth, feminist critiques have highlighted the trends toward commercialization and for-profit lending in microfinance, as well as the questionable effects of such loans on women's empowerment, poverty rates and community development. They further point out that it draws women into global finance and debt relations, individualizes poverty, takes attention away from broader structural anti-poverty efforts and attempts to produce neoliberal self-managing subjectivities among its recipients (see Keating et al., 2010, for a comprehensive overview). As many of these critics have pointed out, the understanding of the causes and indicators of empowerment in relation to microcredit is quite distant from women's realities in situated contexts. What has not been explored much up until now in this critical literature—at least not beyond recognition of women's nonmarket care work as a restricting factor to microcredit success—are the contexts of the diverse economic practices and livelihood activities in which financialization and microcredit occur in gender and development.

However, an emerging scholarship is beginning to explore the diverse economies of microfinance. Kunz and Ramírez (Chapter 5, this volume) demonstrate that attempts to draw women into global commercial finance and indebtedness can sometimes fail because they land in a diverse economic landscape. They offer a case study of women remittance senders in Mexico who face pressures from government agencies, banks and NGOs to use commercial financial services for saving and borrowing. They then highlight the various ways that these "subjects to be financialized" negotiate and resist those pressures. Their account of how women prefer using informal financial resources such as *tandas*, or credit and savings associations in which participants make contributions to a fund that is then given to each participant in a rotation, shows that values of solidarity take precedence over neoliberal entrepreneurial and self-interested values. Women are more likely to trust *tandas* than commercial financial services. And crucially for the purposes of the argument presented here, they also prefer the solidarity economy aspect of *tandas,* viewing the lending relationship as a collective endeavor in which participants are motivated by their sense of responsibility to each other and their community.

Others have shown that even when women are drawn into global commercial financial networks, the result may not necessarily be a deepening of capitalist relations but possibly something different. Hossein (2016), for example, uses a Black feminist and diverse economies frameworks to examine commercial microfinance in the African diaspora communities in the Caribbean and North America. In her close case study research, she finds that microfinance can sometimes be embedded within and foster social and solidarity economy practices that are at odds with neoliberal aims. Such practices reflect the long history of community-focused and cooperative economic practices of the marginalized peoples of the African diaspora. Her findings remind us of the importance of contexts and histories in tracing the effects of development interventions while creating space for imagining economic differences and potential differential impacts on poor women's livelihoods and empowerment.

Moving away from commercial microfinance, another example of how neoliberal aims can get transformed into something different on the ground to foster diverse economies (as well as alternatives to individualized notions of women's empowerment) is found in Valle's (2018) account of a UN Women-funded gender and technology project in Costa Rica. This project, Valle demonstrates, simultaneously embodies both entrepreneurial models of gender and development and explicitly feminist ideas of solidarity and collective purpose. In this project, a cooperative mostly constituted by women offered training to incorporate women into technology fields. The stated goal of the funding agency, and a key focus of the cooperative itself, is fostering a cadre of self-employed women entrepreneurs in the field and, therefore, reducing women's poverty. While those goals resonate with "business case" discourse regarding women's untapped potential, entrepreneurship as empowerment, individualized solutions to poverty and so forth, there is also much more going on here. The women in the cooperative see themselves as activists who want women in their community to be financially independent while simultaneously instilling values of solidarity, social justice and collective action through their training. These feminist values are the ones that guide the women in the cooperative as they ethically negotiate the expectations of funders, the conflicting values of their clients and their own internal conflicts in their work toward building solidarity between women and solidarity economies (Valle, 2018, p. 340). Such commitments challenge neoliberal rationalities of individualism and personal responsibility, and in this way, as Valle (2018, p. 339) writes, "depart from the broad-brush critiques of how neoliberalism has co-opted feminist principles."

This example recasts gender and development as an ethical negotiation around economic differences rather than submission to the dominant logic of capitalism. It also calls into question the sharp distinctions made between feminist resistance and neoliberal co-optation in many of the feminist critiques of the subsumption of feminist politics to capitalist mandates by smart economics. As Eschle and Maiguashca (2014, p. 648) write in their own challenge to broad-brush accounts of neoliberal co-optation of feminisms, "(n)o practice should be assumed to be progressive – or not – in advance of empirical study." While there are no guarantees that these or any attempt at fostering economic difference will not be usurped by other agendas, not acknowledging and supporting solidarity practices that can wrest potentially transformative ends from neoliberally inclined initiatives can only mean that things will remain as they are.

Conclusion

While not minimizing the shortcomings of the smart economics approach to gender and development—with its fetishization of market efficiency and essentialist framings of gender roles—this chapter has emphasized the possibility of nurturing alternatives grounded in the recognition of economic difference expanded by that approach. By letting go of the monolithic view of the capitalist economy held by both business case advocates and their feminist critics, a new picture of the economy emerges that recognizes the potential fragility of the neoliberal project and the diversity of viable economic forms and related motivations of care, solidarity and cooperation. This allows us to think more expansively about the possibilities for feminist engagements with gender and development.

References

Altan-Olcay, Ö. (2016) "The entrepreneurial woman in development programs: Thinking through class differences," *Social Politics: International Studies in Gender, State & Society*, 23(3), pp. 389–414.

Altan-Olcay, Ö. (2020) "Politics of engagement: Gender expertise and international governance," *Development and Change*, 51(5), pp. 1271–1295.

Batliwala, S. (2007) "Taking the power out of empowerment: An experiential account," *Development in Practice*, 17(4–5), pp. 557–565.

Bedford, K. (2009) *Developing Partnerships: Gender, Sexuality and the Reformed World Bank*. Minneapolis: University of Minnesota Press.

Bergeron, S. (2011) "Economics, performativity and social reproduction in global development," *Globalizations*, 8(2), pp. 151–161.

Bergeron, S. and Healy, S. (2015) "Beyond the business case: A community economies approach to gender, development and social economy," in Utting, P. (ed.) *Social and Solidarity Economy: Beyond the Fringe*. London: Zed Press, pp. 72–85.

Calkin, S. (2017) "Disrupting disempowerment: Feminism, co-optation, and the privatised governance of gender and development," *New Formations*, 91(91), pp. 69–86.

Chant, S. (2012) "The disappearing of smart economics? The World Development Report 2012 on gender equity, some concerns about the preparatory process and prospects for paradigm change," *Global Social Policy*, 12(2), pp. 198–218.

Chant, S. and Sweetman, C. (2012) "Fixing women or fixing the world? 'smart economics', efficiency approaches, and gender equality in development," *Gender & Development*, 20(3), pp. 517–529.

de Jong, S. and Kimm, S. (2017) "The co-optation of feminisms: A research agenda," *International Feminist Journal of Politics*, 19(2), pp. 185–200.

Dinerstein, A. (2012) "Interstitial revolution: On the explosive fusion of negativity and hope," *Capital and Class*, 36 (3), pp. 521–540.

Elias, J. (2013) "Davos woman to the rescue of global capitalism: Postfeminist politics and competitiveness promotion at the world economic forum," *International Political Sociology*, 7(2), pp. 152–169.

Eschle, C. and Maiguashca, B. (2014) "Reclaiming feminist futures: Co-opted and progressive politics in a neo-liberal age," *Political Studies*, 62(3), pp. 634–651.

Eschle, C. and Maiguashca, B. (2018) "Theorising feminist organising in and against neoliberalism: Beyond co-optation and resistance?" *European Journal of Politics and Gender*, 1(1–2), pp. 223–239.

Escobar, A. (1992) "Imagining a post-development era? Critical thought, development and social movements," *Social Text*, 31/32, pp. 20–56.

Ferguson, J. (2009) "The uses of neoliberalism," *Antipode: A Radical Journal of Geography*, 41(1), pp. 166–184.

Ferguson, L. (2018) "Feminist political economy perspectives on gender expertise," in Elias, J. and Roberts, A. (eds.) *Handbook on the International Political Economy of Gender*. Cheltenham, UK: Edward Elgar Publishing, pp. 298–310.

Fisher, M. (2012) *Wall Street Women*. Durham: Duke University Press.

Fraser, N. (2009) "Feminism, capitalism and the cunning of history," *New Left Review*, 56, pp. 97–117.

Gibson-Graham, J.K. (2006) *A Post-Capitalist Politics*. Minneapolis: University of Minnesota Press.

Gibson-Graham, J.K., Cameron, J. and Healy, S. (2013) *Take Back the Economy: An Ethical Guide for Transforming Our Communities*. Minneapolis: University of Minnesota Press.

Graham, J. and Amariglio, J. (2006) "Subjects of economy," *Rethinking Marxism*, 18(2), pp. 199–204.

Gregoratti, C. (2016) "Cracks in the corporatisation of feminism," *Globalizations*, 13(6), pp. 922–924.

Holloway, J. (2010) *Crack Capitalism*. London: Pluto Press.
Hossein, C. S. (2016) *Politicized Microfinance: Money, Power, and Violence in the Black Americas*. Toronto: University of Toronto Press.
Kabeer, N. (2020) "Women's empowerment and economic development: A feminist critique of storytelling in 'randomista' economics," *Feminist Economics*, 26(2), pp. 1–16.
Karim, L. (2011) *Microfinance and its Discontents: Women in Debt in Bangladesh*. Minneapolis, MN: University of Minnesota Press.
Keating, C., Rasmussen, C. and Rishi, P. (2010) "The rationality of empowerment: Microcredit, accumulation by dispossession, and the gendered economy," *Signs: Journal of Women in Culture and Society*, 36(1), pp. 153–176.
Lagarde, C. (2014) "The economic power of women's empowerment." Available at https://www.imf.org/external/np/speeches/2014/091214.htm (accessed January 26, 2021).
Moeller, K. (2019) "The ghost statistic that haunts women's empowerment," *New Yorker*. Available at https://www.newyorker.com/science/elements/the-ghost-statistic-that-haunts-womens-empowerment (accessed January 7, 2021).
Molyneux, M. (2006) "Mothers in the service of the new poverty agenda: progresa/opportunidades," *Social Policy Administration*, 40(4), pp. 49–70.
Morduch, J. (1999) "The microfinance promise," *Journal of Economic Literature*, 37(4), pp. 1569–1614.
Porter, D. (1995) "Scenes from childhood: The homesickness of development discourses," in Crush, J. (ed.) *Power of Development*. London: Routledge, pp. 63–86.
Prügl, E. (2015) "Neoliberalising feminism," *New Political Economy*, 20(4), pp. 614–631.
Prügl, E. (2017) "Neoliberalism with a feminist face: Crafting a new hegemony at the World Bank," *Feminist Economics*, 23(1), pp. 30–53.
Prügl, E. and True, J. (2014) "Equality means business? Governing gender through transnational public-private partnerships," *Review of International Political Economy*, 21(6), pp. 1137–1169.
Rankin, K.N. (2001) "Governing development: Neoliberalism, microcredit, and rational economic woman," *Economy and Society*, 30(1), pp. 18–37.
Resurrección, B.P. and Elmhirst, R. (2020) *Negotiating Gender Expertise in Environment and Development: Voices from Feminist Political Ecology*. London: Taylor & Francis.
Roberts, A. (2008) "Privatizing social reproduction," *Antipode: A Radical Journal of Geography*, 40(4), pp. 535–560.
Roberts, A. (2015) "The political economy of 'transnational business feminism'," *International Feminist Journal of Politics*, 17(2), pp. 209–231.
Roy, A. (2010) *Poverty Capital: Microfinance and the Making of Development*. London: Routledge.
United Nations. (2020) "*The impact of COVID-19 on women*," *UN Chronicle*. Available at https://www.un.org/en/un-chronicle/impact-covid-19-women (accessed January 20, 2021).
Valle, F.S. (2018) "Moving beyond co-optation: gender, development, and intimacy," *Sociology of Development*, 4(4), pp. 325–345.
World Bank. (2012) *World Development Report 2012: Gender Equality and Development*. Washington DC: World Bank Group.
World Bank. (2020) *Gender dimensions of the COVID-19 pandemic*. Available at: https://documents.worldbank.org/en/publication/documents-reports/documentdetail/618731587147227244/gender-dimensions-of-the-covid-19-pandemic (accessed January 20, 2021).

Index

For Product Safety Concerns and Information please contact our EU representative GPSR@taylorandfrancis.com
Taylor & Francis Verlag GmbH, Kaufingerstraße 24, 80331 München, Germany

www.ingramcontent.com/pod-product-compliance
Ingram Content Group UK Ltd.
Pitfield, Milton Keynes, MK11 3LW, UK
UKHW020147200926
475702UK00016B/2589

* 9 7 8 0 3 6 7 4 7 7 5 8 5 *